Fodor's

VIETNAM

FODOR'S
TRAVEL PUBLICATIONS

NEW YORK • TORONTO
LONDON • SYDNEY • AUCKLAND

WWW.FODORS.COM

CONTENTS

KEY TO SYMBOLS

- ✚ Map reference
- ✉ Address
- ☎ Telephone number
- ◐ Opening times
- ✋ Admission prices
- Ⓜ Underground station
- 🚌 Bus number
- 🚉 Train station
- ⛴ Ferry/boat
- ⬛ Driving directions
- ℹ Tourist office
- ◪ Tours
- 📖 Guidebook
- 🍴 Restaurant
- ☕ Café
- 🍷 Bar
- 🏬 Shop
- ① Number of rooms
- ✪ Air conditioning
- 🏊 Swimming pool
- 🏋 Gym
- ❓ Other useful information
- ▷ Cross reference
- ★ Walk/drive start point

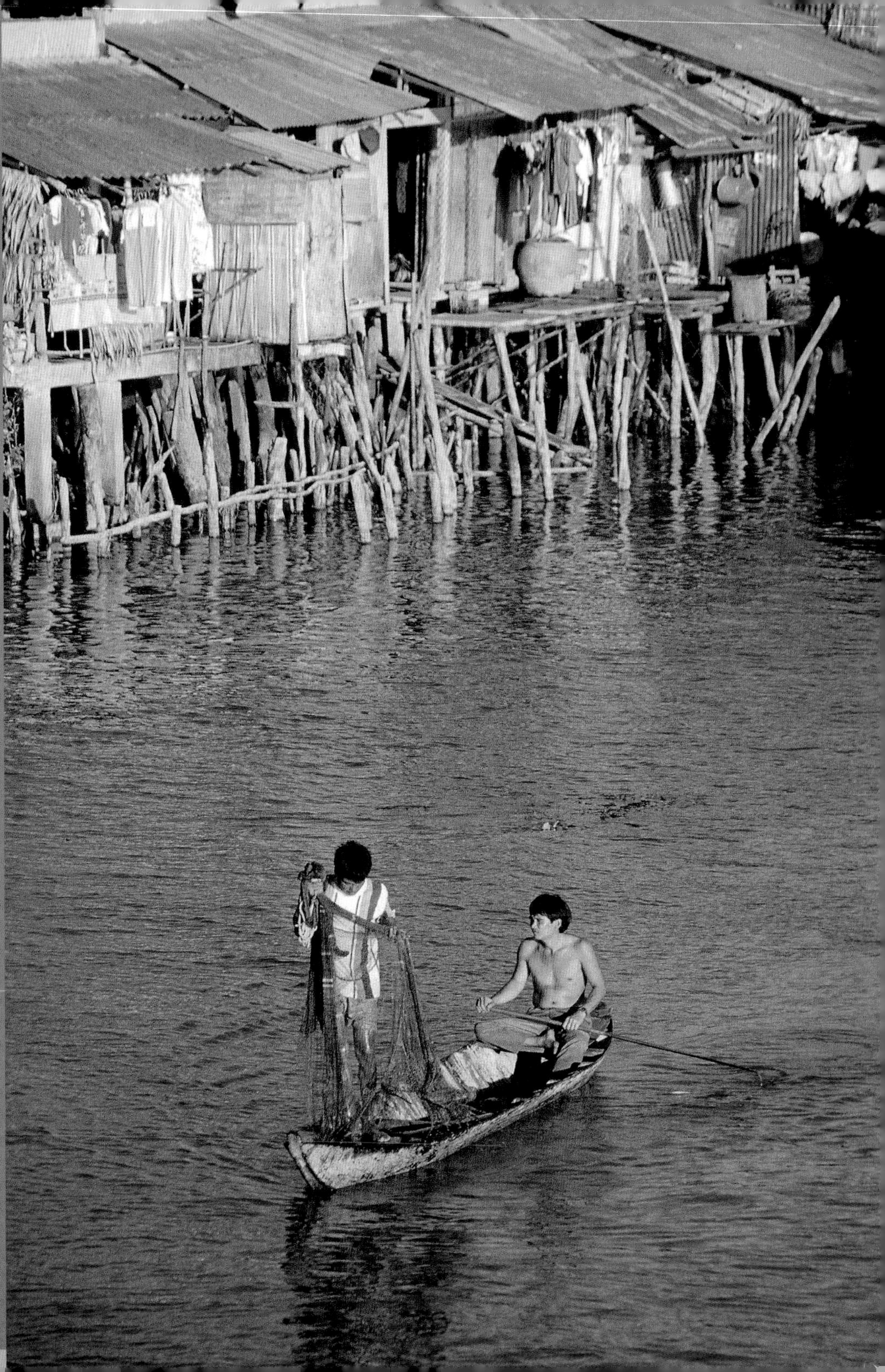

UNDERSTANDING VIETNAM

Understanding Vietnam is an introduction to the country, its geography,
economy, history and its people, giving a real insight into the nation.
Living Vietnam gets under the skin of Vietnam today, while the Story of
Vietnam takes you through the country's past.

UNDERSTANDING VIETNAM

Vietnam is a seductive place; it is an intriguing mix of a country steeped in Marxist creed yet embracing capitalist economic reform. The country has worked hard to shake off its reputation as a war zone and has put a great deal of effort, too, into building up a name for itself as an unusual and offbeat visitor destination. In both respects it has won much success, with visitor numbers increasing annually, and by around 15 percent in 2011.

CONTEMPORARY LIFE AND CULTURE

Many Westerners go to Vietnam to see and experience a completely different way of life that contrasts strongly with their own. Here is a society where family loyalties and obedience to parents are paramount, but where a city café culture is emerging; where some people make do on next to nothing and endure backbreaking work day after day under a cruel sun, knee-deep in mud, yet retain enormous pride and dignity.

Discovering at first hand something of the interesting history and culture of this ancient civilization is a priority for many visitors. Few countries' histories have been rewritten as many times as Vietnam's, when successive victors reinterpreted the events of the past to portray themselves in the most flattering light.

However, some events are beyond distortion by propaganda, and some facts are visible for all to see. Historic towns, scarred battlefields, dusty museums, ransacked palaces, vernacular architecture, junk shops, venerable places of worship and elderly people with long and vivid memories provide vital repositories of Vietnam's history and culture.

Vietnam has made spectacular progress in reducing levels of poverty, largely through egalitarian land reforms, and in the provision of education and health services. In 1993, 63 percent of the population was living on US$1 per day; by 2006 this figure had fallen to 22 percent. Infant mortality dropped from 56 to 14 per 1,000 between 1990 and 2008, and Vietnam's literacy rate is now more than 90 percent. Per capita income in 2010 was just over US$1,000, and with half of the country's nearly 90 million people under the age of 30 the country's future truly belongs to its youth.

Progress has brought its problems, not least in the traffic congestion that afflicts the country's two main cities—especially Hanoi, where the narrow streets seem permanently clogged with lines of vehicles and speedy motorcycles darting in and out of every available space.

CUISINE

Vietnam is a fertile country, and food is plentiful, though malnutrition through poverty is still a problem. It is not regarded as a sin to enjoy the fruits of the land and sea, and restaurants tend to place greater emphasis on food than on decor. The culinary tradition is a fusion of Vietnamese, Chinese and French cuisine, and meals are likely to be of very good quality whether they're served in luxury hotels, floating restaurants, workers' cafeterias or streetside eateries, or even at noodle carts or seaside barbecues.

Above *Traditional life in the backstreets of Hoi An*

LANGUAGE

Jesuit Alexandre de Rhodes (▷ 33) romanized the Vietnamese script in the 17th century, so although Westerners may find the language daunting, it is a fairly straightforward matter to read the names of hotels and streets. English is learned and spoken by many young Vietnamese, and French is spoken to a lesser degree among the older generation. This applies mainly to the cities and visitor resorts; neither language is likely to be an aid to communication anywhere remote.

Many Vietnamese face similar problems when traveling within their own country, as the northern, central and southern dialects and accents are mutually almost incomprehensible.

RELIGION

Vietnamese people are generally open-minded and pragmatic on spiritual and metaphysical matters. Many people are animist, seeing living spirits in the objects and landscapes around them. Respect for, and even worship of, ancestors is a way of life instilled by the elderly in the young.

Buddhism and Christianity are widely represented; Buddhism was brought over from China and Roman Catholicism was introduced from France. Cao Daism, Vietnam's homegrown system of belief (▷ 16), borrows ideas from all the major religions, hoping one day to transcend borders and become the one true global religion.

ETHNIC MINORITIES

Vietnam is home to 54 ethnic groups, including the Vietnamese (Kinh) themselves. Groups vary in size from the Tày, with a population of about 1.3 million, to the O-Du, who can be counted in the hundreds. Ethnic groups belonging to the Sino-Tibetan language family, such as the Hmông and Dao, and the Tibeto-Burman language group, such as the Ha Nhi and Phu La, are more recent arrivals, having migrated south from China within the past 250 to 300 years. These people live almost exclusively on the upper mountain slopes, practicing swidden agriculture (clearing land for cultivation by slashing and burning vegetation) and posing little threat to their more numerous lowland-dwelling neighbors, notably the Thai.

Life has been hard for many of the minorities, who have had to fight not only the French and Vietnamese but often each other in order to retain their territory and cultural identity. Traditions and customs have been eroded by outside influences, although some alien ideas have been successfully accommodated. Centuries of Viet population growth and decades of warfare have taken a heavy toll on minorities and their territories; increasingly, population pressure from the minority groups themselves poses a threat to their way of life.

The highland areas of Vietnam are among the most linguistically and culturally diverse in the world. In total, the highland peoples number just over eight million. The generic term for these diverse peoples of the highlands is Montagnard (from the French for "mountain people") or, in Vietnamese, *nguoi thuong* (highland citizen). The highland peoples themselves identify with their village and tribal group, and not as part of a wider "highland citizens" grouping.

Potentially, tourism can be a serious threat to the minorities' way of life, and any visitors to minority villages should be aware of the extent to which they contribute to this process. Traditional means of livelihood may be quickly and understandably abandoned when a higher living standard can be obtained from the tourist dollar.

Long-standing societal and kinship ties can also be weakened by the intrusion of outsiders. Young people may question their society's values and traditions, which may seem archaic and anachronistic by comparison with those of the modern visitor, and dress and music are in danger of losing all cultural significance if they become mere tourist attractions.

ECONOMY

The stereotypical image of a one-party Communist state is not very evident in the economic sphere. This has occured since Vietnam initiated a period of reform that saw the introduction of market forces and an active encouragement of the private sector in ways that would have been unthinkable 25 years ago.

The minimum wage in Hanoi and Ho Chi Minh City is around US$75 a month, significantly less than the prevailing rate in China's factories, and this is attracting large international companies. Within government ranks, though not in public, there is discussion and disagreement about how best to manage a system of "market forces with a socialist orientation" and, in particular, the future role of the country's large-scale and not always cost-effective public industries.

HUMAN RIGHTS

Human Rights Watch has condemned Vietnam for its treatment of those trying to spread information about democracy via the internet. Its recent report stated: "The Vietnamese government tightened controls on freedom of expression during 2010, harassing, arresting, and jailing dozens of writers, political activists, and other peaceful critics."

Statements from Amnesty International concur with this and draw attention to the widespread hacking of dissidents' websites and blogs. In August 2010, for example, a mathematics professor in Ho Chi Minh City was arrested for contributing to a website criticizing Chinese-run bauxite mines in the Central Highlands. In March 2011, a high-profile political trial of a scholar, Cu Huy Ha Vu, lasted half a day and concluded with a sentence of seven years in prison following his conviction for conducting propaganda against the state.

VIETNAM'S REGIONS

Vietnam's name derives from the one adopted for the country by Emperor Gia Long in 1802: Nam Viet. This means, literally, the Viet (the largest ethnic group) of the south (Nam), and replaced the former name, Annam.

The country covers a land area of 127,246sq miles (329,565sq km) and has a coastline of 2,157 miles (3,471km). The French subdivided Vietnam into three regions, administering each separately: Tonkin or Bac Ky (northern region); Annam or Trung Ky (central region); and Cochin China or Nam Ky (southern region). These administrative divisions have been abolished, but the Vietnamese still recognize their country as consisting of three regions, distinct in terms of geography, history and culture. Their new names are Bac Bo (north), Trung Bo (center) and Nam Bo (south). There are 58 administrative provinces ($\triangleright$ map, opposite).

The most important economic zones, containing the main concentrations of population, are focused on two large deltaic areas. In the north, there are the rice fields and settlements of the Red River, and in the south is the fertile alluvial plain of the Mekong. In between, the country narrows to less than 31 miles (50km) wide, with only a thin ribbon of fertile lowland suited to intensive agriculture. Much of the interior, away from the coastal belt and the deltas, is mountainous. Here, minority hilltribes (Montagnards), with some lowland Vietnamese resettled in New Economic Zones since 1975, eke out a living. The rugged terrain means that only a quarter of the land is cultivated. Of the remainder, somewhere between about 20 and 25 percent of the area is forested, although some of this is heavily degraded.

THE NORTH

In the far north are the Northern Highlands, which ring the Red River Delta and form a natural barrier with China. The rugged mountains on the west border of this region—the Hoang Lien Son—exceed 9,800ft (3,000m) in places. The tributaries of the Red River have cut deep, steep-sided gorges through the Hoang Lien

Son, which are navigable by small boats. The eastern portion of this region, bordering the Gulf of Tonkin, is far less imposing; the mountain peaks of the west have diminished into foothills, allowing easy access to China. The principal towns and cities in this region are Lao Cai and Dien Bien Phu in the northwest and Haiphong and Halong in the east.

The Red River Delta lies in the embrace of the hills of the north, with Hanoi at its core. The delta covers almost 5,800sq miles (15,000sq km) and extends 150 miles (240km) inland from the coast. Rice has been grown on the alluvial soils of the Red River for thousands of years. Yet despite the intricate web of canals, dikes and embankments, the Vietnamese have never been able to tame the river completely, and the delta is the victim of frequent and sometimes devastating floods. The area is very low-lying, rarely more than 10ft (3m) above sea level, and often less than 3ft (1m). Although the region supports one of the highest agricultural population densities in the world, the inhabitants have frequently had to endure famines—most recently in 1989.

CENTRAL VIETNAM

South of the Red River Delta region lie the central lowlands and the mountains of the Annamite Chain. The Annam Highlands, now known as the Truong Son Mountain Range, form an important cultural divide between the Indianized nations to the west and the Sinicized cultures to the east. The northern rugged extremity of the range is in Thanh Hoa Province. From here the Truong Son stretches more than 750 miles (1,200km) south, to gradually end 50 miles (80km) north of Ho Chi Minh City (formerly Saigon). The Central Highlands form an upland plateau, occupied by the hill resorts of Buon Me Thuot and Dalat. On the plateau, plantation agriculture and hill farms are interspersed with stands of bamboo and tropical forests. To the east, the Annamite Chain falls off steeply, leaving only a narrow and fragmented band of lowland suitable for settlement—the central coastal strip. In places the mountains advance all the way to the coast, plunging into the sea as dramatic rockfaces and making north–south communication difficult. The region extends some 40 miles (64km) inland and covers 2,605sq miles (6,750sq km). The soils are often rocky or saline, and irrigation is difficult. The main centers of population are Vinh, Huê, Danang, Hoi An, Nha Trang and Vung Tau.

THE SOUTH

The Mekong Delta is not as prone to flooding as the Red River Delta, and consequently rice production is more stable. The reason for this less severe flooding is the regulating effect of the Great Lake of Cambodia, the Tonlé Sap. During the rainy season, when the water

Left *Terraced paddy fields near Bac Can, in the north of the country*

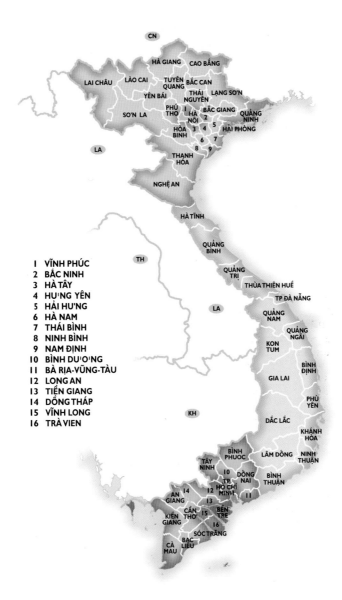

CN

HÀ GIANG   CAO BẰNG

LAI CHÂU   LÀO CAI   TUYÊN QUANG   BẮC CAN

YÊN BÁI   THÁI NGUYÊN   LANG SO'N

SO'N LA   PHÚ THỌ   1   HÀ NỘI   BẮC GIANG   QUẢNG NINH

HÒA BÌNH   3   4   5   HẢI PHÒNG

6   7

8   9

THANH HÓA

LA

NGHỆ AN

HÀ TĨNH

QUẢNG BÌNH

TH

QUẢNG TRỊ

THỪA THIÊN HUẾ

TP ĐÀ NẴNG

LA

QUẢNG NAM

QUẢNG NGÃI

KON TUM

BÌNH ĐỊNH

GIA LAI

PHÚ YÊN

DẮC LẮC

KH

KHÁNH HÒA

LÂM ĐỒNG   NINH THUẬN

BÌNH PHUOC

TÂY NINH

10   ĐỒNG NAI   BÌNH THUẬN

TP HỒ CHÍ MINH

12   11

AN GIANG   14

13   CẦN THƠ'   15   BẾN TRE

KIẾN GIANG

16

SÓC TRĂNG

CÀ MAU   BẠC LIÊU

1   VĨNH PHÚC
2   BẮC NINH
3   HÀ TÂY
4   HU'NG YÊN
5   HẢI HU'NG
6   HÀ NAM
7   THÁI BÌNH
8   NINH BÌNH
9   NAM ĐỊNH
10   BÌNH DU'O'NG
11   BÀ RỊA-VŨNG-TÀU
12   LONG AN
13   TIỀN GIANG
14   ĐỒNG THÁP
15   VĨNH LONG
16   TRÀ VIEN

flowing into the Mekong becomes too great for even this mighty river to absorb, rather than overflowing its banks, the water backs up into the Tonlé Sap, which quadruples in area. The Mekong Delta covers 25,900sq miles (67,000sq km) and is drained by five branches of the Mekong, which divides as it flows toward the sea. The vast delta is one of the great rice bowls of Asia, producing nearly half of the country's rice, and over the years has been cut into a patchwork by the canals that have been dug to expand irrigation and hence the area given over to cultivation. The region was largely forested until the late 19th century, when the French supported its settlement by Vietnamese peasants, recognizing that it could become enormously productive. The deposition of silt by the rivers that cut through the delta means that the shoreline is continually advancing—by up to 260ft (80m) each year in some places. To the north of the delta lies Ho Chi Minh City (HCMC or Saigon). The main towns of the delta itself are My Tho, Can Tho, Rach Gia, Ha Tien and Chau Doc. Offshore is the large unspoiled island of Phu Quoc, while farther south is the protected marine environment of the Con Dao archipelago.

HANOI

Hoa Lo (▷ 73) This legendary prison housed American POWs during the Vietnam War.

Ho Chi Minh Mausoleum (▷ 76) The mausoleum contains the preserved body of Ho Chi Minh.

Old City (▷ 65–67) Markets, flower-sellers, restaurants, traders' quarters and decaying shop houses are crammed into the most vibrant part of the capital.

B-52 Museum (▷ 69) The downed aircraft of the American fighting machine has found its final resting place in the yard of this curious museum.

Vietnam Museum of Ethnology (▷ 70) The museum is dedicated to Vietnam's 54 ethnic minorities.

Opera House (▷ 77, 87) Step out for an evening performance inside the elegant, iconic Opera House.

Shopping (▷ 84–85) Duck in and out of the hundreds of clothing, handicraft and souvenir stores in Hanoi, indulging in a riot of bright patterns and varied textures.

Bobby Chinn (▷ 88–89) Step out for a hip dining experience at this fashionable (and expensive) restaurant, where you'll enjoy innovative dishes, good wine and chic decor.

Dining out (▷ 88–92) Sample any of the multitude of excellent and, happily, inexpensive restaurants that fill Hanoi's streets.

Moca Café (▷ 91) Sip coffee in a window seat and watch the locals pull up onto the sidewalks with their motos. Follow the wisps of exhaust smoke as they curl skyward in the rain.

Above Hanoi Opera House illuminated at night

THE NORTH

Dien Bien Phu (▷ 104–105) The Vietnamese victory over the French here in 1954 heralded the collapse of their Indochinese empire.

Perfume Pagoda (▷ 102) This popular pilgrimage spot is dedicated to the guardian spirit of mother and child, and is built amid caves peppered with hundreds of incense sticks.

Cuc Phuong National Park (▷ 113) Walk here in April or May to be encircled by thousands of green and yellow butterflies.

Halong Bay (▷ 114–117) Sail out to enjoy the jade-green, silken waters of this UNESCO World Heritage Site, studded with thousands of limestone outcrops.

Highland walking (▷ 108, 109, 110, 111, 112, 118–119) Around Mai Chau, Sapa, Son La and other areas of northwest Vietnam, you'll see stilted houses, terraced paddies and vibrant ethnic minority dress.

Sapa (▷ 109–111) Home to the Hmông ethnic minority, Sapa is surrounded by some stunning scenery.

Tam Coc (▷ 113) Glide down the Ngo Dong River through a magnificent limestone landscape.

CENTRAL VIETNAM

My Son (▷ 156) The glories of the Champa kingdom are immortalized in stone here at what was the empire's core spiritual seat.

Museum of Cham Sculpture, Danang (▷ 138–139) Admire sculptural body art and depictions of Hindu deities in some of the most perfect examples of Champa creativity.

Hoi An (▷ 142–146) Wander around the silk emporiums and Chinese temples and indulge in glorious food in this quaint mercantile town.

Huê (▷ 147–154) Absorb the atmosphere of this imperial capital, its tombs and the Perfume River.

Dalat (▷ 134–137) Inhale the mountain air at this highland retreat, a former French colonial hill station and now the Vietnamese honeymoon capital.

Mui Ne (▷ 155) Wind down in luxury resorts with lots of facilities on a perfect strip of palm-studded sand.

Nha Trang (▷ 157–158) The pleasures of travel can be found at this beachside hangout, with restaurants, bars and cafés, plus diving, watersports and spas for pampering.

HO CHI MINH CITY

Reunification Hall (▷ 197) One of the most historically significant buildings in Vietnam.

War Remnants Museum (▷ 190) This collection of Vietnam War military equipment and photographs presents a graphic account of the conflict.

Museum of Vietnamese History (▷ 191) Spend some time at this important museum, which houses an extensive collection of artifacts and sculptures within its elegant walls.

Ben Thanh Market (▷ 189) Slip down to the night market and slurp on a bowl of *pho* (noodle soup) while watching the world go by.

Cholon (▷ 192–194) Ho Chi Minh City's Chinatown has some interesting pagodas and attractive Chinese assembly houses.

Below An idyllic beach villa at Nha Trang
Right Cao Dai Great Temple, Tay Ninh

Lam Son Square (▷ 199) If you're feeling brave, climb on a motorcycle, either as a driver or passenger, and cruise around the square at night in the balmy air amid the roar of thousands of other motos.

Sky drinking (▷ 211–213) Take to one of the city's skyscraper hotels for a nighttime drink and marvel at the energy of this new powerhouse, while overlooking its glittering nightscape.

Shopping (▷ 202–203) Head for Dong Khoi Street and District 1 to pick up silk souvenirs, trinkets and other unmissable purchases.

THE SOUTH

Cu Chi Tunnels (▷ 224) This extensive tunnel complex was the home of some 16,000 resistance fighters during the Vietnam War.

Cao Dai Great Temple, Tay Ninh (▷ 220–221) A fantastical building, dedicated to an indigenous Vietnamese religion that combines elements of other world religions.

Can Tho Markets (▷ 218–219) Motor up the river from Can Tho and enter the busy world of the floating market—brightly painted boats crammed with fruit and vegetables on the Mekong River.

Phu Quoc (▷ 225) Sunbathe, snorkel, eat and drink in one of the small number of resorts on this unspoiled island off the Cambodian border.

Eat *heo quay* and *com tam* **(anywhere)**—broken rice with barbecued pork makes a delicious breakfast, lunch or dinner.

Have Sunday champagne brunch in Opera at the Park Hyatt in Ho Chi Minh City (▷ 209), one of the country's top hotels—be sure to make a reservation.

Kayak around the island-studded waters of Halong Bay (▷ 114–117), exploring caves and deserted beaches.

Relax in a resort at Mui Ne (▷ 179–180), the sandy peninsula near Phan Thiet, which has Vietnam's best selection of beach resorts.

Swim at China Beach (▷ 139), one of Vietnam's most spectacular beaches, with golden sand, wonderful surf and clear, blue water.

Take a boat on the Perfume River (▷ 147, 168), which connects many of the historical sites of enchanting Huê.

Take an early evening boat ride on the Thu Bon River in Hoi An (▷ 143) while swallows dip over the water and the town's lights twinkle in the distance.

Treat yourself to a piece of original art (▷ 21). Contemporary Vietnamese art is making a serious impression on the international scene.

Visit Minh Mang's mausoleum in Huê (▷ 152), for gardens, pavilions, gatehouses and statues.

Walk around Hoan Kiem Lake (▷ 74); as the sun sets in Hanoi, couples come here to huddle on the benches, and walkers come to enjoy the fresh air.

Warm yourself by a log fire on the cold winter nights in Sapa (▷ 109–111), an especially memorable experience at Christmas.

TOP EXPERIENCES

Bargain with the ethnic minority vendors in Sapa (▷ 110), who dangle their charms and souvenirs under your nose, with calls in French of *"jolie, jolie!"*

Be dazzled by the verdant greens of a Mekong paddy; in spring, the young rice shoots up through the murky waters and transforms the landscape.

Bicycle around the paddy fields of Mai Chau (▷ 108), an attractive small town surrounded by Thái ethnic minority villages.

Drive a motorcycle around Saigon—not for the faint-hearted but a novel way to see the sights.

Eat fish on the quayside in Hoi An (▷ 171)—some of the tastiest around.

Eat *pho bo* in Hanoi (▷ 88–92); this beef noodle soup is warming, nourishing and tasty.

Above left *Minh Mang's Tomb in Huê*
Below *Boating on the Suoi Yen River against a dramatic backdrop of densely forested hills*

LIVING VIETNAM

PEOPLE AND SOCIETY

Vietnam is changing fast. Apart from China, it has the fastest annual growth rate in Asia—a leap forward that came of bleak necessity. When the war ended in 1975, Vietnam was starving. In 1986, a desperate government announced a policy of *doi moi* (renovation): decollectivizing agriculture and encouraging small private businesses. The constitution of 1992 announced privatization of state-owned enterprises, and in 2000 a trade agreement was signed with the US. Subsidies on consumer goods were reduced, wages increased and foreign investment was actively encouraged. Vietnam is now the world's second-largest exporter of both rice and coffee, while garments and seafood are other major exports. Electrical appliances spill out of shops, and for the first time many Vietnamese are taking jobs outside the family. Meanwhile, the limits of political reform seem to have been reached. There is no open political debate, and official disapproval makes it difficult to get the police reference required for a university place, a passport or a job. The future is uncertain. The population is growing rapidly, and the rural poor—75 percent of the population—resent the cities' economic gains. While the economies of Hanoi and Saigon grow at about 20 percent a year, the countryside lags far behind.

GRANNY RULES, OK?

The family is all important in Vietnamese society. To some extent, poverty has kept families together, with three generations typically living under one roof. Nearly every house has an ancestral altar where photos of great-grandma and grandpa are propped up among the food and sometimes alcoholic offerings. Vietnamese families generally have very traditional values, a legacy of Confucianism: the ideal of children's loyalty to their parents. This means that even grown-up children bring their earnings home to the family, and very often the grandmother controls all. If a son needs to take a course, everyone in the family contributes, and spouses are drawn into this network of interdependence and support.

Clockwise from above *A woman from a White Thái minority village employs traditional weaving methods; a Muslim Cham village elder; choosing a kumquat tree for New Year celebrations, Hanoi*

FIRST MILESTONES

A two-child directive is still government policy in Vietnam even though it is not always followed. Not surprisingly, Vietnamese families celebrate two important milestones in the early lives of their children. *Day thang* (full month) is celebrated one month after birth. Traditionally, after staying in bed with her baby for the first month, the mother would go out to introduce her baby to the village. Today, parents hold a small party for friends and neighbors. *Thoi noi* is celebrated at the end of the first year. At the party the baby is presented with a tray holding items such as a pen, a mirror, scissors, soil and food. Whichever item the baby takes first indicates its character and likely job: scissors for a tailor, pen for a teacher, soil for a farmer and so on.

KUMQUATS AND FIRST-FOOTERS

A few weeks before *Tet*, Vietnam's important New Year festival, bicycles with mini-orchards of kumquat trees bound to the back begin to appear on the streets. Choosing a kumquat tree is a serious matter. It must have ripe fruit, unripe fruit and buds to represent the three generations of a family; it must have dark green leaves, bright new leaves and leaf buds. During *Tet* visitors call to appraise and admire one another's trees. Another *Tet* tradition is first-footing, where the first person to call by in the new year determines the household's luck. To be sure of a good outcome, families invite their first-footers, who must be distinguished and preferably rich, and must not be divorced or have lost a member of the family in the past year.

FRIENDS AND EX-FOES

Vietnamese people do not hold grudges and this is especially evident in contemporary attitudes toward the United States and, as they call it, the American War. Museums in Vietnam record with brutal realism the sufferings endured under colonial rule and its evolution into the 1960s war, but American visitors are always warmly welcomed. Many Vietnamese now regard the US as an ally—just as Russia once was—that helps buffer their country, geopolitically, against the rising power of China, a country that occupied and ruled Vietnam for nearly 1,000 years. A new generation of overseas Vietnamese, whose embittered parents fled their country in the mid-1970s, are also returning. With an entrepreneurial spirit and much needed capital, they are also finding a place in a country which is embracing Westernization with zeal.

"IF YOU LOVED ME…"

Karaoke has become a national pastime, and lively karaoke parlors now abound in every town throughout the country. These are the places where mixed groups of people can meet in private for courtship, singing their favorite romantic songs to one another. This is a modern echo of a mountain tradition that is still in practice, whereby the young men of one village go to visit the young women of another village and sing impromptu love songs, to which the girls improvise a sung reply—sometimes full of licentious puns.

A strong element of romance and sentimentality exists within Vietnamese culture as well as a long tradition of poetry-writing. Emperors used to hold poetry competitions for their ministers, and examinations for aspiring mandarins included writing poetry to a strict form—within the examination time.

VIETNAMESE RELIGION

Historically, the Vietnamese have taken a pragmatic view toward religion. Whenever a new one comes along, they simply fuse it with what they have and carry on. Even Ho Chi Minh has been added to the pantheon, his statue appearing in a village temple just outside Hanoi. For a time, Communism frowned on all religions and statues were hidden away, but now they are reappearing. This fusion of faiths means that temples may hold the statues of deities of several religions, all of which still influence the Vietnamese psyche. From animism, possibly the oldest, come the goddesses of heaven, forests and waters, revered in villages where small spirit houses hang in the trees. The black-and-white S-shape designs on "worry balls" for arthritic hands are taken from the yin (passive) and yang (active) symbols of Taoism. Confucianism's structure of loyalties—of ministers to emperor, of children to parents, of wives to husbands— is still a strong influence in Vietnamese filial piety and respect for elders. Buddhism, too, is an important religion in the country. Christianity, imported by Portuguese and French priests, has left a legacy of temple-like churches. Hinduism has also made an impact, and there are pockets of Islam.

ASIAN SPECTACULAR
Officially titled The Third Great Universal Religious Amnesty, Cao Daism has grown from a vision witnessed by one man in 1919 to a religion with more than five million followers, making it the third biggest faith in Vietnam. Cao Daism synthesizes elements from other world religions, and by 1948 had fostered a 10,000-strong army that fought against both the French and the Communists.

Since independence, the Cao Dai church has peacefully struggled against the government, which seized all its assets in 1997 as part of "official recognition."

Cao Daists today continue to practice their visually spectacular rituals openly and to petition the authorities with demands for religious freedom.

Clockwise from above *Two men dressed in red robes outside Cao Dai Great Temple; a young monk at a pagoda in Soc Trang; a Jarai spirit effigy from Kontum*

HYPNOTIC FESTIVALS

Buddhism is an enigma in Vietnam; it is the largest organized religion in the country and it is a cultural constant that means different things to different groups of people.

Many Buddhists' beliefs are heavily influenced by Taoism and Confucianism. Vietnamese Buddhism is subdivided into various groups, the biggest belonging to the Mahayana vehicle, which easily conforms to the Vietnamese idea of religion, combining folklore with the veneration of enlightened beings. Temples began to decline after 1975 owing to a state policy discouraging people from becoming monks or nuns. However, attendance at festivals and pilgrimages is now climbing, and about half of all Vietnamese practice some form of Buddhism. Urban temples often have electronic music, powerful incense and hypnotic light shows, providing an entrancing atmosphere during festivals.

POPULAR BELIEFS

Formal religions had to build on the foundations of ancient animist beliefs to get a foothold in Vietnam, and the old traditions are still running strong and perhaps even blossoming as society changes.

Since the late 1980s, village pagodas have undergone a frenzy of refurbishment. In one village near Hanoi, a local woman who lived some 200 years ago is revered for instigating the now prosperous pharmaceutical industry; another village temple is devoted to a Vietnamese princess who developed the silk industry.

One village faith features the unusual courtship ritual of grabbing eels from a jar. A young man and woman try to catch the eel without looking into the jar. The young man has to keep one hand on the young woman's breast while a committee of judges watches closely, along with fellow villagers who continue to call out and tease the couple.

CHRISTIAN TROUBLES

Christianity first came to Vietnam in the 16th century and Roman Catholicism has been a political force here since the French missions of the early 19th century. Catholics have played a part in many national events, creating the national script, for instance. There are more than six million Roman Catholics in Vietnam, mainly in the south, where the former government was Catholic-dominated. Protestants make up only 1 percent of the population, mostly in the central highlands. Evangelical Christianity is less tolerated, and some priests who spoke against the authorities have been jailed. Nevertheless, the government has said it regards Christianity as a "positive force," and in 2004 introduced its Ordinance Regarding Religious Beliefs and Religious Organizations, proclaiming freedom of belief for all faiths that cooperate with the state.

OTHER BELIEFS

The doctrines of Confucius pervade every aspect of Vietnamese life, stressing the importance of family and lineage and the worship of ancestors, but they do not constitute an organized religion. Likewise Taoism, while having several temples and sects devoted to its principal historical figures, has no formal clergy or church, but still exerts its influence on national culture, particularly through pilgrimages. Famous Taoist temples by the West Lake and on Hoan Kiem Lake in Hanoi continue to be popular. Cults such as Tran Hung Dao and Chu Vi feature blood and mutilation rituals and female spirit-mediums. Hoa Hao is a Buddhist sect that has grown into a major religion in its own right, its leaders now joining Christian and Buddhist clergy in opposition to government controls. Small Muslim, Hindu and Bahai communities also exist.

THE ENVIRONMENT AND THE LAND

Vietnam is dominated by water: oceans, rivers, canals, lakes, monsoons and floods. Mountains form the spine of the country, running north to south, broken by steep valleys that create mini-climates. The dense primary tropical rainforest that originally covered the entire peninsula had by 1982 been depleted to only 23 percent of the land. The government's reforestation program has increased this to 28 percent, but just 10 percent is primary rainforest. Scientists and overseas conservation agencies are enumerating, cataloging and protecting Vietnam's flora and fauna, with some remarkable success—such as the rescue of the U-Minh forest in the Mekong Delta from the damage of wartime defoliants. The Javan rhinoceros, one of the rarest large mammals in the world, thought to survive only in West Java, Indonesia, was discovered here in 1989, and an even more astonishing discovery followed: two completely new species of mammal. In 1992, the Vu Quang ox, known to locals as *sao la*, was the first new large mammal species to be found in 50 years. In 1993, a new species of deer, the giant muntjac, was spotted in the Vu Quang Nature Reserve. Since 1962, when Cuc Phuong National Park was created, 87 nature reserves have been established in all, covering 3.3 percent of Vietnam's land area.

Clockwise from above *Sunrise in the Mekong Delta; crossing a hanging bridge near Dalat; a black gibbon in the Endangered Primate Rescue Center, Cuc Phuong National Park*

BUFFALO BOYS
The ubiquitous round-bellied gray water buffalo is a symbol of Vietnam, often the subject of paintings and statues. It is the all-purpose beast of burden, pulling the plough through muddy rice paddies, or carts laden with bags of rice or farm produce along dirt tracks or even into Hanoi and Ho Chi Minh City. Every young country boy must do his stint as a buffalo boy, minding the creature, which is often a family's most precious possession. The image of a boy on the back of the water buffalo, or a white bird perched on its back plucking insects, is a familiar one. The water buffalo may look docile but, with a weight of more than 1,300lb (up to 600kg) it is not an animal to annoy; there have been very occasional incidents of one injuring and even killing villagers.

UNDERSTANDING LIVING VIETNAM

18

THE MEKONG

The Mekong River is one of the 12 great rivers of the world and is the source of much of Vietnam's agricultural wealth. It stretches around 2,800 miles (4,500km) from its source on the Tibet Plateau to its mouth in the Mekong Delta, where it deposits fertile silt. The first European to explore the Mekong was French naval officer Francis Garnier. His Mekong Expedition (1866–68) followed the river upstream from its delta in Cochin China (southern Vietnam). Of the 6,188 miles (9,960km) that the expedition covered, 3,144 miles (5,060km) were charted for the first time. The river is navigable only as far as the Laos–Cambodian border, where the Khone rapids make it impassable.

PULLING UP POPPIES

Opium poppies have long been a significant source of income for Vietnam's poorer ethnic minority areas. However, the extent of plantation is a matter of dispute. Vietnam's official estimate is that only 778 acres (315ha) are used for poppy cultivation; the Ministry of Agriculture and Rural Development claims that in Son La 9,419 acres (3,812ha) out of 9,884 acres (4,000ha) of crop have been destroyed. The UN Office of Drugs and Crime believes there to be 5,683 acres (2,300ha) of poppies, a reduction from the 1993 figure of 31,876 acres (12,900ha). The state has invested more than 38 billion dong in alternative crops such as fruit trees, rice, maize and tea.

THE SCRAP ECONOMY

Scavenging for metal and other recyclable materials is an activity undertaken by many of the poorest of the Vietnamese people to boost their incomes. According to a report by Michael DiGregorio, of Hawaii's East-West Center, some 6,000 people in Hanoi earned a living scavenging for scrap in 1992, this figure rising to 8,000 in 1996. As a result, 275 tons of "garbage" from the waste economy were fed back into the productive economy every day—more than a third of the capital's daily refuse. In the 1990s, an itinerant junk buyer could earn US$1.41 a day—five times more than comparative agricultural wages. However, nearly 40,000 people have died while scavenging for scrap since 1975, after "discovering" some of the 35 million landmines and 300,000 tons of unexploded ordnance that remain scattered across this beautiful country.

TREKKER'S DELIGHT

Vietnam's forests provide great trekking opportunities and unusual sights. The mountain slopes of Nghe An Province on the Laos border harbor some of the rarest animals in the world, notably the Saola antelope, discovered in the 1990s. Although you have to get really lucky to spot a wild elephant or gibbon, there is still plenty of breathtaking forest to walk through. Serious work is now going on to try to preserve and regenerate the woodland of this densely populated country. Dr. Nguyen Van Sinh, of Hanoi's Institute of Ecology and Biological Resources, takes visitors around Cuc Phuong National Park, where he is running a project to restock the area with local plant life. Restoring native tree species will take the pressure off remaining primary and secondary forests, benefiting both wildlife and the Vietnamese people.

Before *doi moi* (▷ 40), the arts in Vietnam were state-funded and censored. Since 1987 there has been a relaxation of control; two-way cultural projects have been launched between Vietnam and the US, limitations on movie production have been lifted (though film scripts are still monitored) and art galleries, once forbidden, flourish in Ho Chi Minh City and Hanoi. However, sources of funding can prove elusive in the newly liberalized economy. One initiative that has emerged to fill the gap is a government program, assisted by international agencies, to train staff in arts and heritage management. Traditional arts such as carving are encouraged, as in Kim Bong village, near Hoi An, where UNESCO supports a master sculptor and 15 apprentices. Other cultural traditions have survived—such as *cai luong* theater and water puppetry, Huê's court dances, and the traditional music performed on Vietnam's unique instruments, the *danh ba*, a huge bamboo-tube xylophone, and the vertically strung bamboo xylophone.

CAI LUONG THEATER
Performed in Hanoi and Ho Chi Minh City, *cai luong* (reform) theater is madcap musical farce. "Reform" merely means a newer incarnation of *cheo*—comic folk theater that originated in villages of the south a century ago. The plots originally made fun of feudal mandarins—feudalism persisted until 1945 and the abdication of Vietnam's last emperor (▷ 31). Dialogue, mostly sung, is now updated to make fun of contemporary powers, in one of the few venues where such criticism is tolerated. Costumes are bright, wildly elaborate and outrageous, there are pretty women and dancers, and it is clear even to foreigners who are the good guys and the bad guys, making this an unforgettable experience even for those without a word of Vietnamese.

Clockwise from above *A young girl taking part in the religious processions to the Ngoc Son Temple in Hanoi; chef Bobby Chinn; propaganda posters have been elevated to an art form*

WATER PUPPETRY

Green bamboo blinds serve as curtains behind a watery "stage." Shiny gilt dragons, spouting water, pop up from beneath the surface, bobbing up and down as dragons do. A fisherman comes rowing along. The puppets, 15in (38cm) high, are so engaging that it is easy to forget the puppeteers manipulating them from behind the blinds, using strings passed through underwater bamboo poles. Best known of the water puppet troupes is the Thang Long in Hanoi, which has made many tours abroad. To join the Thang Long theater troupe—a coveted position, as puppeteers are well paid and have a chance to travel abroad—boys and girls go through a four-year course at Hanoi's College of Arts, then serve an apprenticeship in one of three villages.

PICTURES OF VIETNAM

Recognized by both the Vietnamese Association of Photographic Artists (VAPA) and the International Federation of Photographic Art (FIAP), photographer Long Thanh from Nha Trang is one of the most distinguished in his field. Working only in black and white, he takes many of his famous images in and around his native Nha Trang. The city lies in the old kingdom of Champa, and the Cham villages and people provide most of the subject matter. Long Thanh first started taking pictures at the age of 13 and has since collected some 18 international awards. His pictures have been shown around the world, and are exhibited and sold in Nha Trang (▷ 157–158). See www.elephantguide.com/longthanh.

POSTER ART

Vietnam's countryside and towns are peppered with propaganda and health and safety billboards, where posters have been elevated to an art form. They cover a range of subjects, including government policy, elections, road safety, the danger of HIV, while some commemorate historical events. The Mekong Delta, in particular, is littered with boards expounding the dangers of intravenous drug use and unprotected sex. In the north, remarkable billboards depict the Vietnamese victory at Dien Bien Phu in 1954. At election time, the country is covered in images of the Viet Kinh, ethnic minorities and military at the ballot box. Luong Anh Dung, an official government painter for 30 years, produced many of the nationalist images. Today, propaganda and advertisement painting is taught at fine arts schools as part of an applied graphic arts program.

BOBBY CHINN MAKES WAVES

Restaurateur Bobby Chinn has been making waves ever since he came to Vietnam in 1995. Born in New Zealand, Chinn is half Egyptian, half Chinese, was educated in England and grew up in the US. Inheriting an interest in food from his Chinese and Egyptian grandmothers, Chinn learned his culinary trade while working in restaurants in San Francisco before going on to apprentice in France. He settled in Saigon and managed a number of well-regarded restaurants. His attempts at running his own restaurant in Vietnam were almost defeated by bureaucracy and business practices, but, unwilling to give up, he opened his eponymous restaurant in Hanoi, originally opposite Hoan Kiem Lake. It has now moved to a new location beside West Lake (▷ 88–89). The change of locale has not, however, diminished its popularity.

You need to keep your wits about you when strolling the streets of Vietnam's cities. The sidewalks are crowded with people seeking relief from the heat in any trifling breeze. Add the areas stringed off for parking bicycles and motorcycles, the clutter of "dust cafés" and pedestrians ambling arm in arm, and the squatting itinerant vendors selling lottery tickets, cigarettes, oranges or mangoes, and there's little chance of getting anywhere in a hurry. On any blank wall a barber might hang a mirror and a limp towel and unfold a chair, while a corner bicycle repair shop may advertise itself by displaying an inner tube and a bottle of motorcycle oil. As you stroll along, a scooter may come zooming out of a house across the sidewalk in front of you at any moment, its driver looking neither right nor left. And shouts from hawkers waft through the air as they approach, either doing the rounds or on the way to a spare patch of shade.

COFFEE CABARET
Forget Starbucks or the Left Bank in Paris: Vietnam is the place to find café culture. The country is now a major coffee exporter and overflows with an amazing variety of cafés. Some offer 30 gourmet varieties, including fox coffee—apparently, the beans are collected from fox dung. There is a haven of bohemian cafés near Hanoi's small lake, thick with the literati set and the international editions of famous newspapers. Almost anywhere in Vietnam you can wander into a café, take a wooden chair with a view of the street and choose a hot or iced coffee. Hot coffee, served in a traditional drip filter, takes so long to drip through that your glass stands ready in a bowl of hot water. This keeps the coffee warm— and it's well worth the wait.

Clockwise from above *Hanoi street life; a stand at Binh Tay Market, Ho Chi Minh City; locals at a* bia hoi *bar in Hanoi*

BIA HOI

Walking around Vietnam's cities is great fun, but when the sensory overload starts to bite, take a rest in a *bia hoi* bar. The Vietnamese are never shy of passing a few minutes with a visitor who's not afraid to mingle, and the famous *bia hoi* bars are some of the best places to mix and pick up some real local tips. *Bia hoi* (fresh beer) is the mildly alcoholic local draft brew, sold at prices as low as 4,000d for a half-pint glass in thousands of tiny street bars across the country. It's brewed overnight and is served in stylish bottle-green jugs. The cheaper and dingier the bar, the better it often is, and side dishes of dog or shots of snake whiskey add some spice.

DUST CAFÉS

Vietnam's city sidewalks are full of small cafés, where tiny, low plastic stools are set around equally low tables. The Vietnamese call these "dust cafés," and they are the talking shops of the country. Even when most people should be working, dust cafés are busy. The usual order is a beer or tea, sometimes coffee, or the standard Vietnamese fast food for breakfast, lunch, supper or a late-night snack —a bowl of *pho* (noodle soup). Nothing discourages the customers. Come the monsoons, when city streets are awash with mud, or the bitterly cold winter months of the north, the cafés are still going strong and the *pho* is consumed as eagerly as ever.

CULT OF THE HONDA

Every aspiring chic miss and smart lad in Vietnam's cities yearns for a Honda Dream —the more expensive the model, the better. Vietnam's sea of gently moving bicycles has evolved into a noisy cacophony of motors, as riders race through the streets around Hoan Kiem Lake in Hanoi or up and down Dong Khoi Street in Ho Chi Minh City, wearing the latest Western fashions and cool-looking sunglasses. And during weekends in the major cities, the Vietnamese youth come out in force to show off their gleaming steeds. Honda now have a factory in Hanoi and sell their machines for around US$900, five times less than ones made in Japan. Chinese motorcycles sell for only US$300 but tend not to last long before requiring repairs.

THE OTHER SIDE

Crossing the street in Vietnam's cities is an extreme sport. One popular story goes that the wife of a foreign visitor refused to leave the hotel throughout her husband's two-year contract because she couldn't cross the street outside their hotel. Traffic lights are more or less obeyed—except by bicycles, which go anywhere, anytime. Pedestrians are marooned on the curb while the light turns yellow, red and green, and the bicyclists carry on their journeys regardless. Cautious beginners position themselves on the off-traffic side of Vietnamese pedestrians for protection; veterans stride slowly into the oncoming traffic, looking straight ahead. The traffic weaves around them, all eye contact is avoided, and it's everyone for him or herself.

Few countries have provided as much material for celluloid tales as Vietnam. In the post-Vietnam War era, US film studios made some of the most harrowing, soul-searching and cinematically exciting films of the 20th century, focusing on the nation's involvement in the war. In the 1990s, French-made films covered the colonial era in Vietnam before the French withdrawal in 1954. Vietnamese-made films, however, have suffered arrested development. After World War II, Ho Chi Minh encouraged the production of propaganda documentaries. In 1959, the first film was released — *On the Same River* — about a couple who were divided when the border along the 17th parallel was created in 1954. Post-1975, when the country was reunified, all Vietnamese films were state-funded and monitored at the script stage by the Ministry of Culture. In 2002, however, the ministry relaxed its rules, though Vietnamese film directors are still not fully at liberty to criticize the Vietnamese regime through the medium of film.

DIVIDED OPINIONS

Don Duong, a Vietnamese film actor, angered national censors in 2002 by appearing in what the Vietnamese government regarded as a movie with a pro-US stance.

Duong starred in Hollywood's *We Were Soldiers* (directed by Randall Wallace), which depicts the Battle of Ia Drang in 1965 — the first major battle of the Vietnam War. During the battle, 400 US troops, led by Lieutenant-Colonel Harold Moore (Mel Gibson), and 2,000 North Vietnamese soldiers, commanded by Nguyen Huu An (Duong), met in bloody hand-to-hand combat, leaving severe casualties on both sides. Vietnamese authorities claimed that the movie distorted history, and the National Film Censorship Council moved to ban the actor from appearing in productions, and to fine him. Duong emigrated to the US in 2003.

Clockwise from above *A scene from Stanley Kubrick's movie* Full Metal Jacket *(1987); French-Vietnamese director Tran Anh Hung; Don Duong in* We Were Soldiers *(2002)*

SAIGON STARS

The 2001 film version of *The Quiet American*, Graham Greene's novel of love, war, murder and betrayal set in 1950s Saigon, was filmed in Vietnam—the first Hollywood blockbuster made in the country since the end of the war. It stars Sir Michael Caine as journalist Thomas Fowler, Brendan Fraser as American aid worker Alden Pyle and Do Thi Hai Yen as Fowler's lover, Phuong. The Hotel Continental, the social pivot of the time, is replicated on screen by the Hotel Caravelle (▷ 211), which faces the real thing across Lam Son Square (Place Garnier). The La Fontaine milk bar on Dong Khoi Street (rue Catinat), frequented by Phuong, is now the Givral café and patisserie. The infamous double bomb scene in front of the Opera House and La Fontaine used hundreds of Vietnamese people as extras.

CROSSING BOUNDARIES

Director Le Hoang's film *Gai Nhay (Bar Girls)*, about sex, drugs and HIV, has rocked cinema audiences since it was released (in Vietnam only) in 2003.

HIV and drugs are serious social problems in Vietnam, with 80,000 reported HIV cases at present and rates as high as 65 percent among intravenous drug-users.

Produced by Ho Chi Minh's Liberation Studios, which is run by the army, the film tackles such contemporary social taboos as prostitution and drug addiction. It is a disturbing portrayal of the awful lives of two prostitutes, Hoa (My Duyen) and Hanh (Minh Thu), with scenes of gang rape and murder.

The film cost US$78,000 to make but raked in more than a million dollars in box office sales and is Vietnam's biggest grossing movie to date.

CINEMATIC CENTURY

Vietnam has undergone a cinematic revolution in the 21st century. With the help of an American donation of US$100,000, some 13 Vietnamese directors took a cinematography course in the US and visited Hollywood studios to learn more about moviemaking. The country's filmmakers are also keen to improve sound quality to boost international sales. Since 2002 the Ministry of Culture has reversed much of its policy on censorship and has encouraged private film studios to open up. The 2003 movie *Bar Girls* (▷ left), about drug abuse and HIV, was one result; another was *Luoi Troi (Heaven's Net)*, directed by Phi Tien Son and tackling corruption and crime. Its subjects are Nam Cam, executed in 2004 for a 15-year killing spree in Ho Chi Minh City, and the party officials and local police officers that were indicted during his trial.

NEW PERSPECTIVES

American filmmakers' attempts to come to terms with their country's involvement in Vietnam have produced some classic movies. Francis Ford Coppola's *Apocalypse Now*, substituting Vietnam for the Africa of Joseph Conrad's novel *Heart of Darkness*, won two Oscars in 1979. *The Deer Hunter* (1978), starring Robert de Niro, charts the horrors into which three tough steelworkers are plunged in Vietnam; it won five Oscars. Stanley Kubrick's *Full Metal Jacket* (1987) followed GIs to the Tet Offensive, and *Good Morning Vietnam* (1987) starred Robin Williams as a DJ working for the armed services radio. Oliver Stone's trilogy, *Platoon* (1986), *Born on the Fourth of July* (1989) and *Heaven and Earth* (1993), deals with the war and its aftermath, in the first two from a US soldier's perspective, and in the third from the viewpoint of a Vietnamese woman.

VIETNAMESE FASHION

The new entrepreneurial streak in Vietnam has proved a catalyst for fabulous fashion design and ingenuity. Although known for the beautiful *ao dai*, the classic-cut trouser tunic of local women, Vietnam was not previously renowned for its haute couture. Nowadays, fashionistas flock here to see the latest in desirable clothes, bags, shoes and other accessories from the country's own designers. From the inception of ideas to fabrication, and to the clothes racks, this has been fashion development on steroids. Since economic liberalization, designers have gained national and international fame, some selling to such halls of sartorial fame as Harrods and Henri Bendel.

ASIAN FUSION

Most fashion designers using Vietnam as their creative hub are women. The exception to this rule is the maître d' of the ubiquitous Khaisilk empire, Hoang Khai. His label is synonymous with silk and seduction, and his creativity now spans restaurants and hotels, as well as his silk empire. Christina Yu, a lawyer from Hong Kong, created glitzy label Ipa-Nima. Her bags and sequinned shoes fill two shops in Hanoi (▷ 85) and in Ho Chi Minh City. Frenchwoman Valerie Gregori-McKenzie produces ethereal clothes, embroidered cushions and bags under the label Song. She has two shops, in Hanoi (▷ 85) and Saigon (▷ 203). Sylvie Tran Ha set up SXS in Saigon, specializing in suede. Many designers combine native materials with the ideas, methods and motifs of ethnic minority communities.

THE SILK ROAD TO SUCCESS

Khaisilk began as a workshop in Hanoi in 1980. Since then the empire has expanded, with shops in Hanoi, Saigon and Hoi An. Owner Hoang Khai's entrepreneurialism seems limitless. His stylish restaurants and hotels exhibit interior design that is among the most glamorous in Vietnam. Mr. Khai, who dresses in black, wins award after award for his silk output and uses intriguing advertisements showing a glimpse of a bag or silk shoe-clad foot, to ensure Khaisilk's place as the number one boutique.

TOP TUNIC

Vietnam's national women's costume, the *ao dai*, has been successfully exported worldwide, and is worn by hotel receptionists and office workers in humid Saigon. The name means long dress, and the costume consists of a long, flowing tunic of diaphanous fabric worn over a pair of loose-fitting white pants; the tunic has splits from the waist down. It dates to the mid-18th century, when both men and women wore trouser suits buttoned at the front. The modern design was created by the literary group Tu Luc Van Doan in 1932, and is based on ancient court costumes and Chinese dresses. In traditional society, decoration and complexity of design indicated the wearer's status; gold brocade and dragons were for the sole use of the emperor.

Above left *Fashion from label Ipa-Nima*
Above right *A silk store in Hanoi*

THE STORY OF VIETNAM

Between 5000 and 3000BC, two Mesolithic cultures occupied north Vietnam: the Hoa Binh and Bac Son. The Vietnamese trace their origins to 15 tribal groups known as the Lac Viet, who settled in north Vietnam at the beginning of the Bronze Age. Chinese cultural influence over the north began in the second century BC, and the Chinese dominated Vietnam for more than 1,000 years, until the 10th century. The Ly Dynasty (1009–1225) was the first independent Vietnamese dynasty, based at Thang Long, now Hanoi, and following the Chinese Confucian model of government and social relations. In south Vietnam, where the dynastic lords achieved hegemony only in the 18th century, the most significant power was the kingdom of Champa (AD200–1720), focused on the lowlands running down the Annamite coast. Champa built its power on the maritime trading route through Southeast Asia, and for more than 1,000 years the Cham resisted the Chinese and the Vietnamese. Finally, in 1471, the Cham were defeated by the Vietnamese, and the kingdom shrank to a small territory around Nha Trang until 1720, when surviving members of the royal family and many subjects fled to Cambodia.

DONG SON DRUMS

Dong Son (Bronze Age) culture thrived on the coast of Annam and Tonkin between 500 and 200BC. Its craftsmen produced an iconic instrument that is now seen all over Vietnam: the squat, bronze Dong Son drum, which can measure more than 3ft (1m) in height and width. Decoration is both geometric and naturalistic, notably on the finely incised drum head. Most excavated drums are associated with human remains and other precious objects, and the drums may have symbolized power and prestige. Some are surmounted with bronze figures of frogs, and may have been used in ceremonies to summon the rain.

Clockwise from above *An exhibit in the Museum of Champa Sculpture in Danang; the statue of Tran Hung Dao in Saigon; a Champa tower at Duong Long*

UNDERSTANDING THE STORY OF VIETNAM

FEMALE WARRIORS

The Trung sisters are among the most revered of Vietnamese heroines. In AD40, the Lac Lords of Vietnam agitated against Chinese control, encouraged by Trung Trac, wife of Lac Lord Thi Sach, and her sister, Trung Nhi. Both did battle while pregnant, having donned gold-plated armor over their bellies.

Although there was an independent kingdom for a short time, the uprising proved fruitless. A large Chinese army defeated the rebels in AD43, captured the two sisters, executed them and sent their heads to the Chinese Han Dynasty court at Lo-yang.

An alternative version of events describes the sisters throwing themselves into the Ha Giang River to avoid capture, and turning into statues, which were washed ashore and taken to Hanoi's Hai Ba Trung Temple (▷ 72).

THE BATTLES OF BACH DANG RIVER

In AD938, unable to confront the powerful Chinese fleet on equal terms, the Vietnamese General Ngo Quyen sank sharpened iron-tipped poles into the bed of the Bach Dang River. When the Chinese fleet appeared off the mouth of the river, Quyen sent shallow-draft boats to taunt the enemy into attack. As the tide fell, the heavy ships were impaled on the stakes, and more than half the Chinese were drowned.

Legendary warrior Tran Hung Dao (1225–1300) repeated the trick centuries later (▷ right). In 1283 he was appointed commander of the Dai Viet forces and twice faced Mongol invasion from the north, under Kublai Khan's command. In 1284, a 500,000-strong Mongol army was warded off with superior tactics, and withdrew.

Three years later a Mongol Chinese fleet of 400 ships appeared off the coast, and Tran Hung Dao copied the 10th-century strategy of laying stakes beneath the water—to equally devastating effect.

CHAMPA CUSTOMS

An anonymous manuscript compiled in Manila about 1590–95 described a gruesome custom apparently followed during the tiger hunt that marked the last of the Champa year's six seasons. It was possibly part of the documentation assembled by Don Luis Perez Dasmariñas in justification of his scheme for the conquest of Indochina. According to this account, the king and his wife would send out 100 or more highland people along the roads with the express order that they should not return without filling two gold basins with human gall, which was to be from people of their own nation and not foreigners. Anyone caught on the road was tied to a tree, where their attackers would cut out the gall bladder. The king and his wife would then bathe in the human gall to cleanse away their sins.

WILY WARRIOR

The name of legendary warrior Tran Hung Dao is etched on the memory of all Vietnamese and is inscribed on street names across the land. He was born in Nam Dinh, nephew to King Tran Thai Ton of the Tran Dynasty, and in 1283 became commander of the Dai Viet forces. The expansionist policies of the Mongols posed a constant threat to Vietnamese security, and twice on his watch, Kublai Khan invaded Vietnam from the north. In 1284, the Mongols crossed the border at Lang Son. General Tran Hung Dao evacuated the capital and called for national unity in the face of the attack. The military trounced the Mongols and forced them to withdraw. The Mongols again invaded in 1287. This time the general devised a copy-cat tactic similar to that used in the 10th century (▷ left).

LE DYNASTY TO NGUYEN DYNASTY

After 1,000 years of Chinese domination and centuries of dynastic squabbles, one man harnessed nationalistic sentiment and molded the country into a powerful fighting force. In 1426 Le Loi, together with tactician Nguyen Trai, led a campaign to remove the Chinese from Vietnamese soil and, following victory against the Ming Dynasty (1368–1644), claimed the throne in 1428. Between 1460 and 1497 his successor, Le Thanh Ton, established the system of rule that was to guide Vietnamese emperors for 500 years. However, an ambitious extension of territories, all ruled from distant Hanoi, eventually led to the disintegration of imperial rule. Noble families, locally dominant, challenged the emperor's authority, and the Le Dynasty gradually dissolved into deadly conflict and regional fiefdoms: Trinh in the north, Nguyen in the south. There were numerous peasant rebellions, of which the most serious was the Tay Son rebellion of 1771. Eventually, in 1802, the Nguyen Dynasty was established when Emperor Gia Long ascended to the throne in Huê.

NGUYEN TRAI

Nguyen Trai, mandarin, poet and nationalist, rose to prominence as an adviser to Le Loi during the 10-year campaign to eject the Ming. His counsel "better to win hearts than citadels" was heeded by Le Loi, who aroused patriotic fervor in his countrymen to achieve victory on the battlefield. It was on Nguyen Trai's suggestion that 100,000 defeated Ming troops were given food and boats to make their way home. After the war he accepted a court post, although later resigned. He was a prolific composer of verse, which is considered some of the finest in the national annals. On an overnight visit to Nguyen Trai, Emperor Le Thai Tong (Le Loi's son and heir) died unexpectedly. Scheming courtiers blamed Nguyen Trai, who in 1442, along with three generations of his family, was executed, a punishment known as *tru di tam tôc*.

Clockwise from above *Performers reenact the victory over the Chinese by Quang Trung Nguyen Hue in 1789; a statue of Nguyen Trung Truc; Bao Dai, the last emperor of Vietnam*

TAY SON REBELLION

In 1771, the famine-stricken peasantry rallied to the three Tay Son brothers, whose army of clerks, farmers, hill people and scholars swept through the country fighting Trinh and Nguyen lords. Through brilliant strategy the brothers extended their control south to Saigon and north to Thang Long. Taking advantage of this disorder, the Chinese sent a 200,000-strong army south in 1788. In the same year, one of the brothers, Nguyen Hue, proclaimed himself emperor Quang Trung, and on the fifth day of Tet in 1789 the brothers attacked and defeated the Chinese near Thang Long. Quang Trung introduced policies of land reform, wider education and fairer taxation, but died in 1792, failing to provide the dynastic continuity necessary for Vietnam to survive the impending French arrival.

EUNUCH INTRIGUE

Eunuchs were key members of the Nguyen Dynasty court in Huê. They were the only men allowed inside the Purple Forbidden City, to serve the "Son of Heaven" —the emperor—and his wives and concubines. These castrated men, who wore green and red floral gowns and flat oval hats, arranged the emperor's nightly activities and took bribes from concubines in exchange for choosing them as the night's favored companion. In 1836, Emperor Minh Mang limited the eunuchs' powers, preventing their rise to the powerful position of mandarin, and graded their services. Premier eunuchs (clerks) were paid six times more yuan and four times more rice than the lowly errand boys. The employment of eunuchs was abolished in 1914 by Emperor Duy Tan (reigned 1907–1916).

DEATH OF THE SON OF HEAVEN

The death of the Nguyen Dynasty emperors was always accompanied by elaborate burial rites. After the death of the penultimate emperor Dai-Hanh-Hoang-Khai-Dinh in 1925, seven diamonds were placed in his mouth and his red and gold lacquered coffin was covered with young tea leaves. Official mourning began with animal sacrifices and lasted 60 days. When Emperor Gia Long died in 1820, a three-year mourning period was inaugurated. It is said that three days after his death, a messenger was sent to the Hoang Nhon Pagoda to tell the Empress, who was already dead, that her husband was deceased. Ten days before his funeral, the tomb was opened, and a week later the dead king was informed of his burial.

LAST EMPEROR OF VIETNAM

Bao Dai, born in 1913, was the 13th and last emperor of the Nguyen Dynasty, crowned in 1926 while the French still ruled Indochina. During World War II, Japanese occupiers declared Vietnam independent under Bao Dai, but he was forced to relinquish his role in favor of Ho Chi Minh, leader of the nationalist Viet Minh. After his abdication on August 25, 1945, Bao Dai was made an adviser in the new Hanoi government, but subsequently left the country. He returned, with French backing, in 1949, as emperor and leader of the southern government in Saigon. In 1955, a republic was established and Bao Dai was deposed. He lived out the remainder of his days in exile, and died in Paris in 1997.

UNDERSTANDING THE STORY OF VIETNAM

In 1825, Emperor Minh Mang (reigned 1820–40) issued an imperial edict outlawing the dissemination of Christianity. The Christian faith had a large following among the poor peasantry and, fearing revolt, his successor Emperor Tu Duc (reigned 1847–1883) ordered a mass execution of Catholics between 1848 and 1860. In response, the French attacked and captured Saigon in 1859. In 1862, Tu Duc signed a treaty ceding the three southern provinces; subsequently the French conquered the north, hoping to control trade routes to China. In 1883 and 1884, the French forced the Emperor, and after his death his officials, to sign treaties making Vietnam a French protectorate, and in 1885 the Treaty of Tientsin recognized the French protectorates of Tonkin (North Vietnam) and Annam (Central Vietnam), to add to the colony of Cochin China (South Vietnam). Colonial rule was opposed by nationalists such as Phan Boi Chau (1867–1940) and Phan Chau Trinh (1871–1926). Vietnam Quoc Dan Dang (VNQDD), founded in 1927, was the country's first nationalist party, and the first significant Communist group was the Indochina Communist Party (ICP), established by Ho Chi Minh in 1930. Both organized resistance. Japan occupied Vietnam from August 1940, although the French remained in administrative control. After Japan's surrender in 1945, Ho declared himself president of the Democratic Republic of Vietnam (▷ 34).

FROM SERVANT OF CHRIST TO SAINT

François-Isidore Gagelin of Les Missions Etrangères de Paris (the Paris Foreign Missions Society) was the first European priest to be executed in Vietnam. The 32-year-old was strangled by six soldiers as he knelt on a scaffold in Huê in 1833. Three days later, having been told of the Christian belief in resurrection, Emperor Minh Mang had the body exhumed to confirm the man's death.

Between 1848 and 1860, 25 European priests, 300 Vietnamese priests and 30,000 Vietnamese Roman Catholics were executed. Ten missionaries, including Gagelin, known as the martyrs of Vietnam, were canonized by Pope John Paul II in June 1998.

Clockwise from above *Vietnamese prisoners in French stocks, 1907; Alexandre Yersin; a depiction of the French Governor General's arrival at Saigon in 1902*

PREACHER AND TRANSLATOR

Even before the 19th century, the French had an influence on Vietnam. Alexandre de Rhodes, one of the Jesuit founders of the Paris Foreign Missions Society, was based in Cochin China and Tonkin between 1624 and 1645. He converted the Vietnamese writing system from Chinese characters *(Chu Nom)*, as it had existed since the 13th century, to Romanized script, building on the work of Portuguese missionaries. Rhodes' Vietnamese—Portuguese—Latin dictionary was published in Rome in 1651, but the conversion was not fully in use until it was officially adopted by the French in the early 20th century. De Rhodes was expelled four times from Vietnam: The final, permanent expulsion was in 1645, when Rhodes left for Macao.

ALEXANDRE YERSIN

Alexandre Yersin was born in Switzerland in 1863. He completed his medical education in Paris, becoming assistant to Louis Pasteur, and took French citizenship in 1888. As a ship's doctor, he traveled to Vietnam, where he recommended the temperate Dalat Plateau for development as a hill resort. In 1894, on a visit to plague-stricken Hong Kong, Yersin identified the causative agent of the plague, the bacillus now called *Yersinia pestis*. In 1895 he set up a laboratory in Nha Trang that, in 1902, became the first Institut Pasteur outside France. Here, Yeshin developed a plague treatment, and at Suoi Dau, 16 miles (25km) south, he established a cattle farm to produce serum and vaccines, and to improve breeding stock. He died in 1943.

HO CHI MINH

Ho Chi Minh (approximately meaning "He Who Enlightens") was born in 1890 to a poor scholar-gentry family. In 1911, while in France, he converted to Communism, and in 1923 he moved to Moscow to train as an activist. From there, Ho traveled to China to help form the Vietnamese Communist Movement, culminating in the creation of the Indochina Communist Party in 1930.

In the following years, he was a Buddhist monk, served six months in Hong Kong for subversion, traveled to China several times and, in 1940, returned to Vietnam—his first visit in nearly 30 years. Ho went on to declare Vietnamese independence on September 2, 1945 (▷ 34), but took on a largely ceremonial role after the country split in 1954. He died in 1969, aged 79.

THE JAPANESE IN VIETNAM

In June 1940, France fell to Nazi Germany. From August of that year the Japanese occupied Vietnam, and were then granted full access to military facilities in exchange for allowing continued French administrative control. In March 1945, the Japanese seized power from the French and forced Emperor Bao Dai to declare independence.

Between March and September 1945, a famine struck Tonkin, killing some two million people. The Viet Minh stepped in to attack rice stocks and to rally support for liberation from Japanese and French control. The Japanese finally surrendered in 1945 and the Viet Minh seized power before the French could regain control. The First Indochina War (▷ 34) soon followed.

The First Indochina War started in September 1945 in the south and in 1946 in the north. These years marked the onset of fighting between Ho Chi Minh's Viet Minh and the French. The Viet Minh proclaimed the creation of the Democratic Republic of Vietnam on September 2, 1945, when Ho Chi Minh read out the Vietnamese Declaration of Independence in Hanoi. In the south, British troops fought the Viet Minh. When 35,000 French reinforcements arrived, Ca Mau, at the southern extremity of the country, fell on October 21. From that point on, the war in the south became an underground battle of attrition, with the north providing support to their southern comrades. In February 1946, the French and Chinese signed a treaty leading to the withdrawal of Chinese forces, and in March Ho concluded a treaty with France recognizing Vietnam as a free state within the French Union and the Indochinese Federation. The French controlled the cities, but the Viet Minh were dominant in the countryside. By the end of 1949, with the success of the Chinese Revolution and the establishment of the Democratic People's Republic of Korea (North Korea) in 1948, the US was offering support to the French in an attempt to stem the "red tide" of Communism.

THE VIET MINH

The Viet Minh, or Doc Lap Dong Minh Hoi (League for the Independence of Vietnam), was imported from China by Ho Chi Minh in 1941. The group took control of Hanoi when the Japanese withdrew in 1945, with the initial support of the Office of Strategic Services (the wartime precursor to the CIA). In the north, the Viet Minh had to deal with 180,000 Nationalist Chinese troops, while preparing for the imminent arrival of a French force. Unable to confront both at the same time, and deciding that the French were probably the lesser of two evils, Ho Chi Minh decided to negotiate with France.

Clockwise from above *Relief mural showing the torture of Vietnamese prisoners by the French at Hoa Lo Prison; Ta Quang Buu of the Viet Minh resistance signs a ceasefire agreement on July 20, 1954; Vo Nguyen Giap, former general of the North Vietnam Army*

HAIPHONG CUSTOMS INCIDENT

One episode is usually highlighted as the flashpoint that led to resumed hostilities after the March 1946 treaty with the French. The French seized customs control in Haiphong in November 1946; the Vietnamese resisted and fighting broke out. The port city was bombarded by French naval guns, air bombing ensued and tanks rolled into the streets. After a few days, the French had control of the city, harbor and airport. They claimed 5,000 Vietnamese casualties and five French; the Vietnamese put the toll at 20,000 Vietnamese dead. In December, the Viet Minh attacked the French garrison in Hanoi, justifying it by citing the earlier French bombing. For the French, this December incident marks the beginning of the First Indochina War.

DIEN BIEN PHU

The decisive battle of the First Indochina War was at Dien Bien Phu. At the end of 1953, the French, led by Colonel Christian de Castries, with American support, parachuted 16,000 men into the area in an attempt to protect Laos from Viet Minh incursions. The narrow valley was thought to be impregnable. But Vietnamese General Vo Nguyen Giap moved his 55,000 men into the surrounding area, manhandling heavy guns (with the help of 200,000 porters) up the mountainsides until they had a view over the French forces. From the surrounding highlands, Giap had the French at his mercy. On May 7, 1954, the French surrendered — one of the most humiliating French colonial defeats — marking the end of the French presence in Indochina.

AMERICAN ASSISTANCE

US involvement in Vietnam began when the Office of Strategic Services (OSS) sent the Deer Mission from its southern China base to Vietnam in the last days of World War II, to help the Viet Minh resist the Japanese and to assist American airmen who had been shot down. Between 1950 and 1954, however, a shift in American policy saw a substantial increase in financial, military and advisory aid given to the French, in an effort to prevent the spread of Communism in Asia. During this time about US$2.6 billion was spent by the US on military and economic aid, and from July 1954 money was also pumped in to support the newly formed southern government of Vietnam headed by Hgo Dinh Diem.

GENEVA CONFERENCE

After their defeat at Dien Bien Phu, the French sued for peace in Geneva. On July 20, 1954, Vietnam was divided along the 17th parallel into the northern Democratic Republic of Vietnam (DRV) and South Vietnam — with a view to reunifying elections in 1956. These were never held. The border was kept open for 300 days and about 900,000 Vietnamese traveled south, while nearly 90,000 Viet Minh troops and 43,000 civilians went north. A provision under the Geneva Accords to honor the dead of both sides in an ossuary was never fulfilled. During nine years of war between the Viet Minh and the French, between 250,000 and a million civilians, 200,000 to 300,000 Viet Minh and 95,000 French colonial troops had been killed.

In 1954, Vietnam was split in two, with the Communists in control in the north. The Communists, under Ho Chi Minh, were confident that their sympathizers in the south would soon overthrow the government there. This changed with the rise of Ngo Dinh Diem, President of the Republic of South Vietnam, who undermined the strength of the Communist Party in the south. From 1959, the north shifted its strategy toward military confrontation, leaving armed resistance largely to guerrillas belonging to the Cao Dai religion and the Hoa Hao Buddhist millenarian sect. The establishment of the National Liberation Front (NLF) of Vietnam in 1960 was an important development in creating an alternative to Diem. Its military wing was the Viet Cong. The conflict intensified from 1961 when armed forces under the Communists' control were unified under the People's Liberation Armed Forces (PLAF). The north infiltrated 44,000 sympathizers into the south between 1959 and 1964, while the number recruited in the south was between 60,000 and 100,000. The election of US President John F. Kennedy in 1961 coincided with the Communists' decision to widen the war in the south. Kennedy dispatched 400 special forces troops and 100 military advisers to Vietnam—in contravention of the 1954 Geneva Accords—and began arming the Army of the Republic of Vietnam (ARVN). By the end of 1962, there were 11,000 US personnel in the south, but the US had so far avoided large-scale, direct confrontation with the Viet Cong.

Clockwise from above *Former President Ngo Dinh Diem at the Presidential Palace; Buddhist monks protesting against Ngo Dinh Diem's religious policies in August 1963; bombshells displayed in the Demilitarized Zone*

NGO DINH DIEM

Ngo Dinh Diem was born in 1901 to a Roman Catholic, Confucian family and held a post at the court of Emperor Bao Dai. In 1946, Ho Chi Minh offered him a post in the DRV government, which he declined.

Eight years later, Diem returned from self-imposed exile in the US to become Premier of South Vietnam under Bao Dai's government. After two rigged elections, Bao Dai was deposed and Diem became President of the Republic of South Vietnam in 1955. He proceeded to suppress all opposition in the country and refused to hold elections for reunification. Security forces led by his brother, Ngo Dinh Nhu, terrorized much of Vietnamese society. On November 2, 1963, Diem and his brother Nhu were both assassinated during an army coup.

THE HO CHI MINH TRAIL

The Ho Chi Minh Trail (Truong Son Trail), along which supplies and troops were moved by the North Vietnamese Army from the north to the south via Laos, was established in 1959. There were, in fact, eight to 10 roads, camouflaged in places and maintained by 300,000 full-time and 200,000 part-time workers. Initially, supplies were carried on bicycles; later, trucks were used, provided by China and the Soviet Union. By the end of the conflict the trail comprised 9,544 miles (15,360km) of all-weather and secondary roads. One hero of the People's Army is said, during the course of the war, to have carried and pushed 60 tons of supplies a distance of 25,491 miles (41,025km) — roughly the circumference of the world.

STRATEGIC HAMLETS

An important element in Ngo Dinh Diem's military strategy in 1962 was the establishment of "strategic hamlets," a plan designed by his brother, Ngo Dinh Nhu, and modeled on British antiguerrilla warfare during Malaya's Communist insurgency (1948–60). The aim was to deny Communists rural support bases, and involved surrounding villages with barbed wire and forcing many peasants to relocate from their ancestral lands.

By September 1962, more than four million people (34 percent of the population) had been moved. Of the 7,000 to 8,000 villages sealed in this way, only a fifth could ever have been considered watertight and the methods used to isolate the settlements often just increased PLAF support.

THE BATTLE OF AP BAC

In January 1963 at Ap Bac, not far from the town of My Tho in the Mekong Delta, the Communists scored their first significant victory in the south.

Facing 2,000 well-armed troops of the Army of the Republic of Vietnam (ARVN), a force of just 300 to 400 People's Liberation Armed Forces (PLAF) inflicted heavy casualties, killing 63 ARVN and three Americans, wounding 109 ARVN and three Americans, and downing five helicopters.

American advisers were scathing about the performance of their South Vietnamese allies, and it was this defeat that led them to conclude that the ARVN needed the direct intervention of US troops.

Implementation of this began in 1964 and by late 1965 American combat units began activity in Vietnam.

SELF-IMMOLATION AND DISCONTENT

On 11 June, 1963, 66-year-old Thich Quang Duc committed assisted suicide in protest at the regime and US involvement in Vietnam. He sat in the lotus position as companions poured gasoline over him, then set himself alight. Pedestrians prostrated themselves at the sight, and pictures of the monk in flames appeared in newspapers around the world. Some 30 monks and nuns followed Thich's example. Around 15,000 demonstrators gathered at Saigon's Xa Loi Pagoda in August 1963 as speakers denounced the religious discrimination of the Diem regime. Two nights later ARVN forces raided the pagoda, wounding 30 and killing seven people. Soon after Diem declared martial law; the pagoda became a focus of discontent.

THE VIETNAM WAR

According to US government files, President Lyndon B. Johnson (in office 1963–69) was a reluctant warrior, who doubted the wisdom of intervention but who believed the US must honor its pledge to help South Vietnam. In March 1965 he launched aerial war against the north, and by June there were 74,000 troops in Vietnam. By mid-1967 the Communist leadership in the north escalated hostilities in the south in an attempt to regain the initiative. During the early morning of February 1, 1968—New Year *(Tet)*—84,000 Communist troops, almost all Viet Cong, simultaneously attacked targets in 105 urban centers. The Tet Offensive concentrated American minds. The costs by that time had been vast, and thousands of men had been killed for a cause that, to many, was becoming less clear by the month. Negotiations began in Paris in 1969 to try to secure an honorable settlement for the US. Against the wishes of South Vietnam's President Nguyen Van Thieu, the US signed a treaty on January 27, 1973; the last combat troops left in March 1973. The North's Central Committee formally decided to abandon the Paris Accord in October; by the beginning of 1975 they were ready for the final offensive. On April 30 the Communists achieved total victory.

GULF OF TONKIN

Two American destroyers, the USS *Maddox* and USS *C. Turner Joy*, were attacked—apparently without provocation—by North Vietnamese patrol craft in international waters on August 2, 1964. The US responded by bombing shore installations, and the Gulf of Tonkin Resolution, requesting greater military involvement, was presented to Congress for approval. Only two Congressmen voted against the resolution, and President Johnson's poll rating jumped from 42 percent to 72 percent.

In 1971 some Pentagon papers were leaked to the *New York Times*. According to these, the USS *Maddox* had been involved in intelligence-gathering, while supporting clandestine raids by South Vietnamese mercenaries placed well inside North Vietnamese territorial waters.

Clockwise from above *A parade in Ho Chi Minh City to commemorate the 40th anniversary of the Tet Offensive; a bust of Lyndon B. Johnson; the monument to the victims of the My Lai Massacre*

OPERATION ROLLING THUNDER

Operation Rolling Thunder, the most intense bombing campaign any country had yet experienced, began in March 1965 and ran through to October 1968. In three and a half years, twice the tonnage of bombs was dropped on Vietnam (and Laos) as during the whole of World War II. At the campaign's peak in 1967, 12,000 sorties were being flown each month; a total of 108,000 were flown throughout 1967. North Vietnam claimed that 4,000 out of its 5,788 villages were hit. B-52s dropped their bombs from such altitude—55,700ft (17,000m)—that the attack could not be heard until the bombs hit their targets. By the end of the war in 1973, 15 million tons of all types of munitions had been used in Indochina, an explosive force representing 700 times that of the atomic bomb dropped on Hiroshima in Japan in 1945.

AFTER THE TET OFFENSIVE

Although the Tet Offensive was a strategic victory for the Communists, it was also a tactical defeat. They may have occupied the US embassy in Saigon for a few hours but, except in Huê, Communist forces were soon repulsed by US and ARVN troops. However, US Forces commander General William Westmoreland's request for more troops was turned down, and US public support for the war slumped further, as people grew dismayed by the scale and intensity of the offensive. The aim of the Viet Cong incursion into Saigon was, in fact, not to take the embassy but to make a psychological gesture—and indeed from that date the Johnson administration began to search seriously for a way out of the conflict. Robert Kennedy spoke of the illusion of victory, liberal opinion moved to support him and thousands of Americans voiced their agreement.

THE PHOENIX PROGRAM

The Phoenix Program was established in the wake of the Tet Offensive with the aim of destroying the Communists' political infrastructure in the Mekong Delta. Named for the Vietnamese mythical bird the Phung Hoang, which could fly anywhere, the program sent CIA-recruited and trained Counter Terror Teams into the countryside to capture Communist cadres. By 1971, the program was estimated to have led to the capture of 28,000 members of the Viet Cong Infrastructure, the death of 20,000, and the defection of a further 17,000. By early 1970s, the Mekong Delta towns, previously strongholds of the Viet Cong, had reverted to the control of the local authorities.

MY LAI MASSACRE

On March 16, 1968, Charlie Company, under the command of Lieutenant William Calley, was dropped into the village of Son My. In the hamlet of My Lai, 504 unarmed villagers were massacred. Some of Calley's men refused to participate. The story of the massacre was filed by Seymour Hersh, but not until November 1969. In 1971, a court martial convicted Calley of the murder of 22 people. No one else was convicted. His life sentence was commuted to house arrest, and three years later President Nixon granted a pardon. In 1998, Lawrence Colburn and Hugh C. Thompson Jr., who stopped the massacre, were awarded the highest medal for bravery not involving enemy conflict.

THE LEGACY

The Socialist Republic of Vietnam was established on July 2, 1976 when Vietnam was reunified. It was the beginning of a collective struggle to *come* to terms with the war, build a nation, reinvigorate the economy, and exorcize the ghosts of the past. Thousands of South Vietnamese were sent to re-education camps; many fled, first illegally and then legally through the Orderly Departures Program. In 1986, at the sixth party congress, the Vietnamese Communist Party launched its economic reform program, *doi moi*. Under this program, much of the economy has been freed up, while the party has ensured that it retains ultimate political power. The Asian economic crisis of 1997 to 1998 slowed the pace of change, but—while political tensions have come to the fore—economic growth in Vietnam since the 1990s has been unprecedented.

ENTENTE CORDIALE

From 1975 the US imposed a trade embargo on Vietnam and blocked its attempts to gain membership to the International Monetary Fund and similar agencies. The former countries of the Eastern Bloc filled the gap, providing billions of dollars of aid and technical expertise. But in 1990 the Soviet Union halved its assistance to Vietnam, making improved relations with the West a matter of urgency. In 1991, the US opened an official office in Hanoi to assist in the search for MIA (Missing in Action) personnel; three years later the trade embargo was lifted, and in 1995 fully normalized relations were resumed. In 1997, Douglas "Pete" Peterson, the first post-war American ambassador to Vietnam—and a former POW—took up his post in the capital. The National Assembly finally ratified the trade treaty in 2001, heralding a substantial increase in bilateral trade. In 2003, the US imported US$4.5 billion worth of Vietnamese goods, roughly four times more than it exported to Vietnam.

VIETNAMESE EXODUS

After reunification many political refugees fled Vietnam in boats—some paying between US$500 and US$3,000 to secure a place—in the hope of reaching other Southeast Asian countries. It is estimated that at least a third died at sea, from drowning, dehydration or at the hands of pirates. Despite the risks, Vietnamese continued to leave in huge numbers: By 1980 there were 350,000 awaiting resettlement in refugee camps. Soon the process became semi-official. From 1982 there was an exodus of economic refugees, and more than 40,000 refugees moved into camps in Hong Kong. A program of forcible repatriation, instigated at the end of 1989, was suspended in the face of international protests. In the mid-1990s, and with the US lifting its trade embargo with Vietnam in 1994, the refugee situation eased considerably. More than one million Vietnamese have been resettled since 1975, the majority in North America, Australia, France, the UK and Germany.

Above left *Modern buildings in Ho Chi Minh City*
Above right *Shipbuilding in North Vietnam*

ON THE MOVE

On the Move gives you detailed advice and information about the various options for traveling to Vietnam before explaining the best ways to get around the country once you are there. Handy tips help you with everything from buying tickets to renting a car.

ON THE MOVE | VIETNAM

ARRIVING BY AIR

Vietnam is relatively well served by international airlines, but be prepared for a connecting flight in Europe, Asia or the Middle East. Paris is the main departure point from Europe, with code-shared Vietnam Airlines/Air France flights. Singapore and Bangkok are often used as stopover points. International airports are: Tan Son Nhat Airport (SGN) in Ho Chi Minh City, Noi Bai Airport (HAN) in Hanoi and Danang Airport (DAD), where some international flights from the region land.

The principal national and international carrier is Vietnam Airlines, which has a virtual monopoly on domestic routes. Other major international carriers are Air France, Cathay Pacific, KLM, Lufthansa, Malaysian Airlines, Qantas, Singapore Airlines, Thai International and United Airlines. The only other domestic carrier is Jetstar Pacific Airlines.

AIRPORTS

Tan Son Nhat Airport is 4 miles (7km) north of downtown Ho Chi Minh City, or Saigon, the economic powerhouse of the country and its largest city. It is well connected with the wider world—indeed, more airlines fly here from more places

GETTING DOWNTOWN FROM THE AIRPORT		
FROM	**TAN SON NHAT AIRPORT TO HO CHI MINH CITY**	**NOI BAI AIRPORT TO HANOI**
TAXI	There is a taxi rank outside both terminals. Airport taxis are metered; a tip is requested on payment. Journey time: around 20–30 min. Price: 120,000d	Metered taxis line up outside the terminal but pre-booking is available online at www.hantaxi.com and www.noibaitaxi.com. Journey time: 45 min–1 hour. Price: US$13. Pre-booked taxis US$18.
AIRPORT BUS	No. 152 runs from the airport to Ben Thanh market. Frequency: every 15 min between 5.20am and 8.55pm. Price: 3,000d	The Vietnamese Airlines Minibus (tel 04-38250872) runs from outside the Noi Bai Airport main terminal. There are two stands—one on the far left and one on the far right of the exit behind the airport information desk. Passengers are delivered to the Vietnam Airlines office on 1 Quang Trung Street. The minibus runs in both directions daily 5am–6.20pm (5, 5.30, 6, 7.30, 8, 8.30, 9, 9.30, 10.20, 3, 4, 5.30, 6.20) Frequency: daily from airport every 30 min or when full. Journey time: 45-min–1 hour. Price: 40,000d

than do to Hanoi. The airport is in the process of being upgraded: A new international terminal was completed in 2006.

Airport facilities in the arrivals lounge include visitor information, branches of Vietcombank and First Vinabank, and a post office. Inside the departures area there is a branch of Vietindebank, a post office, a first-aid office and a telephone service. There are duty-free shops both on arrival and departure.

International departure tax is US$12 for adults and US$6 for 2- to 16-year-olds. Pay at the desk to the right of the Vietnam Airlines check-in.

The small domestic airport terminal is the building on the far right. There are toilets, a shop and a small seating area. Vietnam Airlines closes check-in 30 minutes before departure. Jetstar Pacific Airlines also uses this terminal.

In the departure lounge there is a shop and a magazine stall, a telephone booth, toilets and a Sasco restaurant selling fresh juices, breakfast, lunch and dinner. Note that there is a 5,000d premium for taxis to enter the airport area.

Noi Bai Airport, Hanoi's modern airport, is 22 miles (35km) from the city, about a 45-minute drive. There are banks and ATM machines but other facilities are meager or non-existent and eating at the airport's café has little to recommend it. When it comes to departure, Noi Bai's signposting is very poor and at busy times sorting out which line is yours requires a little patience.

First-time Visitors
If this is your first trip to Vietnam, the hassle-free way of reaching your hotel from Tan Son Nhat Airport is to contact your hotel or tour operator and arrange a pickup.

Otherwise, be prepared to deal with persistent taxi touts, especially at night, who will steer you away from metered taxis. Be patient and persistent yourself and look for

USEFUL TELEPHONE NUMBERS AND WEBSITES		
VIETNAM AIRLINES		
Ho Chi Minh City	116 Nguyen Hue Boulevard	
	tel 08-38320320	
	Mon–Fri 8–6.30, Sat 8–12, 1.30–5;	
	www.vietnamairlines.com	
Hanoi	25 Trang Thi Street	
	tel 04-38320320	
	Mon–Fri 8–5, Sat-Sun 7–6;	
	www.vietnamairlines.com	
AIRPORTS		
Tan San Nhat, Saigon		tel 08-38485383/488448358
Noi Bai, Hanoi		tel 04-38866527
Danang		tel 0511-3830339

taxis from reputable companies like Vinasun (tel 08-38272727) or Mai Linh (tel 08-3838-3838) with their telephone numbers displayed on their vehicles.

The service at Noi Bai Airport is better organized and taxis can be pre-booked online (see Getting Downtown from the Airport panel, opposite).

ARRIVING BY TRAIN
International rail connections exist only with China. There are connections with Beijing via Nanning to Hanoi crossing at Lang Son, and from Kunming to Hanoi via Lao Cai. For further information, see www.seat61.com.

ARRIVING BY ROAD
There is a road crossing at Moc Bai on Highway 1 connecting Phnom Penh in Cambodia with Ho Chi Minh City. A second route to Phnom Penh via Chau Doc includes a boat crossing. A further road crossing into Cambodia is at Tinh Bien, approximately 14 miles (22km) south of Chau Doc. The road crossing at Lao Bao, north of Huê, allows travel through to Savannakhet in Laos, and there is a road crossing to Laos from Dien Bien Phu, though few people take it.

There are three land crossings between China and Vietnam: at Lao Cai, Dong Dang and Mong Cai.

ARRIVING BY SEA
There are no regular sea crossings into Vietnam although an increasing number of cruise ships sail into Vietnamese waters.

The only other international connection by boat is the Mekong River crossing from Chau Doc to Phnom Penh.

Opposite Phu Quoc Airport
Below The sleeper service from Hanoi

GETTING AROUND

Vietnam is a large country and some patience is required when trying to get around. If you plan to visit for two weeks or less and want to cover a lot of ground, it's important to factor in some flights; Open Tour buses are also a useful and inexpensive way of bridging important towns. Local bus services are for hardy travelers, who want to get right off the beaten track. Overnight train journeys are another good way of covering long distances.

HOW TO GET AROUND
Because of the lack of self-drive car rental, the slow speed of public transportation and the remoteness of some areas, many visitors use tour operators (▷ 256) to take them on day- and week-long trips. This option has the benefit of an English-speaking guide and safe vehicles, and some of the most popular trips include week-long journeys around northwest or northeast Vietnam or into the Mekong Delta. Getting around within cities involves

renting cyclos (bicycle carriages), xe ôms (pronounced "shay oms;" motorcycle taxis), metered taxis and buses.

The entire country is on the move over Tet (Vietnamese New Year, ▷ 269), and transportation—both international and national—is reserved for a week either side. Christmas, Easter and the Western summer vacation periods are also popular with visitors, and all travel during these times is best reserved in advance.

ON THE ROAD
The main highway is Highway 1, a single-lane road that runs from Lang Son, near the Chinese border, down to Hanoi, then all the way down the coast to Ho Chi Minh City. Highway 5 is another major route—a two-lane highway to Haiphong. Roads in Vietnam are notoriously dangerous. According to Vietnam's National Committee for Traffic Safety, an average of 32 people were killed each day in 2008. However, there are signs of growing attention to

Opposite *Getting around by road in Saigon*
Below *Motorcycles in Saigon*

road safety. There are far more traffic lights, road dividers and traffic police on the intersections ready to pounce on offenders.

Open Tour buses connect the main cities and visitor centers in Vietnam on a daily basis for a reasonable fare. There's also a network of public buses, but journeys are slow and uncomfortable and can be dangerous. Minibuses ply more regular routes, but are often alarmingly overladen.

CROSSING THE ROAD
Vietnam's streets, especially in Saigon and to a lesser extent in Hanoi, may look anarchic but in fact a strict code of conduct applies. Unlike Westerners, the Vietnamese do not wait for a lull in the traffic, but launch themselves straight into the flow, eyes ahead, alert to the endless tide of motorcyclists. Responsibility for their safety rests entirely with the oncoming drivers. To make it easier for bicyclists to avoid them, pedestrians walk at a steady, even pace with no deviation from a clearly signaled route, as

any slight change in trajectory or velocity would spell certain disaster. The only vehicles that will not maneuver their way around pedestrians are buses.

Rush hour is generally all day in Vietnam, but peaks between 6.30am and 9.30am and between 4pm and 6.30pm. In Ho Chi Minh City the roads are only really quiet between about 2am and 5am.

FLIGHTS
Domestic flight coverage is good in Vietnam, with regular flights to many destinations. Prices are reasonable considering the distances covered, and flights may be altered without penalty. The dominant carrier is Vietnam Airlines, but there are also Jetstar Pacific Airlines and Air Mekong, a new domestic carrier, which covers fewer routes than its competitors.

Online booking is available through the websites of all three airlines (for more information on domestic flights ▷ 49).

TRAINS
The Vietnamese rail network is run by Vietnam Railways (www.vr.com. vn) and extends the length of the country from Hanoi to Ho Chi Minh

City. Its branch networks include Hanoi to Haiphong, Hanoi to Dong Dang in the northeast, and Hanoi to Lao Cai in the northwest. It is an economical and comfortable way to travel if you opt for soft class or sleepers. Take care not to leave luggage unattended on the train, and if possible lock it away. See www.seat61.com for train information and how tickets can be booked in advance through agents.

BOATS
Boat services in Vietnam include connections between Ho Chi Minh City, Can Tho and Chau Doc; between Ha Tien and Chau Doc; between Ha Tien and Phu Quoc; and between Rach Gia and Phu Quoc. Ho Chi Minh City is connected by boat to Vung Tau; a ferry service runs between Halong Bay, Haiphong and Cat Ba Island.

VIETNAMESE ADDRESSES
Odd numbers on houses usually run consecutively on one side of the street, evens on the other; "bis" after a number, as in 16 bis Hai Ba Trung Street, means that there are two houses with the same number; "ter" indicates that there are three houses with the same number.

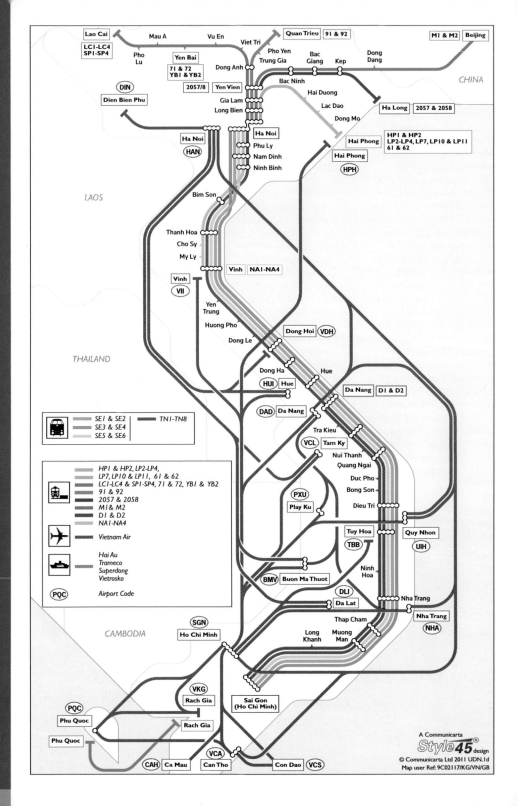

Lao Cai
LC1-LC4
SP1-SP4
Mau A
Vu En
Viet Tri
Quan Trieu 91 & 92
M1 & M2 Beijing
Pho Lu
Yen Bai
71 & 72
YB1 & YB2
Pho Yen
Trung Gia
Bac Giang
Kep
Dong Dang
Dong Anh
Bac Ninh
Hai Duong
Lac Dao
CHINA
DIN
Dien Bien Phu
Yen Vien
2057/8
Gia Lam
Long Bien
Dong Mo
Ha Long 2057 & 2058
Ha Noi
HAN
Ha Noi
Phu Ly
Nam Dinh
Ninh Binh
Hai Phong
HP1 & HP2
LP2-LP4, LP7, LP10 & LP11
61 & 62
Hai Phong
HPH
Bim Son
LAOS
Thanh Hoa
Cho Sy
My Ly
Vinh NA1-NA4
Vinh
VII
Yen Trung
Huong Pho
Dong Le
Dong Hoi VDH
THAILAND
Dong Ha
Hue
HUI Hue
Da Nang D1 & D2
DAD Da Nang
Tra Kieu
VCL Tam Ky
Nui Thanh
Quang Ngai
Duc Pho
Bong Son
PXU
Play Ku
Dieu Tri
Tuy Hoa
TBB
Quy Nhon
UIH
Ninh Hoa
BMV Buon Ma Thuot
DLI
Da Lat
Nha Trang
Nha Trang
NHA
Thap Cham
SGN
Ho Chi Minh
Long Khanh
Muong Man
CAMBODIA
VKG
Rach Gia
Sai Gon
(Ho Chi Minh)
PQC
Phu Quoc
Phu Quoc
Rach Gia
CAH Ca Mau
VCA
Can Tho
Con Dao VCS

SE1 & SE2   TN1-TN8
SE3 & SE4
SE5 & SE6

HP1 & HP2, LP2-LP4,
LP7, LP10 & LP11, 61 & 62
LC1-LC4 & SP1-SP4, 71 & 72, YB1 & YB2
91 & 92
2057 & 2058
M1 & M2
D1 & D2
NA1-NA4

Vietnam Air

Hai Au
Trameco
Superdong
Vietrosko

PQC Airport Code

A Communicarta
Style 45® design
© Communicarta Ltd 2011 UDN.1d
Map user Ref: 9C02117/KG/VN/GB

GETTING AROUND HO CHI MINH CITY

Ho Chi Minh City, or Saigon as it is still often called, has an abundant choice of transportation—which is very fortunate, because it is a hot, large and frenetic place. While metered taxis, motorcycle taxis and cyclos compete for travelers' business, many visitors who prefer some level of independence opt to rent (or even buy) a bicycle or motorcycle.

BICYCLES AND MOTORCYCLES

Bicycles and motorcycles can be rented from some of the low-budget hotels and cafés, especially in Pham Ngu Lao Street. Bicycles should always be parked in the roped-off compounds *(gui xe)* that are all over town; they will be looked after for a small charge (1,000d by day, 2,000d after dark; 2,000d for a motorcycle, 3,000d after dark; always get a ticket).

BUSES

The bus service in Ho Chi Minh City (HCMC)/Saigon has become more reliable and frequent in recent years. Buses are green or yellow and are a safer, less expensive and, in some cases, more convenient alternative to other modes of transportation in the city. They run at intervals of 10 to 20 minutes, depending on the time of day. In rush hours they are jammed with passengers and can run late. There are bus stops every 550 yards (500m).

The same price applies to all routes: 3,000d per person. All these buses start from or stop by the Travel Information Center opposite Ben Thanh Market (tel 08-8214444). A free map of all bus routes can be obtained here.

Right *A cyclo in Ho Chi Minh City*

CYCLOS

Cyclos (bicycle carriages) are a peaceful way to get around the city. They can be rented by the hour (approximately US$4 per hour) or to reach a specific destination. Some drivers speak English, and each tends to have his own patch, which is jealously guarded. Expect to pay more outside the major hotels—you can save some of the fare by walking around the corner.

Cyclos are being banned from more and more streets in the center of Saigon, and as a result some journeys are becoming longer and more expensive.

MOTORCYCLE TAXIS

Motorcycle taxis (Honda or *xe ôm*) are the quickest way to get around town and are less expensive than cyclos; agree on a price and hop on the back. *Xe ôm* drivers can be recognized by their baseball caps and tendency to chain smoke; they congregate on most street corners, and often shout "moto" to attract custom. Prices vary according to distance; a short journey should cost from around 25,000d. Try to haggle the fare down a little.

When you dismount, do so on the side without the exhaust pipe, to avoid being scalded by the fumes. Keep all belongings on the bicycle (hold your bag in front of you, resting behind the driver); flapping baggage is dangerous and is a target for thieves. If targeted, do not resist as you may be pulled off and the result may be far worse than losing a camera or bag.

TAXIS

Saigon has quite a large fleet of metered taxis. There are more than 14 taxi companies and competition has brought down prices, so that a taxi ride for two or more is less expensive than a cyclo or *xe ôm*. The standard of vehicle and service vary widely, and some companies are more expensive. Ensure that the meter is set after you get in. All taxis are numbered; in the event of forgotten luggage or other problems, ring the company and quote the number of your taxi.

USEFUL BUS ROUTES

No. 1 Saigon—Chinatown; from the bus stop you can walk to Cholon Coach Station *(ben xe Cho Lon)*; runs 5am–9pm.

No. 2 Saigon—Eastern Coach Station *(ben xe mien dong)*; from here buses go to provinces in the Mekong Delta; runs 4.45am–7pm.

No. 26 Ben Thanh Market—Western Coach Station *(ben xe mien tay)*; from here buses go to all provinces in other parts of Vietnam; runs 5am–6.40pm.

No. 28 Ben Thanh Market—Tan Son Nhat Airport (stops beside SuperBowl, near the airport); runs 5.30am–6.40pm.

No. 152 Ben Thanh Market—Tan Son Nhat Airport (straight to the airport—very often empty); runs 5.15am–8.55pm.

TAXIS

COMPANY	TELEPHONE
Airport Taxi (white or blue)	08-38446666
Mai Linh Taxi (green and white)	08-38262626
Festival (gray)	08-38454545
Saigon Tourist (red)	08-38222206
Vinataxi (yellow)	08-38111111
Vinasun (white)	08-38272727

GETTING AROUND HANOI

Hanoi is getting more frenetic by the minute as its growing wealth is invested in the internal combustion engine, but its elegant tree-lined boulevards make walking and bicycling a delightful experience nonetheless. If you like the idea of being pedaled, then a cyclo is the answer, but be prepared for some concentrated haggling. There are also motorcycle taxis (xe ôm), self-drive motorcycles to rent, and a fleet of metered taxis.

BICYCLES
» Bicycling is the most popular form of local mass transportation and is an excellent way to get around the city.
» Bicycles can be rented from most visitor cafés and hotels; expect to pay about US$1 per day. For those staying longer, it might be worth buying a bicycle.

CYCLOS
» Hanoi's cyclo drivers charge twice the price of a taxi journey, and consequently most cyclo journeys are for leisurely rides rather than as a mode of transportation from A to B.
» Drivers also have a tendency to forget the agreed fare and ask for more; some travelers ask that the price be written down if communication is a problem.
» Some drivers will ask for more if it is raining; tip at your discretion.
» A trip from the railway station to Hoan Kiem Lake should not be

more than 20,000d. The same trip on a xe ôm would be 15,000d.

MOTORCYCLES
» Renting a motorcycle is a good way of getting to some of the more remote places. Visitor cafés and hotels rent a variety of machines for around US$10 per day. Note that rental shops insist on keeping the renter's passport. As hotels also want to keep visitors' passports it can be hard to rent other than at your hotel.

RACING
A recent trend in contemporary society has manifested itself in the form of young male Hanoians racing each other on powerful motorcycles around the city streets. Up to 400 racers take part, and the more reckless cut their brake cables. A number of racers and spectators have died, and police have so far been unable to prevent the clandestinely organized events.

A team of police riders equipped with fast bikes, guns and electric cattle prods has at least been assembled to maintain order. The Hanoi People's Committee also put forward the suggestion of building a special racetrack, presumably with the hope that the legalization and management of the "sport" will help to control it.

DOMESTIC FLIGHTS
» There are three airlines offering domestic routes and they all have the same checked baggage allowance of 41lb (20kg), with

Above A cyclo driver and passengers

TAXIS	
COMPANY	**TELEPHONE**
Hanoi Taxi	04-38535353
Hanoi Tourist Taxi	04-38565656
Mai Linh Taxi	04-38222666/
	04-38616161
Airport Taxi	04-38866666

varying charges for excess baggage. Vietnam Airlines offers the most routes and have different ticket classes.

The main hubs are Hanoi in the north, Ho Chi Minh City (Saigon) in the south and Danang in the middle. There are air connections to: Hanoi, Haiphong, Na San (Son La), Quang Ninh, Lao Cai and Dien Bien Phu in the north; Vinh, Huê, Danang, Pleiku, Quy Nhon, Buon Me Thuot, Dalat, Quang Binh and Nha Trang in the central region; and Saigon, Phu Quoc, Rach Gia, Ca Mau, Can Tho, Dong Nai and Con Dao in the south.

» Tickets for all domestic flights should be reserved as soon as possible, but during low season it is perfectly possible to secure seats just a few days before flying or even the day before.

» Vietnam Airlines has different types of tickets, from business class

Above *A domestic plane*

down to super-saver class. There is a fee for changing a flight already booked (at the time of writing, between US$12 and US$24) except for economy flexible tickets. Super-saver tickets do not allow for any changes to be made to an existing reservation. Jetstar Pacific allows changes to be made if an extra US$9 is paid at the time of booking the ticket.

DOMESTIC CARRIERS

Vietnam has two domestic carriers:

Vietnam Airlines
www.vietnamairlines.com.vn

Jetstar Pacific Airlines
www.Jetstar.com.vn

New domestic airlines, like VietJetAir (www.vietjetair.com), are likely to open in the near future.

SAMPLE AIRLINE PRICES

AIRLINE	CLASS	ONE WAY (US$)
Vietnam Airlines		
Hanoi–Danang	B	120
	EF	71
Saigon–Danang	B	120
	S	50
Saigon–Hanoi	B	183
	EF	107
Saigon–Dalat	EF	53
	S	33
Saigon–Huê	EF	71
Saigon–Nha Trang	EF	53
	SF	43
Jetstar Pacific Airlines		
Hanoi–Saigon	E	77
Saigon–Haiphong	E	77
Saigon–Huê	E	59
Air Mekong		
Hanoi–Saigon	EF	66
Saigon–Dalat	EF	36

Key:
B = business
E = economy
EF = economy flexible
S = super saver
Round-trip fares are double the figures shown.

BOOKING OFFICES

AIRLINE	TELEPHONE
Vietnam Airlines	
Buon Me Thuot: 19 Ama Trang Long	50-03954442
Can Tho: 66 Nguyen An Ninh	71-03844320
Dalat: 02 Ho Tung Mau	63-3833499
Danang: 58 Bach Dang	511-3832320
Dien Bien Phu: Dien Bien Phu Airport	063-3833499
Dong Nai: 25–27 Pham Van Thuan, Bien Hoa	33-3511550
Haiphong: 30 Tran Phu Street	31-3810 890
Hanoi: 25 Trang Thi Street	04-38320320
Ho Chi Minh City: 116 Nguyen Huê Boulevard	08-38320320
Huê: 23 Nguyen Van Cu	54-3824709
Lao Cai: 2 Fansipan Road, Sapa	20-3873404
Nha Trang: 91 Nguyen Thien Street	58-3826768
Phu Quoc: 291 Nguyen Trung Truc Street	77-3996677
Pleiku: 18 Le Lai	59-3823058
Quang Binh: 35 Tran Hung Dao	05-2385082
Quang Ninh: Hong Gai hotel, Bai Chay Road, Ha Long	33-3511550
Quy Nhon: Nguyen Tat Thanh Street	511-3832320
Rach Gia: 16 Nguyen Trung Truc	77-3924320
Son La: 419 Chu Van Thinh Street	04-38320320
Vinh: 2 Le Hong Phong Street	31-3810890
Jetstar Pacific Airlines	
Danang: 35 Nguyen Van Linh Street	0511-3583583
Hanoi: 152 Le Duan Street, Dong Da District	04-38515350
Haiphong: 36 Hoang Van Thu Street	031-3559550
Ho Chi Minh City: 177 Vo Thi Sau Street, District 3	08-62907349
Nha Trang: Nguyen Ai Quoc Street	058-2228266
Air Mekong	
Ho Chin Minh City	08-38463666/08-38463999
Hanoi	04-37188199/04-37186399

BUSES

Although distances are great, journeys uncomfortable and roads dangerous, the majority of visitors to Vietnam travel over land. It is possible to travel the length of the country in this way, by both train (▷ 52–54) and bus. Since Highway 1 is dangerous and public buses are slow, most visitors opt for the inexpensive and regular Open Tour bus, which runs from Ho Chi Minh City (Saigon) to Hanoi and back, stopping off at several towns en route.

PUBLIC BUSES

Public buses, in general, are slow, old and cramped, but they usually arrive at their destination. It is not uncommon to see buses being totally disassembled at the side of the road, and it is rare to travel through the country by public transportation without experiencing several breakdowns or punctures. Speeds average no more than 22mph (35kph); public road transportation can be a long and tiresome (sometimes excruciating) business, but it is also fascinating and one of the best ways to meet and spend time with ordinary Vietnamese people.

A bewildering array of contraptions pass for buses, from old French jalopies to Chevrolet, Ford and DMC vans and Soviet buses. Many have ingenious cooling systems, in which water is fed into the radiator from barrels strapped to the roof; along the route there are water stations to replenish depleted barrels (look for the sign *nuoc mui* or *do nuoc*).

» Most bus stations are on the outskirts of town; in bigger places there may be several stations.
» Long-distance buses leave very early in the morning (4am to 5am).
» Buses are the least expensive form of transportation, although sometimes foreigners are asked two to three times the standard price.
» Prices are normally prominently displayed at bus stations.

OPEN TOUR BUSES

One of the best and most popular ways to travel by road is by traveler-café minibus, also known as the Open Bus or Open Tour bus. Many

SHORT DISTANCES	
JOURNEY	**PRICE**
Hanoi–Ninh Binh	US$4.50
Hanoi–Huê	US$8
Hanoi–Ho Chi Minh City	US$30
Huê–Hoi An	US$3.50
Hoi An–Nha Trang	US$9
Nha Trang–Dalat	US$9
Dalat–Ho Chi Minh City	US$7

Above *Traveling by bus in Ho Chi Minh City*
Opposite *A new-style bus in Hanoi*

tour operators or travelers' cafés run a minibus service or act as an agent. Operators match their rivals' prices and itineraries closely; indeed, many operate a clearing system to consolidate passenger numbers to more profitable levels.

» The popular Open Tour bus ticket is a flexible, one-way ticket from Ho Chi Minh City to Hanoi or Hanoi to Ho Chi Minh City. Buses run daily and include the following stops: Saigon, Mui Ne, Nha Trang, Dalat, Hoi An, Huê and Hanoi. You can join at any stage of the journey, paying for one trip or several as you go.

» The Hanoi to Huê section and vice versa is an overnight trip.

» Open Tour buses depart and arrive at their own offices. They often take passengers to their own or associated hotels; if you do not want to stay there, be firm about it.

» Buses stop at tourist destinations along the way. Stops can include Lang Co, Hai Van Pass, Marble Mountains and Po Klong Garai.

HO CHI MINH CITY BUS STATION

» Since the completion of a new road around Ho Chi Minh City, long-distance public buses, unless specifically signed "Saigon" or "ben xe Mien Dong," do not come into the city. Instead, passengers are dropped off on the ring road at Binh Phuoc bridge. From here it is a 45-minute xe ôm journey into town.

» There are two main bus stations and a fleet of air-conditioned buses connecting central Ho Chi Minh City with the bus terminals (3,000d). These leave the bus station opposite Ben Thanh Market.

» Buses north to Dalat, Huê, Danang and all points on the road to Hanoi leave from the Mien Dong terminal, north of town on Xo Viet Nghe Tinh Street.

» Buses south to the Mekong Delta (Ca Mau, Rach Gia, Ha Tien, Long Xuyen, My Tho, An Long, Can Tho and elsewhere) leave from the Mien Tay terminal, some distance southwest of town on Hung Vuong Boulevard.

» There is also a bus station in Cholon, which serves destinations such as Long An, My Thuan, Ben Luc and My Tho.

» Minibuses for Vung Tau depart from Ham Nghi Street; hop in quickly as they are not meant to pick up passengers in town.

HANOI BUSES

» The Southern bus terminal is out of town, but linking buses run from the north shore of Hoan Kiem Lake. The terminal serves destinations south of Hanoi: Ho Chi Minh City, Buon Me Thuot, Vinh, Danang, Thanh Hoa, Nha Trang and Dalat.

» Express buses usually leave at 5am; reserve seats in advance.

» Buses to Haiphong depart from Gia Lam bus station (across Chuong Duong Bridge); journey time is 2.5 hours.

» Other routes such as Hoa Binh, Son La and Dien Bien Phu go from My Dinh bus station, some miles to the west of Hanoi.

» Buses can be flagged down on Tran Quang Khai Street before they cross the bridge.

» Ha Dong station, in the southwest suburbs, has buses to Hoa Binh. Get to the station by local bus or xe ôm.

» Giap Bat station on Giai Phong Street serves destinations south.

TRAINS

Vietnam Railways (www.vr.com.vn) runs the 1,615-mile (2,600km) national network. The website lists timetables and fares across the land and is easily navigable (see also www.seat61.com). The rail link between Hanoi and Ho Chi Minh City (Saigon) passes through many of the towns and cities worth visiting, including Huê, Danang and Nha Trang. Other than going by air, the train is the most comfortable way to travel—but this applies only to first-class seats. With overnight stays at hotels along the way to see the sights, a rail sightseeing tour from Hanoi to Ho Chi Minh City, or vice versa, should take a minimum of 10 days, but you need to buy tickets for each separate journey.

FARES

Fares are inexpensive, and because the difference in price between first and second class is small, it is worth paying extra. Children under five travel free, and children between five and nine years of age pay 50 percent of the ticket price.

TRAINS

There are three seating classes and four sleeping classes on the network:
» First class: air-conditioned soft seat; long-distance tickets also include meals.
» Second class: soft seat.
» Third class: hard seat.

For overnight trips there are four classes:
» Hard-berthed cabin sleeping six.
» Air-conditioned hard-berthed cabin for six.
» Soft-berthed cabin for four.
» Air-conditioned soft four-berthed cabin.

» Prices vary according to the class of cabin chosen, the berth (lower berth is more expensive than top berth) and the time the train leaves.

» The slow local trains are entertaining if you have the time and want to enjoy the company of the local people.

» The kitchen on the Hanoi to Saigon route serves soups and simple, but adequate, rice dishes (it is a good idea to take additional food and drink on long journeys).

HANOI TO HO CHI MINH CITY

» Six trains daily leave Hanoi for Ho Chi Minh City and vice versa.
» Odd-numbered trains—SE1, SE3, SE5, TN1, TN3, TN7—travel south.

» Even-numbered trains—SE2, SE4, SE6, TN2, TN4, TN8—travel north.

» The SE9 and SE10 run for the *Tet* festival and peak public holidays, stopping at important destinations along the way such as Vinh, Dong Hoi, Huê, Danang, Nha Trang and Ho Chi Minh City.

» The express trains (known as the Reunification Express) take 29 to 39 hours, but delays are possible.

» The SE1 from Hanoi to Ho Chi Minh City takes 29 hours and the SE3 takes 39 hours. The chart below details fares for these trains, which cover the length of the country.

HANOI TO HUÊ AND DANANG

» Livitrans Express Train (www.livitrantrain.com) is a train service offering a higher standard of comfort than the state railway carriages.

» Trains depart Hanoi at 7pm, arriving at Huê at just after 8am the next morning and at Danang just after 10.30. In the other direction, trains depart Danang at noon, reach Huê at 3pm and Hanoi at 4am the next morning.

» Fares in a deluxe four-berth cabin are US$53 per person for Hanoi to Hue and US$13 for Hanoi to Danang.

» Food is served in the dining car but is not included in the fare.

HANOI TO SAPA

» Sapa can be reached by overnight train from Hanoi to Lao Cai in a journey lasting between 8.5 and 10 hours.

» A fleet of minibuses ferries passengers from Lao Cai rail station to Sapa.

» There are numerous classes of seat or berth on the trains, and various companies have their own private cars.

» The Victoria Express, for hotel guests only, runs Sun–Fri. This is the most expensive of the private rail carriages to Jao Cai (from US$136 to US$328).

» Information about the various travel companies who run their own carriages on the Hanoi to Lao Cai route can be found at www. sapatrains.com and online bookings can be made. The following fares are for one person return to Lao Cai and do not include meals or drinks, but do include a pick-up from your Hanoi hotel to the train station. One-way fares are also available. King Express: 2-berth cabins, US$136; 4-berth cabins, US$65. Tulico Express: 2-berth cabins, US$130; 4-berth cabins, US$65. Livitrans Express: 2-berth cabins, US$135; 4-berth cabins, US$68. Fanxipan Express: 2-berth cabins, US$138; 4-berth cabins, US$68. Royal Express: 4-berth cabins, US$60. TSC Express: 2-berth cabins, US$136; 4-berth cabins, US$60. Pumpkin Express: 4-berth cabins, US$60. Friendly Express: 4-berth cabins, US$60. Hara Express: 2-berth cabins, US$125; 4-berth cabins, US$62. Ratraco Express: 4-berth cabins, US$60.

» There are two cars, each with six superior cabins (four berths) and two deluxe cabins (two berths with a bedside table and ample luggage rack). All are air-conditioned, with wood paneling.

HANOI TO HAIPHONG

» There are four trains daily to Haiphong: one from the central station, and three from Long Bien station, at the western end of Long Bien Bridge near the Red River. Get there by taxi or *xe ôm*.

HO CHI MINH CITY TO NHA TRANG

» There is a luxury train service between Ho Chi Minh City and Nha Trang, called Golden Trains, that consists of deluxe cars attached to the normal Vietnamese Railways slow train running this route. Trains depart around 8pm from Ho Chi Minh City and arrive in Nha Trang at 5.15am; the return times are departure at 7pm and arrival at 4.45am. Ticket prices range from US$38 to US$65 and can be booked though any travel agent.

BUYING TICKETS

» All tickets must be bought in advance.

» Most ticket offices have some staff who speak English.

» Lines can be long and sometimes confusing, and some offices keep unusual hours. If you are short of time and short on patience it may well pay to get a tour operator to reserve your ticket for a small fee.

» All sleepers should be reserved three days in advance.

SAMPLE TRAIN FARES

ROUTE	CLASS	FARE
Ho Chi Minh City–Hanoi	Air-conditioned soft sleeper	US$54–US$80
Hanoi–Ho Chi Minh City	Air-conditioned soft seat	US$36–US$54
Ho Chi Minh City–Danang	Air-conditioned soft sleeper	US$33–US$50
	Air-conditioned soft seat	US$22-US$32
Ho Chi Minh City–Huê	Air-conditioned soft sleeper	US$36–US$54
	Air-conditioned soft seat	US$23–US$35
Ho Chi Minh City–Nha Trang	Air-conditioned soft sleeper	US$16–US$24
	Air-conditioned soft seat	US$10–US$14
Hanoi–Huê	Air-conditioned soft sleeper	US$26–US$40
	Air-conditioned soft seat	US$16–US$24
Hanoi–Danang	Air-conditioned soft sleeper	US$29–US$43
	Air-conditioned soft seat	US$18–US$28
Huê–Danang	Air-conditioned soft sleeper	US$4–US$6
	Air-conditioned soft seat	US$2–US$4
Danang–Hua Trang	Air-conditioned soft sleeper	US$18–US$28
	Air-conditioned soft seat	US$12–US$18

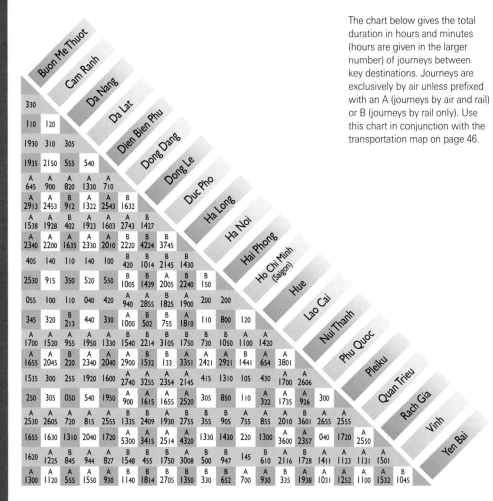

The chart below gives the total duration in hours and minutes (hours are given in the larger number) of journeys between key destinations. Journeys are exclusively by air unless prefixed with an A (journeys by air and rail) or B (journeys by rail only). Use this chart in conjunction with the transportation map on page 46.

To ↓ / From →	Buon Me Thuot	Cam Ranh	Da Nang	Da Lat	Dien Bien Phu	Dong Dang	Dong Le	Duc Pho	Ha Long	Ha Noi	Hai Phong	Ho Chi Minh (Saigon)	Hue	Lao Cai	Nui Thanh	Phu Quoc	Pleiku	Quan Trieu	Rach Gia	Vinh
Cam Ranh	330																			
Da Nang	110	120																		
Da Lat	1930	310	305																	
Dien Bien Phu	1935	2150	555	540																
Dong Dang	A645	A900	A820	A1330	A710															
Dong Le	A2913	A2453	B912	B1322	A2543	B1632														
Duc Pho	A1538	A1928	B402	A1923	A1603	A2743	B1427													
Ha Long	A2340	A2200	1635	A2330	A2010	2220	B4224	B3745												
Ha Noi	405	140	110	140	100	B420	B1014	B2145	B1430											
Hai Phong	2530	915	350	520	550	B1005	B1439	A2005	B2240	B150										
Ho Chi Minh (Saigon)	055	100	110	040	420	A940	B2855	A1825	B1900	200	200									
Hue	345	320	B213	440	330	A1000	B502	B755	B1810	110	800	120								
Lao Cai	A1700	A1520	955	1950	A1330	1540	B2214	B3105	1750	730	1050	1100	1420							
Nui Thanh	A1655	A2045	220	A2340	A2040	2900	1532	133	3351	2421	2921	1441	654	A3801						
Phu Quoc	1535	300	255	1920	1600	A2740	A3255	A2354	2145	415	1310	105	430	A1700	A2606					
Pleiku	250	305	050	540	1950	A900	1615	1655	2520	305	850	110	A322	A1735	926	300				
Quan Trieu	A2530	A2605	720	815	2555	B1335	A2409	1930	B2755	355	905	755	855	2010	B3601	2655	2555			
Rach Gia	1655	1630	1310	2040	1720	B5300	A3415	2514	B4320	1330	1430	220	1300	A3600	2357	040	1720	A2550		
Vinh	1620	1225	845	944	827	1548	455	1750	3008	500	947	145	610	2116	1728	1411	1123	1131	1501	
Yen Bai	A1300	1120	555	1550	930	1140	1814	2705	1350	330	652	700	930	335	1938	1031	1252	1100	1532	B1045

HANOI STATION

» 120 Le Duan Street, Hanoi, tel 04-39423697.
» The central station (ga Hanoi) is at the end of Tran Hung Dao Street (a 10-minute taxi ride from town).
» For trains to Ho Chi Minh City and the south, enter the station from Le Duan Street; for trains to Haiphong, Lao Cai and China, enter from Tran Quy Cap Street.
» Platform tickets are 1,000d.

HO CHI MINH CITY (SAIGON) STATION

» Thong Nhat Railway Station, 1 Nguyen Thong Street, Ward 9, District 3, Ho Chi Minh City, tel 08-38436528.
» The station (nha ga) is 1 mile (2km) from the middle of the city at the end of Nguyen Thong Street.
» Facilities for the visitor include an air-conditioned waiting room, post office, bank (no travelers' checks) and toilets.
» The ticket office is open daily 7–7; tel 08-39310666/39318952.
» There is a Train Booking Agency at 275c Pham Ngu Lao Street (open daily 7.30–11.30, 1.30–4.30; tel 08-38367640/38367660), which saves an unnecessary journey out to the station.
» Alternatively, for a small fee, most travel agents will obtain tickets.

OTHER PRINCIPAL STATIONS

» Danang Station, 122 Haiphong Street, Danang, tel 0511-3823810.
» Huê Station, 2 Bui Thi Xuan, Huê, tel 054-3822175.
» Nha Trang Station, 17 Thai Nguyen Street, Nha Trang, tel 058-3822113.

RENTED TRANSPORTATION

Self-drive car rental is not available in Vietnam. It is, however, possible to rent cars with drivers, and this is a good way of getting to more remote areas with a group of people. Prices vary across the country and according to the period of rental. Motorcycles can be rented easily and are an excellent and exhilarating way of getting off the beaten track. Bicycles can also be rented by the day in the cities and are useful for getting out into the countryside. Within cities, cyclos (bicycle carriages), *xe ôms* (motorcycle taxis) and metered taxis will all be used at some point in your trip to get around large areas or, in the case of a cyclo, for a leisurely ride.

CAR RENTAL

Cars with drivers can be rented for around US$50 to US$70 per day, depending on the distance traveled and the car rental company. It pays to shop around. Many tour operators and travelers' cafés will rent out cars with drivers.

Note that car rental prices increase by 50 percent or more during *Tet*. Some companies rent by the day or by the day plus distance covered. Others charge by the kilometer. Prices vary according to whether a four-seat car or a minibus is rented. Cars are usually four- and seven-seaters. All are modern and air-conditioned.

» In and around Hanoi and the north a standard, air-conditioned modern car including the driver, gasoline, tolls and food, and accommodations for the driver costs around US$420 for one week. A larger car with seats for seven costs around US$75 a day or US$490 a week.

» Tolls are applicable where motorists cross new bridges or new roads. A four-seater car is charged 10,000d.

» For driving the length of the country from Hanoi to Saigon, the cost for an air-conditioned, standard car rises to around US$1,200 for a week, including gas and driver, and food and accommodations for the driver. A discount may be offered for a one-way service where a company has multiple branches throughout the country.

» A round trip works out as a less expensive option. For example, Hanoi to Huê and back within four days costs around US$250.

BICYCLES AND MOTORCYCLES

In cities and towns often the best (and least expensive) way to get around is to rent a bicycle or motorcycle. There has been some tightening up of regulations regarding motorcycle driver's licenses, but for the time being, the police and the rental agencies do not apply them to foreigners (but check before you rent). Take time to familiarize yourself with road conditions and ride slowly. Most towns are small enough for bicycles to be an attractive option, but if you are taking in a sweep of the surrounding countryside (touring around the Central Highlands, for example) a motorcycle allows you to see more. Bicycles are pretty hard work in Dalat and Kontum.

» Hotels often have bicycles to rent, and there is usually someone willing to lend their rental for a small charge (around 20,000d per day).

» Many travelers' cafés rent out bicycles and motorcycles, the former for around 20,000d a day, the latter for 150,000d per day.

» Motorcycles are rented out with helmets and bicycles with locks. Some longer-stay visitors buy bicycles which they then sell on or give to Vietnamese friends.

» Always park your bicycle or motorcycle in a guarded parking place *(gui xe)*. Ask for a ticket.

» It is possible to book bicycles on to trains, but this must be done at least two days in advance. The cost from Nha Trang to Danang, for example, is US$6.

» Foreigners do not currently need a driver's license or proof of motorcycle training to rent a motorcycle in Vietnam.

Opposite *Buying tickets in Hano.* **Below** *A motorcycle rental store*

FINES AND REGULATIONS

» Traffic police stand on every street corner collecting fines for supposed breaches of traffic law, and may confiscate your motorcycle keys.

» The wearing of crash helmets is compulsory. Motorcycle taxis carry a spare helmet for their passengers.

» In some cities you can turn right on a red light. Pedestrians, especially, need to know this.

MOTORCYCLE TAXI (HONDA ÔM OR XE ÔM)

Ôm means to cuddle, which gives some idea of the style of this ubiquitous and inexpensive transportation. Motorcycle taxis are found on most street corners, outside hotels or in the street. With their uniform baseball caps and dangling cigarettes, xe ôm drivers are readily recognizable. If they see you before you see them, they will shout "moto" to get your attention. In the north and upland areas the Honda is replaced with the Minsk, that Russian workhorse of the hills. A xe ôm around the middle of Saigon or Hanoi costs around 20,000d but you will need to stick to your price and have it confirmed before donning your crash helmet.

CYCLOS

Cyclos are a slow and leisurely form of transportation. Cyclo drivers charge double a xe ôm, which, when multiplied by the premium levied on foreign visitors, makes the journey more expensive than a drive in an air-conditioned taxi, especially if there are two or three of you. A number of streets in the central areas of Saigon and Hanoi are one-way or out of bounds to cyclos, necessitating lengthy detours that add to the time and cost. Many cyclo drivers regale their passengers with their life stories, give potted histories of all the pagodas visited and then pedal them to a little diner for a wonderful, inexpensive meal. Taxi drivers are unlikely to do this.

» The cyclo is a wonderful way to get around the Old City of Hanoi, and is ideal for anyone with plenty of time to spare, especially in smaller towns.

» Do not take a cyclo after dark unless the driver is well known to you or you know the route.

» A cyclo from the New World Hotel to the Zoo in Saigon should be around 35,000d, but is often more; a cyclo tour of Cholon could cost as much as 400,000d.

TAXIS

Taxis ply the streets of Hanoi and Saigon and other large towns and cities. If you are new to the country your best bet is to go to a hotel wherever you may be and take one of the taxis waiting there, or ask the hotel to call you one. Although they are found in virtually every large town in the country, taxis sometimes need to be summoned by telephone.

» Fares are inexpensive—around 12,500d per kilometer after a start-up charge of 15,000d—and the drivers generally know their way around and speak some English.

» You will probably need to know the right quan (district) for your destination.

» Always keep a varied selection of notes with you so that when the taxi stops you can round the fare up to the nearest small denomination. Normally, short trips earn a tip of between 2,000 and 5,000d.

» At night use the better known taxi companies rather than the unlicensed cars that often gather around popular nightspots.

Above *A motorcycle taxi or* xe ôm
Opposite *Boat traffic on the Mekong*

BOATS

Boats and hydrofoils make important crossings and journeys in several parts of Vietnam. Boats run regularly and are less expensive (although slower) than flying where plane routes also exist. There are four principal sea crossings—one in the north and three in the south—and two main river journeys in the Mekong Delta, plus some short crossings linked by regular ferry services throughout the Mekong Delta.

HALONG CITY, HAIPHONG AND CAT BA ISLAND

» Ferries depart for Haiphong from Hon Gai (Halong City) at 6am, 11am and 4pm, price 60,000d, duration 3 hours. The trip itself is worthwhile: The ferry is packed with people and their produce, and threads its way through the limestone islands and outcrops that are so characteristic of the area, before winding up the Cua Cam River to the port of Haiphong. For Cat Ba take the Haiphong ferry to Cat Hai and either transfer to the Haiphong–Cat Ba ferry or hop over to Phu Long and take a *xe ôm* from there.

» The air-conditioned Greenlines hydrofoil from Haiphong to Cat Ba departs twice a day, fare 240,000d, duration 1 hour. The timings vary slightly depending upon season, but usually there is one boat in the morning, at 9am, returning at 4pm or 3.15pm in winter. If it is not running late, the 6am train from Hanoi will get you to Haiphong just in time to take a *xe ôm* across town for the morning boat.

» The ferry from Haiphong via Cat Hai (usually crowded) to Cat Ba departs 6.30am and 1pm, fare 160,000d, duration 2 hours 30 minutes, and from Cat Ba departs 5.45am and 1pm. Alternatively, take the Hon Gai ferry at 9am, stopping off at Cat Hai; from there, take a small boat to Phu Long on the west of Cat Ba Island and a *xe ôm* or bus (erratic service) to Cat Ba town.
Contact details: Greenlines, 4M Tran Hung Dao Street, Hong Bang District, Haiphong; tel 031-3747370.

HA TIEN TO CHAU DOC

The ferry wharf is just to the northeast of the pontoon bridge on Nguyen Van Hai Street in Ha Tien. Ferries to Chau Doc depart at 6am, price 180,000d, duration 7–10 hours. Take food and water.

HA TIEN, HON CHONG AND RACH GIA TO AN THOI TOWN, PHU QUOC

» The Duong Dong Express departs daily from Rach Gia at 7.45am and arrives at Phu Quoc at 10.15am. The boat from Phu Quoc departs at 12.45pm and arrives at Rach Gia at 3.15pm. One-way adult fare 270,000d, child (5–11) 200,000d.
Contact details: Duong Dong Express; tel 77-3990747 (An Thoi), 77-3879765 (Rach Gia); www.duongdongexpress.com.vn.

» The Super Dong Express departs daily from Rach Gia at 8am and from An Thoi at 1pm. Unless your onward travel has been arranged in advance you may have to spend the evening in Rach Gia after disembarking from the An Thoi boat. Adult fare 150,000d.
Contact details: Super Dong Express; tel 77-3846180 (An Thoi), 77-3877742 (Rach Gia).

» Trameco departs daily from Rach Gia (Duong and Dong) at 1.30pm and from An Thoi at 8.30am. Adult fare 150,000d.
Contact details: Trameco; tel 77-3980666 (An Thoi), 77-3878655 (Rach Gia).

» Hai An (Seagull) departs daily from Rach Gia at 1.30pm and from An Thoi at 8.30am. Adult fare 150,000d.
Contact details: Hai An; tel 77-3981000 (An Thoi), 77-3879455 (Rach Gia).

HO CHI MINH CITY TO VUNG TAU

Competing companies operate hydrofoils from the Bach Dang wharf at the end of Ham Nghi Street, District 1, in Saigon to the Halong Street jetty in Vung Tau. Crossings take about 1 hour 15 minutes.

» The Petro Express service operates from 7am–5pm; it returns from Vung Tau from 8am–5pm. Price 200,000d, one-way. Ticket office open daily 5.30am–5pm.
Contact details: Petro Express, on the Saigon jetty; tel 08-38215609; in Vung Tau, tel 064-3810625.

» The Greenlines service operates with Petro Express. Children aged under 6 travel free. Booking office open daily 7am–8pm.
Contact details: Greenlines, office on the jetty and at 1A Ham Nghi Street; tel 08-38215609; Vung Tau, tel 64-3810202.

» The Vina Express operates from 6am–4.30pm both ways, with seven departures daily. Price 200,000d adults, 100,000d children. Booking office open daily 6–5.30.
Contact details: Vina Express, on the jetty; tel 08-38253333; Vung Tau, tel 064-3856530; www.vinaexpress.com.vn.

There are very few amenities in Vietnam for visitors with disabilities. City streets are cluttered with vendors, motorcycles and street furniture, and the poor paving presents even more obstacles to anyone with restricted mobility. Generally, however, restaurant and hotel staff are accommodating and helpful.

Above *A wheelchair user waits to board a flight*

AROUND TOWN

» Wheelchair access is improving, and more shopping malls, hotels and restaurants provide ramps for easy access, although most sites are still some way behind.

HOTEL ROOMS

» Some of the better hotels have designated rooms for guests with disabilities; these are listed in the individual Staying entries for each region. However, they are few and far between, so it's advisable to reserve early.

» Wheelchair-designated rooms can be found at the Hilton Hanoi Opera, Nikko Hanoi, Sofitel Metropole, Sofitel Plaza Hanoi and Sunway Hotel in Hanoi; at the Furama Resort in Danang; at Lang Co Beach Resort, Lang Co in the central region; at the Caravelle, Legend, Renaissance Riverside, Rex and Sheraton in Saigon; and in the Saigon-Phu Quoc Resort on Phu Quoc in the south.

TOURS

» High-quality tour operators can arrange visits with suitable transportation for those with a disability. Note, though, that wheelchair-users can be accommodated only in hotels with designated rooms.

USEFUL ORGANIZATIONS

CANADA
THE EASTER SEALS SOCIETY
One Concorde Gate, Suite 700, Toronto
ON M3C 3N6
tel 416 421-8377
www.easterseals.org

UK
RADAR
12 City Forum, 250 City Road
London, EC1V 8AF
tel 020 7250 3222
www.radar.org.uk

US
SATH
347 Fifth Avenue, Suite 610
New York City, NY 10016
tel 212/447-7284
www.sath.org

REGIONS

This chapter is divided into five regions of Vietnam (▷ 9). Region names are for the purpose of this book only and places of interest are listed alphabetically in each region.

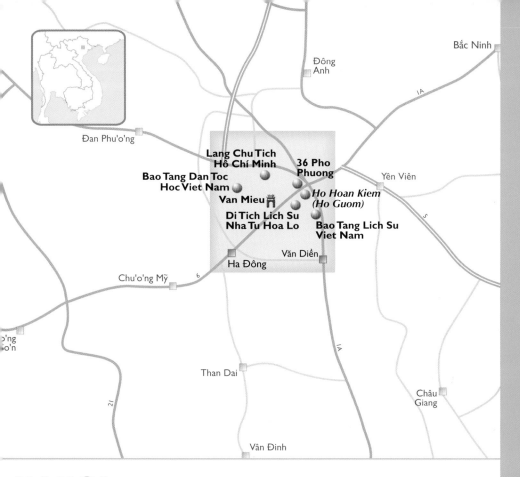

Bắc Ninh

Đông Anh

Đan Phu'o'ng

Lang Chu Tich
Hồ Chí Minh   36 Pho
                          Phuong   Yên Viên
Bao Tang Dan Toc
Hoc Viet Nam
Van Mieu   Ho Hoan Kiem
                          (Ho Guom)
Di Tich Lich Su
Nha Tu Hoa Lo   Bao Tang Lich Su
                          Viet Nam

Chu'o'ng Mỹ   Văn Diễn
                      Ha Đông

'ng
o'n

Than Dai
                                              Châu
                                              Giang

Vân Đinh

HANOI

Slumbering quietly for half a century before weathering the B52s, absorbing the Russian assistance and relishing the peace of the 1980s, and the gradual economic growth of the 1990s, Hanoi is now approaching its 1,000th birthday. The venerable City of the Soaring Dragon has awoken and soars once again, not perhaps in the way that Uncle Ho envisaged but in a way that reflects its ancient culture, its French colonial past and its modern aspirations.

The city has qualities pertaining to the perfect tourist destination. Its busy, noisy, ancient heart is intact, its French colonial architecture gives an air of elegant calm, and Hoan Kim Lake and park provide a haven from the herds of motorcycles and seemingly crazy traffic rules. Hanoi's markets are filled with strange and colorful goods, gorgeously perfumed flowers and all the basic necessities you might want. In the old city specialist streets offer temple goods, funeral items and luscious silk garments and fabrics.

If the architecture displays the city's diverse cultural past, so too does its food, a glorious mix of Vietnamese, Chinese and French cuisines. Here you can eat spring rolls one day and croissants the next, delicate French pastries loaded with fresh cream, or luridly colored riceflour cakes sweetened with palm sugar and perhaps swimming in coconut milk and green beans.

Special places to visit include the mausoleum of Ho Chi Minh, his home and the museum dedicated to him, the museums of ethnology and history, and Hoa Lo Prison, known as the Hanoi Hilton to the many Vietnamese and American people who were incarcerated there. The city is also the starting point for trips into the north, to Sapa, to Halong Bay and to the stunning high mountains of the northwest.

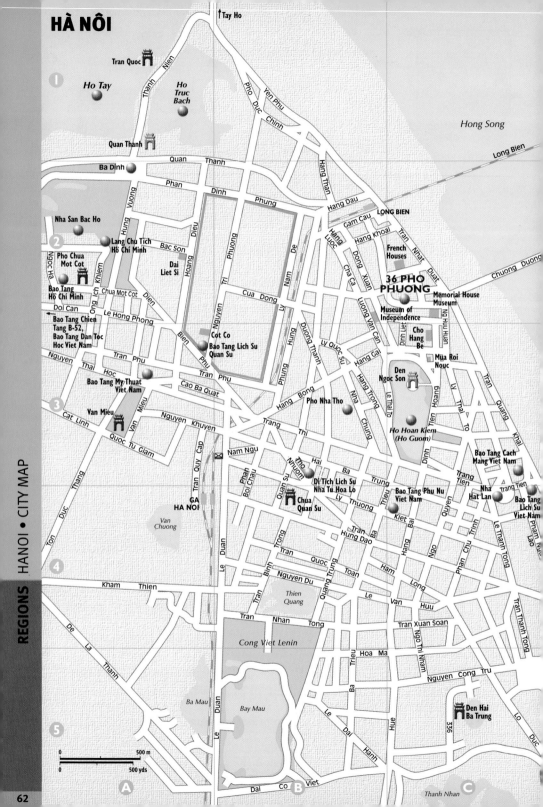

HÀ NỘI

Tran Quoc

Ho Tay

Ho Truc Bach

Hong Song

Long Bien

Quan Thanh

Thanh

Nien

Pho Duc Chinh

Yen Phu

Ba Dinh

Quan Thanh

Phan

Dinh

Phung

Hang Than

Hang Dau

LONG BIEN

Nha San Bac Ho

Lang Chu Tich Ho Chi Minh

Pho Chua Mot Cot

Bao Tang Ho Chi Minh

Bac Son

Dai Liet Si

Chua Mot Cot

Doi Can

Bao Tang Chien Tang B-52, Bao Tang Dan Toc Hoc Viet Nam

Le Hong Phong

Gam Cau

Hang Khoai

French Houses

36 PHO PHUONG

Memorial House Museum

Museum of Independence

Cho Hang Be

Mua Roi Nouc

Nguyen Thai Hoc

Bao Tang My Thuat Viet Nam

Tran Phu

Cao Ba Quat

Cot Co

Bao Tang Lich Su Quan Su

Tran Phu

Hang Bong

Pho Nha Tho

Den Ngoc Son

Ho Hoan Kiem (Ho Guom)

Van Mieu

Cat Linh

Nguyen Khuyen

Quoc Tu Giam

Trang

Thi

Nam Ngu

Hai

Ba

Bao Tang Cach Mang Viet Nam

Trang Tien

Nha Hat Lan

Bao Tang Lich Su Viet Nam

Ton Duc Thang

GA HA NOI

Phan Boi Chau

Quang Trung

Di Tich Lich Su Nha Tu Hoa Lo

Chua Quan Su

Ly Thuong Kiet

Bao Tang Phu Nu Viet Nam

Tran Hung Dao

Van Chuong

Le Duan

Tran

Quoc Toan

Nguyen Du

Ham Long

Tran Nhan Tong

Thien Quang

Tran Xuan Soan

Kham Thien

De La Thanh

Cong Viet Lenin

Hoa Ma

Nguyen Cong Tru

Ba Mau

Bay Mau

Hue

Le Dai Hanh

336

Den Hai Ba Trung

Tran Thanh Tong

0   500 m
0   500 yds

Dai Co Viet

Thanh Nhan

REGIONS   HANOI • CITY MAP

A   B   C

1 2 3 4 5

HANOI STREET INDEX

REGIONS   HANOI • CITY MAP

INTRODUCTION

Hanoi life is at its most vibrant in this beautiful, busy maze of old shops, houses and temples. Small streets are packed with popular restaurants and interesting stores in this shabby but chic district.

Hanoi's Old City, also known as the Thirty-Six Streets, is a delightful warren of lanes inhabited by tinkers, tailors, shoemakers, stone engravers, florists and innumerable other traders, though the crafts and trades of the past have given way in large part to karaoke bars, video rental shops and souvenirs. Nevertheless, this is still the city's liveliest area, humming with the sounds of birds, cyclo drivers, revving motorcycles and women selling their wares from baskets balanced on their shoulders. Forming its boundaries are Hoan Kiem Lake to the south, the Citadel to the west, the Red River to the east, and to the north the vast indoor Dong Xuan Market, devastated by fire in 1994 but rebuilt and operating again within two years. Cyclos are available to take visitors around the Old City, but by far the best way to explore it is on foot.

The original Old City grew up as a squalid, dark, cramped and disease-ridden labyrinth of streets to the east of the Citadel, where the emperor had his residence. This part of Hanoi has survived surprisingly intact, and today is the most beautiful area of the city. By the 15th century there were 36 short lanes here, each specializing in a particular trade and representing one of the 36 trade guilds. Among them, for example, were the Phuong Hang Dao (Dyers' Guild Street) and the Phuong Hang Bac (Silversmiths' Street). The 36 streets have interested European visitors since they first started coming to Hanoi. In 1685, Samuel Bacon noted that "all the diverse objects sold in this town have a specially assigned street," remarking how different this was from "companies and corporations in European cities." The streets in question not only sold different products, but were also usually populated by people from different areas of the country. They would live, work and worship together because each occupational guild had its own temple and support networks.

Some of this past is still in evidence. At the south end of Hang Dau Street, for example, is a mass of stalls selling nothing but shoes, while Tin Street is still home to a community of tinkers.

INFORMATION

www.ticvietnam.com

✚ 62 C2 🛈 Tourist Information Center, 7 Dinh Tien Hoang Street ☎ 04-39263366 Ⓒ Mon–Fri 7–11.30, 1.30–5 🍴 Restaurants serving Vietnamese, Chinese, French and international food ☕ Many cafés serving Vietnamese and international food; some also provide tour information 🍺 Lively bars with music, pool, dancing and long opening hours

Above *Tiny houses in the Old City nestle tightly together in the narrow lanes*
Opposite *Conical hats and bicycles are ubiquitous on the streets of Hanoi*

Above *Shuttered houses in the Old Quarter*
Right *Bright street stalls*

WHAT TO SEE
TUBE HOUSES

Narrow dwellings known as *nha ong* (tube houses) are characteristic of this whole area. Although they may have shop fronts only 10ft (3m) wide or less, the main body of the houses can be up to 160ft (50m) long. Whereas in the Vietnamese countryside the dimensions of houses were calculated on the basis of the owner's own physical dimensions, in urban areas no such regulations existed, and tube houses evolved so that each house owner could have an area—albeit very small—of shop frontage facing onto the main street. Traditionally built of bricks stuck together with sugar-cane juice, the tube houses tend to be interspersed by courtyards or "wells" to allow light inside and provide some space for outside activities such as washing and gardening. Houses also have a natural air-conditioning system, a consequence of the air flow created by the difference in ambient temperature between the inner courtyards and the street outside. The longer the house, the greater the velocity of the flow. It's still possible to see a shared wall in between some of the tube houses. These shared walls were built in a step-like pattern and not only marked land boundaries but also acted as fire breaks. House frontages were not given regulated positions until the early 20th century and as a result some streets have a wonderfully irregular appearance.

Older houses tend to be lower, as commoners were not permitted to build higher than the emperor's own residence. Other regulations prohibited attic windows looking down onto the street (a precaution against assassination attempts, and a means of preventing residents from looking down on a passing king). Purple and gold were shades strictly reserved for royal use, as was the decorative use of the dragon.

FRENCH HOUSES

By the early 20th century, inhabitants of the tube houses had started replacing their traditional dwellings with buildings inspired by French architecture. Many fine structures from this era remain, and these can be best appreciated by standing back and looking upward. Shutters, cornices, columns, wrought-iron balconies and balustrades are common decorative features. An ornate facade sometimes conceals the pitched roof behind.

Some conservationists fear that this unique area will be destroyed as residents who have made small fortunes in the wake of the liberation of the economy redevelop their houses without reference to the traditional

surroundings. However, the desire to build new homes is understandable, as the tube houses are cramped and squalid, and many have no facilities.
✛ 62 C2 ✉ Nguyen Sieu Street and nearby

MEMORIAL HOUSE MUSEUM
The house at 87 Ma May Street is a splendidly preserved example of an original shop house, and is now open to the public. The house was built in the late 19th century as a home for a single family, and given the restricted space available it soon becomes clear that the shop houses' miniature interior courtyards, giving light and fresh air, and their little gardens were of fundamental importance. The wooden upper floor and pitched, fish scale-tiled roofs are typical of the style once followed by most of the houses in this area. From 1954 to 1999 no fewer than five families shared the building on Ma May Street as the urban population rose and living conditions declined.
✛ 62 C2 ✉ 87 Pho Ma May ☎ 04-39285604 ⓧ Daily 8–5.30 ✋ 5,000d ❓ Much of the explanatory text is in French only

MUSEUM OF INDEPENDENCE
Ho Chi Minh lived at 48 Hang Ngang Street, at the north end of Hang Dao Street (before it becomes Hang Duong Street), and this is the spot where he drew up the Vietnamese Declaration of Independence in 1945, modeled on the US Declaration of Independence. The modern building now houses a small museum with black and white photographs of Ho.
✛ 62 B2 ✉ 48 Hang Ngang Street ⓧ Mon–Sat 8–5 ✋ Free

CHO HANG BE
A walk through Hang Be Market reveals just how far Hanoi has developed over the past decade. There is a wonderful variety of food on sale—live, dead, cooked and raw. Quacking ducks, newly plucked chickens, saucers of warm animal blood, pigs' trotters, and freshly picked and pickled vegetables are among the produce whose quality is a remarkable testament to the rapid strides made by Vietnamese agriculture. There are also beautiful cut flowers on sale in this market and the surrounding streets.
✛ 62 C3 ✉ Gai Ngu Street ⓧ Daily 5–5

TIPS
» The best way to explore and experience Hanoi's Old City is on foot ▷ 82–83.
» Don't be put off by shops with only a solitary mannequin in the narrow window. These are tube houses—enter the shop and walk down the passageway into much larger showrooms at the back, where there is plenty of stock.
» Many budget cafés offer reasonably priced tours and places to stay, and are also a good way to meet other travelers.

Below *A variety of fresh produce for sale at Hang Be Market*

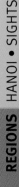

REGIONS • HANOI • SIGHTS

BAO TANG CACH MANG VIET NAM

The Museum of the Vietnamese Revolution, housed in a beautiful old French villa next to the Opera House, traces the struggle of the Vietnamese people to establish their independence. It leaves the impression that American involvement in Vietnam has been just one episode in a centuries-long struggle against foreign aggressors.

The 3,000 dryly presented exhibits are arranged throughout 29 rooms, and cover the fight for independence, 1858–1945 (halls one to nine); the national independence movement, 1945–75 (halls 10–24); and modern Vietnam (halls 25–27). Of most interest are photos of opium smokers and beggars in Hanoi at the turn of the 20th century; displays relating to the founding of the Vietnamese Communist Party; a French guillotine, chains and clubs used to beat nationalists jailed at Hoa Lo (▷ 73); and exhibits relating to the formation of the Viet Minh and those connected to Dien Bien Phu (▷ 35, 104–105). The final rooms illustrate a reunified country of bountiful harvests, large civil engineering projects and smiling peasants. Presents given to Ho Chi Minh and congresses of the Vietnamese Communist Party are also on display.

✚ 62 C3 ✉ 216 Tran Quang Khai Street ☎ 04-38254151 ◴ Tue–Sun 8–11.45, 1.30–4.15 ✋ 10,000d ❓ Labeling in English and French

BAO TANG CHIEN TANG B-52

US B-52 Stratofortress bomber plane remains have been hawked around Hanoi over many years, but some have found a final resting place at the B-52 Museum. Here visitors can walk over the wings and tail of a shattered B-52 in the yard. The size and strength of the B-52 is incredible — with a capacity to hold 60,000lb (27,000kg) of explosives in its undercarriage, it is, in capability terms, still the world's biggest bomber aircraft.

As in most Vietnamese museums, enemy weapons and objects are literally heaped up while native pieces are painted, tended and carefully signed with the names of their heroic units. These include antiaircraft guns, the devastating SAMs that wreaked so much havoc on the US Air Force, and a MiG-21.

✚ Off map 62 A2 ✉ 157 Doi Can Street ✋ Free

BAO TANG DAN TOC HOC VIET NAM (VIETNAM MUSEUM OF ETHNOLOGY)

▷ 70.

BAO TANG HO CHI MINH

www.baotanghochiminh.vn
The innovative Ho Chi Minh Museum is an architectural monument in its own right. Large, white and modernist, it opened in 1990 in celebration of the centenary of Ho Chi Minh's birth. Stairs lead from the foyer to a bronze statue of Ho Chi Minh against a background of sun and trees. Displays trace Ho's life and work from his early travels around the world to his final victory over the south and his death. Exhibits show the Vietnamese plight versus colonial life, juxtaposing straw huts and bowls and a French officer uniform, a carved screen and an upholstered cyclo. Interpretative work also includes a totem pole, which symbolizes the power of the global national liberation movement.

✚ 62 A2 ✉ 3 Ngoc Ha Street ☎ 04-38455435 ◴ Tue–Thu, Sat–Sun 8–11.30, 2–4 ✋ Adult 10,000d ☐ ❓ Labeling in English and French

BAO TANG LICH SU QUAN SU

Battles and episodes in Vietnam's fight for independence are illustrated in the Military History Museum, from the struggles with China to the French defeat at Dien Bien Phu and the Vietnam War. It's also worth seeking out the striking propaganda poster images commemorating the 50th anniversary of Dien Bien Phu, by Le Hoang Anh. Overall, the political

Above *The Ho Chi Minh Museum*
Opposite *The Military History Museum*

poster work is the museum's most interesting element, and includes commemorations of every anniversary since the battle of Dien Bien Phu in 1954.

An untouched MiG-21 stands at the museum entrance, while the wrecked remains of B-52s, F1-11s and Q2Cs are piled up in courtyards at the back. Some of the wreckage belongs to a plane shot down in Halong Bay on August 5, 1964. The pilot, Everett Alvarez, Jr., was the first US aviator captured in the Vietnam War and was sent to Hoa Lo Prison for eight-and-a-half years.

In the museum precincts is the Cot Co, a flag tower raised on three platforms. Built in 1812, it is the only substantial remaining part of a citadel built by Emperor Gia Long (reigned 1802–19); it was destroyed by the French in 1894–1897. There are good views over Hanoi from the top, but other parts of the citadel are in the hands of the Vietnamese army and are out of bounds.

✚ 62 A3 ✉ 28 Dien Bien Phu Street ☎ 04-38234264 ◴ Tue–Thu, Sat–Sun 8–11.30, 1–4.30 ✋ 20,000d, cameras 5,000d ☐ ❓ Random translation of exhibit labels into English and French

INFORMATION

✚ Off map 62 A2 ✉ Nguyen Van Huyen Street, Cau Giay District ☎ 04-37562193 🕒 Tue–Sun 8.30–5.30. Discovery Room: Tue–Sun 8.30–11.30, 1.30–4.30 💵 25,000d 🎫 Guided tours in French and English 50,000d 🎁 Postcards, metalwork, lacquerware and fabric gifts 🥤 Water, soft drinks and snacks ❓ Labeling in English and French; wheelchair access; water puppet performances take place at 10, 11.30, 2.30 and 4 during the third week of each month (10,000d–20,000d)

TIPS

» Plan to spend at least a couple of hours here if you want to watch the absorbing videos recording cultural rites and see the house recreations in the grounds.
» In the Discovery Room children are taught to make such objects as accessories used to decorate houses for the dead.

Above *A replica Bahnar house at the Ethnology Museum*

BAO TANG DAN TOC HOC VIET NAM

Outstanding collections here span the ethnographic spectrum that makes up the Vietnamese nation. The items and photographs reflecting Vietnam's 54 ethnic minorities are presented in an informative, interesting and lively manner. Displays include clothes, cultural implements, social rites and full-size model ethnic houses in the grounds.

The Vietnam Museum of Ethnology was established in 1981 and now contains some 25,000 objects and 15,000 photographs, arranged on two floors and beginning with an overview of the majority Kinh people and the other designated minority peoples. Exhibits include functional items—hats, baskets, fishing implements—and other intriguing objects, such as water puppets and paper toys. Pictures and quotes are used to explain how and why various items are made.

On the museum's upper level, displays concentrate on the hill tribes of Vietnam and its borders. Elaborately decorated and vibrantly dyed costumes are on show, including a very impressive bamboo vest, as well as everyday tools and illustrations of the villages themselves.

PAST AND PRESENT

Much of the work on display is historical, but the museum is also attempting to build up its contemporary collection, and there is a particular focus on craftwork—lacquerware, woodcarving and pottery. Perhaps the most memorable items, though, are the ordinary possessions—a Vietnamese pig counter, a money counter, a bamboo lunar calendar from the Muong, or the bicycle belonging to a man who somehow used it to carry more than 800 fish traps at a time.

Fascinating videos show buffalo sacrifice ceremonies, Bahnar and Hmông funerals and Tày shaman rituals. In the grounds is the open-air section, still under development. Here, alongside the modern, purpose-built museum, replicas are being created of ethnic buildings to illustrate their remarkable range of styles. There are steeply pitched roofs of tile, thatch or local timber, walls of bamboo or no walls at all, a long house from the Ede community, a Tày stilt house, a half-raised, half-grounded Dao house, and a burial ground of the Gia-rai people.

Regular performances of folk singing and dancing are laid on at the museum, and there is often a craftsperson at work there producing traditional items on the spot.

BAO TANG LICH SU VIET NAM

Vietnam's foremost history museum, in a former French colonial institute, houses Dong Son drums, sculpture from the creative powerhouse of the Champa Empire (▷ 28–29) and other relics.

Ernest Hébrard, responsible for many colonial-era structures, designed the building housing the Vietnam History Museum in 1931 as the home of the École Française d'Extrême-Orient, a distinguished archeological, historical and ethnological research institute. He employed a distinctly Indochinese style appropriate to the building's original and, indeed, its current function. The École Française d'Extrême-Orient played an important role in the preservation and restoration of ancient Vietnamese structures and temples, many of which were destroyed or threatened with demolition by the French to enable the growth of their colonial city. Today, the museum remains a center of cultural and historical research, and its collection spans Vietnamese history from the Neolithic Age to the 21st century.

MUSEUM LAYOUT

On the second floor, galleries trace the country's past from the Neolithic Age (Bac Son), represented by stone tools and jewels, through the Bronze Age (Dong Son), with finely engraved ceremonial bronze drums (▷ 28), symbolizing wealth and power. Wooden stakes used to impale invading Chinese forces in 1288 were found in 1976 at the confluence of the Chanh and Bach Dang rivers, and a giant oil painting depicts the famous battle. A replica of the country's oldest Buddha Amitabha statue dominates the far end. Amitabha is the Buddha of Infinite Light, and the original, from 1057, was from Phat Tich Pagoda in Bac Ninh Province. Facing the statue are the country's oldest minted coins, Dinh Dynasty currency from AD968. In contrast is a collection of outsized paper currency from 1875.

The next floor up spans the 15th century to the present day. Champa (▷ 28–29) is represented by some remarkably well-preserved stone carvings of *apsaras* (mythical dancing girls) and a head of Garuda, found at Quang Nam. There are relics such as 18th-century bronze pagoda gongs and urns of successive royal dynasties (some are reproductions).

Also, look out for a giant turtle, symbol of longevity, which supports a vast stela praising the achievements of Le Loi (reigned 1428–1433), founder of the Le Dynasty, who harnessed nationalist sentiment and drove back the Chinese.

INFORMATION

✚ 62 C4 ✉ 1 Pham Ngu Lao Street
☎ 04-38242433/38241384 🕐 Tue–Sun 8–11.30, 1.30–4.30 💶 Adult 15,000d, child (5–15) 2,000d, camcorder 30,000d, camera 15,000d 🎫 Occasional personal tours given by curators for a small gratuity ❓ Individual exhibit labels in English and French; larger, introductory text in Vietnamese

TIPS

» Avoid classroom hours, as this is a popular venue for school trips.
» If you can, take a personal tour, as exhibit descriptions are brief.

Below *The Indochinese-style Vietnam History Museum*

Above *Worshipers in the Ambassador's Pagoda*

This dual approach is carried on throughout, with accounts of the role of women at Dien Bien Phu, pictures of women in tiger cages on Con Dao Island, and models and reconstructions of women in the Cu Chi Tunnels (▷ 224). Other exhibits focus on peasant women, women's involvement in national defense and the development of the Vietnam Women's Union.

✚ 62 C4 ✉ 36 Ly Thuong Kiet Street
☎ 04-38259935 ⏰ Tue–Sun 8–4
✋ 20,000d ❓ Labeling in French and English

CHUA QUAN SU

In the 15th century, a guesthouse for Buddhist ambassadors stood on the site of the Ambassador's Pagoda, hence its name. Today's pagoda, built between 1936 and 1942, contains stone sculptures of past, present and future Buddhas. Scholars, pilgrims and beggars crowd into this hub of Buddhist learning. A short distance south are Thien Quang Lake and Lenin Park (Cong Vien Lenin), which has a statue of Vladimir Lenin (admission is 1,000d to 10,000d, depending on the entrance you use and how wealthy you look). Nearby, on Le Duan Street south of the train station, stalls sell US, Soviet and Vietnamese army surplus kit.

✚ 62 B4 ✉ 73 Quan Su Street
☎ 04-38252427 ⏰ Daily 7.30–11.30, 1.30–5.30 ✋ Free

DEN HAI BA TRUNG

The Hai Ba Trung Temple overlooks a lake and is dedicated to sisters, Trung Trac and Trung Nhi, who are said to have drowned themselves in the first century AD, rather than surrender to the Chinese. The temple was built in 1142 and has been restored a number of times. It contains crude statues of the sisters, which are carried in procession each February (▷ 87).

✚ 62 C5 ✉ Tho Lao Street ✋ Free

HO HOAN KIEM LAKE AND ENVIRONS
▷ 74.

BAO TANG MY THUAT VIETNAM

www.fineartsmuseum.org.vn
The Fine Arts Museum has some 20,000 items, more than 2,000 of which are on show at any one time. The first-floor galleries display pre-20th century art, including Dong Son bronze drums, fine stone Buddhas, and Nguyen Dynasty art. Folk art, on the next floor, includes delicate lacquer paintings and woodblock prints. On the top floor is 20th-century Vietnamese work, including contemporary watercolors and oil paintings. There is also a large collection of overtly political work, posters and propaganda. A collection of ethnic minority clothes is exhibited in an annex.

✚ 62 A3 ✉ 66 Nguyen Thai Hoc Street
☎ 04-7332131 ⏰ Tue, Thu–Fri, Sun 8.30–5, Wed, Sat 8.30–9 ✋ 10,000d
🎧 Tours in English or French, 8.30–5, 70,000d; audio tours 7,000d per person. Tour office right of main entrance ❓ Labeling in French and English

BAO TANG PHU NU VIET NAM

The Vietnam Women's Museum, designed by female architect Tran Xuan Diem, pays tribute to the role of women in war, motherhood, nation-building and daily life. Sculpture, photographs and everyday items illustrate their lives and there are research facilities for the women of today.

The entrance hall ensemble alone is worth the entry fee—a marble-floored space dominated by a statue of the Mother of Vietnam by sculptor Nguyen Phu Cuong. The dome lighting above the sculpture graphically symbolizes a mother's breast, with a giant nipple inverted and producing milk, represented by droplets of sparkling stones.

Spread out over four floors, the displays juxtapose tributes to women's success in public life and to their role in the family and home life. The chronological display starts with a piece of stone from Nghia Linh Mountain (Pho Tho province), where, according to legend, Mother Au Co gave birth to her children (▷ 103). It continues with a bas-relief of the popular uprising against foreign aggression led by the Trung sisters in the first century AD (▷ 29).

DI TICH LICH SU NHA TU HOA LO

Hoa Lo Prison, better known as the Hanoi Hilton, is the prison where American prisoners of war were incarcerated, some for up to six years, during the Vietnam War. Up until 1969, captives were also tortured in this notorious French-built prison.

Rather than face torture, two US Air Force officers, Charles Tanner and Ross Terry, concocted a story about members of their squadron who had been court-martialled for refusing to fly missions against the north. Thrilled with this piece of propaganda, the prison authorities told visiting Japanese communists the story and it filtered back to the US. Unfortunately for Tanner and Terry, they had called their imaginary flyers Clark Kent and Ben Casey (both TV heroes). When the Vietnamese realized they had been fooled, the two prisoners were again tortured. The Hilton's final prisoners were not released until 1973, some having been held in the north since 1964.

THE MUSEUM

In 1992, a US mission was shown around the prison where 2,000 inmates were housed in cramped and squalid conditions. Despite pleas from war veterans and party members, the site was sold to a Singapore–Vietnamese joint venture and is now a hotel and shopping complex, Hanoi Towers. As part of the deal, the developers had to leave part of the prison for use as a museum and, now dwarfed by the modern towers, it is an eternal witness to the horrors of torture. Infamous cell conditions, punitive equipment and escape features are displayed, and in the first outdoor passageway is an almond tree with a hollow in which political prisoners left messages.

Maison Centrale is the legend over the main gate that leads to the museum. Conditions under colonial rule, when the French incarcerated patriotic Vietnamese, are replicated; by 1953 they were holding 2,000 in a space designed for 500. Cell reconstructions, with the fetters control on the outside, are still in place, and parts of the sewers used by escapees can be seen, as can female torture equipment.

Less prominence is given to the holding of US pilots (although there are propaganda displays of good treatment, clean clothes and POWs exercising), but Douglas "Pete" Peterson, the first post-war American Ambassador to Vietnam (in office 1997–2001), who was one such occupant (imprisoned 1966–73), has his mugshot on the wall, as does John McCain (imprisoned 1967–73), the 2008 Republican candidate for the American presidency.

INFORMATION
✚ 62 B3 ✉ 1 Hoa Lo ☎ 04-38246358
🕐 Tue–Sun 8–11.30, 1.30–4.30
✋ Adult 10,000d 📖 Pamphlet included in admission price ❓ Labeling in English

TIPS
» Photography is forbidden in the prison.
» One block east of the prison is the Cho 19–12, a market selling fresh fruit, vegetables and meat.

Below *A mural in the museum showing the torture of Vietnamese prisoners by the French*

REGIONS HANOI • SIGHTS

INFORMATION

✚ 62 C3 ✉ Dinh Tien Hang ⏰ Daily 7.30–6 🎫 3,000d to enter Ngoc Son Temple

TIPS

» Get up at dawn to see the locals practicing tai chi around the lake.
» Photography is also better very early in the day, when there are few visitors and the light is clearer.
» To the side of the Jade Hill Temple is a room containing a preserved tortoise and a collection of photographs of the creatures in the lake.

Above *Early-morning tai chi on the lakeside*

HO HOAN KIEM AND ENVIRONS

The serene focal point of central Hanoi is framed by branches and cloaked in a filmy haze after the clarity of the dawn light. Dominating the lake is the elegant, red Sunbeam Bridge.

Hoan Kiem Lake (Lake of the Restored Sword, also known as Ho Guom), is named after an incident that is said to have occurred during the 15th century. Following a momentous victory against an army of invading Ming Chinese, Emperor Le Loi (Le Thai To, reigned 1428–1433) was sailing on the lake when a golden turtle appeared from the depths to take back the charmed sword with which he had secured the victory and restore it to the lake from whence it came. Reminiscent of the story of the sword in the stone, of British Arthurian legend, Le Thai To's sword assures the Vietnamese of divine intervention in times of national crisis. It is a story that is graphically portrayed in water puppet theaters *(mua roi nuoc)* across the country. On a small island in the southern part of the lake there is a modest and somewhat dilapidated tower (the Tortoise Tower, Thap Rua), which commemorates the event.

In actual fact, the lake does contain some very large tortoises. One that was captured in 1968 is reputed to have weighed 550lb (250kg). The creatures that inhabit the lake are believed to be a variety of the Asian softshell tortoise.

DEN NGOC SON AND SUNBEAM BRIDGE

When the French first set foot in Hanoi in the latter part of the 19th century the lake was an unhealthy lagoon surrounded by so many huts that it was impossible to see the shore. Today, the lake is encircled by an attractive park—a beauty spot that is much loved by city residents and used by them every morning for jogging and the practice of tai chi.

In the northeast corner of the park is Den Ngoc Son (Jade Hill Temple), which was built in the early 19th century on a small, tree-shrouded island, on the foundations of the old Khanh Thuy Palace (built in 1739). The temple is dedicated to Van Xuong, the God of Literature, but the 13th-century hero Tran Hung Dao, the martial arts genius Quan Vu and the physician La To are also worshiped here. Local people can usually be seen playing board games in the temple precincts. The island is linked to the shore by a red, arched wooden bridge—the Sunbeam Bridge (The Huc), constructed in 1875.

HO TAY

Sprawling along the northwestern fringe of the city is West Lake, once a meander in the Red River. On its eastern shores a walkway leads from the causeway to the Tran Quoc Pagoda, Hanoi's oldest pagoda, which was originally built on the banks of the Red River in the sixth century AD. The existing building, including the triple gate, largely dates from 1815, but contains a stela dated 1639 recounting its unsettled history. A few miles north, on the tip of a promontory, stands Tay Ho Pagoda, dedicated to Thanh Mau, the Mother Goddess, and notable chiefly for its setting. It is reached along a narrow lane lined with stands selling fruit, roses and paper votives, and a dozen restaurants serving giant snails with noodles *(bun oc)* and shrimp cakes.

As development has spread northward this area has become a middle-class suburb, with new houses in an unplanned and uncoordinated sprawl. The lake has shrunk by 20 percent, from 1,200 acres (500ha) to 1,000 acres (400ha), as residents and hotel and office developers have reclaimed land. The lake is also suffering encroachment by water hyacinths, which are fed by organic pollutants from factories and untreated sewage. The view from Nghi Tam Road, which runs along the Red River dike, presents a contrasting spectacle of sprawling houses interspersed with the remaining plots of land, currently intensively and attractively cultivated market gardens that supply the city with flowers and vegetables.
➕ 62 A1

HO TRUC BACH

White Silk Lake was created during the 17th century with the construction of a causeway across the southeast corner of Ho Tay (West Lake). This was the site of an 18th-century royal palace that had, so it is said, 100 roofs; all that is left now is the terrace of Kinh Thien, with a dragon staircase, and a number of stupas, bridges, gates and small pagodas. The palace was subsequently used as a prison for concubines who had broken the rules. While held in custody the women were obliged to weave a delicate silk fabric, whose beauty was well known and gave the area its name.

At the southwest corner of the lake is the very beautiful Quan Thanh Pagoda, originally built during the early years of the Ly Dynasty (1010–1225) in honor of Huyen Thien Tran Vo, the Northern God, whose emblems are the tortoise and the snake. The pagoda has since undergone many alterations and now houses a large bronze statue of General Tran Vo, as well as a bell dating from 1677. The Taoist temple is a famous martial arts school, and students can sometimes be glimpsed practicing their moves and skills in the courtyard.

Across the causeway is West Lake (▷ left), a popular recreation area, with opportunities for shoreline bicycle rides, boat rentals and birdwatching—notably egrets and cranes. A number of privately owned luxury villas line the lakeshore, and further development for tourism seems to be inevitable.
➕ 62 A1 🚩 Thanh Nien Street 🕐 5,000d

Left Relaxing by White Silk Lake
Below Swan boats on West Lake

INFORMATION

✚ 62 A2 ✉ Hung Vuong Street
☎ 04-38455128/39421061 🕐 Apr–Oct
Tue–Thu 7.30–10.30, Sat–Sun, public
holidays 7.30–11; Dec–Mar Tue–Thu
8–11, Sat–Sun, public holidays 8–11.30
✋ Free ❓ No photography allowed

TIPS

» Before entering the mausoleum you
must leave possessions at the office
(ban to chuc) on Ong Ich Khiem Street,
to the south.
» If you take your camera you will be
ushered to a drop-off point and you can
collect it from a kiosk at the exit, saving
the trip across Ba Dinh Square before
visiting Ho Chi Minh's house, the
One Pillar Pagoda and the Ho Chi
Minh Museum.
» Do not take anything into the
mausoleum that might be construed as
a weapon, such as a pocket knife.
» Dress neatly, walk quietly and do
not talk.

Above *The Ho Chi Minh Mausoleum
contains Ho Chi Minh's embalmed body*

LANG CHU TICH HO CHI MINH

The Vietnamese have made Ho Chi Minh's place of rest (Ho Chi Minh
Mausoleum) a site of pilgrimage, where visitors march solemnly in file to
see his embalmed corpse inside the mausoleum—a Communist ritual now
practiced in very few nations. However, this is contrary to Ho Chi Minh's
wishes. Ho wanted to be cremated and his ashes, placed in three urns, to be
left on three unmarked hills in the north, center and south of the country. He
once wrote: "Cremation is not only good from the point of view of hygiene,
but it also saves farmland."

The mausoleum, built from 1973 to 1975, is a huge, square, columned and
forbidding structure and must be among the best constructed, maintained
and air-conditioned (for obvious reasons) buildings in Vietnam. Ho lies in a
low-lit glass coffin, dressed in simple clothes, and a guard stands at each
corner of his bier.

In front of Ho Chi Minh's Mausoleum, on Bac Son Street, is a memorial to
those who died fighting for Vietnam's independence.

PRESERVATION

The embalming of Ho's body was undertaken by the chief Soviet embalmer,
Dr. Sergei Debrov, who tended to many other Communist leaders. He was
flown to Hanoi from Moscow as Ho lay dying, bringing with him two transport
planes packed with air-conditioners and other equipment. To escape US
bombing, the team moved Ho to a cave, where it took a full year to complete
the embalming process. Russian scientists still check up on their handiwork.
Their embalming methods and fluids are still a closely guarded secret; in an
interview, Debrov once noted the poor state of the body of China's Chairman
Mao, which was embalmed without Soviet help.

BA DINH SQUARE

From Ho Chi Minh's Mausoleum walk north up Hung Vuong Street then
onto Ba Dinh Square, where Ho read out the Vietnamese Declaration of
Independence on September 2, 1945. Subsequently this date became
National Day—and it was also the date on which Ho died in 1969, although
the announcement was postponed so as not to mar people's enjoyment of
National Day in the beleaguered north.

NHA HAT LAN

The grand, art nouveau Opera House is an iconic symbol of Hanoi. It was built between 1901 and 1911 by François Lagisquet and is one of the finest French colonial buildings in the capital. Shutters, wrought-iron work, balconies, and a tiled frieze cover the exterior, and the upper balustrade is topped with griffins. Below, some 35,000 bamboo piles were sunk into the mud to provide foundations. After years of neglect, the Opera House saw a lavish US$14 million restoration in time for the Francophone Summit in 1997. Original drawings were consulted and experts brought in to supervise craftsmen. Slate was carried from Sin Ho to retile the roof, Italians oversaw the relaying of the lobby's mosaic floor, and French artists repainted the auditorium.
✚ 62 C4 ✉ 1 Trang Tien Street ☎ 04-39330113 🕐 During performances only ✋ Depends on performance; average 200,000d

NHA SAN BAC HO

The residence of the governors general of French Indochina, now a Communist Party guesthouse, was built in the compound of the former Presidential Palace between 1900 and 1908. In 1954, when North Vietnam achieved independence,

Ho Chi Minh declined to live here, saying it belonged to the people. Instead, he stayed in what is said to have been an electrician's house in the same compound from 1958 to 1969. The modest, wooden house (Ho Chi Minh's House) is airy, personal, and immaculately kept. Ho conducted meetings underneath the house, which is raised on wooden pillars, and slept and worked above (his books, slippers and telephones remain). Behind the house is Ho's bomb shelter and the hut where he died in 1969.
✚ 62 A2 ✉ Presidential Palace Memorial Site, 1 Bach Thao ☎ 04-38234760 🕐 Tue–Thu, Sat–Sun, 7.30–11.30, 2–4 ✋ 10,000d

PHO CHUA MOT COT

The tiny and exquisitely formed One Pillar Pagoda was built in 1049 by Emperor Ly Thai Tong (reigned 1028–1054); it has since been rebuilt several times, most recently in 1955 after the French destroyed it before withdrawing from the country. Smoking stalks of incense sitting in a giant red bowl at the top of the small staircase create a peaceful atmosphere. The Emperor built a little lotus-shaped temple in the center of a water-lily pond after dreaming of the Goddess of Mercy, Quan Am (Vietnam's equivalent of the Chinese goddess Kuan-yin), sitting on a lotus and holding a

young boy, whom she handed to him. Shortly afterwards his wife gave birth to a son.

As the name suggests, the pagoda is supported on a single (concrete) pillar with a brick and stone staircase running up one side. Dragons run along the apex of the elegantly curved tiled roof, but the ungainly concrete pillar and the pond of green slime in which it is embedded detract from the enchantment of one of Vietnam's most revered monuments.
✚ 62 A2 ✉ Ong Ich Kiem Street ✋ Free

PHO NHA THO

West of Hoan Kiem Lake in a little square, the twin-towered neo-Gothic St. Joseph's Cathedral, built in 1886, was one of the first colonial buildings in Hanoi, completed just one year after the Treaty of Tientsin gave France control over Vietnam. Some fine stained-glass windows remain. On holy days the building is covered in billboards depicting the subjects of the commemoration. The square in front is dominated by a sculpture of the Virgin Mary, ringed by a wrought-iron fence.
✚ 62 B3 ✉ 40 Nha Chung Street ☎ 04-38285967 🕐 During Mass (daily 5–7am, 5–7pm); at other times 5am–10pm, if not open, ring at side door for entry ✋ Free

Below *The One Pillar Pagoda*

VAN MIEU

INFORMATION

✚ 62 A3 ✉ Pho Van Mieu, corner of Pho Quoc Tu Giam 🕐 Apr 15–Oct 15 7.30–5.30; Oct 16–Apr 14 8–5 ✋ Adult 12,000d, child under 15 free 🎧 Guided tour (45 min) in French or English 50,000d 🎁 Small gift shop inside temple 📖 Brochure 3,000d

Above *Two bronze storks guard the sanctuary honoring Confucius*
Opposite *A red-robed image of Confucius at the temple*

INTRODUCTION

The peaceful complex of the Temple of Literature—the largest temple in Hanoi—is set in a walled garden containing a number of graceful buildings and bordered by Nguyen Thai Hoc, Tong Due Thang, Van Mieu and Quoc Tu Giam streets. The temple and its compound are arranged north–south, and visitors enter at the southern end. Walls divide the five courtyards, which are linked by paths and gates originally reserved for the emperor; walkways to each side were used by administrators and mandarins. From the main gate a path leads through the Cong Dai Trung to the Van Khue Gac Pavilion, built in 1805 and dedicated to the Constellation of Literature; beyond lies the Courtyard of the Stelae. North of here is the Great Success Gate (Dai Thanh Mon), leading to a courtyard flanked by two 1954 buildings whose predecessors (destroyed in 1947) were reserved for 72 disciples of the Chinese philosopher and teacher Confucius. Facing it is the Great House of Ceremonies, and adjoining this is the Great Success Sanctuary (Dai Thanh), which contains a statue of Confucius.

The temple was founded in 1070 by Emperor Ly Thanh Tong (reigned 1054–1072), dedicated to the Chinese philosopher Confucius (who had a substantial following in Vietnam), and reputedly modeled on a temple in Shantung, China, the birthplace of the sage. Some researchers, while acknowledging the date of foundation, challenge the view that it was built as a Confucian institution, pointing to the ascendancy of Buddhism during the Ly Dynasty. Confucian principles and teaching rapidly replaced Buddhism, however, and Van Mieu subsequently became the intellectual and spiritual center of the kingdom, as a cult of literature and education spread among the court, the mandarins and then the common people. At one time there were said to be 20,000 schools teaching the Confucian classics in northern Vietnam alone.

WHAT TO SEE
CONG VAN MIEU MON

On the sidewalk approaching the main gate, two pavilions house stelae bearing the inscription *ha ma* ("climb down from your horse"), a reminder that even the most elevated dignitaries had to proceed on foot. Van Mieu Gate is adorned with 15th-century dragons; traditionally, the large central gate was opened only on ceremonial occasions.

COURTYARD OF THE STELAE

At the heart of the Courtyard of the Stelae is a rectangular pond, the Cieng Thien Quang (Well of Heavenly Clarity). Arranged around it are the stelae themselves, on which are recorded the names of 1,306 scholars who passed the temple's triennial examinations *(tien si)*. Of the 82 that survive (30 are missing), the oldest dates back to 1442 and the most recent to 1779. Each stela is carried on the back of a tortoise, the symbol of strength and longevity, but they are arranged in no specific order. Three chronological categories can, however, be identified. There are 14 from the 15th and 16th centuries —recognizable as the smallest in the courtyard and embellished with floral motifs and yin-yang symbols. These have a noticeable lack of dragon emblems, which at the time were a royal preserve. Dragons were permitted by the 17th century and can be seen on the 25 stelae from that period, along with pairs of phoenix and other creatures mythical or real. The remaining 43 stelae are of 18th-century origin; they are the largest and are decorated with pairs of stylized dragons, some merging with flame clouds.

Passing the temple examinations was not easy. In 1733, out of some 3,000 entrants, only eight passed the doctoral examination *(thai hoc sinh)* and

Below *The Van Mieu Gate is the main entrance to the temple*

REGIONS HANOI • SIGHTS

became mandarins—a feat that took 35 days. The practice of recording the successful doctoral entrants' names was begun in 1484 on the instruction of Emperor Le Thanh Tong (reigned 1460–1498), and continued through to 1878, during which time 116 examinations were held. The Temple of Literature was not used only for examinations, however: Rice was also distributed to the poor and infirm, in rations of 18oz (500g). In 1880, French Consul Monsieur de Kergaradec recorded that 22,000 impoverished people came to receive this meager handout.

DAI BAI DUONG

Although the Great House of Ceremonies was built relatively recently—in the 19th century—it was designed in the far earlier style of the Le Dynasty. Inside the building is an altar on which sit statues of Confucius and his closest disciples. The carved, wooden friezes inside it are a riot of ornament, with dragons, phoenix, lotus flowers, fruits, clouds and yin-yang disks vying for attention. All are symbolically charged, depicting the order of the universe and by implication reflecting the god-given hierarchical nature of human society, each in his or her place. Not surprisingly, the Communist government held reservations for a long time about preserving a temple that extolled such heretical doctrine.

Above *Stelae mounted on tortoises are inscribed with the names of graduates*
Below *Traditional music at the temple*

AROUND OLD HANOI

Hanoi was founded in 1010, when it was called Thang Long, or City of the Ascending Dragon. Before its colonial transformation in the 19th century it consisted of a citadel and a number of temples surrounded by a small village of merchants. By the 15th century this had evolved into the area now called the Old City or the 36 Streets (36 Pho Phuong). Each of the streets was named after a trade or product, starting with the word *hang* (merchandise). Thus tin-makers hammered out their ware on Hang Thiec, silversmiths on Hang Bac and so on. Each of the trades built a temple, many of which still survive, including Bach Ma, or White Horse Temple, the oldest in the city.

THE WALK
Distance: 1.5 miles (2.5km)
Allow: 2 hours
Start at: Ngoc Son Temple
End at: Thuy Ta Café, 1 Le Thai To

HOW TO GET THERE
Go to Hoan Kiem Lake between Old Hanoi and the downtown area focused on Pho Trang Thi. Ngoc Son Temple is on an island at the northern edge of the lake, accessible by the beautiful Sunbeam Bridge.

★ Ngoc Son Temple (Den Ngoc Son), dating from the 18th century, is one of the loveliest and best preserved in Hanoi. Like so many Vietnamese temples, it has been dedicated to a national hero—in this case Tran Hung Dao, who defeated the Mongols in the 13th century (▷ 29).

From Ngoc Son Temple head over Sunbeam (or The Huc) Bridge toward the Socialist Realist-style Martyr's Monument. Turn left up Pho Hang Dau. Continue for about 88 yards (80m) past the shoe bazaar and north along Pho Hang Be, passing Pho Gia Ngu fresh produce market on your left, until you reach Pho Hang Bac at a T-junction.

❶ Pho Hang Bac's specialty lies in selling marble gravestones (at the eastern end of the street) and jewelry (at the western end). The marble gravestones generally have a photograph of the deceased melded into the stone. It's a trade that caters to the ancestor-conscious Vietnamese and a headstone from here is a necessary (and prestigious) way of honoring the deceased. Jewelry is Pho Hang Bac's other

specialty. Now that the Communist prohibitions on wearing gold jewelry have been lifted, the goldsmiths' trade is again flourishing.

Turn left, continuing for about 22 yards (20m), before turning right onto Pho Ma May.

❷ Pho Ma May is a tiny sidestreet that is home to the Memorial House Museum, a museum in a restored tube house that was formerly the home of a Chinese merchant. The building was lovingly restored in 1999 and now provides an excellent idea of how well-to-do traders lived in the 36 Streets in times past.

Retrace your steps from the Memorial House Museum to Pho Hang Bac. Turn right, to the west, and continue for about 110 yards (100m) to the second of two small crossroads. Turn right (north) along Pho Hang Ngang.

❸ Pho Hang Ngang is devoted to the rag trade, with clothing of all kinds cluttering the sidewalks and entrances to narrow shops. A small shop to look out for is Portrait Painting at No. 47, where Nguyen Bao Nguyen, a portrait artist, is usually to be seen at work. His finely executed drawings are based on photographs supplied by customers and you can see for yourself the quality of his work. It takes about five days and costs around US$50 to complete a commission.

After about 55 yards (50m) turn left at another small crossroads, along Pho Lan Ong.

❹ The narrow sidewalk at the eastern end of Pho Lang Ong is dedicated to the sale of towels and linen, while the western end specializes in the sale of fresh herbs and spices. Vietnamese use a wide variety of fresh green leaves in their cuisine, and the stalls here also sell medicinal herbs from the traditional Sino-Vietnamese pharmacopeia.

Halfway along Pho Lang Ong, on the north (right) side, is Pho Cha Ca. Turn up this narrow street.

❺ On the west side of Pho Cha Ca, about 44 yards (40m) north of the junction with Pho Lang Ong, is Cha Ca La Vong Restaurant. It serves the roasted fish for which the street was named. At No. 15, Golden Land is an air-conditioned café where a break can be taken.

When you reach Pho Hang Ma running west and Pho Hang Chieu running east, turn sharp left down Pho Thuoc Bac, continuing into Pho Hang Thiec.

❻ This area is given over to the production and sale of tin and aluminum items, as well as the

sale of mirrors. The noise of the tinsmiths can be heard despite the busy traffic.

At the junction of Pho Hang Thiec and Pho Hang Non turn left (east). Continue along into Pho Hang Quat.

❼ Colorful Buddhist altars and other religious paraphernalia clutter this street, with auspicious red and gold colors predominating. Several musical instrument shops selling drums and traditional Vietnamese stringed instruments may also be found in the area, especially at the point where Pho Hang Non meets Pho Hang Hom.

Continue east along Pho Hang Quat until you reach Luong Van Can. Turn right (south) and continue until you reach the northwestern side of Hoan Kiem Lake. Thuy Ta Café is here, at 1 Le Thai To.

❽ Thuy Ta Garden, facing the lake, is a good place to enjoy an after-walk drink or refreshing ice cream. If you are in the mood for shopping, the sidestreet opposite Thuy Ta, leading west toward St. Joseph's Cathedral (Pho

Nha Tho), has many art shops, interesting souvenir stands and excellent small restaurants.

WHEN TO GO
Any time of the year except during the New Year *Tet* festivities, when most businesses are closed. Commerce is at its busiest in the early morning, and the Old City is most pleasant during the warm autumn months.

WHERE TO EAT
There are numerous small restaurants and bistros throughout the Old City. Try especially Cha Ca La Vong fish restaurant on Pho Cha Ca ("Roasted Fish Street"). The Thuy Ta Café, on the northwestern side of Ho Hoan Kiem, serves excellent Western and Vietnamese cuisine. Nearby Pho Hang Hanh has restaurants and coffee shops.

PLACES TO VISIT
MEMORIAL HOUSE MUSEUM
✉ 87 Pho Ma May ☎ 04-39285604/ 39285605 🕐 Daily 8–5 💷 5,000d

PORTRAIT PAINTER
✉ 47 Hang Ngang Street ☎ 09-3260364; email: nguyenbaonguyen@hn.vnn.vn

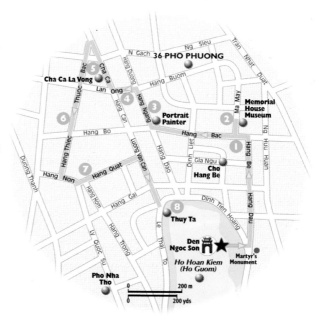

WHAT TO DO

SHOPPING

APRICOT GALLERY

www.apricotgallery.com.vn
Prices are high at this gallery
southeast of the Citadel. It is run by
the owners of the Ancient Gallery,
but the paintings it sells are more
arresting and mainly on larger
canvases. There are some beautiful
works by Nguyen Dieu Thuy, who
sometimes uses silver leaf as a
highlight in her creations. The
enchanting work of Le Thanh Ton
captures Vietnamese life and scenes
in French Impressionistic style.
✉ 40B Hang Bong Street ☎ 04-38288965
🕐 Daily 8–8

AROMA

This small store sells a good range
of local and imported dried fruits,
like guava, jackfruit and Iranian figs,
as well as nuts and Vietnamese
lotus tea. It takes 2.2lb (1kg) of
anthers from 1,000 lotus flowers
to produce 1kg of dry lotus tea
and the result is that 1lb (50g)
will cost US$15. Across the road
from Aroma, a stall in front of a
hairdresser's and No. 100, sells jars
of Vietnamese honey.
✉ 71 Hang Trong Street ☎ 04-39289774
🕐 Daily 8–8

CHI VANG

This shop, which occupies a
beautifully restored building, sells
exquisitely embroidered cloth,
babies' bed linen and clothing,
cushion covers, tablecloths and
unusually shaped cushions. The
goods are artfully arranged in a
spacious interior that is fitted out
with large, wooden dressers. The
store is conveniently close to the
Opera House and is managed by
helpful staff.
✉ 17 Trang Tien Street ☎ 04-39360027
🕐 Daily 8am–9pm

CO

This tiny clothes store has a very
narrow entrance on a popular street
in the Old Quarter and is a good
example of a tube house, with
lots of cloth and materials neatly
stacked along the narrow passage
entrance, which opens out at the
back. In addition to being able to
whip up some quality conventional
items for shoppers, Co has some
unusual and hugely appealing
prints, quite often used for winter
coats. The craftsmanship of the
finished garments is superb.
✉ 18 Nha Tho Street ☎ 04-38289925
🕐 Daily 8.30–7

CODO GALLERY

www.codogallery.net
This private gallery sells the work of
contemporary Vietnamese artists.
A lot of what you see is lacquer on
wood but oil paintings on canvas
are also displayed, as are occasional
pieces painted on rice paper.
✉ 46 Hang Bong Street ☎ 04-38258573
🕐 Daily 9–8

DOME

www.dome.com.vn
Some of the merchandise sold
here is too large to take home but
there are lovely cushion and duvet
covers that could be squeezed
into a suitcase. There are larger
Dome stores at 10 Pho Yen The
Street (tel 04-8436036) and at
Level 2, Building A, Me Linh Plaza
(tel 04-8868055), but the small
store in Hang Trong Street is the
most conveniently located in
the city center.
✉ 71 Hang Trong Street ☎ 04-39287677
🕐 Daily 8.30–8.30

HADONG SILK

If shopping for silk in Hanoi, then
Hang Gai Street is the place to go
and Hadong Silk is one of the finer
places to check out before making

your final decision on what to buy. Prices are fixed but the quality is assured. The same can be said of Kenly Silk just a few doors down at No. 108 (tel 04-8267236), and they also have an outlet at the Nikko Hotel.

✉ 102 Hang Gai Street ☎ 09-285056
🕐 Daily 8.30–7.30

IPA-NIMA
www.ipa-nima.com
Step into the glittering world of Hong Kong native Christina Yu (▷ 26), the creative force behind this increasingly successful designer label. Clothes, bags, exquisitely embroidered jewelry boxes and a limited range of sparkling shoes are available at this sought-after shop. Occasionally, the range of shoe sizes is limited. There are two more stores in Ho Chi Minh City.

✉ 34 Han Thuyen Street ☎ 04-39334000
🕐 Mon–Sat 9–7, Sun 10–6

KHAISILK
www.khaisilkcorp.com
This is the *crème de la crème* of silk shops. Launched by Hoang Khai in 1980, the brand is synonymous with elegance, style and superior quality (▷ 24). All Khaisilk shops display a range of clothes for men (ties, shirts and suits) and women (scarves, ao dai and blouses), plus stunning handbags and other accessories. This store, west of the Vietnam Fine Arts Museum, is the main branch; there is another branch to be found in the Old City at 113 Hang Gai Street (tel 09-289883).

✉ 26 Nguyen Thai Hoc Street ☎ 04-37333991 🕐 Daily 8.30–7.30

MARIE-LINH
www.marie-linh.com
In Hanoi's Old City quarter, this shop retails French-style designer clothing, using Vietnamese fabrics. New collections appear on a seasonal basis.

✉ 74 Hang Trong Street ☎ 04-39286304
🕐 Daily 9–7

MOSAIQUE
This treasure trove, furnished in warm shades, sells embroidered table-runners, box lamps and stands, beautiful silk flowers for accessorizing, silk curtains, metal ball lamps, pillow cushions and lotus flower-shaped lamps. A little more lighting would allow customers to see the sometimes subtle differences in the silk tones. The shop is in the heart of the Old Quarter.

✉ 22 Nha Tho Street ☎ 04-39286181
🕐 Daily 9–8.30

NGUYEN FRÈRES
It's a delight to wander around this artfully cluttered shop, where you'll be served a cup of jasmine tea on arrival. In addition to the usual silk items, from cushion covers to place mats, you can buy old books inscribed with Chinese calligraphy, desks carved with Chinese iconography, porcelain, bronzes, lacquerware and small wooden statues of Christ and the Virgin Mary. The store is southwest of the Opera House.

✉ 3 Phan Chu Trinh Street
☎ 04-39331699 🕐 Daily 9–8

SONG
The Song shop, on Nha Tho Street, is run by friendly and helpful staff. French designer Valerie Gregori-McKenzie (▷ 26) has produced some beautiful, ethereal designs in cottons, linens and silks. She also makes hats, bags, lamps, bed linen and cushion covers, which are exquisitely embroidered. Gregori-McKenzie has also produced a Vietnamese cookbook. Its other store in Ho Chi Minh City (▷ 203) has a larger retail space than the Hanoi outlet.

✉ 27 Nha Tho Street ☎ 04-39288733
🕐 Daily 9–8

TAN MY
www.tanmydesign.com
This shop, in Hanoi's Old Quarter, is stacked full of very affordable goods over two floors. It displays the full range of silk and

embroidered clothes found in many stores in this area. In addition, it sells underwear, nightwear, chenille scarves, children's clothes and plain, unembroidered silk evening purses, which are surprisingly hard to come by, as the millions of bags found in the shops of Vietnam are usually decorated. There is also a café serving good coffee, wine by the glass and light meals.

✉ 61 Hang Gai Street ☎ 04-39381154
🕐 Daily 9–7

THINGS OF SUBSTANCE
A stylish store, in the shadow of St. Joseph's Cathedral, selling swimwear, a small line in clothes for mostly expat men and women, silk jewelry bags, attractive jewelry, leather goods and other unusual gifts. This small shop, with excellent service, offers something a little different.

✉ 5 Nha Tho Street ☎ 04-38286965
🕐 Daily 9–8

TINA SPARKLE
www.ipa-nima.com
A funky boutique, Tina Sparkle sells bags in a glittering array of colors and patterns—from tropical prints to sequinned flowers. The shop, on the popular cathedral street, also sells sequinned shoes by Hong Kong lawyer-turned-designer Christina Yu (▷ 26). Most bags retail for around US$50 and shoes for US$60, although occasional sales will leave half those amounts in your purse.

✉ 17 Nha Tho Street ☎ 04-39287616
🕐 Daily 9–8

TROPICAL
This shop on a busy main road in the Old Quarter has room for only a few customers at a time. It sells plain, flowing silk skirts (a rarity), mother-of-pearl jewelry, hair accessories, lacquerware, buffalo horns and other unusual items in its tiny premises, cluttered with gifts and clothes. The staff are particularly helpful.

✉ 65 Hang Gai Street ☎ 04-39287203
🕐 Daily 9–7

ENTERTAINMENT AND NIGHTLIFE

21°N CLUB

Known as the 21 North Club (the city's latitude as the name for a club hardly rolls off the tongue), this club has views of West Lake from its upper floor, enhancing the appeal of the cocktails, microbeer, comfy sofas, bar food and live music.

✉ 49 Lang Yen Phu ☎ 04-37154034
🕐 Sun–Thu 5pm–midnight, Fri–Sat 5pm–1am

BOOKWORM AND HANOI COOKING CENTRE

www.bookwormhanoi.com
www.hanoicookingcentre.com
Bookworm is a bookshop and café, in the courtyard of the Hanoi Cooking Centre, selling new and used English books, and holding a varied program of evening events with writers and book launches. The Cooking Centre runs classes and courses in Vietnamese cookery.

✉ 44 Chau Long ☎ 04-37153711 (Bookworm); 04-37150088 (Hanoi Cooking Centre) 🕐 Daily 9–7

DALUVA

www.daluva.com
This smart and stylish bar and restaurant in the West Lake area, near the InterContinental and Sheraton hotels, attracts a sociable crowd in the evenings when various promotions—Tapas Night, Ladies' Night, Happy Hour (from 5pm)— draw in a stream of expatriates and a smattering of locals.

✉ 33 To Ngoc Van ☎ 04 37185831
🕐 Daily 8am–11pm

FUNKY MONKEY

This popular, lively bar has changed its address more than once but thas not changed its style. There is good music, with darts, pool and bar football to keep the regulars happy. It attracts both Vietnamese and Westerners. Happy hour is from 4pm to 7pm for beer and from 7pm to 9pm for cocktails.

✉ 31 Hang Thung Street ☎ 04-39286113
🕐 Daily 10am–1.30am

HANOI GRAPEVINE

www.hanoigrapevine.com
This useful web-based guide to Hanoi's cultural scene features a calendar of events, exhibitions, film screenings, art shows, festivals and concerts that are scheduled at cultural institutions like the Goethe Institut (www.goethe.de/ins/vn/han/enidex) and Institut Français de Hanoï (www.ifhanoi-lespace.com) and venues like Hanoi Rock City.

HANOI ROCK CITY

www.hanoirockcity.com
Hanoi Rock City is a live music and arts venue that opened at the end of 2010 and, given its program of Vietnamese and international performers, quickly established itself as a place worth knowing about. The music is upstairs, and there are two bars and a quiet outdoor area with seating.

✉ 25/52 To Ngoc Van, Tay Ho ☎ 0188 7487426 🕐 Daily 6pm–11pm

HO GUOM XANH

There's a lively imagination at work at this nightclub: Few people passing by outside would envisage a wild interior with a nightly spectacle of operatic shows. The upstairs entrance is like a submarine tube. Drinkers can hang out in this capsule before entering the main arena to be entertained by the laser and live music show nightly at 10pm. It is always packed and popular with locals. Drinks are fairly expensive for what is predominantly a Vietnamese venue.

✉ 32 Le Thai To Street ☎ 04-38288806
🕐 Daily 6pm–midnight

I-BOX

www.iboxcafe.com
Decadent looking decor and leather armchairs characterize this popular nightspot in the center of the city. The live bands kick off at 8.30pm on Monday, Wednesday, Friday and Saturday, and the happy hour for drinks is from 4–7pm. Food, Western and Asian, comes in the form of pizza, pasta, steak, stir fries and curries.

✉ 32 Le Thai To Street ☎ 04-38288820
🕐 Daily 8am–1am

LEGEND

One of Hanoi's popular microbreweries is housed in a building that dominates the area at the tip of Hoan Kiem Lake, and offers tremendous views. The German *helles bier* (light) and

Right *A water puppetry show*

particularly the *dunkles bier* (dark) are strong and tasty. The machinery for brewing and ingredients are all imported from Germany. An extensive food menu is available, and this is also a good place for snacks and ice cream. There is another branch of Legend at 4 Vu Ngoc Phan Street (tel 04-37761666), which enjoys a convivial atmosphere, especially on Thursday to Sunday evenings between 7.30–9.30, when live bands perform on stage.

✉ 1–5 Dinh Tien Hoang Street ☎ 04-39360345 🕐 Daily 9am–11pm

LIBRARY BAR
www.hanoi-pressclub.com
The Library Bar is a small venue, decorated as a pastiche of an English country house, with wall-to-wall shelves stacked with old books and leather chairs with a veneer of racing green. This is a tranquil setting in which to tipple a few malts while smoking a fine Havana, and is very popular with older expatriates. It is conveniently situated inside the Press Club, close to the Opera House. For a more gregarious evening, visit the Press Club's top floor, The Terrace, on a Friday night for its weekly bash with live music and expatriates letting their hair down.

✉ Press Club, 59 Ly Thai To Street ☎ 04-39340888 🕐 Daily 6pm–11pm

OPERA HOUSE
www.ticketvn.com
A variety of Vietnamese and Western concerts, operas and plays are staged in this magnificent former French colonial palace of entertainment. Events are not held on a regular basis, so check listings in the daily publication *Vietnam News* or at the box office. Evening dress is required. Occasionally children are not allowed to attend shows. Photography is forbidden during performances.

✉ 1 Trang Tien Street ☎ 04-39330113/09-13489858; fax 04-9330116 🕐 Box office: 8–5 ▨ Ticket prices vary; around 200,000d for a performance

FESTIVALS AND EVENTS

JANUARY–FEBRUARY
DONG DA HILL FESTIVAL
This festival celebrates the Battle of Dong Da, in which Nguyen Hue (self-appointed Emperor Quang Trung) routed 200,000 Chinese troops in 1789. A procession, which includes the carrying of the flaming Thang Long Fire Dragon of straw, accompanied by music, makes its way through Hanoi to Dong Da hill in southwestern Hanoi.

🕐 Fifth day of *Tet* (27 Jan 2012)

MARCH
HAI BA TRUNG FESTIVAL
The Hai Ba Trung Festival celebrates the Trung sisters, who led a revolt against the Chinese in AD41 (▷ 27). On the third day the temple doors are opened; on the fourth, a funeral ceremony

POLYGON MUSIK CAFÉ
A good sound system does justice to the Vietnamese bands and singers who belt out rock and pop favorites from past decades. A downside is the café's small space which can make it feel cramped (and too smoky to suit everyone) on a busy night.

✉ 67A Nui Truc ☎ 89987900936 🕐 Music from 9pm

SUNSET BAR
This is one of the more romantic spots for a quiet evening in Hanoi, watching the sun set over West Lake from rattan couches or daybeds, with a gentle breeze from the water, which makes you forget you're in a large, noisy city. Sunset Bar is reached by a short walkway from the entrance area of the hotel. Cocktails, beer, wine and light food are on the menu but being part of a 5-star hotel prices are not pitched at budget travelers.

✉ Intercontinental Hotel, 1A Nghi Tam, Tay Ho ☎ 04-32708888 🕐 Daily 3pm–11pm

begins; on the fifth, their statues are removed for a bathing ceremony (the most important day); and on the sixth, a ritual ceremony is held.

🕐 Third to the sixth day of the second lunar month

SEPTEMBER
NATIONAL DAY
This public holiday marks the Declaration of Independence by Ho Chi Minh on September 2, 1945. Parades take place in front of his mausoleum in Ba Dinh Square and boat races are held on Hoan Kiem Lake.

🕐 Sep 2

DECEMBER
Christmas is celebrated in Hanoi and is a public holiday. Midnight Mass is popular at St. Joseph's Cathedral.

SPORTS AND ACTIVITIES
HIDDEN HANOI
www.hiddenhanoi.com.vn
At Hidden Hanoi's cookery courses, the first person to book for the day gets to choose from seafood, monsoon, street food, village food or vegetarian.

✉ 137 Nhgi Tam Road ☎ 09-12254045 🕐 Mon–Sat 11–2 ▨ US$40 per person

FOR CHILDREN
WATER PUPPETRY HOUSE
www.thanglongwaterpuppet.org
A performance here, at the northeast corner of Hoan Kiem Lake, is unmissable. Shows have live music, and the puppeteers' technical virtuosity is astonishing. First-class seats near the water stage provide photo opportunities. The troupe has performed in Japan, Australia and Europe.

✉ 57 Dinh Tien Hoang Street ☎ 04-39364335 🕐 Box office: 8.30–12, 3.30–8. Performances: daily 4.30, 5, 6.30, 8, 9.15pm; additional performance on Sun at 9.30am ▨ Tickets: 60,000d and 100,000d

EATING

REGIONS HANOI • EATING

PRICES AND SYMBOLS

The restaurants are listed alphabetically (excluding Le, La, Il and The). The prices given are the average for a two-course lunch (L) and a three-course dinner (D) for one person, without drinks. The wine price is for the least expensive bottle.

For a key to the symbols, ▷ 2.

AL FRESCO'S

It's only a short walk from Hoan Kiem Lake to this popular Australian grill bar serving ribs, steak, pasta, pizza and fantastic salads. Giant portions and a lively atmosphere make it a memorable experience. A Greek salad followed by jumbo ribs and apple crumble leaves you more than full. It serves food between 11am and 10pm, and is one of only a few places in Hanoi serving ice cream.

✉ 23L Hai Ba Trung Street ☎ 04-38267782 ⊕ Daily 8.30am–11pm
✋ L 170,000d, D 350,000d, Wine 320,000d

AU LAC HOUSE

The setting, an elegantly renovated French-style colonial mansion, is hard to beat for a relaxed evening meal if a table is available outside on one of the balconies (air-conditioned rooms inside the house). The Vietnamese food is equally stylish—try the banana flower salad—and the cocktails are not too bad either. Au Lac is situated at the junction of Tran Hung Dao and Han Thuyen.

✉ 13 Tran Hung Dao ☎ 04-9333533
⊕ Daily 8am–11pm ✋ L 150,000d, D 300,000d, Wine 250,000d

LE BEAULIEU

www.sofitel.com
Le Beaulieu is a good French and international restaurant whose Sunday brunch buffet is regarded as one of the best in Asia. Take your pick from a great selection of French seafood, oysters, prawns, cold and roast meats, and cheese, all piled high on platters. A dress code insists on long trousers and shoes for men.

✉ Sofitel Metropole Hotel, 15 Ngo Quyen Street ☎ 04-38266919 ext 8206
⊕ Daily 6.30–10.30, 11.30–2, 6.30–11
✋ L 360,000d, D 780,000d, Wine 270,000d

BROTHER'S CAFÉ

www.brothercafe.com
Part of the pleasure of dining here is the sumptuous surroundings. Brother's is set in a beautifully restored villa close to the Fine Arts Museum, and its leafy patio with umbrella-shaded tables is a haven of peace, filled with stands offering tempting dishes. The buffet lunch, with a range of starters, main courses and desserts, is one of the best-value meals in the country. Dinners are nightly barbecue buffets (seafood on weekends).

✉ 26 Nguyen Thai Hoc Street ☎ 04-37333866 ⊕ Mon–Sat 11–2, 6.30–10,

Above *Restaurant Bobby Chinn (▷ 92)*

Sun 6.30–10 🖐 L 256,000d, D 370,000d (472,000d at weekends), Wine 330,000d

CAY CAU RESTAURANT

www.desyloia.com

Popular with well-to-do Vietnamese, this small restaurant offers excellent set-price meals and a huge range of delicious food. After an appetizer of eel and mushroom soup or beef and bindweed salad, try the full crab menu—fried, soft-shell crab with butter—or simmered pigeon with garlic in a clay pot. Tofu dishes figure prominently on the menu. If room remains, death by chocolate or blueberry cheesecake are tempting. Eat outdoors or inside under a decorated wooden ceiling. There is live music from 7.30pm to 9.30pm daily.

✉ De Syloia Hotel, 17A Tran Hung Dao Street ☎ 04-38245346 🌐 Daily 11–2, 6–10 🖐 L 150,000d, D 200,000d, Wine 380,000d

CHA CA LA VONG

This is a deservedly popular spot with some tour groups—an eating house that looks to be at least a century old and with few changes made over that time. The wooden tables quickly fill up, leaving only elbow room, but this is all part of the culinary fun. The set meal arrives in a clay pot sizzling with fish and spluttering over hot charcoal: Spoon out a portion, add to it from the bowls of parsley, dill, vegetables and sauces and throw some noodles and peanuts on top for a hearty repast.

✉ 14 Pho Cha Ca Street ☎ 04-73253929 🌐 Daily 10–2, 4–9 🖐 L and D 150,000d

CLUB DE ORIENTAL

Just a short walk from the Sofitel Metropole, the Club de Oriental uses a three-story building to create a luxurious restaurant on different levels. The basement has tables surrounded by over 300 different wines, the first level has an open kitchen in the middle and the second level, with its own bar and lounge area, is more private in tone and dedicated to a fine-dining experience. *The New York Times* once lauded the restaurant's spring rolls as the best in Asia and, despite there being some seriously expensive items on the menu, there are plenty of reasonably priced dishes, like steamed, rolled rice pancakes filled with cinnamon-flavored pork, tiger prawns with passion fruit sauce, and chicken with lemon grass. There is live music on Tuesday, Thursday and Saturday nights.

✉ 22 Tong Dan Street ☎ 04-38268801 🌐 Daily noon–11 🖐 L 320,000d, D 480,000d, Wine 750,000d

CLUB OPERA

An extensive Vietnamese menu is on offer in this small and intimate restaurant in the attractive setting of a restored French villa, close to the Opera House. Tables are beautifully laid, and the food is appealingly presented with exquisitely carved vegetables. The grapefruit salad with shrimp and dried shredded squid is delicious. Beef, chicken and fish (fried grouper fillet with ginger sauce, for example) complete the repertoire. The dessert menu is decidedly uninspired, however, considering the varied savory menu on offer.

✉ 59 Ly Thai To Street ☎ 04-38246950 🌐 Daily 11–2, 6–midnight 🖐 L 300,000d D 420,000d, Wine 480,000d

COM CHAY NANG TAM

This popular little vegetarian restaurant is down an alley off Tran Hung Dao Street, near the Ambassador's Pagoda. It serves excellent and inexpensive dishes in a small, family-style dining room. The set meals range in price from 30,000d to 200,000d. Dishes incorporate a wide range of ingredients: sweetcorn cakes, beef salad with banana flower, star fruit and pineapple, and snowballs (light potato and mushroom croquettes). To accompany the 59 vegetarian options there are lots of freshly squeezed juices (wine is not served). Keep some room for the delicious banana and chocolate crêpes.

✉ 79A Tran Hung Dao Street ☎ 04-39424140 🌐 Daily 11–2, 5–9.30 🖐 L 30,000d, D 100,000d

DAKSHIN

Southern Indian *dosas*—pancakes served with different sauces—are the specialties in this popular Indian vegetarian restaurant. The menu provides a useful glossary of the many unusual dishes served in the dining room, which is elegantly laid out with rattan furniture. There are nearly 100 dishes, such as cauliflower fritters, *dosas* and curries, all served on stainless-steel platters lined with a banana leaf. Prices are reasonable; set meals with five options are available for 120,000d. Desserts include *gulab jamun, khoya* balls immersed in cardamom- and saffron-flavored syrup. Wine is not served.

✉ 94 Hang Trong Street ☎ 04-39286872 🌐 Daily 10–2.30, 6–10.30 🖐 L and D from 120,000d

THE DELI

www.hanoi-pressclub.com

Keep The Deli delivery menu by the telephone for pizza, pasta, healthy salads and sandwiches, especially during the rainy season or if you fancy a quick lunch on the move. There is free delivery within a 6-mile (10km) radius. Edible goodies include the flame-grilled Greek lamb kebab sandwich and the colossal double chocolate brownie. The same menu is available to eat in on the third floor of the Press Club.

✉ The Press Club, 59A Ly Thai To Street ☎ 04-38255337 🌐 Daily 7am–10pm 🖐 Take-out meal: 150,000d

FANNY

This is just the place to escape the busy streets—but sit well back from the open entrance. It is convenient for the offices of Vietnam Air and Air France. Try the delicious mango sherbet, mocha ice cream or a version with Bailey's, ice cream cakes and milkshakes.

✉ 47 Le Thai To Street ☎ 04-38285656 🌐 Daily 8am–11pm 🖐 Ice creams around 15,000d

GREEN MANGO

www.greenmango.vn

Green Mango is a delightful restaurant in Hanoi's old quarter, especially after dark when the interior is lit by subdued red lighting and a relaxing atmosphere prevails. Dishes include smoked scallop salad, curries and Asian favorites like roasted chicken with coconut and flavored with pandan leaves. Green Mango is a culinary and, on the nights when live music is played, a cultural oasis in this part of the capital.

✉ 18 Hang Quat Street ☎ 04-39289916/17/18 ⏰ Daily 11–11 ✋ L 250,000d, D 350,000d, Wine 350,000d

IL GRILLO

Despite stiff competition from newer places, this long-established Italian restaurant remains popular. Two giant liquor bottles sit on its big, dark bar; the floor is tiled and the tables laid with checked tablecloths. Classic dishes, served to the sound of opera, include Parma ham with melon and carpaccio di vitello (thinly sliced veal), followed by homemade pastas, veal, chicken, dumpling filled with roasted beef, pork, and ham served with a light ham and cream sauce.

✉ 116 Ba Trieu Street ☎ 04-38227720 ⏰ Mon–Sat 10–2, 5.15–11, Sun 5.15–11 ✋ L 200,000d, D 300,000d, Wine 270,000d

HANOI GOURMET

For lovers of fine wine, cheese and cold cuts, this delicatessen south of Hoan Kiem Lake, with a couple of tables at the back, is a great discovery. Find a free afternoon, go short on breakfast, then come here for a long, leisurely lunch. Stocks are replaced from France every few weeks. The counter displays an array of salads, baguettes and other breads, smoked salmon, cheeses and assorted terrines (in winter, fondue and raclette). A second outlet is opening across the street.

✉ 6T and 1B Pho Ham Long Street ☎ 04-39431009 ⏰ Daily 8.30am–9pm ✋ L 100,000d, D 170,000d, Wine 205,000d

HIGHWAY 4

www.highway4.com

Enter this restaurant through red swing doors to enjoy ethnic minority dishes from the north. Highway 4 is the most northerly road in Vietnam, running along the Chinese border, and is much used by owners of Minsk motorcycles. The restaurant itself is a visual and culinary treat. Superb fruit and rice wines are sold, the latter displayed in large medicinal bottles stuffed with preserved cobra, silkworm and gecko. You may need some rice wine for courage to face the exciting but alarming menu. Dishes include ostrich sautéed with cashews, mushrooms and onions; fried scorpions with chili and lemon grass; sauerkraut sautéed with pigs' intestines; and the pièce de résistance: bull's penis steamed with Chinese herbs. For the fainthearted, there are less challenging dishes such as curried chicken.

✉ 5 Hang Tre Street ☎ 04-39260639 ⏰ Daily 10am–1am ✋ L 60,000d, D 75,000d, Wine 36,000d

JASPAS

Expatriates, children and older, professional Vietnamese customers form much of the clientele of this noisy restaurant serving Western food. Starters include lamb roti and the salads are above-average. There's a good choice of steaks, an appealing vegetarian section as well as old favorites such as fish (wasabi-breaded barramundi) and fries, and a wine list and cocktails. The chocolate mud pudding or Mars bar cheesecake will delight young ones. For the adults, there's a big TV screen for sporting events. The one drawback is air-conditioning that is usually too cold.

✉ 4th floor, Hanoi Towers, 49 Hai Ba Trung Street ☎ 04-39348325 ⏰ Daily 6am–11pm ✋ L 220,000d, D 400,000d, Wine 400,000d

KOTO

www.koto.com.au

Koto is a training restaurant next to the Temple of Literature for underprivileged young people. There is a vegetarian menu, but nonmeat dishes like tofu wrapped in mushrooms and vegetables and served with noodles and black bean sauce appear on the main menu. Nonvegetarians have a wide choice: sautéed scallops, beer-battered fish and chips, sandwiches, wraps, salads, and the Vietnamese food includes bun bon am bo (fried beef on rice noodles with a delicate blending of herbs and sauces). Desserts are mainly fruit based, with dishes such as tropical fruit in ginger and lime syrup served with sorbet. Sandwiches are also sold.

✉ 61 Van Mieu Street ☎ 04-37470337 ⏰ Mon–Sat 7am–4pm, Sun 7am–9.30pm ✋ L 110,000d, D 130,000d, Wine 450,000d

LITTLE HANOI

Little Hanoi is perfectly positioned on a busy corner of the Old City. The sandwiches are outstanding; so too are the cappuccinos, the homemade yogurt with honey and the apple pie. Shop till you drop and then dive in here for a cup of Earl Grey tea and a glance at the English-language newspapers and magazines, relaxing amid the wooden floors, rattan furniture and the wooden ceiling fans. Healthy and not-so-healthy breakfasts are also served.

✉ 21–23 Hang Gai Street ☎ 04-38288333 ⏰ Daily 7.30am–11pm ✋ L 110,000d, D 130,000d, Wine 450,000d

MILAN

The open kitchen and fine contemporary decor provide a stylish setting for a stylish meal under the direction of the Italian chef. Appetizers feature truffle tapenade, marinated artichokes, Portabello mushrooms, Gorgonzola sauce and garlic focaccia bread. Grilled steaks share menu space with pastas (linguine pasta with mussels, clams, squid, scallops and prawns is one of the chef's recommendations), pizzas and a superb risotto Arborio with radicchio scallops.

✉ InterContinental West Lake, 1A Nghi Tam ☎ 04-62708888 ⏰ Daily noon–10.30pm ✋ L 200,000d, D 900,000d, Wine 550,000d

MOCA CAFÉ

With its exposed, dark, red-brick wall and chrome flue, Moca Café would look more at home in Chicago or Manchester than in Hanoi. Its high open space, big windows, wafting fans and marble-topped tables are very inviting. Cinnamon-flavored cappucccino, smoked salmon and Bengali specials are all served on pretty, floral crockery.

✉ 14–16 Nha Tho Street ☎ 04-38256334 ⏰ Daily 7am–midnight ✋ L 120,000d, D 250,000d, Wine 300,000d

OLD HANOI

www.oldhanoi.com

Launched by British chef Gordon Ramsay in 2010, Old Hanoi is in a restored French villa, stylishly decorated to reflect a bygone age. The Vietnamese food includes a clay pot dish and beef served in a tube of bamboo as well as old favorites like spring rolls and grilled fish. The service can be a little haphazard and the wine is on the expensive side. Old Hanoi is a nonsmoking restaurant.

✉ 4 Ton That Thiep, Hoan Kiem ☎ 04-37478337 ⏰ Daily 11–2, 5–11 ✋ L 164,000d, D 200,000d, Wine 513,000d

PANE E VINO

The branch in Hang Trong Street is the easiest to find but this makes it all the more busy; Nguyen Khac Street is tucked away on the block behind the Sofitel Metropole. Pane e Vino enjoys a pleasant, family-friendly atmosphere with tables outside on the sidewalk in addition to the main dining area upstairs. The food is Italian, there is a range of set menus for two and the wine list is surprisingly good.

✉ 98 Hang Trong Street / 3 Nguyen Khac Street ☎ 04-39286329/04-38269080 ⏰ Daily 7.30am–10pm ✋ L 240,000d, D 320,000d, Wine 260,000d

PUKU CAFÉ

A bright and cheerful place with comfortable seating for Western-style food, and conveniently close to the railway station for early morning arrivals in the city. The food is average, and includes sandwiches, burritos, nachos, dishes such as tuna in a mushroom sauce with mashed potatoes, and some vegetarian bites. There is free WiFi.

✉ 16 Tong Duy Tan ☎ 04-39285244 ⏰ Daily 24 hours ✋ 50,000d–150,000d

THE RESTAURANT

www.hanoi-pressclub.com

The Restaurant has consistently remained one of the most popular dining experiences in Hanoi. Set in a smart complex close to the Opera House, it is luxuriously furnished, with polished, dark wood floors and print-lined walls. The menu is expensive: Start with crisp veal sweetbreads with langoustine and artichoke-heart purée on lobster essence. Then move on to the gimmicky deconstructed Vietnamese *pho* with lobster, foie gras and truffle, or chargrilled squab with wild forest mushroom tossed pasta. The delicious chocolate pavlova with passionfruit ice cream is a highlight of the chocolate-heavy dessert menu. Alfresco dining is also possible.

✉ The Press Club, 59A Ly Thai To Street ☎ 04-39340888 ⏰ Mon–Fri 11–2, 6–11, Sat, Sun 6–11 ✋ L 190,000d, D 500,000d, Wine 510,000d

Above *Green Mango restaurant*

RESTAURANT BOBBY CHINN

www.bobbychinn.com

This most famous of restaurants has moved from its former location, but the glamour (silk-lined dining rooms) and the adventurous cuisine remain constants. The menu covers a judiciously global range of dishes but with inventive touches. Steamed crab salad is soaked in sake, cod glazed with miso, ginger chicken wrapped in lotus leaf, duck smoked in hickory. Vietnamese favorites such as spring rolls are given an equally imaginative treatment. Nonmeat diners will enjoy the mezze platter. It is worth making a reservation to be sure of a table when you want it.

✉ 77 Xuan Dieu Street ☎ 04-37192460 🕐 Daily 11–11 🖐 L 525,000d, D 840,000d, Wine 630,000d

SAIGON SAKURA

The set lunch consists of pork or squid, with ginger or deep-fried, with *kobachi* (small dishes), steamed eggs and pickles, rice and miso. Dinner is a choice of sushi, sashimi and tempura. The excellent food is served at a straight row of tables amid uninspiring decor.

✉ 17 Trang Thi Street ☎ 04-38257565 🕐 Daily 11–2, 5–11 🖐 L 140,000d, D 350,000d, Sake 200,000d

LA SALSA

www.lasalsa-hanoi.com

La Salsa is a French–Spanish enclave in the middle of Hanoi, with perfect views of the cathedral and a pleasing menu. The chorizo and warm goat's cheese salad, with olive oil and thyme toast, is divine. Overall the food is a broad European mix, with the likes of beef tenderloin, French sausage and white beans, duck leg confit and paella on the menu, and is enhanced by a full range of tapas.

✉ 25 Nha Tho Street ☎ 04-38289052 🕐 Daily 8am–11pm 🖐 L 110,000d, D 230,000d, Wine 340,000d

SAN HO

www.sanho-seafood.com

Hanoi's most popular seafood restaurant offers a series of set meals with nine or ten courses, or an à la carte selection. The fruits of the sea dish includes winkles with garlic-butter sauce, oyster porridge and raw oysters served with wasabi sauce and ginger in vinegar, grilled oyster with scallions (spring onions), as well as winkles, cockles, clams and scallops. For dessert, try the sweetened bird's-nest delicacy with gingko nut. This is a pleasant, airy restaurant, with live piano music between 7pm and 9pm.

✉ 58 Ly Thuong Kiet Street ☎ 04-39349184 🕐 Daily 10–2, 5–10 🖐 L 280,000d, D set courses from 822,000d Wine 360,000d

SEASONS OF HANOI

www.seasonsofhanoi.com.vn

Seasons of Hanoi is housed in a finely restored and authentically furnished colonial villa with a small patio fringed by a hedge and fairy lights. The food is fresh and delicious, but service can be slack. Dine on stewed eel with red wine, fish kebabs with satay sauce and stewed duck in tofu sauce. The dessert list is disappointing after the extensive mains and appetizers menu, with only the coconut ice cream proving a temptation. Reservations are recommended.

✉ 95B Quan Thanh Street ☎ 04-38435444 🕐 Daily 11–2, 6–10 🖐 L 280,000d, D set courses from 822,000d, Wine 360,000d

SONG THU

www.hoasuaschool.com

This is a French training restaurant for disadvantaged youngsters, close to the Hanoi Cook Centre. At Song Thu visitors can eat French and Vietnamese cuisine in an attractive and secluded courtyard setting. It is popular, reasonably inexpensive and offers a children's menu. As it is a training school, service can be a little awkward at times. A variety of traditional daily specials are also available.

✉ 28A Ha Hoi Street ☎ 04-39424448 🕐 Daily 11–10 🖐 100,000d, D 150,000d, Wine 220,000d

TANDOOR

www.tandoorvietnam.com

Exceptional Indian food is freshly prepared at this small but long-standing restaurant. Authentic curries, tandooris and breads are served by the same family who run Dakshin (▷ 89). Tuck into onion *pakora*, chili potato *bhaji*, chicken *irani* (marinated in a rich mixture of yogurt, cream, lime juice, cashew paste and green chilies), kebabs, masalas and curries. Set lunches are available for under 100,000d, and Halal food is also served. No wine.

✉ 24 Hang Be Street ☎ 04-38245359 🕐 Daily 11–2.30, 5–10.30 🖐 L 110,000d, D 150,000d

VERTICALE

www.verticale-hanoi.com

The entrance to this 1930s French villa, where original features like the tiled floors and the clunky fan switches have been retained, resembles an apothecary but with shelves of spices and herbs. The charming dining rooms are upstairs, reached by outside stairs or by passing through the kitchen and up the original staircase. The colonial-style lounge bar is on the top floor. The food is modern Vietnamese and many of the ingredients, like rolls of cinnamon bark, can be purchased. Cookbooks by the French chef, Didier Corlou, are also on sale.

✉ 19 Ngo Van So Street ☎ 04-39446317 🕐 Daily 11.30–2, 6.30–10.30 🖐 L 248,000d, D 679,000d and 900,000d, Wine 570,000d

Below *Several restaurants in Hanoi serve delicious seafood dishes*

REGIONS HANOI • EATING

PRICES AND SYMBOLS

The prices are for a double room for one night including breakfast, unless otherwise stated. All the hotels listed accept credit cards unless otherwise stated. Note that rates can vary widely throughout the year.

For a key to the symbols, ▷ 2.

CAMELLIA 4

www.camellia-hotels.com

The location, in the middle of the Old Quarter, is convenient and the rooms which are a good size come equipped with a computer. Rooms on the lower floors are more affected by noise from the nightclub next door than those higher up. For guests newly arrived in Vietnam, Camellia 4 has a helpful travel service when it comes to planning journeys and tours.

✉ 44 Hang Giay Street ☎ 04 38243667 ✋ US$32–$55, including taxes 🚪 24 ♻

CHURCH HOTEL

www.churchhotel.com.vn

This is a small, characterful and cozy hotel in the city's Old Quarter. Rooms are well presented, with mini bar and free Internet access. The hotel's travel desk is convenient for booking journeys and tours. Try to book a room at the back of the hotel to avoid noise from the street.

✉ 9 Nha Tho Street ☎ 04-39288118 ✋ US$57–$90, including taxes 🚪 26 ♻

CLASSIC STREET HOTEL

www.classicstreet-phocohotel.com

In a good location in the Old Quarter, the hotel is quieter than you might expect for this part of the city. The good-sized rooms are clean and comfortable, with a small fridge and WiFi (two computers in the lobby are free to use). There is a neat little breakfast room. Staff are helpful and travel arrangements and tours can be booked through the hotel. A reasonably priced pickup from the airport can be arranged in advance.

✉ 41 Hang Be Street ☎ 04-38252421 ✋ US$33–$38, including taxes 🚪 20 ♻

DE SYLOIA

www.desyloia.com

This small hotel, south of Hoan Kiem Lake, is within walking distance of the Opera House and the Vietnam History Museum. Facilities include a restaurant, Cay Cau (▷ 89), babysitting, satellite and cable TV, in-house movies, free WiFi and a laundry service as well as use of a rattan bicycle. The daily set lunch is excellent value. Guests are welcomed with roses and complimentary fruit.

✉ 17A Tran Hung Dao Street ☎ 04-38245346 ✋ US$70–$90, excluding taxes 🚪 33 (16 nonsmoking) 📺 ♻

EDEN

http://edenhanoihotel.vn

This popular mini-hotel, which has its own restaurant, open-air breakfast terrace and bar, is on a very busy street close to the Hoa Lo Prison (▷ 73). The less expensive rooms are small, but the discounts they offer can halve the price of the room. Some bedrooms have wedge-shaped baths, and satellite TV; phones and minibars are standard. There is also a free Internet and e-mail service.

Above *The Hilton Hanoi Opera*

✉ 78 Tho Nhuom Street ☎ 04-39423273
✋ US$45–$75, including taxes ⓘ 36 ⬡

GALAXY
www.galaxyhotel.com.vn
The only recommended hotel north
of the Old City is this well-run,
3-star business hotel built in 1918,
facing Hanoi's squat water tower
and only a few minutes' walk from
the middle of town. Suites are
comfortably carpeted and fully
equipped, and they have satellite
TV and minibars. The bathrooms
come with a shower and a bathtub,
and bedside reading lights are
provided—a considerate luxury.
✉ 1 Phan Dinh Phung Street ☎ 04-
38282888 ✋ US$109–$119, excluding
taxes ⓘ 60 ⬡

GREEN MANGO
www.greenmango.vn
A true boutique hotel and probably
one of the nicest places in which
to spend a night in Hanoi. Satin
sheets, silk curtains, laminated
floors and a complimentary bottle
of wine (in the "Sweet Deluxe"
rooms) are part of the attraction of
staying here. The seven rooms are
tastefully and individually decorated
and the staff are attentive and
considerate. Pickup from the airport
costs US$25.
✉ 18 Hang Quat Street, Hoan Kiem District
☎ 04-39289916 ✋ US$49–$99, excluding
taxes ⓘ 7 ⬡

HANOI BACKPACKERS HOSTEL
www.hanoibackpackershostel.com
This Australian-run hostel is in
the heart of the city and has a
good reputation for friendliness,
cleanliness and contact with other
young travelers. Internet use, as
well as tea and coffee, is always
freely available, there is a restaurant
serving mostly Western food and
a bar that becomes busy and
sociable at night. The air-
conditioning is turned on in the
evening but not throughout the day.
As well as the mixed dorm rooms
there is a dorm room for women
only (all dorm beds have their own
lockers) and there are also double

and triple rooms available. Success
has brought expansion and the
owners have now opened a second
hostel near Hoan Kiem Lake in the
Old Quarter.
✉ 48 Ngo Huyen Street ☎ 04-38285372
✋ US$26–$36 ⓘ 18 ⬡

HANOI BOUTIQUE HOTEL 1
www.hanoiboutiquehotel1.com
The bedrooms may be a tad too
small for some guests—but in other
respects this is a good-value hotel
with some sophisticated touches,
such as flat-screen televisions. It
also has a spa, sauna, safe-deposit
boxes and a restaurant.
✉ 07 Ngo Gach Street ☎ 04-39290366
✋ US$46–$90, excluding taxes ⓘ 30 ⬡

HANOI DAEWOO
www.hanoi-daewoohotel.com
The Hanoi Daewoo is one of
Vietnam's most luxurious hotels,
a huge building with an adjoining
apartment complex and office
tower. Rooms are plushly decorated
and have private bathrooms with
marble bathtubs and showers, plus
satellite TV, safe-deposit boxes,
minibars and Internet. Guests can
swim in the large pool, browse in
the shops and dine in one of four
restaurants: The Café Promenade,
serving international food; La
Paix, which has an Italian menu;
Silk Road, for excellent Chinese
food; and the Edo, serving some
of the finest Japanese food in
town. Alternatively, there's the
delicatessen, Le Gourmet, serving
pastries and cakes, and two bars,
Palm Court Lobby Lounge and Lake
View Rooftop Lounge—the lake
in question being Lu Lake, in Ba
Dinh District, the diplomatic and
government quarter. The hotel has
a large collection of Vietnamese
modern art.
✉ 360 Kim Ma Street ☎ 04-38315000
✋ US$94–$126, excluding breakfast and
taxes ⓘ 411 ⬛ ▼ ⬡

HANOI HORISON
www.hanoihorisonhotel.com.vn
A tall chimney stack stands in front
of the Hanoi Horison—a relic of

the brickworks that once stood on
this site. The busy, popular hotel is
conveniently placed for the Temple
of Literature (▷ 78–81), and has
very comfortably furnished rooms
with satellite TVs, minibars, music
systems, coffee- and tea-making
equipment, and private bathrooms
with both a bathtub and a shower.
The circular swimming pool is in
rather an exposed position. There
are several restaurants, a lobby bar,
a casino, high-speed Internet access
and an ATM.
✉ 40 Cat Linh Street ☎ 04-37330808
✋ US$98–$195, including taxes ⓘ 250
⬛ ▼ ⬡

HILTON HANOI OPERA
www.hilton.com
Built adjacent to, and architecturally
sympathetic with, the Opera
House, the Hilton Hanoi Opera is a
lofty edifice with large bedrooms.
Its foyer is in art deco style, with
marbled flooring, enormous
decorated columns and an elegantly
curved balcony. Rooms—with views
of the Opera House or the city—are
furnished in traditional Vietnamese
style and have coffee-makers,
mini-refrigerators, TVs, broadband
Internet access, minibars and
bathrooms with tubs and showers.
Two rooms are specially adapted
for guests with disabilities. There
is a set lunch available at the Chez
Manon restaurant and the hotel
also has the Ba Mien Vietnamese
restaurant, a bakery and a sports
bar. Other amenities include a
florist, a gift shop, an airline desk
and a laundry and valet service.
✉ 1 Le Thanh Tong Street ☎ 04-39330500
✋ US$175–$190, excluding taxes ⓘ 269
(nonsmoking on one floor) ⬛ ▼ ⬡

HONG NGOC 1
www.hongngochotel.com
This small family-run hotel, one of
a trinity in the Old City (▷ below),
is spotlessly clean throughout,
with cheerful and helpful staff. The
largest rooms, whose balconies
have street views, are huge, so the
heavy imperial-style furniture is not
too oppressive; the 14 rooms at the

back of the hotel are smaller and do not have balconies. All rooms have minibars, satellite TVs and private bathrooms with tubs.

✉ 34 Hang Manh Street ☎ 04-38285053 💳 US$49–$109, excluding taxes 🚪 50 ♿

HONG NGOC 2

www.hongngochotel.com
This small and quiet hotel has amenities similar to those of its sister, Hong Ngoc 1 (▷ above), and sits in a prime location in the heart of the 36 Streets, on the connecting road to Hoan Kiem Lake. In addition to the standard facilities, Hong Ngoc 2 has an elevator and offers baby-sitting services. Pets are allowed.

✉ 14 Luong Van Can Street ☎ 04-38267566 💳 US$42–$75, excluding taxes 🚪 40 (10 nonsmoking) ♿

HONG NGOC 3

www.hongngochotel.com
The third member of the Hong Ngoc group is also in the heart of the Old City. Rooms are small, but not cramped, and some come with both a double and single bed. All are furnished with Huê imperial-style beds and chairs inlaid with mother-of-pearl, and have minibars, satellite TV and private bathrooms with tubs. The seven rooms at the back of the hotel are quieter, and the top room has a good view over the older rooftops of the city. There is an Internet and e-mail service. The restaurant serves Asian, European and Vietnamese food.

✉ 39 Hang Bac Street ☎ 04-39260322 💳 US$31–$47, including breakfast, excluding taxes 🚪 25 (all nonsmoking) ♿

INTERCONTINENTAL

www.intercontinental.com/hanoi
Most of the rooms are set in three island pavilions—the entire hotel is built over the waters of West Lake— and this is what creates the sense of being in a resort hotel, despite being a 10-minute taxi ride away from the city center. All the rooms are generously sized, have balconies

Above *The Nikko Hanoi hotel's contemporary marble lobby*

and superb views of either the lake or the city skyline; showers are separate from the bathtubs. There is a health club, a modestly sized pool, the Milan Italian restaurant, the French brasserie-style Café du Lac and a Sunset Bar positioned out on the water. A very good range of informative tours can be booked through the hotel. The InterContinental is one of the most singular hotels in Vietnam.

✉ 1A Nghi Tam, Tay Ho ☎ 04-32708888 💳 US$310–$393, excluding taxes 🚪 359 (258 nonsmoking) 🖼 ♿

MELIÃ

www.meliahanoi.com.vn
Given its amenities and the impressive list of important people who have stayed here, the 22-story Meliã rivals the Metropole as the most prestigious hotel in Hanoi. Everything seems to be available: business center, babysitting service, travel desk, spa and beauty salon, fitness center, sauna, outdoor pool, WiFi (though only from the 15th floor upward). There is a lovely outdoor pool and plenty of restaurants, including the El Oriental, serving Vietnamese cuisine, and El Patio for international dishes, a daily buffet dinner and Sunday brunch. The CK bar is a

lively place late at night, with a dance floor and live music.

✉ 44 Ly Thuong Kiet Street ☎ 04-39343343 💳 US$103–$129, excluding taxes 🚪 306 🖼 📺 ♿

NIKKO HANOI

www.hotelnikkohanoi.com.vn
Despite its rather forbidding exterior, this hotel has a tranquil air inside, with a cool, marble lobby. It overlooks Lenin Park and Bay Mau Lake, in the south of the city, and is popular with Japanese guests, who appreciate the excellent Japanese restaurant, Benkay. Also here are a Chinese restaurant, Tao-Li, and a brasserie, plus a cake shop and the Portraits bar. Spa, sauna and massage facilities are available. Rooms are large and brightly furnished and have satellite TV, Internet access, safe-deposit boxes and in-room fitness equipment. Some rooms are equipped for guests with disabilities.

✉ 84 Tran Nhan Tong Street ☎ 04-38223535 💳 US$120–$250, excluding taxes 🚪 255 (nonsmoking on request) 🖼 📺 ♿

PRINCE

This extremely friendly hotel on the fringes of the Old City is good value and can offer help with tours and bicycle rental, as well as services such as laundry and dry-cleaning and baby-sitting. The comfortable, double-glazed rooms have simple, dark wood furniture and private bathrooms with showers and/or tubs, plus coffee- and tea-making equipment and satellite TV. All rooms have city views.

✉ 34 Hang Tre Street ☎ 04-39349063
✋ US$25–$35, including breakfast and taxes ⓘ 9 ⌚

QUEEN TRAVEL HOTEL
www.azqueentravel.com
This travel café in the heart of the Old City has beautifully furnished private rooms, each equipped with satellite TV, air-conditioning and a shower. Vietnamese handicrafts decorate the rooms. The travel desk offers a good range of trekking, mountain-biking and kayaking tours. There is free Internet use.

✉ 65 Hang Bac Street ☎ 04-38260860
✋ US$65–$95, excluding taxes ⓘ 9 ⌚

SHERATON HOTEL
www.sheraton.com/hanoi
The opulent and luxurious Hanoi Sheraton is some distance out of town, on a spot overlooking the West Lake. Rooms have satellite TV, coffee-makers, refrigerators and broadband Internet access, and the private bathrooms, furnished in marble, have separate tubs and showers. Other services available to guests include babysitting and laundry, and there is a whirlpool, a hot tub, a sauna and an illuminated outdoor tennis court. The swimming pool is in a courtyard that opens up onto a lawn leading down to the lakeshore. At the Nutz eatery, which serves light snacks, you can sit on a terrace overlooking the West Lake; there are also two other restaurants—the Oven D'Or, serving international food, and Hemispheres, serving fine Southeast Asian cuisine—and a lobby bar.

✉ 11 Xuan Dieu Road, Ho Tay District ☎ 04-37199000 ✋ US$187–$305, excluding taxes ⓘ 229 (nonsmoking on request) ⌚ ⓨ ⌚

SOFITEL METROPOLE
www.sofitel.com
At this elegant and renowned French colonial hotel in the heart of central Hanoi there is a long tradition of catering to the rich and famous. Charlie Chaplin, Graham Greene, Catherine Deneuve and Michael Caine have all been guests at this prestigious hotel, which is, not surprisingly, often fully booked. Staff speak English, French, Japanese and Russian. Le Beaulieu serves French dishes, and Hanoi specialties are on the menu of the Spices Garden, while Angelina's is devoted to Italian cuisine. Evening cocktails are served in the Bamboo Bar overlooking the pool and there's a sidewalk café, La Terrasse du Metropole, in front of the hotel. Among other amenities are a business center, fitness center, a bookstore, beauty salon, spa, hairdresser, car rental desk, and dry-cleaning and babysitting services. Rooms are simply but attractively designed and have satellite and cable TV, safe-deposit boxes, minibars and private marble bathrooms. One room is equipped for guests with disabilities.

✉ 15 Ngo Quyen Street ☎ 04-38266919
✋ US$195–$313, excluding breakfast and taxes ⓘ 363 (163 nonsmoking)
⌚ ⓨ ⌚

SOFITEL PLAZA HANOI
www.sofitel.com
This vast, 20-floor hotel overlooks the West Lake and is a 40-minute drive from the airport. Rooms are generously furnished in pleasing, neutral tones and have writing desks, minibars, safe-deposit boxes and satellite and cable TV. All rooms are reached by glass-walled elevators and have floor-to-ceiling windows affording splendid panoramic views. Ten are equipped for guests with disabilities. The large, all-weather swimming pool has a retractable roof and is bordered by the Pool Garden Café, a gym and a spa. Chinese and Vietnamese food are served at the Ming Palace restaurant, and

a brasserie provides Western and Asian buffets. There are three bars and a nightclub.

✉ 1 Thanh Nien Street ☎ 04-38238888
✋ US$120–$200, excluding breakfast and taxes ⓘ 322 rooms (85 nonsmoking)
⌚ ⓨ ⌚

SUNWAY HOTEL
www.sunwayhotels.com
This extremely comfortable, quiet and friendly hotel is south of Hoan Kiem Lake and close to Hanoi Gourmet, which is an attraction in itself (▷ 90). Breakfast is good and varied at the Sunway, and there is a restaurant for dinner and a lobby bar. All rooms have satellite TV, telephones, minibars, tea- and coffee-making equipment, safe-deposit boxes, plus a very useful control panel by the bed that operates all the room's lighting. There is drinking water in the private bathrooms, and triple-glazed windows give good soundproofing. One room is suitable for guests with disabilities. The restaurant, Allante, serves a good mix of Vietnamese and international dishes, and there is a lobby bar and a business center with high-speed Internet access.

✉ 19 Pham Dinh Ho Street ☎ 04-39713888 ✋ US$66–$200, excluding taxes ⓘ 145 (38 nonsmoking) ⓨ ⌚

ZEPHYR
www.zephyrhotel.com.vn
Small but neat, Zephyr aspires to be chic and boutique-like in its style and decor. The best aspect of Zephyr is its excellent central location, right by Hoan Kiem Lake and within walking distance of the Old Quarter of the city. There is a bar and café at the lobby level, attractively decorated with a small Japanese-style garden as a backdrop. Tea- and coffee-making facilities can be found in all the rooms, and residents have free use of the hotel's gym.

✉ 4–6 Ba Trieu Street ☎ 04-39341256
✋ US$123–$143, excluding taxes ⓘ 40
ⓨ ⌚

Right *The luxurious Sofitel Metropole*

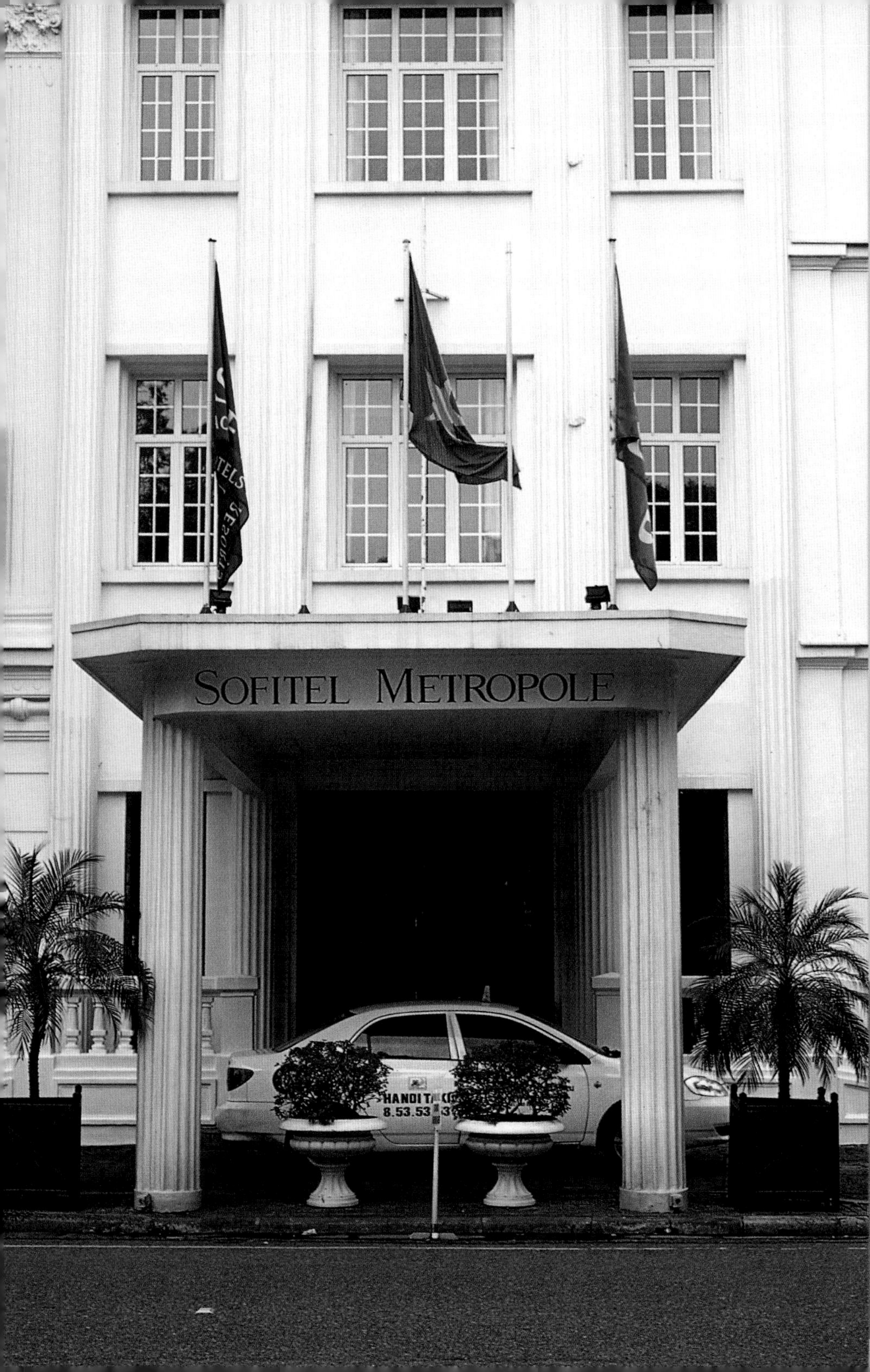
SOFITEL METROPOLE

THE NORTH

Culturally and geographically distinct, the northern area of Vietnam offers the high mountain ranges of the still relatively unexplored northwest, the visually stunning karst landscapes of the northeast, expansive Halong Bay dotted with tiny spiky islands, and the fertile rice paddies of the Red River Delta. At its heart is Hanoi, ancient in its ways while striving toward modernity. The northern region has its own climate and defined seasons: hot and steamy summers, marked by heavy rain and the odd typhoon, balanced by mild, dry winters.

Inaccessible without an uncomfortable journey until recent times, the lofty mountains of the northwest are home to colorfully dressed hill tribes, the beautiful Sapa hill station and deep-sided gorges offering stunning if hair-raising views, hairpin bends, sudden, hidden villages and zany markets where the Hmông bring their wares. Deep in the highlands is the city of Dien Bien Phu where Vietnamese independence was established. The city is unprepossessing in itself but surrounded by a lush valley with stilt-house communities and a sea of paddy fields.

To the east, the mountains are lower, the scenery less dramatic and the roads less demanding. The highlight is huge Halong Bay with its 3,000 limestone pinnacles and Cat Ba Island, a relaxing place to hang out after the thrills of the mountain passes. Here too is Ba Be National Park, home to at least 10 species of endangered mammals, and the vibrant commercial hub city Haiphong, its colonial heart intact and its food stalls second to none.

BAC CAN

The market town and capital of Bac Can Province lies on the River Cau and attracts all the region's main ethnic minority groups to its daily market—the Tày people and local branches of the White Hmông and Red Dao, in addition to Dao Tien (Coin Dao) and Dao Quan Chet (Tight Trouser Dao). Bac Can acquired enormous strategic significance during the First Indochina War as the westernmost stronghold of the Cao-Bac-Lang battle zone. It was captured by the Viet Minh in 1944 and retaken by the French in 1947, but guerilla attacks forced them to abandon the town after two years.

♁ 283 D2 🚌 Bus station on Duc Xuan Street. Connections from Ha Giang, Cao Bang and Hanoi 🍴 Vietnamese food 🎫 Private tours from Hanoi

BAC HA

Hundreds of local minority people flock in from the surrounding districts to shop and socialize at Bac Ha's Sunday market (7am–1pm). Among the regulars are the Flower Hmông, wearing embroidered linen; Phu La, in square aprons embroidered with motifs; La Chi, in turbans (men) or four-paneled dresses (women); and Tày, Vietnam's largest ethnic minority, dressed in black. While the women trade and chat, the men drink rice wine. There are several walks to outlying villages. Pho village of the Flower Hmông is around 2.5 miles (4km) north; Thai Giang Pho village of the Tày is 2.5 miles (4km) east; and Na Hoi and Na Ang villages, also Tày, are 1 mile to 2.5 miles (1.6km to 4km) west.

♁ 282 B1 🚌 Connections from Lao Cai and Pho Lu 🚂 From Lao Cai or Hanoi (10 hours) to Pho Lu 🎫 Minibus tours from some Sapa hotels

BAC SON

Settled mainly by members of the Tày and Nung ethnic groups, this small market town has two claims to significance in the nation's history. The first derives from the

Above *A Hmông woman wearing a headdress sells vegetables in Bac Can*
Opposite *The Black Dao women selling colorful hats and bags*

very large number of prehistoric objects unearthed here by archeologists. The Bac Son period (5000–3000BC) was characterized by the development of pottery and the widespread use of refined stone implements, including distinctive axes, with polished edges.

The second is the Bac Son Uprising of September 1940, when revolutionaries escaped here from Lang Son prison and established the first revolutionary power base in the Viet Bac. The following year French forces launched a campaign of terror, forcing the leaders of the uprising to retreat into the mountains, but the tide later turned steadily against the French throughout the entire region.

The road into town passes a stilted white building, in which the Museum of the Bac Son Rebellion (daily 7–4) has prehistoric tools and weapons, letters and other

documents relating to the uprising, and a number of personal effects.

♁ 283 D2 🚌 Connections from Hanoi, and Lang Son 🎫 Private tours depart from Hanoi

BICH DONG

Bich Dong consists of a series of temples and caves built into, and carved out of, a limestone mountain during the reign of Le Loi (reigned 1428–33). A trail leads up from the lower temple past Buddha's footprints embedded in the rock to the middle temple and a cave with rock forms. There's also a rock that's said to help choose the sex of a baby. The highlight is a scramble to the peak for glorious views. Tours usually include a visit to Tam Coc (▷ 113) and a boat trip to caves.

♁ 283 D3 🚌 Leave Highway 2 9 miles (14km) south of Ninh Binh; Bich Dong is 3 miles (5km) farther west 🎫 Private tours from Ninh Binh and Hanoi

CAO BANG

Cao Bang, set in a narrow valley, has some late-19th-century French buildings. The Exhibition Center (Hoang Nhu Street, tel 026-852616, Wed, Sat 7.30–11, 2–5) records the fight for independence. Ho Chi Minh's headquarters was at Pac Bo, 35 miles (56km) north of Cao Bang; his old staff car has pride of place at the museum.

➕ 283 D1 ℹ️ Phong Lan Hotel, 83 Be Van Dan Street ☎ 026-3852260; Mon–Fri 7–11.30, 1.30–5 🚌 Kim Dong Street

CHUA HUONG

The Perfume Pagoda, dedicated to Quan Am, the Guardian Spirit of Mother and Child, is one of a number of shrines and towers built among limestone caves in one of Vietnam's most beautiful spots. A sampan takes visitors along the Yen River, a 2.5-mile (4km) ride through a flooded landscape, to the Mountain of the Perfume Traces. From here it is a 2-mile (3km) hike up the mountain to the cool, dark cave containing the Perfume Pagoda. The stone statue of Quan Am in the principal pagoda was carved in 1793 after Tây Son rebels had stolen and melted down its bronze predecessor to make cannon balls. This is a popular pilgrimage spot, particularly during the festival months of February through May.

➕ 282 D3 ✉️ 37 miles (60km) southwest of Hanoi ✋ Day tours from Hanoi, including boat trips around US$25

CHUA THAY

The 11th-century Thay Pagoda is a tribute to herbalist Dao Hanh, who was from Sai Son village, and who was reputedly reborn as the son of Emperor Le Thanh Tong (reigned 1460–97). The complex, also known as Master's Pagoda, is divided into three: the outer part is used for ceremonies; the middle is a Buddhist temple; and the inner part is dedicated to the herbalist. There are golden-faced Buddhas with lacquered red garments and an array of demons. Water-puppet shows are staged during holidays and festivals in the middle of the pond Dao Hanh built at the front of the pagoda, which is spanned by two 17th-century bridges.

➕ 282 C2 ✉️ 25 miles (40km) west of Hanoi in the village of Sai Son 🚩 Private tours from Hanoi

DIEN BIEN PHU

▷ 104–105.

Below The gateway to the Perfume Pagoda

DEN HUNG

Myth and history intertwine at the Kings' Temples, a striking hillside site. This was an ancient royal capital and, legend has it, the birthplace of the Viet people. An almost perfectly circular hill rises unexpectedly from the monotonous Red River floodplain, with two lakes at the bottom. This is the site chosen by the Hung Vuong kings as their capital.

The stories say that the Viet people are the product of the union of King Lac Long Quan, a dragon, and his fairy wife, Au Co, who gave birth to 50 boys and 50 girls. Half the children followed their mother to the highlands and half remained with their father on the plains, giving rise to the Montagnards and lowland peoples of Vietnam. Historically easier to verify is the story of the Hung kings (Den Hung), who built a temple in order to commemorate the progenitors of the Vietnamese people.

WHAT TO SEE

The Hung Kings' Museum, at the foot of the hill (daily 8–11.30, 1–4) displays pottery, jewelry, fish hooks, arrowheads and ax heads (dated 1300–1000BC) excavated from the province, as well as bronze drums dating from around the fifth to the third centuries BC.

A track climbs the hill to a memorial to Ho Chi Minh and the Low Temple, dedicated to Au Co, mother of the country. At the back is a statue of the Buddha of a Thousand Arms and a Thousand Eyes. In the Middle Temple, farther uphill, Prince Lang Lieu was crowned seventh Hung king; here, too, kings would play chess and discuss pressing affairs of state. Prince Lang Lieu's most enduring creation is a pair of cakes, *banh trung* and *banh day*, which are still eaten at *Tet* (Vietnamese New Year).

Toward the top of the hill is the oath stone on which the 18th Hung king, Thuc Phan, swore to defend the country. The nearby 15th-century Top Temple is adorned with dragons and gaudily painted mural warriors stand guard outside. Smoke rises from burning incense on the three altars where the kings would pray for peace and prosperity.

Steps lead downhill from the rear right to the mausoleum of the sixth Hung king, then continue to the Well Temple, built in memory of the last princess of the Hung Dynasty, who combed her hair using the reflection in the well inside. Today, worshipers throw money in and, it is said, even drink the water.

INFORMATION

✚ 282 C2 ✉ 62 miles (100km) northwest of Hanoi ✋ Free 🚌 Turn off Highway 2 about 7.5 miles (12km) north of Viet Tri, Vinh Phu Province 🚕 Private tours from Hanoi

TIP

» The temples are particularly busy during the Hung Kings' Festival, a two-week celebration on the 10th day of the third lunar month.

REGIONS | THE NORTH • SIGHTS

Above *Warriors, dragons and lions guard the entrance to the Den Trung Temple*

INFORMATION

www.dienbienphu.org

✚ 282 A2 ✉ Highway 12, near middle of town. Connections with Hanoi, Son La, Lai Chau, Sapa ✈ Airport 1 mile (2km) north; connections with Hanoi ⅋ Near Vietnamese cemetery, market and Airport Hotel; local food ☞ Private tours from Sapa and Hanoi

INTRODUCTION

A crushing defeat inflicted on the French forces here in 1954 heralded the collapse of their Indochinese empire. Historic battle sites, a dazzling bronze commemorative statue and war cemeteries mark the event.

The town of Dien Bien Phu itself came into existence only in 1841 when, in response to continued Lao, Siamese and Chinese banditry in the area, the Nguyen Dynasty ordered the establishment of a royal district governed from a fortified settlement at Muong Thanh. It is a bland, modern town deep in the highlands of northwest Vietnam, close to the border with Laos. Unremarkable though Dien Bien Phu may be, its surroundings are extremely impressive. It sits in the Muong Thanh valley, a heart-shaped basin 12 miles (19km) long and 8 miles (13km) wide and crossed by the Nam Yum River. This is a majestic landscape, with Thái stilt houses nestling around the edges of lusciously green paddy fields. The town itself is quite easy to negotiate on foot, but the battlefield sites are well spread out, most to the west of the Nam Yum River, and are best visited by car or by motorcycle.

WHAT TO SEE

HILL A1

This small hill, known as Eliane 2 to the French, was the scene of the fiercest fighting of the hostilities of 1954, when it formed the foremost French stronghold in the area. It still holds reminders from the decisive battle in which the Viet Minh forces prevailed, marking the end of French influence in the whole of Indochina. These relics include a bunker and a French tank, or bison, named *Gazelle*. There's also a war memorial, dedicated to the Vietnamese who died on the hill, and nearby is the entrance to a tunnel that was excavated by coal-miners from Hon Gai and ran beneath French positions several hundred yards away. The tunnel was subsequently filled with 2,200lb (1,000kg) of high explosives, which were detonated at 11pm on May 6, 1954 as a signal for the final assault. The huge crater that resulted still scars the landscape.

🕐 Daily 7–11, 1.30–5 💰 5,000d ❓ Explanations in Vietnamese only

HISTORIC VICTORY EXHIBITION MUSEUM

In the grounds of the Historic Victory Exhibition Museum (Nha Trung Bay Thang Lich Su Dien Bien Phu) is a wide collection of assorted Chinese, American and French weapons and artillery, ground vehicles and aircraft. Inside, the museum illustrates national resistance from 1945 to 1953, then goes on to cover the 1954 battle, with a comprehensive range of photographs and illustrations and a display that includes a "packbike" with a carrying capacity of 816lb (370kg) that was used to support the troops. There are

Above *Dien Bien Phu as seen from Hill A1*

also displays relating to the battle in Hanoi's Museum of the Vietnamese Revolution (▷ 69).
✉ 7 Thang 5 Street ☎ 023-3824971 ⏱ Daily 7.30–11, 1.30–6 ✋ 5,000d 🗓 ❓ All labels in English and French

REVOLUTIONARY HEROES' CEMETERY

The Revolutionary Heroes' Cemetery (Nghia Trang Liet Sy Dien Bien Phu) contains the graves of some 15,000 Vietnamese soldiers killed during the course of the Dien Bien Phu campaign. A large bas-relief runs along its main front wall; look closely and you'll see Ho Chi Minh flanked by Viet Minh General Vo Nguyen Giap to the left and Hoang Van Thai, Giap's deputy, on the right. Sitting next to Hoang Van Thai is Pham Van Dong, who later became premier of North Vietnam.
✉ 7 Thang 5 Street ⏱ Daily 7.30–11, 1.30–6 ✋ Free

VICTORY MONUMENT

Dien Bien Phu's newest sight towers over the town. The Victory Monument (Tuong Dai Chien Dien Bien Phu), erected at a cost of US$2.27 million, is an enormous, 132-ton (120-tonne) bronze sculpture—the largest monument in Vietnam. It was sculpted by former soldier Nguyen Hai, and depicts three Vietnamese soldiers standing on top of General de Castries' Bunker. Engraved on the flag is the motto "Quyet Chien, Quyet Thang" (Determined to Fight, Determined to Win). One of the soldiers carries a Thái child. The work was commissioned to mark the 50th anniversary of the 1954 victory.
✉ Off 7 Thang 5 Street

GENERAL DE CASTRIES' BUNKER

The command bunker of French General Christian de Castries has been rebuilt on the site of the battlefield as it looked in 1954. Eight of the ten French tanks are scattered over the valley, along with US-made artillery pieces.
✉ Off Highway 12 ⏱ Daily 7–11, 1.30–5 ✋ 5,000d

MORE TO SEE

NGHIA TRANG PHAP

A white obelisk surrounded by a gray concrete wall and black iron gates sits on a bluff overlooking the Nam Yum River near de Castries' command bunker. This is the French War Memorial, inaugurated on July 5, 1994 on the initiative of the French Foreign Legion.
✉ Off Highway 12

TIPS
» Visit the Victory Monument in the late afternoon for the best pictures of the valley and the glowing statue.
» A 15-minute video in the museum uses live footage and a large model to make sense of the battle.

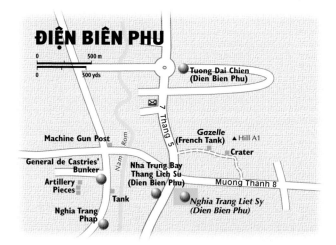

HA GIANG

You can get permits here (at the tourist company) to visit the far northern Dong Van-Meo Vac region. Archeological treasures have been unearthed here, and it also saw a flowering of Bronze Age culture — the most beautiful Dong Son bronze drums originate from and are still made here. There's an interesting daily market.

✚ 282 C1 🛈 Tran Hung Dao Street
☎ 019-3867054 ⏰ Mon–Fri 7–11.30, 1.30–5 🚌 Nguyen Trai Street

HAIPHONG

www.haiphongtourism.gov.vn
The third-largest city in Vietnam, where a customs house incident triggered the First Indochina War, retains an attractive center with colonial-style architecture. In the heart of town, where Tran Hung

Dao and Quang Trung streets meet, is the 1904 Great Theater, where, in November 1946, 40 Viet Minh fighters died in a pitched battle with the French. After visiting the theater, spend time in the surrounding streets where there are many food stalls and shops.

The Haiphong Museum at 66 Dien Bien Phu Street (Tue, Thu 8–10.30am, Wed, Sun 7.30–9.30pm) contains records of the city's turbulent past. On Me Linh Street is the early 20th-century Nghe Pagoda, dedicated to heroine General Le Chan, who fought with the Trung sisters against the Chinese. The 1672 Du Hang Pagoda, south of the center on Chua Hang Street, contains fine woodcarving, and farther south, at 51 Nguyen Cong Tru Street, is Dinh Hang Kenh, a communal house

(dinh), built in 1856 and now serving as a temple.

The main building of Dinh Hang Kenh is supported by 32 ironwood columns; the dramatic roof is decorated in fish-scale style and ornamented with dragons. The roof corners turn up and it appears that the sheer weight is too much, as the roof is now propped up with bricks.

✚ 283 D3 🛈 Haiphong Tourism, 44 Lach Tray ☎ 031-33843782 ⏰ Mon–Fri 7–12, 1.30–5 🚌 Tam Bac station, connections with Hanoi; Niem Nghia station, connections with southern destinations 🚉 Railway station, tel 031-3921333, trains to Hanoi at 8.25am and 6.25pm 🚢 Connections with Cat Ba, Hon Gai ✈ Airport 4 miles (7km) from city; connections with Saigon 🎫 Private tours from Hanoi

Above *Hang Kenh communal house in Haiphong is renowned for its woodcarvings*

HOA LU

Vietnam's 10th-century capital sits amid stunning scenery of rocks towering over rice paddies. Kings once inhabited the now half-ruined citadel of temples.

Hoa Lu was the capital of Vietnam from AD968 to 1010, during the Dinh and early Le dynasties. Its strategic location, in the narrow valley of the Hong River, provided easy defense of passes and views over the northern plains in case of Chinese incursions. Its temple art and architecture is primitive in form and massive in conception, dominated by huge stone carvings of elephants, rhinos and horses.

Much of this former capital, which covered more than 494 acres (200ha), has been destroyed, although archeological excavations have revealed a great deal of historical and artistic interest. The two principal temples at Hoa Lu are those of Dinh Bo Linh, who took the title King Dinh Tien Hoang (reigned AD968–80), and Le Hoan, who became King Le Dai Hanh (reigned AD980–1009).

DINH TIEN HOANG

The 11th-century Temple of Dinh Tien Hoang, reconstructed in 1696, is a series of courtyards, gates and buildings. An ancient inscription on one of its pillars—*Dai Co Viet*—is the derivation of the name Vietnam. The back room is dedicated to Dinh Tien Hoang, whose statue occupies the central position. In the AD960s, Dinh Tien Hoang pacified much of the Red River plain, but banditry continued to plague the kingdom. A large kettle and a caged tiger were placed in the palace courtyard, in which lawbreakers were to be boiled and gnawed. In the ensuing uneasy calm, Dinh Tien Hoang promoted Buddhism and geomancy, arranged strategic marriages and implemented reforms. But in AD979 his infant son, Hang Lang, made heir to the throne, was killed by his adult son, Dinh Lien, and soon afterward both father and surviving son were killed as they lay drunk in the courtyard. They say the assassin's flesh was fed to the citizens. Next to Dinh Tien Hoang's temple is a small hill, and at the top is Dinh Tien Hoang's tomb, reached via 265 steps.

LE DAI HANH

The Temple of King Le Dai Hanh is dedicated to the founder of the Le Dynasty, who seized power after the regicide of Dinh Tien Hoang. Le Dai Hanh also took the throne of his wife, Duong Van Nga, and there are representations of her, Le Dai Hanh and Le Ngoa Trieu (Hanh's eldest son), each occupying its own altar, in the rear temple.

INFORMATION

✚ 283 D3 ℹ Tran Hung Dao Road, Ninh Binh, Hoa Lu District ☎ 030-3875158 💵 15,000d 🚉 Ninh Binh, then car or motorcycle 🍴 At Van Xuan hotel, off Highway 1 🚌 4 miles (6km) north of Ninh Binh, 4 miles (6km) west of Highway 1; follow signs to Truong Yen 🚐 Private tours from Ninh Binh and Hanoi (tours often include a visit to Tam Coc)

TIPS

» Ninh Binh is the base for visits to Hoa Lu; it has rail connections with Hanoi and Ho Chi Minh City and is served by Open Tour buses.

» Guides are available, but the easiest option is to charter a car and driver.

Above *Farm workers head home after a day's work in the fields near Hoa Lu*

Above *The rice fields of Lai Chau*

LAC

The most popular village excursion from Hanoi is to Lac, so its White Thái residents are used to visitors, and many of the women sell clothing. The hope is that by "sacrificing" one village to tourism the industry's impact will be limited. Income generated by visitors has enabled many valley inhabitants to tile their roofs and buy items such as TVs and motorcycles.

Lac is easily accessible from the main road in Mai Chau, along a track past the People's Committee Guesthouse. You can ask stilt-house residents if you can stay the night, and possibly borrow or rent a bicycle for a ride to nearby hamlets, where you may be offered tea made from tree bark. A dance troupe performs most nights, followed by communal drinking of sweet, sticky rice wine from a large pot.
🏠 282 C3 🖐 Dinner, bed and breakfast at stilt house about 100,000d; dances included in tour packages or small contribution 🚌 Mai Chau; connections from Hanoi 🧭 From Hanoi, 2-day/1-night tours US$155

LAI CHAU

Lai Chau occupies a majestic setting in the deep, wide Da River valley, which is cloaked in dense tiers of forest. In 1993 the status of capital of Lai Chau Province was transferred from Lai Chau town to Dien Bien Phu, partly in recognition of the latter's growing importance as a hub of economic and tourist activity, and partly in deference to the side effects of the massive Son La hydroelectric power scheme being planned for the valley (due for completion in 2010).

The history of Lai Chau is entwined with that of the Black Thái seigneurial family of Deo, who achieved ascendancy by the first half of the 15th century. In 1947, the dynasty's descendant Deo Van Long (a tyrant, remembered with loathing by most older inhabitants) was installed as king of the Thái by the colonial government in return for his allegiance. The ruins of Deo Van Long's House, originally a plush colonial mansion and now overgrown with creepers and strangling figs, lie on Road 127 to Muong Te on the opposite bank of the Da River from High Hill (Doi Cao). Some say that before fleeing the country in 1953, Long had his servants poisoned so they could not inform the advancing Viet Minh forces of his whereabouts. Get there by boat from below High Hill or on a 5-mile (8km) road trip, crossing one rickety suspension bridge. At the site, beware of loose masonry and deep vaults covered in creepers.
🏠 282 A2 🚌 Station several miles from town; connections south with Dien Bien Phu, north and east with Sapa 🧭 Private tours from Hanoi and Sapa

MAI CHAU

During the first half of the journey from Hoa Binh to Mai Chau, the turtle-shaped roofs of the Muong houses predominate, but after passing Man Duc the road enters the territory of the Thái, Northwest Vietnam's most prolific ethnic minority, heralding a subtle change in the style of stilt-house architecture. While Thái are encountered in great numbers on this circuit, it is the Black Thái subethnic group who are seen most frequently. What makes the Mai Chau area interesting is that it is one of the few places en route where travelers can encounter their White Thái cousins. Some say visits here and to nearby Lac (▷ left) are a manicured way of encountering village lifestyle without the discomfort, and it is true that Mai Chau, an isolated farming community until 1993, has seen significant change in just a few years. Young Hanoians arrive in large groups at the weekend and appear oblivious to the impact of their presence, sometimes shattering the peace with loud portable music systems. The dignity and elegance of the Thái is all the more evident by contrast, and there is no denying that the tranquil valley setting, engaging inhabitants and superb rice wine make this a worthwhile overnight stop.
🏠 282 C3 🚶 47 miles (75km) from Hoa Binh 🚌 Connections with Hoa Binh, Hanoi, Son La 🍴 Simple eating places near market 🧭 Tours: www.trekmaichau.com

NHA THO CHANH TOA PHAT DIEM

The Red River Delta was the first part of the country to be influenced by Western missionaries: Portuguese priests proselytized here as early as 1627. Christian influence is still strong despite the mass exodus of Roman Catholics to the south in 1954 and decades of Communist rule. There can be up to half a dozen churches in a coastal province village, every one with packed congregations, and not only on Sundays. Phat Diem Cathedral is the most spectacular of the church buildings in the area, partly for its scale but also for its remarkable Asian style. Completed in 1891, it has a bell tower in the form of a pagoda, behind which the nave of the cathedral stretches for 243ft (74m), held up by 52 ironwood pillars. At the base of the bell tower are two carved stone slabs, placed here so that mandarins could sit and watch the Catholic worshipers.
🏠 283 D3 🚶 15 miles (24km) southwest of Ninh Binh in the village of Kim Son 🚏 Tran Hung Dao Road, Ninh Binh, Hoa Lu District ☎ 030-3881958 🕐 Several services a day 🧭 Private tours from Hanoi

INTRODUCTION

Sapa enjoys an impressive natural setting, high on a valley slope with Fansipan, Vietnam's tallest mountain at 10,312ft (3,143m), either clearly visible or brooding in the mist, and the clamor and color of ethnic minorities selling their craftwork and clothes. Buffaloes wander the surrounding valleys where the Hmông minority follow a way of life unchanged for centuries. However, the town's beauty, set amid such alpine grandeur high above the mountain clouds, is a little compromised by the new hotels sprouting up everywhere. Certainly none of the more recent ones can compare with the lovely old French buildings—pitched roofs, window shutters and carefully nurtured gardens. While hilly, Sapa is a fairly compact town and is easy to get around on foot, but at least a basic level of fitness is required for all mountain-trekking. Sapa enjoys warm days and cool evenings in the summer but gets very cold in winter, when snow falls on average every couple of years and settles on the surrounding peaks of the Hoang Lien Son mountains. The wettest months are May through September, with nearly 40in (1,000mm) of rain in July and August alone, the busiest months for Vietnamese visitors. December and January can be pretty miserable, with mist, low clouds and low temperatures. The spring blossom is lovely, but even in March and April a fire or heater may be necessary in the evening.

INFORMATION

🚌 282 B1 🚐 Connections with Lao Cai 🚊 Connections with Lao Cai and Hanoi 🍴 Range of restaurants including Vietnamese, other Asian, French, Italian and English food 🚗 A variety of tours, by car or bicycle or on foot, is available. from Explorer Tours (☎ 04-39231430; www.sapa-vietnam.com)

Above *Hmông girls in Sapa wearing traditional dress*

TIPS

» Weekends are peak tourist time, but during the week the few visitors who remain have the town to themselves.

» It is not possible to buy walking shoes, backpacks, coats, jackets or any mountaineering equipment in Sapa.

» Tourists wanting to trek around Sapa are no longer allowed to go it alone. Visitors must now have a touring card, sightseeing ticket and a licensed tour guide to trek five permitted routes from Sapa: round trip to Cat Cat and Sin Chai; Cat Cat, Y Linh Ho, Lao Chai and Ta Van; Lao Chai, Ta Van, Ban Ho, Thanh Phu and Nam Cang; Lao Chai, Ta Van, Su Pan and Thanh Kim; Ta Phin, Mong Sen, Takco, and climbing Mount Fansipan.

» It is possible to trek just to Cat Cat without a ticket and a guide. Homestays are permitted in six local villages: Ta Van Giay, Ban Den, Muong Bo, Ta Phin commune central area, Sa Xeng cultural village, and Sin Chai and Topas Eco Lodge. Tour guides who violate these rules will have their licenses withdrawn and tourists who do so will be disciplined, according to the People's Committee of Sapa District.

Below *A view of Sapa and its surrounding countryside from the Darling Hotel*

Originally a Black Hmông settlement, Sapa was first discovered by Europeans when a Jesuit missionary visited the area in 1918 and established an order there. By 1932 news of the quasi-European climate and beautiful scenery of the Tonkinese Alps had spread throughout French Indochina. Like Dalat farther south, Sapa was developed as a retreat for French administrators when the heat of the plains became unbearable.

By the 1940s an estimated 300 French buildings—including a prison and the summer residence of the governor of French Indochina—had sprung up, and many parks and flower gardens had been cultivated. During the latter days of French rule the expatriate community steadily dwindled, and by 1953 virtually all had gone.

Immediately after the French were defeated at Dien Bien Phu in May 1954, Vietnamese forces razed a large number of Sapa's French buildings to the ground. More destruction was subsequently wrought by the Chinese, who briefly occupied the town in 1979 before being driven out again.

Since the 1990s, Sapa's population of a little more than 3,000 has been swelled by tourists, attracted by the spectacular mountain scenery, the comfortable climate and the lively weekend market. Their presence brings in much-needed revenue.

WHAT TO SEE
SATURDAY MARKET

Hmông, Dao and other minorities come to Sapa's weekly market to trade, and the Hmông, normally very reticent, have been the first to seize the commercial opportunities presented by tourism. They are engaging but persistent vendors of hand-loomed indigo shirts, trousers, skull caps and other handicrafts such as little brass and bamboo mouth-harps. The women, their hands stained purple by dye, sit on street corners stitching while they wait for a foreigner who might buy their clothing. Meanwhile, the girls roam in groups, bracelets, earrings and necklaces jingling as they walk, and urge their jewelry on passersby, while the little ones sing *muat mot cai di* ("buy one") to a usually responsive audience of visitors.

🕐 Sat 6–6

DRAGON'S JAW HILL

There are outstanding views of the town and valley from the top of Dragon's Jaw Hill (Nui Ham Rong), immediately above Sapa town center. A path winds its way through some interesting limestone outcrops, miniature grottoes, an orchid garden, a peach garden and an ethnic village as it nears the summit.

🕒 Daily 6–6 ✋ Adult 30,000d, child (5–16) 5,000d

SAPA CHURCH

The slate-gray church that sits in the heart of Sapa was originally built in 1930 but was destroyed just 22 years later during hostilities with the occupying French—a troop of French artillerymen were engaged in shelling the adjacent building, in which Viet Minh troops were billeted.

In the churchyard are the tombs of two former priests, including that of Father Thinh, who was brutally murdered. In 1952, Father Thinh confronted a monk named Giao Linh, who had been discovered having an affair with a nun at the Ta Phin seminary. Giao Linh obviously took great exception to the priest's interference, for shortly after this, when Father Thinh's congregation arrived at Sapa church for Mass one foggy November morning, they discovered his decapitated body lying next to the altar.

🕒 Daily 6pm for services, Sat 1.30pm

LAO CHAI AND TA VAN

A guided round-trip of 12 miles (20km), taking in the beautiful scenery along the way, starts by heading out past the Auberge guesthouse in a southeasterly direction. A track leads from the right side of the road down to the valley floor and then across the river by a footbridge, before continuing through the rice fields into the Black Hmông village of Lao Chai. Here you can observe a style of rural life that is led in reasonable prosperity. There is terracing here on an awesome scale, in places with more than 100 steps, the result of centuries of labor to convert the steep slopes into level fields that can be flooded to grow rice. Ta Van, a village of the Zay, is 1 mile (1.6km) farther on.

✚ 282 B2

Above The hills and valley are often
shrouded in mist

INFORMATION

✚ 282 B2 🚌 Connections with Hanoi, Mai Chau, Hoa Binh, Dien Bien Phu, Lai Chau ✈ Na San Airport, 12 miles (20km) southeast 🍴 Near the bridge, along Tinh Doi Street 🚗 Private tours from Hanoi

TIPS

» Son La makes a useful stopover between Hanoi and Dien Bien Phu.
» The Son La Provincial Museum (5,000d) is on Bao Tang Tinh Son La, Youth Hill, just off Highway 6 and near the middle of town.

Above *A minority group in colorful traditional costume*

SON LA

Hill villages surround the provincial capital, which is acquiring gleaming new government buildings. Town sites recall the colonial past and walks lead to natural beauty spots.

The road to Son La passes several particularly attractive Black Thái and Muong villages, each with a suspension footbridge and hydraulic works. Mini hydroelectric generators on the river supply houses with enough power to run a light or television, and water power is also used to husk and mill rice. Cuc Dua village, 52 miles (84km) from town, is highly photogenic, with a bridge spanning the incised river in which fish traps are set and children swim. Up to 100,000 people were displaced in preparation for the building of a dam in the valley, which began producing electricity in 2011.

IN AND AROUND TOWN

Son La began to develop in the 18th century, and in the 19th century was part of the territory controlled by Deo Van Tri, the Black Thái chieftain. In 1888 a French garrison was established here, and in response to subsequent uprisings, the French established detention units, known to the Thái as *huon mut* ("dark houses"), in the area. In 1908 a large penitentiary was built to incarcerate resistance leaders from the northwest and other regions. The Son La Provincial Museum (tel 022-3852022, daily 7–11, 1.30–5.30) is, in fact, the town's old French penitentiary, constructed in 1908, damaged in 1909, bombed in 1952, and now partially rebuilt for tourists. The original dungeon and tiny cells, complete with food-serving hatches and leg irons, can be seen, as well as an exhibition relating the history of the place and the key individuals incarcerated here. The first secretary of the Vietnamese Communist Party, Le Duan, was kept here between 1931 and 1933. The Black Thái village of Ban Co and the Coong caves are nearby (▷ 118–119).

TAM COC

The highlight of a visit here is an enchanting boat ride up the little Ngo Dong River through the three caves, part of the beehive scenery created by limestone towers. Their exact form varies seasonally; when flooded the channel disappears and some caves may be flooded. In the dry season the shallow river meanders between fields of golden rice. Women punt pitch-and-resin tubs through the tunnels or row with their feet.

The villagers have a rowing rota and supplement their earnings by selling visitors embroidery work. On a busy day the scene is like a two-way, nose-to-tail procession, so try to visit early in the day.

⊞ 283 D3 ✉ 6 miles (10km) south of Ninh Binh, west of Highway 1 ⯑ Tran Hung Dao Road, Ninh Binh, Hoa Lu District ☎ 030-3875158 ✋ 30,000d plus 40,000d for the boat ride ⬛ Private tours from Hanoi

TAM DAO

This relaxing hill station, developed by the French from 1902, lies high in the Tam Dao mountains north of Hanoi and is reached by a circuitous route. It is an excellent base for walks and birdwatching, and has a cooler climate than the city.

The resort of Tam Dao lies within a beautiful mountain range that bears the same name, a chain of three peaks that constitute a natural border between Vinh Phu and Thai Nguyen provinces. Protruding from the clouds, the three peaks are said to resemble the "three islands" of Tam Dao's name.

The former colonial hill station has a stunning location at an altitude of 3,050ft (930m) above sea level, lying in a giant rock bowl seemingly bitten out of the side of the mountain. Steep cliffs soar all around it, thickly clothed in a glorious jungle of trees entangled with lianas; the early morning mists and clouds slowly burn off as the sun rises, and the forest comes alive with the sound of birdsong, animal cries and the constant humming of insects. On a good day there are

clear views over the plains below. Lost in the overgrowth are colonial remains—crumbling walls, forlorn bridges, and enticing gateways.

Construction of the town started in 1904. The then governor general resided in an eight-roofed mansion here, and the 130-room Metropole Hotel was busy with a steady stream of expatriates coming to Tam Dao to escape the punishing summer heat of the Red River Delta. Subsequently, the town was almost completely destroyed during the First Indochina War of 1945–54, and now little remains, other than the foundations of old villas and the shell of the old church building (which is now the clubhouse of the Tam Dao Trades Union).

⊞ 282 C2 ⯑ 53 miles (85km) north of Hanoi ✋ 50,000d levied on all visitors' vehicles at checkpoint on Highway 28 🍴 Several, serving local dishes ⬛ Tours from Hanoi

VUON QUOC GIA BA BE

Vietnam's eighth national park, Ba Be National Park, designated in 1992, covers 57,674 acres (23,340ha) on the eastern shore of beautiful Ba Be Lake. Another 19,964 acres (8,079ha) provide an encircling buffer zone. It protects about 417 plant species, 100 butterfly species, 23 amphibian and reptile species and 110 bird species. Of 50 species of mammal, 10 are

seriously endangered, including the Tonkinese snub-nosed monkey (Rhinopithecus avunculus) and the black gibbon (Hylobates concolor). The park has a number of villages inhabited by the Tày, Red Dao, Dao Tien (Coin Dao) and White Hmông ethnic minorities.

⊞ 282 C1 ⯑ 27 miles (44km) west of Na Phac on Highway 279 ☎ 0281-3894026 ✋ 10,000d plus 1,000d insurance per person and 20,000d per car ⬛ Range of English-language guided tours. Private tours arranged from Hanoi

VUON QUOC GIA CUC PHUONG

www.cucphuongtourism.com
This area of deeply cut limestone (Cuc Phuong National Park) reaches peaks of 2,600ft (800m) and is covered by 54,300 acres (22,000ha) of tropical forest. In April and May the park (▷ 120–121) is cloaked in vast swarms of green and yellow butterflies.

The Endangered Primate Rescue Center (tel 030-848002; www.primatecenter.org; daily tours every 30 minutes 9–4) has langurs, lorises and gibbons.

⊞ 282 C3 ⯑ Ninh Binh Tourism Administration, Tran Hung Dao Road, Ninh Binh ☎ 030-3875158 ✋ Adult 20,000d, child 10,000d. Rescue Center: 20,000d ⬛ Tours arranged by Cuc Phuong Tourism

Below Colonial Tam Dao hill station has a glorious mountain setting

INFORMATION

www.halongtravelguide.com

⊞ 283 E3 🛈 Information and Tourist Guide Center, Halong Bay portside

☎ 33-3847481 🚉 Bai Chay station, Halong City; connections with Hanoi

🚢 Haiphong; then bus or ferry

🍴 Range of restaurants in Halong City

🚤 Boat tours from Halong City, Cat Ba Town; tours include caves. Private tours from Hanoi

Above *Limestone rocks and emerald-green waters at Halong Bay*
Opposite *Junks in Cat Ba harbor*

INTRODUCTION

Halong Bay is a sparkling, emerald-green bay dotted with sailing junks and thousands of forested limestone towers. Cat Ba, home to the rare white-headed langur, is the largest island in an archipelago of hundreds.

Spectacular Halong Bay (Vinh Ha Long) and its 3,000 islands cover 580 square miles (1,500sq km), spreading to the Chinese border. At dusk the stars and lights of moored junks ripple across the deep blue water in unearthly silence. There are two bases from which to explore the bay—Halong City or Cat Ba—but many opt for all-inclusive trips from Hanoi, where tourist cafés and operators also offer tours of the bay with one night in Bai Chay. This is the prettier, western side of town (officially Halong City West), which is divided in two by the bay waters. Halong City East is the main port and ferry dock. Full- or half-day trips of the bay can be taken from Cat Ba. The islands of the bay are separated by a broad channel. East are the smaller outcrops of Bai Tu Long, and west are the larger islands, with caves and secluded beaches.

TIPS

» Cat Ba is at its wettest July through August and its driest and coolest (59°F/15°C) November through January.
» Hotel rates double during the school summer break, May through September.
» From July through October leeches are a problem and mosquitoes are at their worst. If trekking in the national park, bring leech socks and plenty of insect repellent. Collars, long sleeves and long pants (trousers) are advisable.

Halong means "descending dragon," a reference to the enormous beast that is said to have careered into the sea at this point, cutting the bay from the rocks. According to another myth, the islands are dragons, sent by the gods to impede the progress of an invasion flotilla. The area was, in fact, the site of two famous sea battles, in the 10th and 13th centuries (▷ 29). It is now a UNESCO World Heritage Site.

Geologically the tower-karst scenery of Halong Bay is the product of millions of years of chemical action and river erosion working on the limestone to produce a pitted landscape. At the end of the last ice age, when glaciers melted, the sea level rose and inundated the area, turning hills into islands. Tools and bones indicate that Cat Ba Island was occupied by humans 6,000 to 7,000 years ago. The population is now about 12,000 and is concentrated in the south.

WHAT TO SEE

CAVES

Vietnamese poets and artists have long drawn inspiration from the crooked islands, seeing the forms of monks and gods in the rock faces, and dragons' lairs and fairy lakes in the depths of the caves. The more spectacular of these are Hang Hanh, 1 mile (1.6km) long and full of stalagmites and stalactites. Hang Luon is another flooded cave, which leads to the hollow core in a doughnut-shaped island. It can be swum or navigated by coracle. Hang Dau Go is where a famous Vietnamese general, Tran Hung Dao, stored wooden stakes in 1288, prior to studding them in the bed of the Bach Dang River to destroy a 400-strong Mongol-Chinese invasion fleet. Hang Thien Cung is a hanging cave, a short 165ft (50m) haul above sea level, with dripping stalactites, stumpy stalagmites and solid rock pillars.
✋ All caves 15,000d

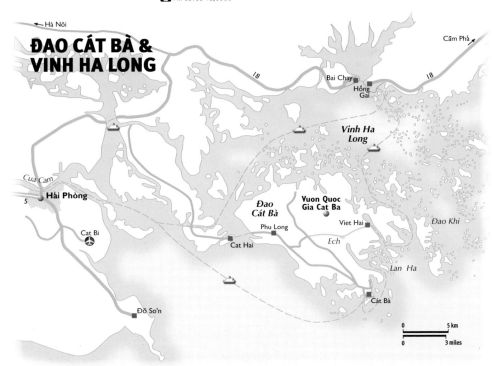

DAO CAT BA

Cat Ba Island occupies a stunning setting in the south of Halong Bay. Much of the island and the seas around are designated a national park (▷ below) and, while perhaps not quite teeming with wildlife, it is pleasantly wild and green. Cat Ba's remoteness has been steadily eroded (it only got electricity in 1999) and it is now a handy weekend break for many Hanoians. Despite the growth of karaoke-loving weekenders, it remains an attractive place. Best of all it is a springboard into the surrounding waters of Halong Bay and an increasingly popular alternative to Halong City. Outside the town there are only a few small villages, and perhaps the greatest pleasure is to rent a motorcycle and explore. The islands around Cat Ba are larger than the outcrops of Halong Bay and generally more dramatic.

🚌 Service to Phu Long 🚤 Connections from Haiphong 🍴 In Cat Ba Town

VUON QUOC GIA CAT BA

Roughly half of Cat Ba Island forms Cat Ba National Park, established in 1986. Of this area a third consists of coast and inland waters. The park is home to 109 bird and animal species, and of particular importance is the world's last remaining troop (about 200) of white-headed langurs. These elusive monkeys are rarely spotted, and then only from the sea, as they inhabit wild and remote cliff habitats. There are also several types of rare macaque (rhesus, pig-tailed and red-faced) and moose deer. Vegetation ranges from mangrove swamps in sheltered bays and densely wooded hollows to high, rugged limestone crags sprouting caps of hardy willows. The marine section of the park is no less bountiful; the high economic value of its fish and crustacea populations keeps the local fishing fleet hard at work and prosperous.

☎ 031-2216350 🕐 Park office: daily 7–5.30 ✋ 15,000d–35,000d depending on distance covered 🎫 Park guide: US$5 for half a day, US$10 for full day. Guide for single (one-way) trips to sites of interest in the park: 50,000d–100,000d depending on distance

Above *A lone farmer working in a paddy field on Cat Ba Island*
Below *Canoeing at sunset in Halong Bay*

THAM COONG AND BAN CO

This walk from the former French military outpost of Son La (▷ 112; ✚ 282 B2) takes you through magnificent highland scenery, two caves and the fascinating Black Thái settlement of Ban Co.

THE WALK
Distance: 3 miles (4.7km)
Allow: 2 hours 35 minutes
Start/end at: Son La

HOW TO GET THERE
Son La is 192 miles (310km) northwest of Hanoi.

TIP
» You may like to take a flashlight for your visit to the cave.

★ Son La (▷ 112), now a provincial capital, was a military outpost during French colonial rule.

Start the walk 2 miles (3km) north of the heart of Son La, at the turning to the caves on the main road (Hoa Ban Street). Opposite a fuel station there's a turning to the left (west) and a signpost marking the caves (Tham Coong). Take this path. Almost immediately, on your right, is a house with a white decoration on its roof.

❶ The curious wooden decoration on this house is shaped into multiple white blobs. This signifies that the family here has produced a lot of male children. Along the path you will see the bright red leaves of poinsettia (Euphorbia pulcherrima).

Continue across a metal bridge where there is a water park on the right. Just after here, look to the far left to see a tiled roof with a similar decoration to the previous house.

❷ The roof decoration has one white blob, showing that this family has one male child. To your left are glistening green rice paddies.

Take a path to the left, by a concrete post, a wooden one-room house surrounded by a fence, and a gray house. The canal is to your right.

At the foot of a tall hill, there is a house on your right with domestic animals in its yard. You need to climb straight up the hill to a concrete walkway. At the walkway, turn left onto a path that leads to the wet cave (you may be allowed to peer into the wet cave but you cannot enter as it is fenced off).

To reach the dry cave, you have a further climb up a limestone face. A woman controlling the passage, at the foot of the limestone face, will point you in the right direction (you pay 15,000d to enter). Clamber up the face for a few minutes to reach the entrance to the dry cave.

❸ The dry cave is 262ft (80m) deep and is full of stalactites; although it is fairly light, there are darker areas around the route and so you may wish to bring a flashlight. At its farthest point there is a dangling rope from which to drink water. Return to the foot of the limestone face and enjoy the view.

❹ Below are fields, ponds and streams, stilt houses, gardens and hibiscus hedgerows. Fish are bred in the ponds, which are covered with watercress *(salad soong)* and what looks like a red algae bloom, but is actually a floating weed *(beo hoa dau)*, fed to ducks and pigs.

Retrace your steps and look for the fish farm just before the water company offices, close to the main road. Turn right onto the main Hoa Ban Street and walk for half a mile (1km) before turning off the main road. This left turning is marked by a road sign on the right-hand side marked "250m." At this point there is a coffin-maker's workshop and a phone booth. Next to the turning is a billboard.

❺ The billboard at the turning translates as: "Protect the forest, plant more to reduce deforestation."

Turn left off Hoa Ban Street toward the Black Thái (Thái Den) village of Ban Co. After 330 yards (300m) you arrive in the village.

❻ Ban Co is a large, fairly typical Thái village. Thái villages *(ban)* have 40 to 50 stilt houses shaded by fruit trees and surrounded by verdant paddy fields. The Thái are excellent custodians of the land. Cabbage, spinach and pole beans are all grown in the fields, and you may also see people fishing.

Walk to the left for a short way and turn right up a concrete path (shortly before you reach the maroon and white government building) between a white house with Chinese symbols on the upper floor, a gray lamppost and house with a gray corrugated-iron roof (with a brick wall on the left). Return to the main street.

Walk a little farther to see the villagers at work, and water buffaloes and horses eating. Turn back the way you came (toward the main Hoa Ban Street) when the

road veers to the right by a big gray rock opposite a bamboo gate. Hoa Ban Street leads back into Son La.

WHEN TO GO
The best time for this walk is late afternoon, when the light is at its best and villagers return home.

WHERE TO EAT
There is a café and *bia hoi* on the main road to the left of the exit from the caves and a snack stall to the right. There are several *bia hoi* opposite the turn off to Ban Co.

THE THÁI
The Thái number around one million and are the second-largest ethnic minority in Vietnam. There are two main sub-groups: the Black Thái (Thái Den), settled mainly in Son La, Lai Chan, Lao Cai and Yen Bai provinces, and the White Thái (Thái Trang), found predominantly in Hoa Binh, Son La, Thanh Hoa and Vinh Phu provinces.

Opposite *Mountains near Co Noi*
Above *Lush green fields outside Ban Co*
Left *A Black Thái woman in Son La*

REGIONS THE NORTH • WALK

CUC PHUONG NATIONAL PARK

This tour takes you to the Cuc Phuong National Park (Vuon Quoc Gia Cuc Phuong; ▷ 113, ✛ 282 C3), where you can see numerous limestone caves, Vuon Thuc Vat Botanic Gardens and a mysterious tree said to change color if poison touches it.

THE TOUR
Distance: 84 miles (135km)
Allow: 8–10 hours
Start/end at: Ninh Binh

HOW TO GET THERE
Ninh Binh is 58 miles (93km) south of Hanoi on Highway 1. It's served by regular buses from Hanoi's southern bus terminal and by train from Hanoi. To drive to Cuc Phuong National Park, either rent a motorcycle or a car and driver for the day (up to 3.5 hours from Hanoi). This can be arranged through a tour agency in Hanoi or Ninh Binh or at the Viet Hung Hotel.

★ Ninh Binh is a useful base for visiting other sights in the north. It is the capital of the province of Ninh Binh.

Head west from Ninh Binh along the road to Hoa Binh. After 7.5 miles (12km), at Gian Khau Bridge,

turn left to Nho Quan. At Nho Quan follow the sign (in English) to Cuc Phuong National Park for a further 9.5 miles (15km) to the park's main gate. Allow about 90 minutes to reach the park's Visitor Center by the main gate.

❶ Buy your entry tickets here (20,000d) and a separate ticket for the Rescue Center (20,000d): A brochure offering an introduction to the main sights of the park, as well as a color map, is included in the price of the ticket. They can also make arrangements for lodgings and organize guided treks.

Park near the Visitor Center and walk back to visit the Endangered Primate Rescue Center, on the right-hand side of the road just before the park gate.

❷ The Endangered Primate Rescue Center (▷ 113) is definitely a

high point of this tour. The center cares for local animals saved from hunters or otherwise injured. It also promotes breeding and conservation programs, and tries to rehabilitate endangered primates for release into the wild. It's a good place to see animals that might otherwise be difficult to locate in the park. The center usually houses several species of langur, as well as gibbons, lorises and monkeys. There is also a 5-acre (2ha) enclosure used to prepare rescued animals for return to their natural environment.

Pass through the main park entrance and almost immediately turn left to visit the Vuon Thuc Vat Botanic Gardens.

❸ The botanic gardens showcase local flora, carefully marked with both Vietnamese and Latin names. Of almost 2,000 identified plant species, more than 400 have

Opposite *A bridge spans Mac Lake in Cuc Phuong National Park*
Below *An orchid in bloom*

useful medicinal qualities, while 300 may be used as sources of human nutrition. A number of animals native to Cuc Phuong may be seen at quite close quarters in the gardens, including deer, civets, langurs and gibbons.

Continue your drive into the park along a narrow but well-surfaced road. After 1 mile (2km) on the right, pass Khu Mo Mac (Mac Lake Place), which has waterside cabin accommodations, a restaurant and a souvenir shop. Continue for a further 4 miles (7km) until you reach a signposted track on the right-hand side of the road leading to one of the largest caves, the Cave of the Prehistoric Man (Doong Nguoi Xua).

❹ The Cave of the Prehistoric Man has a shop where you can rent a flashlight (5,000d) to take inside the cave. Walk along a concrete bridge, then climb 150ft (45m) by ladder to reach the lower cave. Inside there are three sections. The first, where relics of prehistoric humans were discovered, is large, bright and airy. The second is dark and humid, and is inhabited by numerous bats. The third is distinguished by some beautiful stalactites.

Return to the main road and drive a further 9.5 miles (15km) northwest until you arrive at Khu Trung Tam Park Center (which has some souvenir shops, a restaurant and an information center). On the way you will pass a signposted track to the left leading to the Cay Dang Co Thu thousand-year-old tree. About 6 miles (10km) farther on, as you approach Khu Trung Tam Park Center, another tree of venerable age, Cay Vu Huong, stands close by the road on the left-hand side.

The surfaced road comes to an end at Khu Trung Tam, so it's time to park your vehicle and begin to walk.

❺ A circular trek starts from Car Park B, and it will take about five hours to complete the walk. From the rest area, look to the right where you will see a sign for Cay Cho Ngan Nam, the "Thousand Year Old Tree." The cleared track leads for 4.5 miles (7.5km) through dense jungle vegetation, past the 157ft-high (48m) tree, before winding back to Khu Trung Tam. Give yourself three hours to get there and back.

After refreshments and a rest at Khu Trung Tam, head back to the park entrance and retrace your way to Ninh Binh (continue 9.5 miles/15km to Nho Quan; turn right and continue east past the Gian Khau Bridge to Ninh Binh).

Or, if you are feeling energetic, take a guided trek (a guide is compulsory; US$20) for 11 miles (18km) to the northwestern limits of the national park, where you can stay overnight in Kanh Muong, a Muong village.

❻ The trek to Kanh Muong is pretty strenuous, and you should take plenty of liquid to drink on the way. About 5 miles (8km) into the trek, you pass Cay Sau Co Thu, another magnificent old tree, which stands to the right of the track. The Muong minority are the original inhabitants of this area and subsisted by hunting. At the village, you can see their traditional pillar houses, waterwheels and brocade looms. Accommodations (which must be arranged in advance) are simple but adequate, and during the stay visitors will be entertained by displays of the traditional Muong *gong* festival.

In the morning, make the 11-mile (18km) return trek to Khu Trung Tam, starting early to avoid the mid-morning heat. Collect your vehicle and head back to the park entrance. Continue 9.5 miles (15km) to Nho Quan. Turn right and continue east past the Gian Khau Bridge to Ninh Binh.

WHEN TO GO
The best time to visit is winter (November through February): It is relatively dry, there are fewer insects (including mosquitoes) and the leeches are less active. In summer, there are a lot of insects, reptiles, flowers and butterflies—the latter especially in April and May. The best way to get around the park is by hiring a bicycle for US$5 from the Visitor Center.

WHERE TO EAT
There are two restaurants, one at the main gate and another 1 mile (2km) into the park at Mac Lake. There are set menus and à la carte with prices ranging from US$8 to US$14. Simple vegetarian dishes are available.

WHERE TO STAY
There are comfortable cabins at Mac Lake for US$25 per night. A room in a pillar house at Kanh Muong village is US$7. A room in a pillar house at the Park Center is US$12.

PLACES TO VISIT
VUON THUC VAT BOTANIC GARDENS
🕐 Daily 9–4.30 💵 10,000d

CAT BA ISLAND
CAT BA VENTURES
www.catbaventures.com
Take a trek of 2 to 3 hours through the Kim Giao forest in Cat Ba National Park, with the option of spending a whole day in the park. A one-day tour of Cat Ba is also possible, visiting a mangrove forest and Thien Long cave.
✉ Phong Lan Hotel ☎ 031-3888605

FLIGHTLESS BIRD
The Flightless Bird is on the seafront, a short distance to the left of the jetty. It is run by New Zealander Graeme Moore, and as the only real pub in town is a popular meeting point for travelers. There's also a book exchange.
✉ Seafront on Cat Ba Island ☎ 031-3888517 ⊙ Mon–Sat 5.30pm–midnight

HALONG BAY
KAYAKING AND JUNK CRUISES
Kayaking and junk cruises are now regular features in Halong Bay and Lan Ha Bay, especially in the summer. They're best joined via a reputable tour operator in Hanoi.

MAI CHAU
MAI CHAU ETHNIC MINORITY DANCE TROOP
Visitors to Mai Chau are entertained by White Thái dancing, which culminates in communal drinking of sweet, sticky rice wine through straws. The troupe, wearing traditional clothes, performs most nights in Lac in a large stilt house.
✉ Lac village ✋ Admission as part of tour or small contribution

SAPA
DRAGON'S JAW HILL
At the top of Dragon's Jaw Hill there are daily performances of ethnic minority dancing with live music. A flautist and percussionists playing gongs, drums, maracas and cymbals accompany dancing boys and girls, who act out local scenes. The performances last an hour and the admission fee includes a drink.
⊙ Dragon's Jaw Hill: daily 6–6. Performances: daily 9.15am and 3pm
✋ Dragon's Jaw Hill: 15,000d (child 5,000d). Performances: 10,000d

HANDSPAN
www.handspan.com
Handspan organizes mountain bicycling tours to the villages and markets around Sapa and the national parks, lasting from one to three days. It also offers a one-day trip from Hanoi involving an initial coach journey of more than two hours, followed by an hour's cycling and, after lunch, a shorter cycle before a one-hour sampan trip in Halong Bay. An alternative trip, departing from Hanoi, starts with a one-hour coach ride and then three hours of cycling along the Red River.
✉ 8 Cau May Street, Sapa (78 Ma May Street, Hanoi ☎ 04-39262828) ☎ 020-3872110 ✋ A 2-day/3-night trek is US$290 for two people

TAU BAR

The long bar at this place beneath the Tau Hotel is made from a single tree trunk, and it's worth a beer just to be able to see it. The minimalist, subterranean venue, with white walls, bar stools, a dart board and pool table, is welcoming and relaxing.

✉ Tau Hotel, 42 Cau May Street, Sapa ☎ 020-3871322 ⏰ 8pm–late

TOPAS

www.topastravel.vn
Topas offers bicycling and trekking excursions. Bicycling trips range from half a day to eight days and the price includes rental of mountain bicycles, English- or French-speaking guides, water and fruit. Trekking options range from an easy half-day walk to a demanding three-day trip through Ban Ho valley to Jao Cai. Topas also offers some fairly demanding hiking and climbing trips in the Sapa region.

✉ 20 Cau May Street, Sapa ☎ 020-3871331 (✉ 52 To Ngoc Van Hanoi ☎ 04-37151005) 🖐 Bicycling: from US$42 per person (minimum two people) for six hours and including lunch

VICTORIA BEAUTY SALON AND HEALTH CENTER

www.victoriahotels-asia.com
The health center offers everything from traditional massage to reflexology. The US$37 Victoria Massage package is a combination of head, body and foot massages, plus a 10-minute massage with special natural oil.

✉ Victoria Hotel, Sapa ☎ 020-3871522 ⏰ Daily 8am–10pm

WILD ORCHID

There are three outlets of this shop on Sapa's main street. They all sell attractive, well-made wall hangings with embroidered motifs, for around US$15. Cushion covers, clothes and a range of other embroidered souvenir gifts are also available.

✉ Cau May Street, Sapa ☎ 020-3871665 ⏰ Daily 8–8

FESTIVALS AND EVENTS

JANUARY–MAY
THE PERFUME PAGODA FESTIVAL

The Perfume Pagoda Festival, held at the Perfume Pagoda (▷ 102), focuses on the worship of the Goddess of Mercy. There are dragon dances and a royal barge sails on the Yen River.

✉ Huong Son Mountain, 37 miles (60km) southwest of Hanoi ⏰ Sixth day of first lunar month to end of third lunar month (starting 28 Jan 2012)

APRIL
THE HUNG KINGS' TEMPLES FESTIVAL

Visitors from all over Vietnam descend on the Hung Kings' Temples on the Red River floodplain (▷ 103) for this two-week celebration, focusing on the worship of ancestors. The place bursts with vendors, food stands and fairground activities. There are swan boats, incense, drums, bamboo swings, wrestling matches, sword dances and also singing.

✉ Viet Tri, Vinh Phu Province ⏰ Tenth day of third lunar month (starting 31 Mar 2012)

AUGUST–SEPTEMBER
DO SON BUFFALO FIGHTING FESTIVAL

This festival, held in Haiphong and celebrating the God of the Sea, begins with an offering of a buffalo, a pig and some sticky rice. Then 12 men carrying a palanquin lead a procession of musicians, six buffaloes and a further 12 men dressed in red, who wave flags to signal the start of the buffalo fight. The head of the winning buffalo is thrown into the sea.

✉ Haiphong City (Do Son) ⏰ Ninth day of eighth lunar month (24 Sep 2012, 19 Sep 2013)

Below *The Perfume Pagoda Festival*

EATING

PRICES AND SYMBOLS

The restaurants are listed alphabetically (excluding Le, La, Il and The). The prices given are the average for a two-course lunch (L) and a three-course dinner (D) for one person, without drinks. The wine price is for the least expensive bottle.

For a key to the symbols, ▷ 2.

DIEN BIEN PHU

LIEN TUOI

This local restaurant is the only real alternative eatery to the Muong Thanh Hotel (▷ right and 126–126), and is next to Hill A1 (▷ 104). Dishes are served in a vast, impersonal dining room, and cover a wide range, from banana salad to venison and turtle stews. There are no fewer than 14 fish dishes, which include steamed fish with beer, steamed cuttlefish, and steamed sweet-and-sour shrimp. To accompany your meal you can take your pick of soft drinks, a selection of beer and some rice wines.

✉ 64 Muong Thanh 8 Street, Dien Bien Phu ☎ 023-3824919 🕐 Daily 7am–10pm ✋ L 80,000d, D 100,000d, Rice wine 40,000d

MUONG THANH HOTEL

The Muong Thanh Hotel is considered to have the best restaurant in town. It is housed in a massive, bamboo barn, where the tables are set out in long rows, medieval style. The building is open-sided and well ventilated by numerous fans. Dishes are varied and should satisfy all tastes, with several types of omelets for breakfast, Dien Bien Phu spring rolls (mushrooms, meat, onion, carrot and mayonnaise) for starters, spaghetti and other types of pasta, chicken, grilled duck with honey, boar, pork, frog and curry as main dishes, as well as tofu dishes and seafood, which is recommended.

✉ 25 Him Lam-TP, Dien Bien Phu ☎ 023-3810043 🕐 Daily 6am–10pm ✋ L 65,000d, D 115,000d, Wine 250,000d

HAIPHONG

VAN TUE

The exterior might seem too brazen for its own good and the street-level dining area will not appeal to everyone but check out the more congenial basement for a meal. The menu is large and a special draw is the home-brewed, Czech-style beer.

✉ 1a Hoang Dieu Street, Haiphong ☎ 031-3746338 🕐 Daily 10am–11pm ✋ L 155,000d, D 300,000d, Beer 30,000d

SAPA

BAGUETTE & CHOCOLAT

The Baguette & Chocolat is an appealing place with a pleasant

seating area. In addition to the pastries, breakfasts, sandwiches, pasta, pizzas and dishes such as sautéed venison with lemongrass and sautéed Chinese noodles with shrimp are served. Caramelized apple with honey and cinnamon or a selection from the cake cabinet will complete your meal. You can also buy picnic kits from 65,000d. Profits from the sale of the cakes and pastries go toward the Hoa Sua School, which trains local young young women of ethnic minorities to work in hotels and restaurants.
✉ Thac Bac Street, Sapa ☎ 020-3871766 🕐 Daily 7am–9pm 🖐 L 80,000d, D 120,000d, Wine 250,000d

BAMBOO BAR AND RESTAURANT

This spacious hotel restaurant has great views of Mount Fansipan. The extensive menu includes some great breakfast possibilities; the delightfully thin pancakes with chocolate sauce are a must. For dinner, try the special set meals, which offer as many as five courses. Song and dance performances are given by local Hmông groups on weekend evenings.
✉ Cau May Street, Sapa ☎ 020-3871075 🕐 Daily 6.30am–11pm 🖐 L 60,000d, D 80,000d, Wine 180,000d

BON APPETIT

This friendly, central place serves a good mix of Western breakfasts, burgers, French baguette sandwiches, stews and a variety of Vietnamese dishes. The food is certainly aimed at a tourist clientele, so don't expect to find any unusual local dishes on the menu. Try their excellent spring rolls accompanied by a huge pile of edible leaves including mint, lettuce and cilantro (coriander). A small selection of desserts and cakes is on offer, changing on a daily basis.
✉ 25 Xuan Vien Street, Sapa ☎ 020-3872927 🕐 Daily 7.30am–10.30pm 🖐 L 110,000d, D 160,000d, Wine 170,000d

CAMELLIA

Reached through the main market, Camellia is a great place from which to watch local shoppers. The long menu has a full range of Vietnamese fare, which includes some twists on conventional themes. The beef steak is rather dry, but the grilled deer is good and the spicy Camellia salad is excellent. Warm, strong apple wine makes an ideal accompaniment. Recommended dishes include fried beef with garlic, ginger and celery, and stuffed squid with sausage in sauce; apple cake with honey is one of the best desserts. In winter the rice bowls are warmed. There is also a selection of Western food, including pizzas, hamburgers and healthy breakfasts.
✉ Cat Cat Street, Sapa ☎ 020-3871455 🕐 Daily 6.30am–11pm 🖐 L 110,000d, D 200,000d, Wine 230,000d

DELTA

Sapa's popular Italian restaurant serves good portions of pasta, pizzas and warming soups, as well as tasty seafood options such as calamari in *bianco*—squid, anchovies, capers and white wine. If you crave a hearty, meaty meal, order the Australian ribeye steak. There is a particularly good wine list. Photographs hang on the restaurant walls, and the tables are decorated with green and burgundy tablecloths. Delta is on the main road and offers good people-watching vantage points near the windows.
✉ 33 Cau May Street, Sapa ☎ 020-3871799 🕐 Daily 7.30am–10pm 🖐 L 150,000d, D 220,000d, Wine 230,000d

MIMOSA

A path leads off the main road to this small, slightly chaotic, family-run restaurant serving delicious local specialties and occupying an old house. Seating is cozy and comfortable indoors or fresh and airy on the small terrace. A long menu of good Western and Asian dishes should satisfy all palates. Mimosa is very popular; as a result, service can be excrutiatingly slow

during busy periods. The menu lists pizzas, pastas and burgers, as well as a range of dishes containing boar, deer, rabbit, frog, eel, chicken, beef and pork. To finish, try the homemade brownies or crêpes. There is also a reasonably varied vegetarian menu.
✉ 22 Cau May Street, Sapa ☎ 020-3871377 🕐 Daily 8am–11pm, until midnight during high season 🖐 L 90,000d, D 100,000d, Wine 250,000d

THE RED DRAGON PUB

The Red Dragon is furnished like an English tearoom, complete with faux-Tudor beams and checked tablecloths. The friendly owners serve food that will appeal to homesick Brits, including a variety of teas, full English cooked breakfasts, baked potatoes and shepherd's pie. In the pub upstairs, which has a small balcony, you can sup beer or strawberry wine and admire the outstanding valley views. Christmas lunch here is a must.
✉ 21 Muong Hoa Street, Sapa ☎ 020-3872085 🕐 Daily 8am–11pm (bar from 11am, food until 9.30pm) 🖐 L 130,000d, D 180,000d, Wine 260,000d

TA VAN

www.victoriahotels-asia.com
Sitting high above Sapa is this first-class restaurant with three walls that have been replaced by glass doors, so that you can enjoy the views while you eat. A large, central, raised fireplace dominates this restaurant and warms the dining room on cold days. The set dinners for 272,000d are excellent value and provide a vast range of delicious options; a choice of 12 appetizers followed by 14 main course options such as seafood ragout with saffron sauce and grilled spare ribs Latino style with BBQ sauce. The eight dessert options include Brazilian coconut tart and chocolate mousse. The à la carte menu is no less inviting with grilled shrimp and T-bone steaks.
✉ Victoria Sapa Hotel, Sapa ☎ 020-3871522 🕐 Daily 6.30am–10pm 🖐 L 200,000d, D 300,000d, Wine 420,000d

Above *Princes hotel on Cat Ba Island*

PRICES AND SYMBOLS

The prices are for a double room for one night including breakfast, unless otherwise stated. All the hotels listed accept credit cards unless otherwise stated. Note that rates can vary widely throughout the year.

For a key to the symbols, ▷ 2.

CAT BA ISLAND
HOLIDAY VIEW

www.holidayviewhotel-catba.com
The 120 rooms of this efficiently managed hotel, close to Lan Ha bay and beaches, are spread out on 10 floors; most rooms enjoy fine views of the sea, with the rest facing the mountain. Individual air-conditioning is standard. There is a good restaurant, the Redsail, with an open-air terrace and various tours of Cat Ba can be organized at the efficient travel desk.
✉ 1/4 Street, Cat Ba Island ☎ 031-3887200 ✋ US$43–$75, including taxes ⓘ 120 ⬟

PRINCES

www.princeshotel-catba.com
Princes, opposite the hydrofoil ticket office, is currently the most comfortable and best-equipped hotel in Cat Ba. The airy, well-furnished rooms have satellite TV, bathrooms and hot water. The hotel has a laundry service, a lobby lounge and bar, Internet and e-mail access, and there is a pleasant open courtyard at the back.
✉ Nui Ngoc Road, Cat Ba Island ☎ 031-3888899 ✋ US$40–$50, excluding taxes ⓘ 80 rooms ⬟

CUC PHUONG NATIONAL PARK
NATIONAL PARK ACCOMMODATIONS

www.vietnamhotels.biz/cucphuonghotel
Cuc Phuong National Park has several types of accommodations —at the main gate (headquarters), half a mile (1km) from the gate, and at the park center, 12 miles (20km) from the gate. The headquarters' concrete cabins have twin beds, air-conditioning and private bathrooms; less expensive bungalows are available with shared bathrooms and ceiling fans. There are more cabins with private bathrooms and air-conditioning in the center, at a slightly higher rate, as well as wooden stilt houses with no facilities. In addition, you can arrange to camp at the headquarters and in the center, or organize homestays with ethnic minorities in the park.
✉ Nho Quan District, Ninh Binh Province ☎ 030-3848006 ✋ US$16–$40 ⓘ 6 bungalows ⬟

DIEN BIEN PHU
MUONG THANH HOTEL

Dien Bien Phu's best hotel is on the main thoroughfare, some distance from the major sights. All rooms are simply but adequately equipped and ranged around a large courtyard. At one side is the pool, incongruously surrounded by giant African animal sculptures and open to nonresidents for 10,000d. Other facilities include one of the few Western restaurants in town (which also serves Vietnamese food, ▷ 124), Internet access, a souvenir shop, bicycle rental, karaoke, a steam bath and fitness center, and Thai massage. Guests are given free transfers to the airport.

✉ 25 Him Lam-TP, Dien Bien Phu ☎ 023-3810038 👋 US$30–$43, including taxes 🛈 70 🏊 📺 💲

THUY ANH HOTEL
www.thuyanhhotel.com
In the very center of town, Thuy Anh Hotel has plain but clean rooms, a bar and a rooftop garden serving food. Train and bus tickets can be reserved here, cars and bicycles rented and tours arranged. Internet use is free for the higher-priced rooms.

✉ 55A Trung Han Sieu Street, Dien Bien Phu ☎ 030-3871602 👋 US$10–$45, including taxes 🛈 20 💲

HAIPHONG
HARBOUR VIEW
www.harbourviewvietnam.com
Haiphong's largest and most luxurious hotel occupies an elegant French colonial building, slightly out of the center but near the river. Rooms are comfortably and neutrally furnished and have coffee- and tea-making equipment, minibars, safe-deposit boxes, phones, in-house movies and cable TV. The hotel's two restaurants serve Vietnamese and international cuisine, with a daily buffet lunch starting at US$7, and laundry and baby-sitting services are also available.

✉ 4 Tran Phu Street, Haiphong ☎ 031-3827827 👋 US$75–$100, including taxes 🛈 122 📺 💲

HOTEL MONACO
Clean rooms in an inexpensive hotel make Hotel Monaco a place worth considering for a short stay. There is WiFi throughout the hotel and it

is a 10-minute walk to the harbor. Laundry service is available and tours can also be arranged through the hotel.

✉ 105 Dien Bien Phu, Haiphong ☎ 031-3746468 👋 US$25, including taxes 🛈 20 💲

HALONG
HA LONG 1
A shuttered, white French villa set among frangipani along the bay road out of town has been converted to a hotel. Rooms, some with a sea view, have TVs and minibars, and huge private bathrooms with tubs and bidets. The hotel has several restaurants serving Vietnamese and international food, shops, a travel agency and tennis courts.

✉ Halong Road, Bai Chay, Halong City ☎ 033-3846320 👋 US$75–$100, including taxes 🛈 23 🏊 💲

HALONG PLAZA
www.halongplaza.com
This joint Thai-Vietnamese venture has produced an excellent hotel with wonderful sea views, especially from upper floors. The 20-floor building is centrally placed, near the Bai Chay ferry station, and has a bar, a café and three highly rated restaurants serving international and Asian food. There are massage and sauna facilities, and laundry and valeting services. You can reserve a seat on the 300-passenger boat service here. Rooms are luxuriously designed and have vast private bathrooms, minibars, satellite TV and in-house movies, safe-deposit boxes and complimentary fresh fruit, tea and coffee.

✉ 8 Halong Road, Bai Chay, Halong City ☎ 033-3845810 👋 US$70–$100, including taxes 🛈 200 🏊 📺 💲

LAI CHAU
LAN ANH HOTEL
www.lananhhotel.com
The Lan Anh Hotel brings welcome respite in the hottest valley in northwest Vietnam. It has clean and comfortable rooms in stilt houses set around a courtyard. The staff

can organize hotel, bus and airline reservations, as well as jeep, car, moto and bicycle tours; boat trips along local rivers; and treks to Ban Cho, a White Thái village, and to White and Blue Hmông villages. The restaurant has a limited menu and is open from 6am to 9pm. The friendly manager, Thang, speaks English and French.

✉ Lai Chau ☎ 023-3852370 👋 US$20–$50, including taxes 🛈 56 💲

SAPA
AUBERGE DANG TRUNG
The biggest attraction at this hillside hotel is its flourishing garden, tended with pride by Mr. Dang Trung, the French-speaking owner. Sweet peas, honeysuckle, snapdragons and roses grow alongside subalpine flora and a collection of orchids. Rooms are simply furnished, but clean and bright, and have bathtubs, satellite TV and log fires in winter; those higher up are more expensive and have great views. Tours, flight reservations and vehicle rental can be arranged here. There is a laundry service and a restaurant.

✉ 7 Muong Hoa Street, Sapa ☎ 020-3871243 👋 US$28–$42, including taxes 🛈 30 rooms 💲

BAGUETTE & CHOCOLAT
This small hotel, restaurant and café (▷ 124–125), in a quiet part of downtown Sapa, is run as a training hotel offering placements in hotels and restaurants throughout Vietnam for local ethnic minority women. There are only two twin and two double rooms, each with a private shower unit, and the whole operation is well run and extremely clean and comfortable. Gas heaters are provided in winter. Downstairs there's a stylish restaurant and café, with a small boulangerie attached.

✉ Thac Bac Street, Sapa ☎ 020-3871766 👋 US$25–$30, including taxes 🛈 4

BAMBOO SAPA HOTEL
www.bamboosapahotel.com.vn
The very attractive views of mountains and valley from the

room balconies are the plus factor in this otherwise middle-of-the-road hotel. There is a restaurant with discounted prices between 3pm and 6pm. The more expensive deluxe bedrooms are more spacious than the superior rooms, but all are subject to an extra charge if you arrive early in the morning from the night train and wish to book in before 2pm.

✉ 18 Muong Hoa, Sapa ☎ 020-3871076 ✋ US$52–$95 🛏 63 💺

CAT CAT
www.catcathotel.com

Friendly owner Le Loan runs this tall complex of buildings perched on a hill with views of the Sapa valley and Mount Fansipan. Bedrooms are large and plain, with wooden floors and fireplaces, two double beds, bathtubs and very hot water. TVs are available on request. Try to book either room 209 or 309, as they have 240-degree mountain views. Guests can relax in swing chairs, have a massage and eat in the vegetarian restaurant. Half an hour's free Internet access is provided.

✉ Cat Cat Street, Sapa ☎ 020-3871946 ✋ US$27–$30, including taxes 🛏 32

CHA PA GARDEN
www.chapagarden.com

This is one of the better hotels in Sapa and definitely the smallest so expect a degree of personalized service in this renovated French villa. There is a pleasant restaurant with an open fireplace, as well as a garden area for breakfast or dinner in the open air. The bedrooms are heated in the winter. This hotel also boasts a spa.

✉ 23b Cau May Street, Sapa ☎ 020-387290 ✋ From US$72 🛏 4 💺

CHAU LONG
www.chaulonghotel.com

The hotel has an eye-catching location on the side of a hill and, like most of the hotels in Sapa, a free pickup from the railway station is organized for guests but unlike Chau Long they do not all offer

free Internet access. Most of the bedrooms are in a new wing but some of the prices can be steep and it is worth considering the old wing. There is a restaurant and a bar.

✉ 24 Dong Loi, Sapa ☎ 020-3871245 ✋ US$48–$155 🛏 75 💺

DARLING

The top bedroom of the Darling, with its curios—wooden bathtub and large, orange, layered bedside lamps—and vast terrace, enjoys the best view in town. A short walk from central Sapa, the hotel has cozy rooms with ethnic curtains, small balconies, private bathrooms with tubs, fireplaces, free tea, in-house movies, minibars and safe-deposit boxes. Car and motorcycle rental and Internet access are available. The slightly out-of-center location ensures that it is not usually as busy as other hotels.

✉ Thac Bac Street, Sapa ☎ 020-3871961 ✋ US$26–$41, including taxes 🛏 45 🏊 Indoor

MOUNTAIN VIEW HOTEL
www.mountainviewhotelsapa.com

The impressive views and interesting decor help to create an Alpine ambiance and the bedrooms are large; they do however vary in quality and it is advisable to have a look at several before making a decision—some guests have found mattresses less than firm. The place can be chilly in the winter but in summer the hotel earns its name.

✉ Cau May Street, Sapa ☎ 020-3871690 ✋ US$25–$55, including taxes 🛏 23

TOPAS ECO LODGE
www.topasecolodge.com

Adventure tour operator Topas has created an eco lodge perched on a plateau overlooking the Hoang Vien Valley, 11 miles (18km) from Sapa. Solar-powered, palm-thatched cabins, each with its own bathroom and porch, enjoy fantastic views over the valley, home to Red Dao and Tày minorities. Trekking, horseback-riding, mountain-biking and handicraft workshops are organized daily for guests.

✉ Office: 24 Muong Hoa Street, Sapa ☎ 020-3872404 ✋ US$89–$115 🛏 25

VICTORIA SAPA
www.victoriahotels-asia.com

This wooden villa, on a small hill overlooking the town and built in mountain chalet style, is the best hotel in Sapa. The exquisitely decorated, wooden-floored rooms have balconies or terraces at garden level, to take advantage of the spectacular views of Mount Fansipan, satellite TVs, in-house movies, safe-deposit boxes and minibars. In winter there are open fires in the bar and dining rooms. Guests have access to mountain bicycles, an indoor pool, sauna, massage, billiards, petanque and a floodlit tennis court. The hotel has private sleeper carriages on the train from Hanoi to Lao Cai. Packages are available on the web.

✉ Sapa ☎ 020-3871522 ✋ US$155–$235, excluding taxes 🛏 77 🏊 Indoor

SON LA
HOA BAN 2

A stuffed tiger welcomes you to the foyer of this small hotel, where the facilities are basic but comfortable. Rooms have two large beds (one king and one queen), TVs, phones and hot water, but only two of the rooms have bathtubs. There is no restaurant, but the hotel is close to local eateries.

✉ Group 6, Chieng Le Ward, Son La ☎ 022-3853408 ✋ US$17 🛏 16 💺

NHA KHACH UY BAN NHAN DAN TINH SON LA (PEOPLE'S COMMITTEE GUESTHOUSE)

This large hotel in a secluded position, signed Nha Khach, just off Highway 6, has been extended and upgraded, and now has 70 rooms, all with air-conditioning and fans, TVs and minibars. The restaurant serves a range of Vietnamese and Western food. Reservations by phone are necessary.

✉ Highway 6, Son La ☎ 022-3852080 ✋ US$20–$50, including taxes 🛏 40 💺

Opposite A luxury hotel bedroom

CENTRAL VIETNAM

Hundreds of miles long yet narrowing to less than 40 miles (65km) wide, central Vietnam attracts visitors of every kind. Here you will find the ancient sites of My Son, the imperial city of Huê and the old quarter of Hoi An with its peaceful riverside location, long sandy beaches on the west coast, a national park and cave system, the DMZ and Vinh Moc tunnels and some of Vietnam's finest food for everyone to try.

Cooler and rainier than the south, central Vietnam's mountains offer even cooler spots such as Dalat, where Vietnam's last emperor built his summer home, while the bizarre-looking Hang Nga's Crazy House offers some of the strangest accommodation you are likely to see.

Access to the area could hardly be easier with Danang Airport offering a quick entry, and Highway 1 and the railway offering slower but more scenic alternatives. Tour buses, minibuses, rented cars and, for the brave, motorcycles offer easy travel around the area. For really slow travel, there are leisurely boat rides along the tranquil Perfume River, past pagodas, the citadel and temples, taking in the simple age-old lifestyles of the people who live beside the river.

To the west, the mountains are home to ethnic tribal groups who welcome visitors, while for those who enjoy the bustle of city life Danang has urban sights and nightlife. Peaceful Hoi An, one of the four World Heritage Sites in this region, can fulfill all your handmade clothing and footwear needs while also offering a delightful sense of what life in the Vietnam of old must have been like.

BA NA

The rehabilitated Ba Na Hill Station has cool air and spectacular views, and is tucked into the hillside 4,000ft (1,200m) up Chua Mountain (Nui Chua). It was founded in 1902 by the French, whose villas have been restored and rebuilt. Some villas accept guests, but the area is fast being taken over by karaoke bars and similar establishments.
🔹 285 E7 ✉ 24 miles (38km) west of Danang ✋ 10,000d per person, 5,000d per motorcycle, 35,000d cable car ☛ Private tours from Huê, Danang and Hoi An 🔲🔲🔲🔲

BUON ME THUOT

This is a good Central Highlands base for visits to ethnic minority villages and to a national park, where elephants still roam and elephant treks are available.

Buon Me Thuot, unofficial capital of the Central Highlands, is on the Daklak Plateau at an altitude of about 3,300ft (1,000m), surrounded by plantations and large numbers of Montagnards, the ethnic hilltribes. Nearby is Yok Don National Park (▷ 160), where

rare white elephants are said to roam, and there are several minority villages where visitors can spend the night. Coffee has long been the mainstay of the local economy, and the fortunes of the area are highly dependent on the price of the bean.

The Museum of Cultural Heritage on Nguyen Du Street (daily 7.30–5), in Bao Dai's old palace, contains a limited collection of clothes, tools and other objects of the various minority groups that live in the area. In Buon Me Thuot Prison (daily 7.30–5) you can see guardrooms, watchtowers and the tiny cells where revolutionaries were imprisoned from the 1930s to the 1970s. Serene Lak Lake, about 31 miles (50km) southeast, is an attraction in its own right, but all the more compelling for the surrounding M'nong villages. Early morning mists hang above the calm waters and mingle with the columns of wood smoke rising from the longhouses.

The Daklak Tourist Company can arrange overnight stays at the M'nong village of Buon Juin; this is the only way to watch elephants

taking their evening wallow in the cool waters. The M'nong, who are famed elephant-catchers, number about 50,000 and live in a matriarchal society.

The most interesting Ede village is Buon Tur, some 9 miles (15km) southwest of Buon Me Thuot on Highway 14. Apart from the odd TV aerial, life is unchanged in this community of 20 stilt houses and, despite government opposition, Ede is still taught in schools. However, as with all of the villages in this particular region, do not expect English to be spoken here.
🔹 287 E10 ℹ 3 Phan Chu Trinh (within grounds of Thang Loi Hotel) ☎ 050-3852108 Mon–Fri 7–11.30, 1.30–5 🚌 Pleiku, Dalat, Nha Trang ✈ Danang 🚗 For Buon Juin take Highway 27, the Dalat road; turn right down a track just before a sign advising "Dalat 156km" ☛ Private tours from Nha Trang. For those on tours there is little choice as to where to go, but independent visitors on motorcyles have a wide selection of villages to see

Opposite *Jars of rice wine for sale in Ba Na*
Below *Children in Buon Tur, a village near Buon Me Thuot*

INTRODUCTION

Dalat sits on a plateau in the Central Highlands, at an altitude of almost 5,000ft (1,500m). The town, once a French hill station, is centered on a lake—Xuan Huong—amid rolling countryside. To the north are the five volcanic peaks of the Lang Biang mountains, rising to 7,900ft (2,400m), and in the vicinity are forests, waterfalls and an abundance of orchids, roses and other temperate plant life. There are Honda *xe ôms* and taxis for getting about, but walking is by far the best way of getting the most out of a visit to the town.

WHAT TO SEE

DINH BAO DAI

Vietnam's last emperor, Bao Dai, who reigned from 1925 to 1945, had a summer palace about 1 mile (2km) west from the heart of town. Built on a hill between 1933 and 1938, with magnificent views on every side, it is art deco in style both inside and out, and is altogether rather modest for a palace. The stark interior contains little to indicate this was once the home of an emperor—almost all of Bao Dai's personal belongings have been removed.

The impressive dining room contains an etched-glass map of Vietnam, and in the study are Bao Dai's desk, a few personal ornaments and photographs, and a small collection of his books, which include Shakespeare's comedies, works by Voltaire and the Brontës, and a copy of the Bible. The emperor's bedroom and bathroom are open to public scrutiny, and so too is the little terrace that opens out from his bedroom, where, apparently, on a clear night he would gaze at the stars. In the family drawing room a commentary explains who sat on which chair.

According to US reports, by 1952 Bao Dai was receiving an official stipend of US$4 million per year. A considerable amount of this was ferreted away in US and Swiss bank accounts, as insurance against the day when his reign would end. The remainder of the money was spent on his four private planes, which left little to lavish on his home. Surrounding the palace are pretty and well-maintained gardens.

There is also a hunting lodge on Dinh 1, Hung Vuong, past the Lam Dong Museum (open 7–11.30, 1–4.30), which contains a collection of 1930s

INFORMATION

www.dalattourist.com.vn

✚ 287 F10 ℹ 10 Quang Trung Street ☎ 063-3810324 🌐 Mon–Fri 7–11.30, 1.30–5 🚌 Dalat bus station, 1 mile (1.5km) from the city at 3 Thang 4. Buses to Saigon, Nha Trang, Danang, Huê. Served by Open Tour buses 🚩 Dalat Tourist ✉ 10 Quang Trung Street is the state-run tourist agency for the region ☎ 063-3810324. A variety of tours is also available through local tour agencies like Phat Tire Ventures ✉ 109 Nguyen Van Troi Street ☎ 063-3829422; www.phattireventures.com and Sinh Café ✉ 4a Bui Thi Xuan Street ☎ 063-3822663; www.sinhcafevn.com

🍴 Restaurants around town serving Asian, Pacific Rim, Chinese and Continental food 🍽 Places to eat at Dalat Central Market, end of Nguyen Thi Minh Khai

TIPS

» Rent a motorcycle to get around the palace and surrounding countryside.

» Dalat produces some of the finest handmade silk paintings in Vietnam, sold all over town.

» The Pasteur Institute on Le Hong Phong Street was built to produce vaccines for the colonial population. Though small and modest, the yellow-wash institute, opened in 1935, has a striking design, made up of a series of cubes with beveled corners; it's well worth a visit.

furniture and antique telephone switchboards. Although it is by no means sumptuous it does have a feel of authenticity. The gardens are green but lacking in intimacy. You may have the place to yourself.

✚ Off map 137 A2 ✉ Le Hong Phong Street (official name Dinh 3) ◉ Daily 7am–8pm ✋ 5,000d ❓ Visitors must wear covers over their shoes to protect the wooden floors

LAM TY NI PAGODA

Lam Ty Ni Pagoda would be unremarkable were it not for the presence of its resident monk, Vien Thuc. He arrived here in 1968, and by 1987 he was finishing work on the gateway that leads up through a garden to the figure of Quan Am, Goddess of Mercy. Vien Thuc's garden was inspired by the classic Japanese garden of tranquility, and he originally called it An Lac Vien (Peace Garden). He has since decided that the name Divine Calmness Bamboo Garden has a better ring to it.

Vien Thuc is a renowned scholar, poet, artist, philosopher, mystic, divine and entrepreneur, but is best known for his paintings, of which, by his own reckoning, there are more than 100,000. This is easy to believe when you wander through the rustic huts and shacks that are tacked on to the back of the temple, their walls lined deep with suspended sheets that bear the simple but distinctive calligraphy that spells out his philosophy: "Living in the present, how beautiful this very moment is"; "Zen painting destroys millennium sorrows"; "The mystique, silence and melody universal of love" and so on.

Vien Thuc personally shows visitors around, with both a mixture of pride in his achievement ("I work very hard") and disarming, self-deprecating modesty, cheerfully chuckling to himself as he goes. His work is widely known at international levels and he has had exhibitions in Paris, New York and the Netherlands, as well as on the Internet. His paintings and books of poetry are sold at prices that are creeping up all the time.

✚ 137 A2 ✉ 2 Thien My, southwest of town ☎ 063-38227775

HANG NGA'S CRAZY HOUSE

Soviet-trained architect, arty Doctor Dang Viet Nga has, over many years, built up her remarkable hotel in organic fashion. The brightly painted concrete house winds itself around trees—some rooms perch in the bough of a tree, others occupy the gardens, and all resemble scenes taken from the pages of a fairy-tale book. The fantasy continues within, and guests sleep inside crafted mushrooms, trees and giraffes and sip tea under giant cobwebs. There is a honeymoon room, an ant room and plenty more. Intriguing as it is, though, the hotel is not a particularly comfortable or private place to stay (▷ 175).

✚ 137 A2 ✉ 3 Huynh Thuc Khang Street ☎ 063-822070 ◉ Art gallery: daily 7–7 ✋ Art gallery: 8,000d

Above *Dalat sits on a plateau in the Central Highlands*

DALAT CATHEDRAL

This single-tiered cathedral, constructed between 1931 and the 1940s, has a chicken-shaped weather vane on its turret. The colorful stained-glass windows were crafted in France by Louis Balmet, the same man who made the windows in Nha Trang and Danang cathedrals, between 1934 and 1940.

✚ 137 B2 ✉ Tran Phu Street 🕐 Mass: Mon–Sat 5.15am, 5.15pm, Sun 5.15am, 7am, 8.30am, 2.30pm, 4pm

COLONIAL VILLAS

Many of Dalat's large colonial villas are 1930s and 1940s vintage. Some have curved walls and railings and are almost nautical in inspiration; others are more rustic. Perhaps the largest and most impressive is the former residence of the governor general on Tran Hung Dao Street, now the Hotel Dinh 2. The building occupies a magnificent position set among mountain pines.

✚ 137 B2 ✉ Tran Hung Dao Street

XUAN HUONG LAKE

The central Xuan Huong Lake (originally the Grand Lake) was created in 1919 after a small dam was constructed on the Cam Ly River. A road runs all the way round the perimeter of the lake, providing a pleasant and gentle bicycle ride, and paddleboats are available for lake trips.

✚ 137 B2

DALAT RAIL STATION

Dalat's train station was opened in 1938, five years after the completion of the rack-and-pinion track from Saigon, and was closed in 1964. The station is the last in Vietnam to retain its original French art deco architecture—the stained-glass windows remain intact. Its steeply pitched roofs could handle the heaviest of alpine snowfalls, and the waiting room, formerly segregated by race, is in good condition. In 1991, a 4-mile (7km) stretch to the village of Trai Mat, home to the K'Ho ethnic minority, was reopened; a Japanese-built train travels daily here and to the Linh Phuoc Pagoda.

✚ 137 C2 ✉ Nguyen Trai Street 🕐 Daily 8am–5pm ✋ 103,000d per journey

Above *Hang Nga's hotel is constructed around trees and gardens*

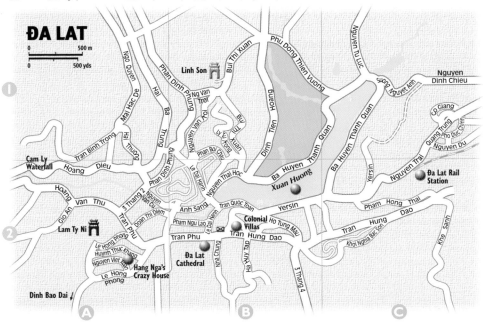

INFORMATION

✚ 285 F7 ℹ An Phu Tourist Company,
5 Dong Da Street ☎ 0511-818366
🚌 Dien Bien Phu Street, 2 miles (3km)
from town; connections with all major
cities; Hung Vuong Street, connections
with Hoi An. Served by Open Tour buses
🚆 Haiphong Street, 1 mile (2km) west
of town; connections with Hanoi, Saigon,
Huê ✈ Danang Airport 1.5 miles (2.5km)
southwest of city 🍴 Seafood, Asian and
Western restaurants; several on Bach
Dang Street 🍺 Cafés and bars on Bach
Dang Street 🚗 Cars and guides arranged
at An Phu Tourist Co, 5 Dong Da Street
☎ 0511-3818366 🕐 Daily 7–6

INTRODUCTION

Vietnam's third-largest port has a frenetic buzz and spectacular beaches on its
doorstep. Its museum houses glorious sculpture and bas-relief works of the
Champa empire in an open-sided French-established institute.

Danang sits on a peninsula at the point where the Han River flows into the
South China Sea. The city is ringed by huge two-lane freeways, and new roads
have been driven out into the empty spaces beyond, which are quickly being
fleshed out with factories, shops and houses. The most important sight in the
city itself—the Museum of Cham Sculpture—sits at the southern end of Bach
Dang Street, which runs along the eastern edge of the center and is lined with
places to stay and eat.

WHAT TO SEE

BAO TANG DIEU KHAC CHAMPA DA NANG

Close to Danang are the ruins of My Son (▷ 156), the holiest of the sites
of Champa, one of the most glorious kingdoms in Southeast Asia, which
reached its apogee in the 10th and 11th centuries. The Museum of Cham
Sculpture contains the largest display of Cham art anywhere in the world,
and testifies to a lively, creative and long-lived civilization. The first Champa
capital, Tra Kieu, was less than 28 miles (45km) from here, but the kingdom's
territories extended far afield—other major sites included Dong Duong, Po
Nagar and Thap Man and Cha Ban.

Each room in the museum is dedicated to work from a different region
of Champa, revealing how these parts flowered artistically at varying times
from the fourth to the 14th centuries, and illustrating outside influences from
Cambodia to Java. Many pieces from My Son illustrate the Hindu trinity:
Brahma the Creator, Vishnu the Preserver and Siva the Destroyer. An altar
is inscribed with scenes from the wedding story of Sita and Rama from the
Hindu epic *Ramayana*. Ganesh, the elephant-headed son of Siva, is well
represented here. At the end of the ninth century AD Dong Duong replaced
My Son as the focal point of Cham art, and Buddhism became the dominant
religion at court, although it never replaced Hinduism. The Dong Duong room
is illustrated with scenes from the life of Buddha. From this period faces

Above *View across the houses of China
Beach from the top of the Marble
Mountains*

become less stylistic and bodies more graceful and flowing. The subsequent period of Cham art is known as the late Tra Kieu style. In this section there are *apsaras*, celestial dancing maidens whose fluid and animated forms are captured in stone. Thereafter Cham sculpture went into artistic decline. The Thap Man style (late 11th to early 14th century) produced mythical beasts whose range and style are unknown elsewhere in Southeast Asia. Also in this room is a pedestal encircled by 28 breast motifs, believed to represent Uroba, mythical mother of the Indrapura (My Son, Tra Kieu, Dong Duong) nation.

✉ Intersection of Trung Nu Vuong and Bach Dang streets 🕓 Daily 7–5 💰 30,000d
❓ Limited labels in French and English

MY KHE BEACH

Once a resort celebrated in rock songs, the white sand and surf of China Beach, so popular with American soldiers, is now quiet, apart from the souvenir and food stands. This was a military retreat for GIs during the Vietnam War, but after 1975 it was given the North Vietnamese Army code T20 Beach; locals call it My Khe. The whole area is developing at a furious pace and a number of international hotel chains are opening along the beach. The water is clean (note that at times there is a dangerous cross-current and undertow) and benefits from a glorious setting—the hills of Monkey Mountain to the north and the Marble Mountains (▷ 155) to the south.

✉ Across Han River Bridge; right then left onto Nguyen Cong Tru Street 🍴

MORE TO SEE

DANANG CATHEDRAL

This single-spired building with a sugary-pink wash was built in 1923. Its stained-glass windows were made in Grenoble in 1927 by Louis Balmet, who also supplied the windows of Dalat Cathedral (▷ 137).

✉ 156 Tran Phu Street 🕓 Mass: daily 5am, 5pm

BAC MY AN BEACH

This is another clean and attractive beach with some seafood stands. Next to it is the Furama Resort (▷ 166–167), which has facilities for water-based and other sporting activities.

✉ 1 mile (2km) south of China Beach, 5 miles (8km) from the middle of Danang

TIPS

»» Danang is too large to explore on foot, but there are plenty of cyclos, taxis and Honda *xe ôms*.
»» Bicycles and motorcycles are available for rent from most guesthouses and hotels.
»» The border with Laos at Lao Bao is open to foreigners; daily buses leave Danang for the Lao town of Savannakhet, on the Mekong. Visas are available from the Laos consulate on Tran Qui Cap Street.

Left *The white sands of My Khe or China Beach*
Below *Danang's pink cathedral*

INFORMATION

www.huetouristvietnam.com

✚ 284 D6 ⓘ Huê Tourist Services, 39 Chu Van An Street, Huê ☎ 054-816263 ⊕ Mon–Fri 7–11.30, 1.30–5 🚌 Khe Sanh, 2 miles (3km) from site of US base; connections with Huê (An Hoa station) 🚗 Private tours from Huê

Above *The Hien Luong Bridge crosses the Ben Hai River*

INTRODUCTION

The incongruously named Demilitarized Zone (DMZ) saw some of the fiercest fighting of the Vietnam War and, in 1968, this is where a key Vietnam War battle took place.

The DMZ covers a 3-mile (5km) strip on each side of the Ben Hai River and the 17th parallel, the one-time boundary between the Communist north and the capitalist south. Sites are scattered around Dong Ha, north of Huê. Highway 9 branches off the main coastal Highway 1 toward the Laos border, passing Khe Sanh (now officially called Huong Hoa), one of the most evocative names associated with American involvement in Vietnam. Close to Khe Sanh are parts of the famous Ho Chi Minh Trail, along which supplies were ferried from the north to the south.

The DMZ was the creation of the 1954 Geneva Peace Accords, marking the armistice between Ho Chi Minh's forces and the French. Although the zone divided the country into two spheres of influence, this was always intended to be a temporary measure. However, the nationwide elections that were planned for July 1956 never took place. The boundary evolved into a national border, separating the Democratic Republic of Vietnam in the north from the Republic of Vietnam in the south. The border remained in force until reunification in 1976.

On 2 January 1968, a North Vietnamese regimental commander was killed while surveying the base at Khe Sanh and the American high command concluded that the North Vietnamese Army (NVA) was planning a major assault. Special forces long-range patrols were dropped into the area around the base and photo reconnaissance was increased. It subsequently became clear that between 20,000 and 40,000 NVA troops were converging on Khe Sanh. The US Marines were surrounded in a place the assistant commander of the 3rd Marine Division referred to as "not really anywhere," and there followed a heavy exchange of fire, during which B-52s carpet-bombed the surrounding area. The 77-day siege cost thousands of lives, but the attack on Khe Sanh was a diversionary tactic, designed to draw US forces away from the cities. On 1 February 84,000 Communist troops attacked 105 urban centers in the Tet Offensive, taking the US and South Vietnam by surprise.

WHAT TO SEE

TACON MILITARY BASE AND KHE SANH

Khe Sanh (Huong Hoa) is the site of one of the most famous battles of the Vietnam War. The remains of the Tacon military base, amid a coffee plantation, have been converted into a museum. In its grounds are a Chinook, an M41 tank and Viet Cong equipment. Dog tags and ID cards of US soldiers are exhibited along with pictures of the battle.

⊞ 284 D6 ✉ Along Highway 9, 2 miles (3km) from Khe Sanh village ⏱ Daily 9–5 ✋ 30,000d

HO CHI MINH TRAIL

The labyrinth of jungle paths used by troops and porters is a popular but inevitably disappointing sight, given that its whole purpose was to be as inconspicuous as possible. Anything you see was designed to be invisible— from the air, at least. Every day up to 60 tons of supplies were carried along these lines, on foot, on ponies or on bicycles. The paths were also used to send soldiers and reinforcements, and as many as 200,000 troops made their way from Hanoi every month. The more the trail was used, the easier progress was, and by 1970 the journey from North Vietnam to Saigon, which had previously taken several months, could be completed in six weeks. Repeated American bombing of the trail failed to disrupt the flow of supplies, but disease was a serious problem, with some 10 percent of the porters falling victim to malaria and other sickness.

ROCK PILE

This 755ft (230m) limestone outcrop was a US observation post in a severely contested zone, and troops, ammunition and beer all had to be helicoptered in to its apparently unassailable position. However, the sheer walls were eventually scaled by the Viet Cong.

✉ Off Highway 9 on the road to Laos

VINH MOC TUNNELS

Families in the heavily bombed village of Vinh Moc dug themselves shelters beneath their houses between 1965 and 1966, and eventually formed a network of interconnecting tunnels. Later the tunnels developed a more offensive role when Viet Cong soldiers fought from them, and they served a similar function to the better known Cu Chi Tunnels (▷ 224). About 5,500ft (1,700m) of the tunnels remain. Offshore is Con Co Island, an important supply depot and anti-aircraft stronghold in the war.

✉ 13km (8 miles) off Highway 9, 4 miles (6.5km) north of Ben Hai River; turn right in Ho Xa village ✋ 25,000d

Left *A helicopter on display at Khe San*
Below *The Vinh Moc Tunnels*

REGIONS • CENTRAL VIETNAM • SIGHTS

INTRODUCTION

Low-slung houses, shops and temples crowd the streets of this ancient mercantile town. At this center of the clothes trade, hundreds of tailors sew gowns, suits, bags and shoes in silks and cottons for fashion emporiums across town.

Hoi An's tranquil riverside setting, its diminutive scale (you can almost touch the roofs of some houses), its friendly and welcoming people and its wide array of shops and galleries have made it one of the most popular destinations for foreigners. The town is divided into five quarters, or bangs, each of which would traditionally have had its own pagoda and supported one Chinese clan group. Most of Hoi An's more attractive buildings and assembly halls (known as *hoi quan*) are found either on or just off Tran Phu Street. Tran Phu stretches west to east from the Japanese Covered Bridge to the market, running parallel to the Thu Bon River, where boat rides are available.

The Chinese, along with some Japenese settled in Hoi An in the 16th century and controlled trade between the islands of Southeast Asia, East Asia (China and Japan) and India. Portuguese and Dutch vessels also docked at the port. By the end of the 19th century the Thu Bon River had started to silt up and Hoi An was gradually eclipsed by Danang as the most important port of the area.

WHAT TO SEE

CAU NHAT BAN (JAPANESE COVERED BRIDGE)

Hoi An's most famous landmark is the covered bridge variously known as the Pagoda Bridge, the Faraway People's Bridge and, popularly, as the Japanese Covered Bridge. Its popular name reflects a long-standing belief that it was built by the Japanese, although no documentary evidence exists to support this. It was built in the 16th century, perhaps even earlier. On its north side there is a pagoda, Japanese in style, for the protection of sailors. Statues represent two dogs at the west end, and two monkeys at the east; it is said that the bridge was begun in the year of the monkey and finished in the year of the dog. Scholars have pointed out that this would mean a two-year period of construction—an inordinately long time for such a small bridge— and maintain that the two animals represent points of the compass, WSW (monkey) and NW (dog). Father Benigne Vachet, a missionary who lived in Hoi An between 1673 and 1683, noted in his memoirs that the bridge was the haunt of beggars and fortune-tellers hoping to benefit from the stream of people crossing over it.

➕ 146 A1 ✉ West end of Tran Phu Street ✋ 1 token; keep ticket to get back

ASSEMBLY HALLS

Chinese traders in Hoi An (as elsewhere in Southeast Asia) established self-governing dialect associations, or clan houses, which owned their own schools, cemeteries, hospitals and temples. A clan house *(hoi quan)* may be dedicated to a god or an illustrious individual and may contain a temple, but is not itself a place of worship. There are five *hoi quan* in Hoi An, four for use by people of specific ethnicities—Fukien, Cantonese, Hainan, Chaozhou—and the fifth for use by any visiting Chinese sailors or merchants.

Merchants from Guangdong would meet at the Quang Dong Hoi Quan (Cantonese Assembly Hall), built in 1786 and dedicated to Quan Cong, a Han Chinese general. Fine embroidered hangings decorate the hall, which is set in a cool, tree-filled compound. Next is the Ngu Bang Hoi Quan (All Chinese Assembly Hall), sometimes referred to as Chua Ba (Goddess Temple).

INFORMATION

www.hoian-tourism.com

➕ 285 F7 ℹ 6 Truong Minh Hung Street ☎ 974-676593 🕐 Mon–Fri 8–6, Sat 8–5. If coming from the beach, a convenient place to buy the tokens is the tourist office in Hoang Dieu Street (🕐 7–6), just past the parking area for the hotel shuttle buses ✋ 90,000d; available from tourist offices. Valid 1 day. Includes tokens for one museum, one old house, one assembly hall, concert, handicraft workshop, and Japanese Covered Bridge. Separate ticket necessary for further sites 🍴 Wide range of restaurants of a high standard, specializing in seafood; several on Bach Dang Street 🚌 0.6 miles (1km) west of town; connections with Danang ✖ Danang

Opposite *Children sitting on a cannon at Hoi An's museum*

Unusually for an assembly hall, this was a mutual aid society open to any Chinese trader or seaman, regardless of dialect or region of origin. The hall helped shipwrecked and sick sailors and performed burial rites for merchants with no relatives in Hoi An. Built in 1773 as a meeting place for all five groups (the four listed above plus Hakka) and for those with no clan house of their own, it now contains a Chinese school, Truong Le Nghia, where children of the diaspora learn the language of their forebears.

The Phuc Kien Hoi Quan (Fukien Assembly Hall), was founded around 1690 and served Hoi An's largest Chinese ethnic group, those from Fukien. Thien Hau, goddess of the sea and protector of sailors, is the central figure on the main altar, clothed in gilded robes; together with her assistants, she hears the cries of drowning sailors. On the right of the temple entrance is a mural depicting Thien Hau rescuing a sinking vessel. Behind the main altar a second sanctuary houses the image of Van Thien, who blesses the lives of pregnant women's unborn children.

The Hai Nam Hoi Quan (Hainan Assembly Hall), was founded in 1883 in memory of more than 100 sailors and passengers who were killed when three ships were plundered by an admiral in Emperor Tu Duc's navy. In his defense the Admiral claimed the victims were pirates, and some sources maintain he even had the ships painted black to strengthen his case. At night the building is illuminated by a man selling lanterns inside the pagoda gates.

Exquisite woodcarving is the highlight of the Trieu Chau Hoi Quen (Chaozhou Assembly Hall), on Nguyen Duy Hieu Street. The altar and its panels depict images from the sea and women from the Beijing court, presumably intended to console homesick traders. Walk into the courtyard, turn around and look up at the two dragons and, below them, beautifully carved phoenixes with multicolored tails and feathers.

✚ 146 B1–146 C1 ✉ Tran Phu Street, east of Japanese Covered Bridge 🕐 Daily 7.30–6 ✋ 1 assembly hall token per hall, unless free entry noted

TAN KY HOUSE

This merchant house was the first to be given special recognition by the Ministry of Culture. It dates from the late 18th century and was built from jackfruit timber by the Tan Ky family. The family had originally arrived in Hoi An from China 200 years earlier, and the building reflects not only the prosperity they had acquired (by trading in silk, rice, beans, cinnamon, apple, areca nut and betel) but also the architecture of the houses of their Japanese and Vietnamese neighbors, whose styles had worked their influence on the younger family members. The interior is intact; all the furniture is mahogany and inlaid with mother-of-pearl. Seven generations have lived there; the fifth-generation member is the owner.

✚ 146 B2 ✉ 101 Nguyen Thai Hoc Street 🕐 Daily 7.30–6 ✋ 1 house token

ONG HOI AN PAGODA

The Ong Hoi An Pagoda is in fact two interlinked pagodas built back-to-back: Chua Quan Cong and, behind that, Chua Quan Am. Their date of construction is not known, although both certainly existed in 1653. In 1824, Emperor Minh Mang made a donation of 300 *luong* (1 *luong* being equivalent to 1.5oz/42g of silver) for the maintenance of the pagodas, which are dedicated to Quan Cong, the God of War and Soldiers, and Quan Am, the Goddess of Mercy, respectively. The brightly painted crimson doors, decorated with serpentine fire-breathing dragons, are particularly striking.

✚ 146 C1 ✉ 24 Tran Phu Street

TRAN FAMILY TEMPLE

Chinese and Japanese styles are fused in this building, which was built by the Chinese mandarin Tran in 1802 and has been owned by the Tran family

Below *The bright façade of the Fukien Assembly Hall*

for 15 generations. The current generation has no son, which means that the lineage has been broken. The temple is entered through a shady and luxuriant courtyard and is roofed with heavy yin-yang tiling, which requires strong roof beams; these are held up by a triple-beamed support in the Japanese style (seen in the roof of the Japanese Covered Bridge). Some beams have Chinese-inspired, ornately carved dragons. The outer doors are Japanese, the inner Chinese. On a central altar rest small wooden memorial boxes that contain the photograph or likeness of the deceased together with biographical details. Beyond, at the back of the house, is a small, raised Chinese herb, spice and flower garden with a row of bonsai trees.

As in all Hoi An's family houses, guests are received warmly and courteously and served lotus tea and dried coconut.

➕ 146 B1 ✉ Junction of Le Loi and Phan Chu Trinh streets 🕐 Daily 7.30–6
✋ 1 house token

Above *A group of women making lanterns in Hoi An*

PHUNG HUNG HOUSE
Just east of the Japanese Covered Bridge is this 200-year-old house which has been in the same family for eight generations. It presents an eclectic mix of Chinese-style balcony and Japanese-style roof, and is supported by 80 columns of ironwood, which stand on marble pedestals. During the floods of 1964, Phung Hung House became home to 160 locals who camped upstairs for three days as the water rose to a height of 8ft (2.5m).

➕ 146 A1 ✉ 4 Nguyen Thi Minh Khai 🕐 Daily 7.30–6 ✋ 1 house token

NHA TRUNG BAY LICH SU VAN HOA HOI AN
A former pagoda houses the Hoi An Museum of History and Culture, which sets the town in its trading context, including sections on all the main cultural influences. Most interesting are the photographs of old Hoi An taken between the 1930s and the 1990s, and the displays of ornamentation depicting watchful eyes, often incorporating the yin-yang symbol, which are believed to ward off evil spirits.

➕ 146 C1 ✉ 7 Nguyen Huê Street 🕐 Daily 8–8 ✋ 1 museum token

BAO TANG GOM SU MAU DICH
The Museum of Trade Ceramics, established with financial and technical support from Japan, contains an interesting range of ancient wares, some of them removed from shipwrecks in surrounding waters. There are also detailed architectural drawings of various houses in Hoi An. Upstairs, from the front balcony, there is a superb roofscape view.

➕ 146 B1 ✉ 80 Tran Phu Street 🕐 Daily 7.30–6 ✋ 1 museum token

BAO TANG VAN HOA SA HUYNH
Housed in an attractive colonial-era building, the Museum of Sa Huynh Culture contains a modest collection, mostly of pottery, unearthed in 1989 at Sa Huynh, 75 miles (120km) south of Hoi An. The objects, dating from around 200BC, are especially significant because they have called into question the previous theory that the only cultures native to Central Vietnam were the Cham and the Viet.

➕ 146 A2 ✉ 149 Tran Phu Street 🕐 Daily 7.30–6 ✋ 1 museum token

CUA DAI BEACH
A few beachfront cafés line this beautiful 2-mile (3km) stretch of white sand. On a clear day the seven islands of the Cham archipelago, 9 miles (15km) offshore, are visible. Deckchairs are available in places and the beach is long enough to offer complete seclusion, especially outside of weekends, and there are resort hotels to drop into for food and drinks.

➕ Off map 146 C1 ✉ 2 miles (4km) from Hoi An, east down Tran Hung Dao Street

TIPS

» Hoi An itself is best explored on foot, but for venturing farther, hotels have two- and four-wheel vehicles to rent.

» On the 14th day of every lunar month, Chinese silk lanterns are hung in town and entertainment is laid on among the houses and streets.

MORE TO SEE

QUANG THANG

A Chinese captain built this house in the early 18th century; it was subsequently used as a shop and a residence. There are pictures of the current owner's ancestors on the walls. A fine arched roof and decorative carvings, aided by the care and attention devoted to its upkeep by the present owners, help make this house an architectural highlight in Hoi An.

✚ 146 B1–B2 ✉ 77 Tran Phu Street ◉ Daily 9–5 ✋ 1 house token

FRENCH HOUSE

This example of a colonial building in the small French quarter was built in 1887 and has belonged to the same family for four generations. It has very high ceilings, mahogany French chairs and an ebony bed. The French-speaking owner is happy to discuss his family's history as well as his country's.

✚ 146 C2 ✉ 25 Bach Dang Street ◉ No set hours ✋ Tip appreciated

CHO HOI AN

At the northern, Tran Phu Street end, Hoi An's market is covered, and sells mostly dry goods. Cloth merchants and seamstresses will produce made-to-measure shirts here in a few hours. The southern, river side is the local fish market, which comes alive from 5am to 6am as boats arrive with the night's catch.

✚ 146 C2 ✉ Between Tran Phu and Bach Dang streets ◉ Daily

DIEP DONG NGUYEN HOUSE

This house, with two Chinese lanterns hanging outside, was once a Chinese dispensary. The owner is friendly and hospitable, and he shows visitors around with pride. He has a beautifully painted doorway, decorated with Chinese characters.

✚ 146 B2 ✉ 80 Nguyen Thai Hoc Street ◉ Daily 7.30–6 ✋ Free

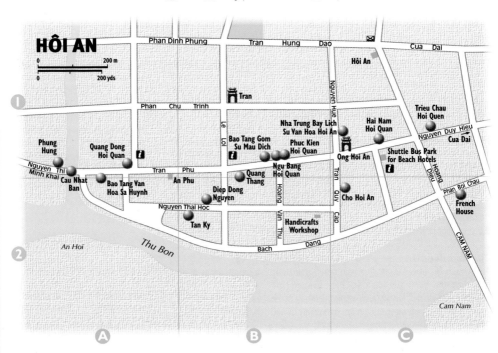

INTRODUCTION

For more than a century the emperors of the Nguyen Dynasty (1802–1945) lived here, in the now war-damaged Imperial City.

Huê straddles the Perfume River (Song Huong), 10 miles (16km) inland of the South China Sea and 62 miles (100km) south of the 17th parallel, and has been given UNESCO World Heritage status. On the western bank is the vast Imperial City, which housed generations of the country's emperors, and inside this complex is the Purple Forbidden City, the private imperial enclosure. Running along the northwestern edge of the Imperial City is the Dong Ba Canal, lined by a commercial district, and beyond the canal are the suburbs of Phu Cat and Phu Hiep, where there are several Chinese pagodas. Huê city itself spreads out from the eastern bank of the river, and to the south of it are the Imperial Tombs (▷ 151–154). Much of Huê is easily negotiated on foot.

WHAT TO SEE

IMPERIAL CITY

Four outer walls, 23–33ft (7–10m) thick, enclose the Imperial City (Kinh Thanh), surrounded by ditches and canals and pierced with towers and 10 gates. Emperor Gia Long (reigned 1802–20) began its construction in 1804, enclosing the land of eight villages and covering 2sq miles (6sq km). It took 20,000 men to construct the walls alone. Chinese custom decreed that the palace should face south, and this is the direction from which visitors approach. Massive 16ft (5m) cannon are grouped just inside the outer wall gates, four through the Hien Nhon Gate and five through the Chuong Duc Gate. These are the Nine Holy Cannon (Cuu Vi Than Cong), cast in 1803 from bronzeware seized from the Tay Son revolutionaries.

To the north, over one of three bridges spanning a second ditch, is the Royal Gate, Ngo Mon (1), built in 1833 during the reign of Emperor Minh Mang (reigned 1820–40) and surmounted by a pavilion where the emperor would view ceremonies. This entrance was opened only for the emperor.

INFORMATION

✚ 285 E6 ℹ A good source of tourist information is Sinh Café, 12 Jung Vuong Street ☎ 054-3845022 🚆 An Cuu station, 43 Hung Vuong Street; connections with Saigon. An Hoa station, northwest corner of citadel; connections with Hanoi. Don Ba station, Tran Hung Dao; connections with local villages and Thuan An Beach. Served by Open Tour buses 🚌 Le Loi Street; connections with Saigon and Hanoi ✈ Phu Bai Airport south of city; connections with Saigon, Danang and Hanoi 🚢 There are numerous private tour operators in town 🍴 Wide range, serving Western and local food ☕ Several on Hung Vuong Street

Above *The Thien Mu Pagoda dates from the 17th century*

HUÊ IMPERIAL CITY PLAN

1. Royal Gate (Ngo Mon)
2. Golden Water Bridge
3. Laterite-lined tanks
4. Great Rites Courtyard (Dai Trieu Nghi) & Palace of Supreme Harmony (Thai Hoa Palace)
5. Red Gate
6. Ta Pavilion
7. Huu Vu Pavilion
8. Central Pavilion, private apartments of the Emperor
9. Quang Minh Palace
10. Royal Reading Pavilion
11. Hien Lam Cac
12. Nine bronze urns
13. Thé Temple
14. Waiting Pavilion (Huu Ta Dai Lam Vien)
15. Royal (East) Theater

 Purple Forbidden City (Tu Cam Thanh)

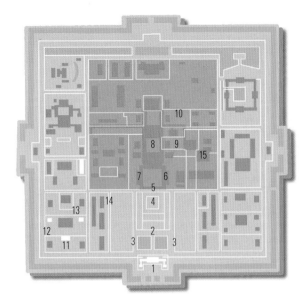

Farther north is the Golden Water Bridge (2), again reserved solely for the emperor, and set between two tanks (3) lined with laterite blocks. This bridge leads to the Great Rites Courtyard, Dai Trieu Nghi (4), on the north side of which is the Palace of Supreme Harmony (Thai Hoa Palace), used for Gia Long's coronation in 1806. Here, sitting on his golden throne, the emperor received visitors on ceremonial occasions. The 18 stone stelae in front of the palace stipulate the correct ranking of officials standing in the Great Rites Courtyard. Only royal princes were allowed to stand in the palace itself, which is perhaps the best-preserved building in the complex, with restored red and gold columns, a tiled floor and a fine ceiling.

Next comes the Purple Forbidden City (Tu Cam Thanh), surrounded by walls 1m (3ft) thick. Following its almost complete destruction during the 1968 Tet Offensive, only two mandarin palaces and the rebuilt Royal Reading Pavilion (10) still stand.

Beyond the Palace of Supreme Harmony two huge bronze urns (Vac Dong), weighing about 3,300lb (1,500kg) each, flank the Ta (6) and Huu Vu (7) pavilions—one now a souvenir shop, the other a mock throne room. At the southwest corner is the well-preserved Hien Lam Cac (11), a pavilion built in 1821, in front of which stand nine massive bronze urns (12) cast between 1835 and 1837. The central, largest and most ornate urn is dedicated to the founder of the empire, Emperor Gia Long. Next to the urns is the Temple of Generations, Thé Temple (13), built in 1821 and housing altars honoring 10 of the emperors of the Nguyen Dynasty (Duc Duc and Hiep Hoa are missing). ✚ 150 A1 🕐 Mid-Apr to mid-Oct daily 6.30–5.30; mid-Oct to mid-Apr daily 7–5 💲 55,000d 📷 90-min tours in English, French, Japanese

HUÊ MUSEUM OF ROYAL FINE ARTS

Housed in the Long An Palace (built 1845), the museum contains a collection of ceramics, furniture and bronzeware. In the front courtyard are stone mandarins, cannon, gongs and giant bells. The elegant building itself was commissioned by Emperor Thieu Tri (reigned 1841–1847) in 1845, and was dismantled and erected on its present site in 1909. Highlights include the imperial sedan chair, covered in red and gold dragons; a beautiful, wooden divan inlaid with mother-of-pearl in a floral design; and the cloth bags used for holding betel and areca belonging to Empress Mother Doan Huy, wife of

Emperor Khai Dinh. One of the ceremonial gowns on display is emblazoned with dragons rising out of a swollen sea amid red, gold and green sequins.

➕ 150 A1 ✉ 3 Le Truc Street ⊘ Oct 15–Apr 13 Tue–Sun 7–5; Apr 14–Oct 14 Tue–Sun 7–5.30 💰 35,000d ❓ No cameras or camcorders; overshoes must be worn; labeling in English

THIEN MU PAGODA

Huê's finest pagoda was built in 1601 by Nguyen Hoang, the governor of Huê, after an old woman appeared to him and told him of the site's supernatural significance. Five Buddhist monks and seven novices still live here. The seven-level Happiness and Grace Tower (Phuoc Duyen), built by Emperor Thieu Tri in 1844, is 69ft (21m) high, each floor housing an altar to a different Buddha. Its summit is crowned with a water pitcher to catch the rain (water represents the source of happiness). Arranged around the tower are four smaller buildings, one of which contains the Great Bell, cast in 1710 under the orders of the Nguyen Lord Nguyen Phuc Chu and weighing 4,850lb (2,200kg). Beneath another of these surrounding pavilions is a monstrous marble turtle on which an 8.5ft high (2.6m) stela recounts the development of Buddhism in Huê. The pagoda entrance, beyond the tower, is via a triple gateway patrolled by six carved and vividly painted guardians. The roof of the sanctuary itself is decorated with Jataka stories, which relate the previous lives of the Buddha. At the front of the sanctuary are a brass, laughing Buddha, an assortment of gilded Buddhas, and a crescent-shaped gong cast in 1677 by Jean de la Croix.

The first monk to commit self-immolation, Thich Quang Duc (▷ 37), came from this pagoda; the gray Austin car in which he drove to Saigon is kept in a garage in the temple garden.

➕ Off map 150 A2 ✉ North bank of Perfume River, 2.5 miles (4km) upstream of city

HO QUYEN

Ho Quyen is an amphitheater built in 1830 by Emperor Minh Mang as a venue for the popular staged confrontations between elephants and tigers. This royal sport had previously taken place on a river island or on the river banks, but by 1830 this was considered too risky for the royal party. The amphitheater was last used in 1904 when, as was usual, the elephant emerged victorious: "The elephant rushed ahead and pressed the tiger to the wall with all the force he could gain. Then he raised his head, threw the enemy to the ground and smashed him to death", wrote Crosbie Garstin in *The Dragon and the Lotus* (1928). Ho Quyen's walls are 16ft (5m) high and the arena is 144ft (44m) in diameter. At the south side, beneath the royal box, is a large gateway for the elephant; to the north are five smaller entrances for the tigers.

➕ Off map 150 A3 ✉ South bank of Perfume River, 2.5 miles (4km) upstream of Huê, 2 miles (3km) west of rail station on Bui Thi Xuan Street; turn left up paved track

TIPS

» Huê has a reputation for bad weather. The rainy season runs from September to January, and rainfall is particularly heavy between September and November. The best time to visit is between February and August.

» Even in the dry season an umbrella is useful, particularly when leaving town to visit pagodas and tombs.

Below *Boats on the Perfume River, as seen from the Thien Mu Pagoda*

REGIONS CENTRAL VIETNAM • SIGHTS

149

MORE TO SEE

CHURCH OF MOTHER OF PERPETUAL HELP

This three-story, octagonal steel tower is 174ft (53m) high and an attractive blend of Asian and European styles. It was completed in 1962, and marble from the Marble Mountain in Danang was used for the altar. The church lies at the junction of Nguyen Huê and Nguyen Khuyen streets. The church's choir sing hymns during the Sunday services.

✚ 150 C3 ✉ Nguyen Khuyen Street ⊙ Mass: Sun 8am

THANH TOAN BRIDGE

Thanh Toan Covered Bridge was built in the reign of King Le Hien Tong (1740–86) by Tran Thi Dao, a childless woman hoping to be blessed with a baby in return for her charity. The bridge, with its shelter for the tired and homeless, attracted the interest of several kings, who granted the village immunity from taxes. The original yin-yang tiles have been replaced with green enameled tube tiles, but the structure is still in good condition, though no longer in use—apart from the shaded parapets that now line both sides of the bridge. Periodically subject to storm damage, Thanh Toan Bridge was substantially renovated in 1991.

✚ Off map 150 C2 ✉ 5 miles (8km) east of Huê

Above *A gateway in the Forbidden City*

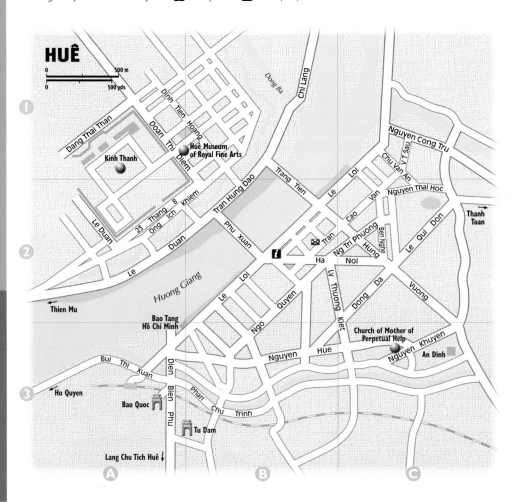

INTRODUCTION

The magnificent tombs of seven former emperors (Lang Chu Tich Huê) and those of various other royal personages and countless courtiers and mandarins dot the countryside to the south of Huê city in peaceful locations along the course of the Perfume River. Each imperial tomb follows the same stylistic formula while reflecting the tastes of the emperor in question. Every one has five design elements to glorify the imperial dead: A courtyard with statues of elephants, horses and military and civil mandarins; a stela pavilion with an engraved eulogy by the king's heir; a Temple of the Soul's Tablets; a pleasure pavilion; and a grave. Geomancers decreed that they should also have a stream and a mountainous screen in front.

WHAT TO SEE

TOMB OF EMPEROR GIA LONG

Gia Long, the first of the dynasty, was crowned with French support. When he died on February 3, 1820, imperial relations and mandarins were given set periods of mourning, with a minimum of three years, and astrologers chose a date for the funeral (May 27).

Gia Long's resting place is the most distant and the most rarely visited mausoleum, but is well worth the effort. The tomb itself is overgrown with venerable mango trees. The only sounds are bird calls and, occasionally, the wind in the trees: otherwise a blessed silence. Devoid of tourists, touts and ticket-sellers, this is the most atmospheric of all the tombs, although, given the historical changes that were to be wrought by the dynasty Gia Long founded, it is arguably also the most significant.

Being the first of the dynasty, Gia Long's mausoleum set the formula for later tombs. There is a surrounding lotus pond, and steps lead up to a courtyard with the Minh Thanh ancestral temple, splendid in red and gold. To the right of this is a double, walled and locked burial chamber, where Gia Long (reigned 1802–20) and his wife are interred. The tomb is perfectly aligned with two huge obelisks on the far side of the lake. Beyond is a courtyard with five now headless mandarins, horses and elephants on each side. Steps lead up to

INFORMATION

✚ Off map 150 A3 🕐 Popular tombs 55,000d; others less expensive or free; camcorders 75,000d extra 🚌 An Cuu station, 43 Hung Vuong Street, Huê; connections with Saigon. An Hoa station, northwest corner of Huê citadel; connections with Hanoi. Don Ba station, Tran Hung Dao, Huê; connections with local villages and Thuan An Beach 🚆 Le Loi Street, Huê; connections with Saigon, Danang and Hanoi ✈ Phu Bai Airport, south of Huê; connections with Saigon and Hanoi 🚤 Tours available from private operators and hotels; boats to rent from outside Huong Giang Hotel, Huê or any berth on south bank, east of Trang Tien Bridge

Above *The tomb of Emperor Minh Mang*

TIPS

» Getting to and around the mausoleums is easiest by motorcycle or car, but all are accessible by bicycle; set out early if taking this option.

» Boat tours travel to a select number of the tombs, but still require a climb up to a road and, occasionally, motorcycle transportation to the tombs; these costs and the entrance fees are excluded from the tour price.

the stela eulogizing the Emperor's reign, a gray monolith engraved in ancient Chinese characters that have remained miraculously undisturbed during two turbulent centuries.

✉ 10 miles (16km) south of Huê ⏰ Daily 6.30–6 🚌 Dien Bien Phu Street from Huê; right at intersection; signed along path from Ben Do 1km milestone; ferry across tributary and 0.6-miles (1km) track on opposite bank

TOMB OF EMPEROR MINH MANG

The Tomb of Emperor Minh Mang (reigned 1820–40) is the finest of all the imperial tombs. Built between 1841 and 1843, it sits among peaceful ponds, and in terms of architectural poise and balance, and richness of decoration, it has no equal in the area. The layout, along a single central sacred axis (Shendao), is unusual in its symmetry; no other tomb, with the possible exception of that of Khai Dinh, achieves the same unity of constituent parts, nor draws the eye onward so easily and pleasantly from one visual element to the next. Today, visitors pass through a side gate, but the traditional approach was through the Dai Hong Mon (15), a gate that leads into the ceremonial courtyard containing an array of statuary. Next is the restored Stela Pavilion (2), with a carved eulogy to the dead Emperor composed by his son, Thieu Tri. Continuing downward through a series of courtyards you reach, in turn, the Sung An Temple (4), dedicated to Minh Mang and his Empress; a small garden with flower beds that once formed the Chinese character for "longevity"; and two sets of stone bridges. The first consists of three spans, the central of which, Trung Dao Bridge (6), was for the sole use of the Emperor. The second, single bridge leads to a short flight of stairs, at the end of which is a locked bronze door leading to the tomb (no access).

✉ 8.5 miles (12km) south of Huê ⏰ Daily 6.30–6 🚌 As for Tomb of Gia Long, but cross Perfume River using new road bridge; on far side turn immediately left 🚩 Guides available for early visitors only, 55,000d an hour

TOMB OF THIEU TRI

When building the Tomb of Thieu Tri (reigned 1841–47) in 1848, the Emperor's son Tu Duc took into account his father's wishes that it be economical

PLAN OF EMPEROR MINH MANG'S TOMB

1. Ceremonial Courtyard
2. Stela Pavilion
3. Hien Duc Gate
4. Sung An Temple
5. Hoang Trach Gate
6. Trung Dao Bridge
7. Thong Minh Chinh Truc Bridge
8. Linh Phuong Pavilion
9. Quan Lan Building
10. Truy Tu Mansion
11. Nghenh Luong Pavilion
12. Minh Lau Pavilion
13. Emperor's Tomb
14. Fishing Pavilion
15. Dai Hong Mon Gate

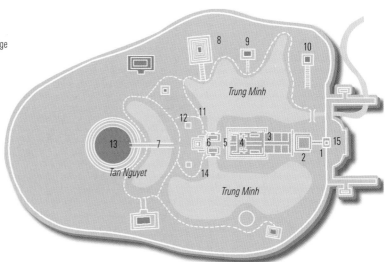

and convenient. Thieu Tri, unlike his forebears, did not start planning his mausoleum the moment he ascended the throne. With no tomb to go to, on his death his body was temporarily interred in Long An Temple (now the Huê Museum of Royal Fine Arts, ▷ 148–149).

The mausoleum is in two adjacent parts, with separate tomb and temple areas; the layout of each follows the symmetrical axis arrangement of Minh Mang's tomb, which inspired the architectural style. The memorial temple area is to the right and reached via a long flight of steps. A gatehouse incorporates Japanese triple-beamed columns and at the back of the courtyard beyond is the temple dedicated to Thieu Tri. The stela pavilion and tomb are to the left. Thieu Tri is buried on a circular island reached by three bridges beyond the stela pavilion.

✉ 4 miles (7km) southwest of Huê in Thuy Bang village ⏰ Daily 6.30–6 ✋ Ticket required for admission beyond gatehouse, 55,000d

Above *Emperor Tu Duc's tomb*

TOMB OF TU DUC

The tomb of Tu Duc (reigned 1847–83), built between 1864 and 1867 in a pine wood, is enclosed by a wall, within which is a lake where lotus and water hyacinth grow.

On a small island in the lake the Emperor built replicas of famous temples (now rather difficult to discern). He often came here to relax, compose poetry and listen to music. The Xung Khiem Pavilion (13), built in 1865, has recently been restored with UNESCO's help and is the most attractive building here. The tomb complex follows the usual formula: ceremonial square, mourning yard with pavilion, and then the tomb itself. To the left of Tu Duc's tomb are the tombs of his Empress, Le Thien Anh (16), and adopted son, Kien Phuc (14). Many of the pavilions are crumbling and ramshackle, lending the tomb a rather tragic air.

Though he had 104 wives, Tu Duc fathered no sons and had to write his own eulogy, a fact that he took as a bad omen. Shortly after his reign, France gained full control of Vietnam.

✉ 3 miles (5km) south of Huê ⏰ Daily 6.30–6 🗣 Guides available speaking German, French, English, Chinese, Japanese; negotiable rates

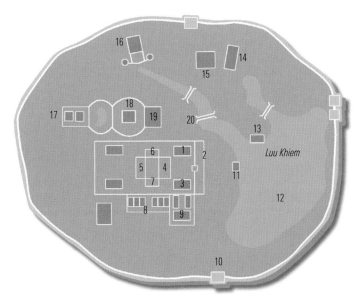

PLAN OF TU DUC'S TOMB

1. Le Khiem House
2. Khiem Cung Gate
3. Phap Khiem House
4. Hoa Khiem Palace
5. Luong Khiem Palace
6. Minh Khiem Royal Theater
7. On Khiem Mansion
8. Harem
9. Chi Khiem Temple
10. Vu Khiem Gate
11. Du Khiem Pavilion
12. Tinh Khiem Island
13. Xung Khiem Pavilion
14. Emperor Kien Phuc's Tomb
15. Chap Khiem Temple
16. Empress Le Thien Anh's Tomb
17. Emperor Tu Duc's Tomb
18. Stela Pavilion
19. Ceremonial Courtyard
20. Tien Khiem Bridge

TOMB OF DUC DUC

Despite ruling for just three days and then dying in prison, Emperor Duc Duc (lived 1852–83) has a tomb, built in 1889 by his son, Thanh Thai, on the spot where the Emperor's body was said to have been dumped by jailers. Emperors Thanh Thai (reigned 1889–1907) and Duy Tan (reigned 1907–16) are buried in the same complex. Unlike Duc Duc, both were strongly anti-French and were, for a period, exiled in Africa. Thanh Thai later returned to Vietnam and died in Vung Tau in 1953. His son Duy Tan was killed in an air crash in Africa in 1945; his body was repatriated in 1945 and interred alongside his father. The tomb is in three parts: The Long An Temple; Duc Duc's tomb, to the south; and Thanh Thai and Duy Tan's tombs, next to each other. The tombs are badly rundown.
✉ 1 mile (2km) south of Huê, on Tan Lang Street 🕐 Daily 6.30–6

TOMB OF DONG KHANH

Built in 1889, this is the smallest of the imperial tombs, but nonetheless it is one of the most individual. Unusually, it has two separate sections. One is a walled area containing the usual series of pavilions and courtyards, plus an historically interesting collection of personal objects that belonged to the Emperor. The second, a short distance away, consists of an open series of platforms. On the lower platform is the honor guard of mandarins, horses and elephants, along with a stela pavilion; the third platform is a tiled area that would have had an awning; and the highest platform is the tomb itself. The tomb is enclosed within three open walls, the entrance protected by a dragon screen (that is supposed to prevent spirits entering).
✉ 550 yards (500m) from Tu Duc's tomb; path on other side of road from main entrance
🕐 Daily 6.30–6

TOMB OF KHAI DINH

The last of the Nguyen Dynasty mausoleums was built between 1920 and 1932. By the time Khai Dinh (reigned 1916–25) was contemplating the afterlife, brick had given way in popularity to concrete.

The tomb occupies a wonderful position on the Chau Mountain, facing southwest toward a large white statue of Quan Am, which was also built by Khai Dinh. Before construction could begin, Khai Dinh had to remove the tombs of Chinese nobles who had already selected the site for its beauty and auspicious orientation. A total of 127 steep steps, lined by four dragons, lead to the honor courtyard; an octagonal pavilion in the mourning yard contains an engraved stone stela; and at the top of more stairs are the tomb and shrine of Khai Dinh, containing a bronze statue of the Emperor sitting on his throne and holding a jade scepter. The interior is richly decorated with ornate murals, floor tiles, and decorations built up with fragments of porcelain. This elaborate tomb took 11 years to build and had to be funded with additional taxes.
✉ 6 miles (10km) south of Huê 🕐 Daily 6.30–6 🚌 As for Gia Long's tomb; continue under river crossing but turn immediately left and go straight across small crossroads

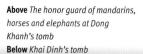

Above *The honor guard of mandarins, horses and elephants at Dong Khanh's tomb*
Below *Khai Dinh's tomb*

DONG PHONG NHA

Visitors are taken by boat only 656 yards (600m) into this UNESCO World Heritage Site (Phong Nha Cave), and are dropped off to explore. The brick foundations of a Cham temple remain in one of the chambers. There are stalagmites and stalactites, and powerful flashlights can pick out ghoulish and godly shapes in the rocks. British divers explored 5.5 miles (9km) of the main cave system in 1990, but less than 0.6 miles (1km) is open to visitors. The nearby Tien Son cave, which was discovered in 1935 in the mountain of Ke Bang, is also accessible up to 440 yards (400m).
🕂 284 D5 ✉ 31 miles (50km) from Dong Hoi 🖐 40,000d admission to each cave and boat rental, which costs US$12.50 for up to 14 passengers 🚍 North on Highway 1 for 12 miles (20km); 19 miles (30km) west to Son River landing stage 🔄 Tours from Huê

MUI NE

www.muinebeach.net

This sandy cape east of Phan Thiet (▷ this page) has two claims to fame: Its *nuoc mam* (fish sauce) and its beaches. It is dominated by sand dunes, some golden, others quite red, reflecting the underlying geology (some areas of the beach may be shifting due to natural erosion). Lining the strip of golden sand are a dozen or so resorts (▷ 179–180). The strong smell pervading the small fishing village at the end of the cape is fish sauce fermenting in wooden barrels. Labels reading *cá com* indicate that the local *nuoc mam* is made from anchovies. The fermenting process takes a year, and the end product is highly regarded—though not as highly as that from the island of Phu Quoc (▷ 225).
🕂 287 F11 🚍 Services from Tran Hung Dao Street, Phan Thiet; Sinh Café bus from Saigon; served by Open Tour bus 🔄 Tours by private operators

MY SON

▷ 156.

Right *Women making fish sauce in Mui Ne*

NGHU HANH SON

The Marble Mountains were named by Emperor Minh Mang on his visit in 1825; they are, in fact, limestone crags with marble outcrops. Their five peaks are important Cham religious sites, and were used by Communist guerrillas during the Vietnam War for their view over Danang air base. Thuy Son, the most visited mountain, has several grottoes and cave pagodas, marked by steps cut into the rock. Tam Thai Pagoda was built in 1825 by Minh Mang on the site of a much older Cham place of worship, and subsequently rebuilt. Its central statue is of the Buddha Sakyamuni (the historic Buddha), flanked by the Bodhisattva Quan Am (a future Buddha and the Goddess of Mercy), and Van Thu, symbolizing wisdom. At the rear of the grotto is the Huyen Khong Cave, originally an animist and later a Buddhist site. The high ceiling is pierced by five holes through which the sun filters and, in the hour before midday, illuminates the central statue. A track leads south to Chua Quan The Am, a grotto with stalactites, stalagmites and pillars.

🕂 285 F7 ✉ 7.5 miles (12km) west of Danang 🕐 Daily 6–5 🖐 20,000d entrance 🚍 Hoi An bus from Hung Vuong Street, Danang 🔄 Private tours from Danang and Hoi An 🏛

PHAN THIET

www.muinebeach.net

This little fishing town on the Ca Ty estuary has an 18-hole golf course designed by British golfer Nick Faldo and it is regarded as one of the best in Vietnam. Until a few hundred years ago the Cham and the Raglai were the region's dominant groups, and there are still some 50,000 Cham and 30,000 Raglai in the area today. The best and most accessible Cham relic is Po Shanu. Situated on the Mui Ne road, these two hilltop towers date from the late eighth century AD. Like other towers in the area, they were constructed of brick bound together with the resin of the day tree.

🕂 287 E11 🚹 Binh Thuan Tourist, 82 Trung Trac Street ☎ 062-3816821 🕐 Mon–Fri 7–11.30, 1.30–5 🚍 Tran Hung Dao Street; connections with Mui Ne, Saigon. Served by Open Tour bus 🚆 Connections with Muong Man for services to Saigon and Hanoi

INFORMATION

⊞ 285 E7 ✉ 40 miles (60km) southwest of Danang 🕐 Daily 8–6 💰 75,000d
🚌 Tours from several operators in Hoi An and Danang ℹ 12 Phan Chu Trinh Street, Hoi An ☎ 0511-3861276; Mon–Fri 7–11.30, 1.30–5

TIPS

» It is not clear how thoroughly the area has been cleared of mines, so it is advisable not to stray too far from the road and path.

» My Son is usually hot and dry; take a hat, sunscreen and water.

» A jeep takes you the 1 mile (2km) from the ticket office to the site; price included in entrance fee.

Above *Some of the 70 ancient monuments in the jungle at My Son*

MY SON

Weather, overgrown jungle and years of fierce warfare have wrought their worst on My Son, which was declared a World Heritage Site by UNESCO in 1999 and is one of Vietnam's most ancient monuments and a tranquil archeological treasure. Arguably, however, the jungle under which it remained hidden for so long may have provided its best protection—more of the structure has been destroyed since the site was uncovered in the 1960s than in the previous four centuries. More than 70 monuments, interlaced with streams and set amid coffee plantations, occupy a valley below Hon Quap mountain. The monuments are in 10 groups, each identified with a letter (A, A', B, C, D, E, F, G, H, K). Within each group, structures are named with that letter and a number.

CHAM STYLE

Much that is known of My Son was ascertained by French archeologists of the École Française d'Extrême-Orient, who rediscovered and excavated the site in 1898. It is one of the most important of the Champa kingdom, along with Tra Kieu and Dong Duong, and was settled from the early eighth to the 15th centuries, the longest constant period of development of any monument in Southeast Asia. It fell strongly under Chinese influence, but there's evidence of Indian culture in its graceful sculptures and buildings. Bricks are laid exactly and held together with a vegetable cement—probably the resin of the day tree. It is thought that each tower was encircled by wood and fired in what amounted to a vast outdoor kiln. Sanctuaries with fine examples of the Cham style of ornamentation through the centuries are C1, with eighth-century AD motifs, and B4, with abstract, wriggling patterns from the ninth century AD.

SITE CONDITIONS

My Son was a Viet Cong field headquarters in the Vietnam War, within one of the US "free fire" zones, and some temples were badly damaged—notably groups A, E and H; groups B and C have largely retained their temples but many statues, altars and linga (phallic symbols) have been moved to the Cham museum in Danang (▷ 138–139). The main sanctuary, A1, was reduced to rubble, after which President Nixon ordered US forces to avoid damaging Cham structures. A stone altar was restored in the 1980s, and it is possible to see some of the 10th-century brickwork. B5, also 10th-century, housed sacred books and ceremonial items used in B1, a temple dedicated to King Bhadravarman I, who started work here in the fourth century AD.

NHA TRANG

INTRODUCTION

There are two Nha Trangs—the sleepy seaside town, with a long, palm- and casuarina-fringed beach and one or two parallel streets, and the commercial town north of Yersin Street. It's the capital of Khanh Hoa Province, with a population of some 200,000 and an active fishing fleet. Several roads lead into the heart of town, which is centered on Yersin and Thong Nhat streets.

WHAT TO SEE

ISLANDS

Several islands lie within reach of Nha Trang. Trips take in Mieu Island and its Tri Nguyen aquarium (20,000d per person), where fish and crustacea are reared. Other nearby islands are Hon Mun, Hon Tam (5,000d per person to dock) and Hon Mot, sometimes called the Salangane Islands after the many sea swallows (*yen* in Vietnamese) that nest here. This bird produces the highly prized nest from which the famous soup is made (▷ 271). Hon Yen (Swallow Island) is strictly out of bounds.

🦐 Mama Linh's Tours, 23c Bier Thu Street ☎ 058-3522844 🦐 Hanh's Green Hat, 44 Ly Thanh Ton Street and 2A Biet Thu Street ☎ 058-3526494 ✋ US$7 (including lunch and pickup from hotel), daily 7am–9pm. Boat tours from Cau Da pier, 123,000d (including lunch and snorkeling equipment), depart 9am

CHAM PONAGAR TEMPLE COMPLEX

On a hill just outside the city is the Cham Ponagar Temple complex, known locally as Thap Ba. Of its original eight towers, four remain, and their styles indicate building periods between the seventh and 12th centuries. The largest, 75ft (23m) high, was built in AD817 and contains a fine and very large linga (phallic symbol) and a statue of Lady Thien Y-ana, also known as Ponagar and said to have re-created the world and taught the local people weaving and new agricultural techniques. The other towers are dedicated to gods: The central tower (now a fertility temple for childless couples) to Cri Cambhu; the northwest tower to Sandhaka, woodcutter and foster-father to Lady Thien Y-ana; and the south tower to Ganeca, Lady Thien Y-ana's daughter.

✚ Off map 158 B1 ✉ 1 mile (2km) north of town on 2 Thang 4 Street 🕐 Daily 6–6 ✋ 5,000d

INFORMATION

✚ 287 F10 🛈 2 Khanh Hoa Tourism, 1 Tran Hung Dao Street ☎ 058-3822753; www.nhatrangtourist.com.vn

🛈 Sinh Café, 90C Hung Vuong Street ☎ 058-3522982 🚌 23 Thang 10 Street; connections with Saigon, Danang, Buon Me Thuot, Dalat, Huê. Served by Open Tour buses 🚌 Thai Nguyen Street; connections with Hanoi, Saigon ✈ Nha Trang Airport 21 miles (34km) to north of town; connections with Hanoi, Saigon and Danang 🍴 Seafood eateries on beach road; also Italian and Indian restaurants ☕ Wide range of cafés and bars

Above *Blue-and-red fishing boats in Nha Trang's harbor*

REGIONS | CENTRAL VIETNAM • SIGHTS

TIPS

» Inter-province buses drop off at intersections on Highway 1, where a *xe ôm* takes passengers to the town center.
» Nha Trang Airport, now used only by small aircraft, is a 5-minute drive from town. There are taxis, *xe ôms* and cyclos, but travelers with light bags could walk it.
» Breakfast in the central market (Cho Dam), at the northern end of Hoang Hoa Than Street, is amazing, with the wealth of sea and land under one roof.

ALEXANDRE YERSIN MUSEUM

This museum is within the Pasteur Institute, founded by the great scientist's protégé, Dr. Alexandre Yersin (1863–1943). Swiss-born Yersin (▷ 33) first arrived in Vietnam in 1891 and spent much of the rest of his life in Nha Trang, where he set up a laboratory to study infectious diseases affecting animals and to produce serum from horses and buffaloes. The museum contains his laboratory equipment, library, stereoscope and microscope.

✚ 158 B1 ✉ 8 Tran Phu Street ☎ 058-3822355 ⊕ Mon–Fri 8–11, 2–4.30, Sat 8–11am
✋ 26,000d 🎫 ❓ Labeling in French and English; no photography

LONG SON PAGODA

An unusual image of the Buddha, backlit with natural light, is the focus of this sanctuary built in 1963. Murals depict the Jataka (birth of the Buddha) stories, and, to the right of the sanctuary, stairs lead to a 29ft (9m) white Buddha perched on a hilltop. The pagoda commemorates monks and nuns who died demonstrating against the Diem government (▷ 37). Behind the pagoda is an impressive 46ft (14m) reclining Buddha, commissioned in 2003.

✚ Off map 158 A1 ✉ 23 Thang 10 Street

MORE TO SEE

NHA TRANG CATHEDRAL

This imposing concrete cathedral, built between 1928 and 1933, has a single, crenelated tower, a vaulted ceiling and stained glass by Louis Balmet.

✚ 158 A2 ✉ Nguyen Trai Street ⊕ Mass: Mon–Fri 4.45am, 5pm, Sat 5pm, Sun 5am, 7am, 9.30am, 5pm

LONG THANH'S STUDIO

This gallery showcases the black-and-white work of one of the country's most distinguished photographers (▷ 21).

✚ 158 A1 ✉ 126 Hoang Van Thu Street ☎ 058-3824875 ⊕ Daily while Long Thanh present

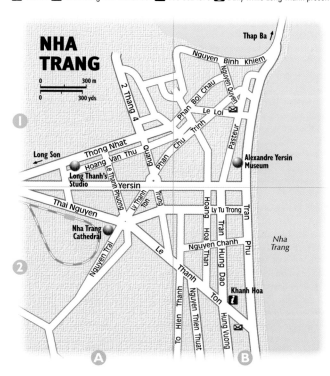

PLEIKU

Pleiku (Play Ku) town, population 35,000, sits high on the Pleiku Plateau, once densely forested and still home to many ethnic minorities. The main attractions lie on the road north to Kontum—a pleasant motorcycle drive, especially early in the year when the white coffee blossom exudes a jasmine-like scent. Bien Ho, 3 miles (5km) north of Pleiku off the Quy Nhon road (Highway 19), is a large volcanic lake (access 1,000d) and Pleiku's main source of water. A platform on a promontory jutting into the water makes a good viewpoint.

Northwest are several Jarai villages, the first being Plei Mrong, which gives a glimpse of Jarai life. Plei Fun, about 12 miles (20km) along the road, has Jarai graves covered by tiled or wooden roofs sheltering possessions of the deceased and guarded by carved hardwood statues. At Plei Mun, another 3 miles (5km) down the road and left 1 mile (2km) down a dirt road, there are even finer examples, as well as a traditional wooden *rong* house with a corrugated-iron roof.

➕ 285 E8 ℹ️ Gia Lai Tourist, 215 Hung Vuong Street (in Hung Vuong Hotel) ☎ 059-3874571 🚌 Connections with Saigon, Buon Me Thuot, Dalat ✈️ Connections with Saigon, Danang ☞ Private tours from Nha Trang and Danang

PO KLONG GARAI

Po Klong Garai is a group of three Cham towers, perhaps the most striking in the country outside My Son (▷ 156). They were built during the 13th century on a cactus- and boulder-strewn hill with commanding views over the surrounding countryside. To the north the remains of Thanh Son, the former US air base, are visible. The towers are raised up on a brick base and have been extensively renovated, but other than the repair work there is no sign of mortar at all, the cohesion of the red bricks being one of the enduring mysteries of the Cham. The central tower has a figure of a dancing Siva (the Hindu god of destruction) over the main entrance. The door jambs are made of what looks like polished sandstone on which (competing with modern graffiti) are ancient Cham engravings. Tucked inside the dimly lit main chamber, full of incense smoke, is Siva's vehicle, the bull Nandi, and some other statues.

➕ 287 F11 ℹ️ 4 miles (6km) from Phan Rang on Highway 27 ✋ 5,000d ℹ️ Ninh Thuan Tourist, 505 Thong Nhat Street, Phan Rang ☎ 068-3822722 🚌 Local services from south side of Phan Rang towards Dalat. Served by Open Tour bus

Above *The 13th-century Po Klong Garai*

VUON QUOC GIA BACH MA

www.bachma.vnn.vn

Bach Ma National Park was established as a hill station in 1932, but after the departure of the French in the 1950s its villas and hotels were forgotten. The ruins are gradually being uncovered, and gardens and ponds cleared, with some of the ruined villas now serving as tourist accommodations. In 1991 the Vietnamese government classified the 54,440-acre (22,031ha) granite and sandstone area a national park. Trails lead past cascades, through rhododendron woods and up to the 4,751ft (1,448m) summit, and wildlife includes buff-cheeked or white-cheeked gibbon and seven of the 12 pheasant species recorded in Vietnam.

✠ 285 E7 ✉ Phu Loc, Thua Tien, Huê ☎ 054-3871330 ◷ Daily ✋ 20,000d ⛴ Guides hired for 200,000d a day. Private tours from Huê, Danang and Hoi An. Six guesthouses (100,000d–300,000d)

VUON QUOC GIA CAT TIEN

www.namcattien.org

The newly created Nam Cat Tien National Park, about 90 miles (150km) north of Saigon on the route to Dalat, is one of the last surviving areas of natural bamboo and dipterocarp forest in southern Vietnam. It is also one of the few places in the country where populations of large mammals can be found—tiger, elephant, bear, and the last few remaining Javan rhino. There are also some 300 species of birds, smaller mammals, reptiles and butterflies.

The park is managed by 20 rangers who, besides helping protect the flora and fauna, also conduct research and guide visitors. (No English spoken.)

✠ 287 E11 ✉ 30 miles (50km) south of Bao Loc on Highway 20; turn off at Tan Phu and follow track for 15 miles (25km) ☎ 061-3669228/3669330 ✋ 50,000d ⛴ Private tours from Saigon and Dalat

VUON QUOC GIA YOK DON

The 284,000 acres (115,000ha) that make up this wildlife reserve, Yok Don National Park, are home to at least 63 species of mammals, 17 of which are on the worldwide endangered list, and 240 species of birds. The reserve is also thought to be the home of several rare white elephants. Five of the world's 25 rarest primates survive here, as does the Asian elephant. Within the park's boundaries 17 different ethnic minority groups make their home.

About 1.5 miles (3km) beyond the Yok Don National Park gate is Ban Don village, which has a long tradition of taming the forest's elephants, and beyond the third sub-hamlet is the tomb of Khun Ju-Nop, known as the King Elephant-Catcher, who died in 1924. Next to his square tomb is a taller, white stupa commemorating his brother, also a famous elephant-catcher, who died in 1950. Both were of Lao origin. Behind is the more modern tomb of a M'nong elephant-catcher, Y Pum B'Ya, a son of Khun Ju-Nop.

✠ 287 E9 ✉ 25 miles (40km) northwest of Buon Me Thuot, Daklak Province ☎ 050-3783049 ◷ Daily 7.30–5 ✋ 45,000d 🍴 ⛴ Guided tours on foot 400,000d an hour; elephant ride for two 515,000d an hour. Trekking and animal spotting by night is also available. Private tours from Buon Me Thuot

Opposite Bach Ma National Park
Below Ea Rong Lake, in Yok Don National Park

HUÊ TO DANANG BY ROAD

This tour takes you down the coast of the central region of Vietnam past spectacular scenery, including the dramatic Lang Co Bay, and along a road pass that leads you through the clouds.

THE TOUR

Distance: 67.5 miles (108km)
Allow: Half a day
Start at: Huê
End at: Danang

HOW TO GET THERE

Rent a car and a driver from one of the many tour operators in Huê, or take an Open Tour bus from Huê to Danang—some stop at Lang Co.

TIPS

» Be prepared: The journey between Huê and Danang is precarious as it winds its way over the Hai Van Pass.
» Clouds gathering on the Pass may obscure your view.
» A 7-mile (12km) tunnel was opened in early 2005 under the Hai Van Pass to smooth the flow of traffic along Highway 1 and reduce the number of accidents on the pass. It links Lang Co and Danang.
» To make the journey by rail, ▷ 164.

★ Huê (▷ 147–150) was the capital of Vietnam between 1802 and 1945 and is a city with a royal heritage. Key visitor attractions include the Imperial City and the Museum of Royal Fine Arts. Flowing through Huê is the "Perfume River" (Huong Giang), which takes its name from a sweet-smelling shrub said to grow at its source.

Leave Huê and head south on Highway 1.

The road from Huê to Lang Co passes through pretty, red-tiled villages, surrounded by bamboo and fruit trees that provide shade and sustenance. Pink-flowered bougainvillea bushes create splashes of color, while windowless jalopies from the French era trundle along picking up passengers. You may spot a station wagon from the American era providing an inter-village shared taxi service.

Continue to the village of Lang Co, about 40 miles (65km) south of Huê.

❶ Lang Co is an idyllic fishing village with a number of inexpensive seafood restaurants. Emperor Khai Dinh apparently visited Lang Co in the first year of his reign (1916) and was so impressed that he ordered the construction of a summer palace here. This, it seems, was never carried out—even by his son Bao Dai, who was so fond of building palaces—but there is the Lang Co Beach Resort to stay in (▷ 179).

Shortly after crossing the Lang Co lagoon, dotted with coracles and fish traps, the road begins the long haul up to Hai Van Pass.

2 Hai Van Pass (Deo Hai Van)—Pass of the Ocean Clouds or, to the French, Col des Nuages—lies 1,630ft (497m) above sea-level and once marked the border between the kingdoms of Vietnam and Champa. The mountains act as an important climatic barrier, trapping the cooler, damper air masses to the north and bottling them up over Huê, which accounts for the city's shockingly wet weather. The mountains also mark a linguistic divide; the Huê dialect (the language of the royal court) to the north is a constant source of bemusement to many southerners. The pass is peppered with abandoned pillboxes and crowned with an old fort, originally built by the dynasty from Huê and used as a relay station for the pony express on the old Mandarin Road. Looking back to the north, stretching into the haze is the shore and lagoon of Lang Co. To the south is Danang Bay and Monkey Mountain (Hon Lao), and at your feet lies a patch of green paddies belonging to a leper colony, accessible only by boat.

The road then passes through the village of Nam O.

3 Nam O was once famous for firework manufacture. Pages of old school books were dyed pink, laid out in the sun to dry, rolled

Opposite *Girls cycling to school in Huê*
Above *The blue waters of Lang Co Bay*

up and filled with gunpowder, but the village has suffered from the government's ban on firecrackers.

Just south of Nam O, you pass Xuan Thieu Beach.

4 Xuan Thieu Beach was dubbed "Red Beach II" by the US Marines who landed here in March 1965, marking the beginning of direct US intervention in the Second Indochina War. The surfaced road and military base's concrete foundations still remain.

Continue on to Danang.

5 Danang (▷ 138–139) is on a peninsula where the Han River flows into the South China Sea. It was an important port during French colonial times. The city's main attraction is the Museum of Champa Sculpture.

WHERE TO EAT
Stock up on food in Huê or visit one of the seafood restaurants in Lang Co.

HUÊ TO DANANG BY RAIL

The rail journey from Huê (▷ 147–150; ⊞ 285 E6) to Danang (▷ 138–139; ⊞ 285 F7) is regarded as one of the most scenic in the world—a leisurely chug around the coast on a line that clings to cliff edges like a limpet to a rock.

THE TOUR
Allow: Half a day
Start at: Huê rail station *(ga xe lua),* west end of Le Loi Street ☎ 054-3822175
End at: Danang rail station, 122 Haiphong Street ☎ 0511-3823810

TRAIN INFORMATION
Trains between Huê and Danang: depart daily 4.48am, 6.12am, 8.02am, 10.50am (journey time 2.5 hours); air-conditioned soft-seat 67,000d.

TIPS
» Timetables change, so consult the train office or Vietnam Railways website www.vr.com.vn/English.
» The booking/ticket office opens daily 7am–10pm, but closes 11–1.30, 6–7.
» Local tour operators charge US$6 to purchase and organize the ticket.

This is an exciting journey, often passing through clouds that temporarily obscure the view. First-class cars have plenty of leg room, luggage racks and Western- and Eastern-style toilets at either end. Each car is staffed by a Vietnam Railways employee.

Between Huê and Danang a finger of the Truong Son Mountains (Day Truong Son) juts eastwards, extending all the way to the sea. This barrier to north–south communication has resulted in some spectacular engineering solutions. The single track, narrow gauge rail track closely follows the coastline, sometimes almost hanging over the sea and making this a nail-biting section.

On foggy days the vegetation that tumbles down from the coastal heights oozes steam; on clear days you can see fishing boats drifting in the water. The magnificent spit of land on which Lang Co sits is decorated around its edge with fine white sand pushing out into the turquoise sea. Palm trees and other vegetation jostle for position on the peninsula. This beautiful view is marred only slightly by the road bridge that crosses it.

Above *A train travels along the Hai Van Pass from Huê to Danang*

TOUR

BICYCLING AROUND CAM NAM ISLAND

This is a peaceful bicycle ride through the countryside that also passes some of the busy areas of Hoi An (▷ 142–146; ✚ 285 F7).

THE TOUR
Distance: 6 miles (10km)
Allow: Around 4 hours, with food stops
Start at: Hoi An Beach Resort, Cua Dai
End at: Cua Dai Road

HOW TO GET THERE
Hoi An is on the coast, 19 miles (30km) south of Danang.

★ Make the 2-mile (4km) ride west from the Hoi An Beach Resort on Cua Dai Beach (crossing a narrow bridge) to the first major left turn in Hoi An town (corner of Cua Dai and Pham Hong Thai (if you pass the post office you've gone too far).

❶ As you bicycle past many paddy fields dotted with cemeteries and huts, you'll also pass the busy restaurants and food stands on the main road.

From the corner of Cua Dai and Pham Hong Thai streets, ride as far as you can go to Phan Boi Chau Street, then turn right. Pass through the French district. At the corner of Phan Boi Chau and Hoang Dieu streets, ride over Cam Nam bridge.

❷ On Cam Nam bridge, look to the right to see the busy activity of Hoi An market.

Stay on the paved road, passing the Van Hoi hotel and later a shoemaker's outdoor workshop, both on your left, until an expanse of the river with vertical fishing poles comes into view on the right by a large blue sign. The tourist shops have petered here and this is a spot where you can turn around. If you want to continue, stay on the paved road until you are ready to turn around.

❸ Ahead is what must be one of the most ramshackle houses you will come across in Vietnam.

At the intersection, take the path to the left and continue along the riverbank. After five minutes you will reach the main road. Turn left here, then follow the main road, which bears round to the left.

❹ Cycle back to Can Nam bridge, continue across it, and turn right into Nguyen Duy Hieu Street.

Only turn right at the bridge, into Phan Boi Chau Street (from where you first came), if you are ready to eat. There are a number of good eateries along Phan Boi Chau. Vegetarians should wait a little longer (▷ right).

❺ Continue to the end of Nguyen Duy Hieu Street until you reach a T-junction. Turn left here onto Le Thanh Tong Street and stay on this street until you reach a set of traffic lights where you turn right.

You are now on the road back to the beach, passing the Phuoc An Riverside Hotel on your left and the Hoi An Riverside Resort on the right. There are a number of attractive riverside restaurants along this stretch of road and it is worth checking some of them out if planning ahead for an evening meal.

❻ Continue back over the narrow bridge you crossed earlier and return to your start point. Note again the rice paddies and fish farms; the large numbers of ducks on your right are part of a duck farm.

On the right side of the road, just across the bridge, there is a vegetarian café by the water's edge.

WHEN TO GO
Start early in the morning to avoid the heat of midday.

Above *Bicycling through the countryside on Cam Nam Island*

CENTRAL VIETNAM • TOUR

REGIONS

WHAT TO DO

DALAT

DALAT PALACE GOLF CLUB
www.dalatpalacegolf.vn
This US-owned, 18-hole golf course, rated by some as the finest in Vietnam, overlooks the Xuan Huong Lake.
✉ Phu Dong Thien Vuong Street, Dalat ☎ 063-3824325 🕓 Daily ✋ Green fee US$95–$110; caddie fees US$21, golf cart rental US$35

GOLF 3 BAR AND CLUB
The bar is in the basement opposite the nightclub and has several pool tables and a varied selection of drinks and bar food, both of which are good value for money. The club has a moderate-sized dance floor.
✉ 4 Nguyen Thi Minh Khai Street, Dalat ☎ 063-3826042 🕓 Daily 6pm–midnight ✋ Admission 40,000d

HAI SON HOTEL BAR
All the hip folk in Dalat come here for the top nightclub in town. The large, modern bar gets full in the evenings with people waiting to enter the adjoining club. There's a good choice of inexpensive drinks, but the food is limited.
✉ 1 Nguyen Thi Minh Khai Street, Dalat ☎ 063-3822626 🕓 Daily 6pm–midnight

LARRY'S BAR
Larry's Bar was named for the late Larry Hillblom, a Californian businessman who, in the 1990s, renovated Dalat's Sofitel, Novotel and golf course. It has live music, drinks and good bar food.
✉ Sofitel Dalat Palace, 12 Tran Phu Street, Dalat ☎ 063-3825444 🕓 Daily 4pm–midnight

PHAT TIRE VENTURES
www.phattireventures.com
This company arranges exhilarating days out. There are two descents in the Datanla Falls area for canyoning, 3 miles (5km) from Dalat. You can go kayaking on Dankia Lake at the base of Lang Bian mountains, 12 miles (20km) north of Dalat. One- or two-day mountain-biking trips are organized around the countryside of Dalat. One-day rock climbing trips are also arranged.
✉ 109 Nguyen Van Troi Street, Dalat ☎ 063-3829422 ✋ Canyoning (no experience necessary) US$40 half day; kayaking in Tuyen Lam Lake US$37 half day; white-water rafting on the Langbian River US$67 1 day; mountain-biking, US$42–$48 1 day; biking and rafting from Dalat to Nha Trang US$107; 1- and 2-day biking trips from Dalat to Mui Ne, US$77–$169

Above A day out with Phat Tire Ventures

SPORTS CAFÉ
The open-air bar has good views over Xuan Huong Lake. There's quite a wide selection of drinks and some reasonably priced bar food.
✉ Empress Hotel, 5 Nguyen Thai Hoc Street, Dalat ☎ 063-3833888 🕓 6.30am–10.30pm

DANANG

CHRISTIE'S COOL SPOT
This popular expatriate venue has a downstairs bar and an upstairs restaurant. Happy hour runs from 4pm to 8pm, and food is also served in the bar.
✉ 112 Tran Phu Street, Danang ☎ 0511-3824040 🕓 Daily 9.30am–10.30pm

FURAMA RESORT
www.furamavietnam.com
Between February and September the 5-star PADI diving center at the resort runs trips out to the sea off Danang. It runs a range of courses from beginners to advanced and its instructors speak four languages. The Furama also has a catamaran, a banana boat and speedboats. Health spa treatments are available.

✉ 68 Ho Xuan Huong Street, Bac My An Beach, Danang ☎ 0511-3847888
✋ 3-day Open Water Diver course US$437; shorter courses US$291 (includes equipment and transportation)

XQ DANANG SILK EMBROIDERY

www.xqhandembroidery.com

At this large embroidery store in downtown Danang, visitors can witness the creative process at work and there is also opportunity to buy a wide variety of beautifully embroidered goods.

✉ 39–41 Nguyen Thai Ho, Danang
☎ 0511-3816847 ⏰ Daily 10.30–8.30pm

HOI AN

41 LE LOI STREET

See the process of silk manufacture, at this silk workshop run by very friendly staff. A 1940s manufacturing machine is on display downstairs. The finished fabrics are on sale.

✉ 41 Le Loi Street, Hoi An ☎ 0510-862164 ⏰ Daily 7.45am–10pm

CHAM ISLAND DIVING

www.chamislanddiving.com

All the diving trips (between mid-February and the end of September) include a pickup from your hotel, snokeling and diving equipment, lunch on the beach and return to your hotel around 5.30pm.

✉ 88 Nguyen Thai Hoc Street, Hoi An
☎ 0510-3910782 ✋ One discovery dive for beginners: US$65; snorkeling: US$40. PADI diving course also available: US$370

COCONUT TOUR

All the hotels in Hoi An offer the same tours (river and town tours, My Son) but with Huynh Huu Phuoc there is an opportunity to enjoy a bicycle excursion into the local countryside and visit a small organic vegetable farm followed by a street-side breakfast, a herbal foot massage and a cooking class. Less expensive morning (6am) and afternoon (3pm) bicycle tours of the market and villages are also available (US$8 and US$10).

☎ 0510 3864376/0905-411184 ✋ US$20

HOI AN HANDICRAFT WORKSHOP

www.hoianhandicraft.com

Musicians sometimes play the Vietnamese monochord at this traditional venue. At the back of the building are craftspeople, including a potter, straw mat-makers, embroiderers and woodcarvers.

✉ 9 Nguyen Thai Hoc Street, Hoi An
☎ 0510-3910216 ⏰ Workshop: daily 7.30am–6pm. Performances: Tue–Sun 10.15am, 3.15pm

LIFESTART FOUNDATION

www.lifestartfoundation.org.au/workshop

This is a nonprofit workshop making and selling arts and crafts by people who need a helping hand. The quality is high and the scarves, jewelry, traditional Vietnamese hats and other knickknacks make ideal small gifts. There are plans to run half-day tours with lessons in lantern-making.

✉ 77 Phan Chu Trinh ⏰ Daily 9am–7pm

LOTUS JEWELLERY

www.lotusjewellery-hoian.com

Lotus has two shops in Hoi An retailing silver jewelry in a variety of styles. If you supply a sketch or photograph, they can match the designs. Prices are not outrageous given the quality of the work.

✉ 82 Tran Phu Street and 100 Nguyen Thai Hoc, Hoi An ☎ 0510-3917889 and 0510-3911664 ⏰ Daily 8am–10pm

PHUC THINH

The prices at this jewelry store with remain fairly fixed unless you purchase more than one item of gold, silver or jade. Before making a purchase, check out another jewelry shop a few doors down at No. 147.

✉ 137 Tran Phu Street, Hoi An
☎ 0510-3864269 ⏰ Daily 9–8

REACHING OUT, HOA-NHAP HANDICRAFTS

www.reachingoutvietnam.com

The arts and crafts, cards, textiles and jewelry on sale here are made by local artisans with disabilities. The shop operates a fair trade policy, and profits support people with disabilities. There is usually someone at work in the shop, and visitors are welcome to watch as they create their products.

✉ 103 Nguyen Thai Hoc Street ☎ 0510-3910168 ⏰ Mon–Fri 8.30am–9pm, Sat–Sun 9.30am–8pm

RED BRIDGE COOKING SCHOOL

www.visithoian.com

Visit the market to see local produce, then take a 20-minute boat ride to the cookery school, where you will be shown around the fabulous herb garden. The demonstration by chefs that follows includes dishes such as warm squid salad served in half a pineapple or grilled eggplant (aubergine) stuffed with vegetables. Inside, you are able to make your own spring rolls and learn Vietnamese food-carving. Then dine at the restaurant while listening to Cuban music and watching ducks swim by on the river.

✉ Thon 4, Cam Thanh, Hoi An ☎ 0510-3933222 ⏰ Daily ✋ US$27 half day; US$43 full day; 2-hour evening class US$16

TAM TAM CAFÉ

http://tamtamcafe-hoian.com

Though mainly a café/restaurant, the Tam Tam also has a good bar. It is in an attractively renovated tea house and the bar has a pool table and a DJ playing music some evenings. The balcony makes a nice spot for a break anytime of the day. Cooking classes are also available.

✉ 110 Nguyen Thai Hoc Street, Hoi An
☎ 0510-3862212 ⏰ Daily 9.30am–1am

VN COLOUR

Browse through one of the catalogs and consider a new garment made to measure in 24 hours. Many tailors in Hoi An operate on a modest scale and it makes sense to compare prices and the service on offer before choosing an outlet.

✉ 79 Nguyen Thai Hoc Street ☎ 0510-3910827

WHITE MARBLE

Regardless of whether you are dining upstairs or not, the street-

level bar in White Marble is a congenial spot for drinks before or after eating. The open windows look out onto a street junction and the world can be watched going by. Check the blackboard for the range of wines available by the glass.
✉ 98 Le Loi Street, Hoi An ☎ 09-11862
🕐 Daily 11–11

YALY

www.yalycouture.com

Professional tailors make very good-quality Thai and Vietnamese silk outfits in this attractive old building. Prices are a little high but you won't be disappointed with the results. Thai silk clothes are more expensive than those made with Vietnamese silk. Other Yaly stores are at 47 Nguyen Thai Hox Street (tel 0510-3861119) and 358 Nguyen Duy Hieu Street.
✉ 47 Nguyen Thai Hoc Street, Hoi An
☎ 0510-3910474 🕐 Daily 7am–8.30pm

HUÊ

DMZ BAR

Huê's first bar is popular with younger travelers as well as locals. Cold beer and spirits are served at low prices, and there's a pool table and patio.
✉ 60 Le Loi Street, Huê ☎ 054-3823414
🕐 Daily 4pm–2am

DRAGONBOATING

Sail up the Perfume River with your own private singers and musicians. Boats are available on the stretch of riverbank between the Huong Giang Hotel and the Trang Tien Bridge, and also from the dock behind the Dong Ba Market. Tour offices and major hotels will arrange trips, including the Sinh Café and Hotel Saigon Morin (▷ 178).
✋ From 50,000d per person

ROYAL (EAST) THEATER (DUYET THI DUONG)

www.nhanhac.com.vn

Highly enjoyable performances of traditional Vietnamese court music are held in the rebuilt Imperial City theater, accompanying elaborate dances by costumed performers.

✉ 23 Thang 8 Street, Huê ☎ 054-514989, 091-5439183 🕐 Daily 9, 10, 2.30, 3, 3.30, 4 ✋ 50,000d

WHY NOT?

Mini conical hats hang from a brick bar and fishing nets hang from the walls at this arty café-bar (not to be confused with the Why Not? restaurant farther down the street). It offers a reasonable selection of food and drink and has a pool table. The special cocktail—Why Not?—is a blend of vodka, Cointreau, blue Curaçao, grenadine and fresh milk.
✉ 21 Vo Thi Sau Street, Huê ☎ 054-3824793 🕐 Daily 7.30–2am. Happy hour is 5–9pm

MUI NE

C2SKY KITECENTER

www.c2skykitecenter.com

Under the same management as the Mui Ne Cooking School (▷ right), C2Sky runs kiteboarding courses in English, French, German, Dutch and Russian. Kites and boards can also be rented and a taxi service from Ho Chi Minh City's airport can be organized (US$120).
✉ Sunshine Beach Resort 82 Nguyen Dinh Chieu Street, Mui Ne ☎ 091-6655241
✋ Courses from 2 hours to 12 hours US$100–$540

JIBE'S BEACH CLUB

www.windsurf-vietnam.com

Jibe's is an importer of sea kayaks, windsurfing, surfboard and kite surfing equipment. Watersports equipment can be purchased or rented by the hour, day or week. Kite surfing lessons are run by instructors certified by the International Kite Surfing Organization; instruction is available in nine languages. There's also a good range of bathing suits for sale.
✉ Full Moon Beach Resort, Mui Ne ☎ 062-3847405 🕐 Daily 7.30am–3am
✋ Varies, check website and email for a quotation

LOTUS DAY SPA

www.sailingclubvietnam.com

Indulge yourself in the open-sided cabins of the spa area in the

lusciously green hotel grounds or in the privacy of your own room. Treatments include a rice body polish, mineral mud wrap and 60-minute skin-purifying facial.
✉ Sailing Club, Mui Ne ☎ 062-3847442
🕐 Daily 10–7pm; after 7pm by appointment only ✋ Body massage US$22; wraps US$28–32; facials from US$22 for 45 minutes

MUI NE COOKING SCHOOL

www.c2skykitecenter.com

Learn to cook in a beach garden after a visit to the local Ham Tien market to collect ingredients. You can skip the market visit if you wish and just join the cooking class that starts at 1.30pm.
✉ Sunshine Beach Resort, 82 Nguyen Dinh Chieu Street, Mui Ne ☎ 091-6655241
✋ US$25 (including market visit); US$20 (cooking class only)

NHA TRANG

COCO DIVE CENTER

www.cocodivecenter.com

This 5-star PADI instructor center is run by the first Vietnamese to qualify as a PADI master instructor. Daily trips and courses are offered from beginner to advanced, and five languages are spoken by the staff. Night dives are run on request. Prices include all equipment and instruction, and there is a 10 percent discount for those who have their own equipment.
✉ 2E Biet Thu Street, Nha Trang
☎ 058-3522900 🕐 Daily 6am–9pm
✋ Two dives US$50–$70; Open Water Diver, 3 days US$270–$360

CRAZY KIM BAR

This place serves bar food and breakfast inside or in a small outdoor eating area at the front. At the back, the Wild East Saloon, complete with swing doors, is an added attraction. The remaining area focuses on the bar in the front room and the low-slung wicker chair area out the back. Happy hour is from noon to midnight, and the bar is deservedly popular with travelers and expatriates.
✉ 19 Biet Thu Street, Nha Trang
☎ 058-3816072 🕐 Daily 10am–1am

EVASON ANA MANDARA SPA

www.sixsenses.com

The wonderful Six Senses Spa experience at the Ana Mandara will leave you feeling pampered and totally relaxed. The helpful, professional staff massage away your aches and pains in beautiful surroundings next to the beach. The Six Senses Spa offers Japanese and Vichy showers, hot tubs and massages. The Vietnamese Experience includes steam and sauna with fresh herbs, foot massage, cupping and pressure-point activation, scalp massage, a Vietnamese facial using aloe vera and a Vietnamese hair wash. The shampoo, used by a former empress of Vietnam, is made from a black bean called *bo ket*, lime and grapefruit peel.

✉ Tran Phu Street, Nha Trang ☎ 058-3522222 🖐 Herbal bath 990,000d, massages 320,000d–1,980,000d, facials from 1,100,000d, body wraps from 650,000, beauty treatments from 660,000d

GUAVA

Guava is a stylish cocktail bar and café with an orange facade, a garden and lounge area. Sit in the large, quarry-tiled courtyard on solid, woodblock chairs with ultra-cool, square white cushions. Earlier in the day Guava enjoys a Zen-like calm. At night the palms are backlit. Burgers, hangover breakfasts and sandwiches are served all day. Happy hour is between 5pm and

9pm for Vietnamese cocktails.

✉ 17 Biet Thu Street, Nha Trang ☎ 058-3524140 🕐 Daily 10.30am–1am

LONG THANH'S GALLERY

Long Thanh, one of Vietnam's most famous black-and-white photographers (▷ 21), will meet enthusiasts and organize special photographic expeditions.

✉ 126 Hoang Van Thu Street, Nha Trang ☎ 058-3824875 🖐 Negotiable with Long Thanh

RAINBOW DIVERS

www.divevietnam.com

A British-owned, 5-star PADI instructor development resort that runs a full range of dives and courses around the islands off Nha Trang. The instructors speak a variety of languages. There are also dives from Whale Island Resort (▷ 181). Price includes pickup, equipment and refreshments.

✉ 90a Hung Vuong Street, Nha Trang ☎ 058-3524351 🕐 Daily 6am–10pm 🖐 PADI courses from US$102 (scuba diving afternoon course) to US$456 (5-day open water course)

THAP BA HOT SPRINGS

www.thapbahotsprings.com.vn

Soak in mineral water or a mud bath, in baths and pools of differing sizes available for individuals, couples and groups. The water is 104°F (40°C) and is salty and rich in sodium silicate chloride. The mineral mud is high in sodium silicate

carbonate, which stimulates the nerves under the skin. Steam baths and massages are also available.

✉ 3 miles (4km) from Nha Trang, past Ponagar Cham towers ☎ 058-3834939 🖐 Mineral mud tub for one 550,000d; for two 950,000d; mineral water bath for two 700,000d, for one 400,000d

VINPEARL LAND

www.vinpearlland.com

A water and amusement park reached from the Phu Quy jetty by ferry (from 8am and last return at 10pm), or by cable car. Vinpearl Land attracts vast numbers of Vietnamese families at weekends. There are five restaurants and, like everything else here, payment is organized by smart cards.

✉ Tre Island, Nha Trang ☎ 058-3598188 🖐 Amusement park and water park 329,000d adult, 236,000d child (1–1.4m/3–4.5ft); set meals at any restaurant 154,000d (aduld and child); fast food ticket 20,000d (adult and child); ferry fare 40,000d (one way)

PHAN THIET

OCEAN DUNES GOLF CLUB

www.vietnamgolfresorts.com

Phan Thiet's US-owned 18-hole golf course was designed by Nick Faldo and is regarded as one of the best in Vietnam. The 6,746-yard (6,169m) par 72 course has a fully equipped clubhouse and restaurant.

✉ 1 Ton Duc Thang Street, Phan Thiet ☎ 062-3823366 🖐 Green fees from US$38 (9-hole Mon–Thu) to US$77 (18-hole Fri–Sat); caddy fees from US$12 to US$18; equivalent green fees if staying at the Novotel hotel US$30–US$57

VICTORIA PHAN THIET

www.victoriahotels-asia.com

This hugely attractive beach resort, close to Mui Ne, has an on-site spa that offers Thai massage, reflexology, traditional Japanese shiatsu and other face and body massages. There is also a sauna, Jacuzzi and beauty salon.

✉ Km 9, Phu Hai, Phan Thiet ☎ 062-3813000 🖐 From US$25 (hand and reflexology) to US$40 (full-body massage)

Left *Parasailing over Nha Trang*

EATING

PRICES AND SYMBOLS

The restaurants are listed alphabetically (excluding Le, La, Il and The). The prices given are the average for a two-course lunch (L) and a three-course dinner (D) for one person, without drinks. The wine price is for the least expensive bottle.

For a key to the symbols, ▷ 2.

BAC MY AN BEACH DANANG
CAFÉ INDOCHINE

www.furamavietnam.com

This resort restaurant, decorated with pink Chinese lanterns, rattan furniture, banana trees and old colonial photographs, enjoys open-sided views over the infinity pool and onto the beach, and has a predominantly Asian menu of Vietnamese, Indian, Japanese and fusion dishes. Try the oyster mushroom soup and the martini shrimp—jumbo shrimp flamed with martini and finished with tomato, and served in a filo basket. The ice creams and sherbets here are hugely popular.

✉ Furama Resort, 68 Ho Xuan Huong Street, Bac My An ☎ 0511-3847888 ⏰ Daily 6.30am–11pm ✋ L 230,000d, D 350,000d, Wine 430,000d

DALAT
LONG HOA

In the best traditions of French family restaurants, this place serves delicious food and superb breakfasts, and is fairly priced. It is popular with Dalat's expatriates and visitors alike. The chicken soup and steak are particularly good, and the vegetarian choices can be recommended. Service is erratic; don't be surprised if your main course comes at the same time as your starter. It's best to arrive early.

✉ 6, 3 Thang 2, Dalat ☎ 063-3822934 ⏰ Daily 10.30am–9.30pm ✋ L 70,000d, D 200,000d, Local wine 130,000d

LE RABELAIS

www.sofitel.com

Eating in the sumptuous dining room of Le Rabelais, with its elegant furnishings, terrace and views down to the lake, is one of the highlights of a visit to Dalat. The restaurant specializes in French cuisine, and there is an excellent wine list. Staff are attentive and knowledgeable. Note that smart dress is required. After dinner retire to the Le Rabelais Piano Bar for live music until 10pm.

✉ Sofitel Dalat Palace, 12 Tran Phu Street

Dalat ☎ 063-3825444 ⏰ Daily 11am–2pm, 6pm–10pm ✋ L 453,000d, D 514,000d, Wine 490,000d

STOP AND GO CAFÉ

This bohemian café, serving coffee, cakes and snacks, is also an art gallery run by the locally distinguished poet Mr. Duy Viet, who was born in the house. Sit inside, enjoying the early morning sunlight that fills the house, or on the terrace as he bustles around rustling up breakfast and pulling out volumes of visitors' books and his own collected works. The garden is an attractively overrun wilderness where tall fir trees sigh in the breeze.

✉ 2A Ly Tu Trong Street, Dalat ☎ 063-3828458 ⏰ Daily 7.30am–8.30pm ✋ L 90,000d, D 125,000d, Wine 220,000d

DANANG
CHRISTIE'S COOL SPOT

Christie's old premises were demolished during the construction of the River Han Bridge; its new location is one block in from the river, where it has merged with the Cool Spot bar. Frequented by expatriates from Danang and outlying provinces, it has a small bar downstairs, and a restaurant above serving cold beer and Western and Japanese food, plus a magnificent all-day breakfast. Its homemade pizzas are tasty, as is its home-made lemon pie. Happy hour runs from 4pm to 8pm, with cocktails during normal hours ringing in at 50,000d.

✉ 112 Tran Phu Street, Danang ☎ 0511-3824040 🌐 Daily 9.30am–10.30pm
✋ L 125,000d, D 180,000d, Wine 280,000d

HOI AN
BROTHER'S CAFÉ
www.brothercafehoian.com

These cloistered French houses were renovated with exquisite taste in 2008. The garden leads down to the river, and dining alfresco is a delight. The menu has good Vietnamese specialties, and at 360,000d the daily set meal (excludes single diners) still offers good value in lovely surroundings with white umbrellas and white-clothed tables. Interior dining, roadside, is also possible. Hoi An spring rolls are beautifully presented, and the Brother's-style steamed shrimp comes bathed in coconut juice inside the coconut.

✉ 27 Phan Boi Chau Street, Hoi An
☎ 0510-3914150 🌐 Daily 10am–11pm
✋ L 220,000d, D 460,000d, Wine 410,000d

CAFÉ DES AMIS

Customers come back again and again to this hugely popular restaurant facing the river, despite the limited range of dishes on offer. The daily set meal consists of four very tasty fish, seafood or vegetarian dishes, concocted by the owner, Mr. Nguyen Manh Kim, who spends several months a year cooking in Europe.

✉ 52 Bach Dang Street, Hoi An
☎ 0510-3861616 🌐 Daily 10–10
✋ L and D 120,000d

CARGO CLUB
www.restaurant-hoian.com

Riverside and streetside vantage points add to the appeal of The Cargo Club, as does its attractive interior. Accommodated within a pair of beautiful old shop houses overlooking the tranquil waters of the Son River, the restaurant serves breakfasts, brunches and sandwiches, homemade ice cream and an array of cakes and desserts from its huge patisserie counter. Among items on the mainly international restaurant menu are goat's cheese and spinach lasagne and a delectable passion mousse with chocolate.

✉ 107–109 Nguyen Thai Hoc Street, Hoi An ☎ 0510-3910489 🌐 Daily 8am–11pm ✋ L 170,000d, D 300,000d, Wine 312,000d

HAI'S SCOUT CAFÉ

Crossing the block between two of the main streets of the old town, there are two entrances: from the Tran Pau side you enter a courtyard with tables set under bamboo trees, while from the other side the entrance immediately accesses the traditional building and dining area. The smoked pork and beef kebabs on the nightly barbecues draw in a steady stream of hungry customers; curried chicken and various stir-fries are also on the menu.

✉ 111 Tran Phu Street/ 98 Nguyen Thai Hoc Street, Hoi An ☎ 0510-3863210 🌐 Daily 7.30am–11pm ✋ L 160,000d, D 185,000d, Wine 260,000d

THE MERMAID (NHU Y)
www.restaurant-hoian.com

Miss Vy turns out local specialties, as well as some of her own. Diners are aided by pictures on the menu. One particularly good choice is the stir-fried prawns with garlic chives; others are the grilled eggplant (aubergine) with ground pork, and mackerel wrapped in banana leaf.

✉ 2 Tran Phu Street, Hoi An ☎ 0510-3861527 🌐 Daily 10–10 ✋ L 44,000d, D 150,000d, Wine 230,000d

TAM TAM CAFÉ
http://tamtamcafe-hoian.com

This is a great little café in a renovated tea house with an attached restaurant serving French and Italian cuisine. Tam Tam is a relaxing place for a drink, an espresso or a meal. Upstairs, in the dining room with white ceiling fans and low-hung lamps (using small fish baskets as shades), customers are offered a series of set meals from 79,000d which could include a large hunk of garlic bread, pasta with a choice of sauces and *crêpes* or ice cream. You'll taste some of the best pesto in Vietnam here—made from freshly plucked Vietnamese basil.

✉ 110 Nguyen Thai Hoc Street, Hoi An ☎ 0510-3862212 🌐 Daily 9.30am–1am ✋ L 110,000d, D 200,000d, Wine 345,000d

THANH

This attractive little Chinese restaurant is in an open-sided old house overlooking the river: It is recognizable by its Chinese style and by the *hoa cat dang*, a purple flowering creeper draped over its walls. Seafood is served here—try the shrimp fried in ginger. You can also order the Hoi An specialties *cao lau* and white rose (rice-flour dumplings with shrimp-meat filling).

✉ 76 Bach Dang Street, Hoi An ☎ 0510-3861366 🌐 Daily 7am–11pm ✋ L 80,000d, D 120,000d, Wine 170,000d

VINH HUNG 1
www.vinhhungrestaurant.com

The riverside setting near the Japanese bridge adds to the attractiveness of this restaurant and so do the local dishes on the menus: *cau lau* (pork and noodles), Quang Nam noodles, white rose dumplings and sweet cakes, which may not be to everyone's liking. There is a good choice of set menus as well as à la carte; no wine list.

✉ 47B Tran Phu Street ☎ 0510-862203 ✋ Set menus 72,000d–206,000d

WHITE MARBLE

A wine and Asian tapas bar, the first of its kind in Hoi An, managed by an Australian and bringing a new kind of dining experience to the town. Chicken salads, yakitori (skewered chicken), *san choy bao* (a Chinese dish), sushi rolls, roasted eggplant (aubergine), pork spare ribs and, well worth trying, Hoi An money bags and *cha-cha* (skewered fish with crushed peanuts).

✉ 98 Le Loi Street ☎ 0510-311862
🕐 Daily 11–11 ✋ L and D 150,000d to 210,000d. Set menus are available for two or more people at US$8.50, US$12 and US$15, Wine 329,000d

HUÊ
LA CARAMBOLE

Huê's most popular restaurant is attractively decorated, with beautiful kites and multicolored feathers adorning its ceiling. Its specialty is a range of Huê imperial-style set meals, starting from as little as 120,000d for nine courses, including soup, rice cakes, steamed fish with five-spice sauce, fried vegetables with squid and *banh khoai*. Á la carte items include a meaty duck à l'orange, pizzas and croque-monsieur for children.

✉ 19 Pham Ngu Lao Street, Huê
☎ 054-3810491 🕐 Daily 7am–11pm
✋ L 120,000d, D 200,000d, Wine 400,000d

DONG TAM

Tucked away in the little *hem* (alley) opposite Century Riverside (▷ 177–178) is Huê's vegetarian restaurant. Sit in a pleasant and quiet little yard surrounded by hanging orchids and topiary, while choosing from the reasonably priced menu, which has fairly simple tofu dishes. The restaurant is a popular choice with the city's resident monks.

✉ 66/7 (7 Kiet 66), Le Loi Street, Huê
☎ 054-3828403 🕐 Daily 10–8
✋ L and D 50,000d

GARDEN RENDEZVOUS

www.morinhotel.com.vn
The nightly buffet in the candlelit courtyard of the Hotel Saigon Morin (▷ 178), accompanied by traditional music, is a vast spread of beef, squid, fish, pork, shrimp pancakes, rice cakes and apple fritters. Diners sit in the courtyard, centered on a fountain, while the musicians sit under an arch of illuminated, hanging Huê conical hats, elegantly attired in

headdresses and deep sapphire-blue and scarlet costumes.

✉ 30 Le Loi Street, Huê ☎ 054-3823526
🕐 Daily 6.30pm–11pm ✋ D 280,000d, Wine 430,000d

LAC THIEN

Lac Thien and its neighbor Lac Thanh are arguably Huê's most famous restaurants and are run, with fierce rivalry, from adjacent buildings by two branches of one family. Lac Thien serves excellent dishes from a wide, inexpensive menu; its Huda beers are long and cold, and the family is riotous and entertaining. Similar reports are given about Lac Thanh, next door. For hungry diners, Lac Thien serves a filling *banh khoai*, Huê's specialty pancake containing a mix of shrimp, meat and eggs served with salad, figs, green bananas and peanut sauce. The restaurant is designed as a cafeteria, its mint-green walls plastered with red graffiti testifying to the success of the food.

✉ 6 Dinh Tien Hoang Street, Huê
☎ 054-3857348 🕐 Daily 7am–10pm
✋ L 130,000d, D 180,000d

LE PARFUM

www.la-residence-hue.com
As befits Hue's best hotel (La Résidence, ▷ 178), Le Parfum is the most stylish place to enjoy an evening meal in the city. Diners come for the European food, fine service and the sense of French colonial elegance that still attaches itself to the restaurant. Enjoy pre-dinner drinks on the terrace.

✉ La Résidence Hôtel & Spa, 5 Le Hoi street, Huê ☎ 054-3837475 🕐 Daily 6pm–11 ✋ D350,000d Wine 430,000d

TINH TAM

This non-touristy vegetarian restaurant is in the heart of Huê's tourist area. There is an English version of the menu, offering a number of mock-meat dishes, using tofu to create convincing sweet-and-sour chicken and the like.

✉ 12 Chu Van An Street, Huê
☎ 054-3823572 🕐 Daily 7am–8.30pm
✋ L and D from 50,000d

THE TROPICAL GARDEN RESTAURANT

Dine alfresco in a leafy garden under a gazebo-like structure in this restaurant, just a short walk from the Perfume River. The staff are attentive and serve dishes such as bitter pumpkin soup with shrimp, mackerel baked in pineapple and an aromatic banana dessert flambéed with wine.

✉ 27 Chu Van An Street, Huê
☎ 054-3847143 🕐 Daily 8.30am–10pm
✋ L 112,000d, D 170,000d, Wine 330,000d

MUI NE
LUNA D'AUTONNO

One of the best Italian restaurants in the country occupies a bamboo-roofed rustic building surrounded by plants, close to the Sailing Club. Portions are huge, the menu is inspired, and there is a full wine list. Choose from daily fish specials, pasta dishes that include *penne in carrozza* (mozzarella, anchovies, cream, tomato and feta cheese) and ravioli, veal, squid, beef and wood-fired pizzas. Barbecues are hosted on Friday and Saturday nights, and there is salsa music on Saturday nights.

✉ Mui Ne ☎ 062-3847591 🕐 Daily 10.30–10.30 ✋ L 140,000d, D 270,000d, Wine 330,000d

SANDALS

www.miamuine.com
This is a beachfront resort restaurant set in lovely lush tropical gardens. The kitchen makes creative use of locally caught seafood, Dalat-grown fruits and vegetables. The African-style calamari (squid) and the tiger prawns are favorites with many, as are the pears with honey and walnuts for dessert.

✉ Sailing Club, 24 Nguyen Dinh Chieu Street, Mui Ne ☎ 062-3847440 🕐 Daily 6.30am–10pm ✋ L 200,000d, D 350,000d, Wine 450,000d

STRAWY

Strawy is set close to the beach and earns its name from the thatching. Guests have plenty of choices from a menu of international food.

✉ Bamboo Village Beach Resort, Km 11.8, Ham Tien, Mui Ne ☎ 062-3847007 🕐 Daily 7am–11pm 🖐 L 130,000d, D 210,000d, Wine 340,000d

NHA TRANG

ANA PAVILION RESTAURANT

Vietnamese and fusion dishes are offered by Jeevan, the Indian chef, in what may be the finest restaurant along this stretch of coast. Buffet breakfasts are a feast, seafood lunch buffets are available in the restaurant as well as à la carte for lunch and dinner. A buffet dinner is also available at the nearby Beach Restaurant (daily 6am–11pm).
✉ Ana Mandara, Tran Phu Street, Nha Trang ☎ 058-3522222 🕐 Daily 24 hours 🖐 L 240,000d, D 380,000d, Wine 410,000d

BREWHOUSE LA LOUISIANE

http://louisanebrewhouse.com.vn
Opposite the turning for the former airport, this large, blue resort complex has canary-yellow and blue iron chairs and small mosaic tables centered on a small swimming

Below Ana Pavilion Restaurant in Nha Trang

pool right on the beach, and is a popular, laidback hangout. It serves a range of homemade Western snacks and Vietnamese meals, as well as homemade ice cream. The brewery's beers are a highlight of the restaurant.
✉ 29 Tran Phu Street, Nha Trang ☎ 058-3812948 🕐 Daily 7.30am–midnight 🖐 L 60,000d, D 90,000d, Wine 180,000d

CYCLO CAFÉ

Italian and Vietnamese dishes are served at this outstanding little restaurant with tables spilling onto the sidewalk. There is real attention to detail in the bamboo furniture and in the cooking. The vodka penne and steamed fish with ginger are popular. There are also vegetarian dishes. Happy hour is between 7pm and 8pm.
✉ 5A Tran Quang Khai Street, Nha Trang ☎ 058-3524208 🕐 Daily 7am–10pm 🖐 L 70,000d, D 115,000d, Wine 130,000d

GOOD MORNING VIETNAM

www.goodmorningviet.com
This popular Italian restaurant in the budget district of Nha Trang is part of a small chain of five. Among the offerings are hot sandwiches, risotto Gorgonzola and heaps of pasta dishes, as well as braised mackerel in a caramelized pepper sauce. Vegetarians have a choice of tofu options. Desserts include tiramisu (layered sponge fingers, soaked in coffee and liqueur with mascarpone) and a great crêpe suzette (a thin pancake in orange sauce and flamed in liqueur, served with ice cream).
✉ 19B Biet Thu Street, Nha Trang ☎ 058-3815071 🕐 Daily 10am–11pm 🖐 L 110,000d, D 200,000d, Wine 350,000d

LAC CANH

This very popular restaurant specializes in beef and beautifully succulent squid, which customers barbecue at their table and dip in a selection of sauces. Fish is also excellent, as is eel mixed with vermicelli. The restaurant itself is smoky and minimally furnished, but the atmosphere is great fun. It can

be hard to get a table as it's often packed with locals, so arrive early. Customers who linger too late are hustled out at closing time.
✉ 44 Nguyen Binh Khiem Street, Nha Trang ☎ 058-3821391 🕐 Daily 9am–9.30pm 🖐 L 40,000d, D 80,000d, Wine 200,000d

NGOC SUONG

A contender for the best seafood restaurant in Nha Trang, evidenced by its popularity with expatriates, Ngoc Suong can be relied on for fresh fish on a daily basis. Tables under thatching are available alfresco or in the cozy, warmly lighted interior, but reservations are sometimes essential to secure a table.
✉ 96 Tran Phu. Nha Trang ☎ 058-3525677 🕐 Daily 10–10 🖐 L 140,000d, D 300,000d, Wine 350,000d

TRUC LINH

Fresh seafood is displayed on large platters on the sidewalk to entice customers to this lovely, open-sided, thatched-roof restaurant next to the Truc Linh Villa Resort. The full culinary spectrum of tasty Asian and Western delicacies can be enjoyed here, from breakfast to dinner. Treats include Earl Grey tea, pork and herbs with peanut dip as an appetizer, and stuffed crab or minced frogs in lemon grass for the main course. Only the excessively loud music detracts from the warmly friendly and welcoming atmosphere.
✉ 21 Biet Thu Street, Nha Trang ☎ 058-3821259 🕐 Daily 7am–11pm 🖐 L 70,000d, D 140,000d, Wine 245,000d

PHAN THIET

L'OCEANE RESTAURANT

Sea views are magnificent from this resort restaurant; the premier position is at a table on the elevated terrace dining area. Guests have plenty of choices from a menu that focuses on Malaysian, Indonesian and Japanese food.
✉ Victoria Phan Thiet Resort, Km 9, Phu Hai, Phan Thiet ☎ 062-3847171 🕐 Daily 6.30am–10.30pm 🖐 L 120,000d, D 220,000d, Wine 400,000d

PRICES AND SYMBOLS

The prices are for a double room for one night including breakfast, unless otherwise stated. All the hotels listed accept credit cards unless otherwise stated. Note that rates can vary widely throughout the year.

For a key to the symbols, ▷ 2.

BACH MA NATIONAL PARK
NATIONAL PARK ACCOMMODATIONS

www.bachma.vnn.vn
There are six guesthouses in the park's 54,000 acres (22,000ha). Two are near the park gate and cost 120,000d with air-conditioning. Four guesthouses are near the highest point, 4,100ft (1,250m) up, where there are several trails taking less than a day; these have private bathrooms. The biggest rooms accommodate six people. There are also campgrounds near the summit of Bach Ma. Credit cards are not accepted. Rooms for US$25–$35 are available in the Morin Bach Ma Hotel in the park; www.huonggiangtourist.com.
✉ 2 miles (3km) from Cau Hai, off National Route 1 ☎ 054-3871330 ✋ 30,000d (dorm room) to 300,000d, excluding breakfast and entrance fee, including taxes 🛈 36 ⬜

BUON ME THUOT
CAO NGUYEN

Daklak Tourist runs this modern hotel with a moderate range of facilities, 490 yards (450m) from the Daklak visitor office in the central part of town. Rooms have minibars, TVs and private bathrooms (which may have no shower curtains); it's worth paying US$10 extra for one of the six large suites. The staff are friendly and helpful and speak some English, and the restaurant, though not large, has a reasonable selection of food. There is a garden where guests can relax.
✉ 65 Phan Chu Trinh Street, Buon Me Thuot ☎ 050-3855960 ✋ From US$18, including taxes 🛈 35 ⬜

DAMSAN HOTEL

www.damsanhotel.com.vn
Some hotels in Buon Me Thuot have left visitors less than satisfied, but the Damsan can be relied on in terms of cleanliness and service. Facilities include free Internet use, a large restaurant and a sauna. The hotel also arranges a number of local tours.
✉ 212 Nguyen Cong Tru Street, Buon Me Thuot ☎ 050-3851234 ✋ US$35–$65, including taxes 🛈 68 ⬜

DALAT
ANA MANDARA VILLAS DALAT RESORT AND SPA

www.anamandara-resort.com
This complex of restored French villas is on a hillside, just a 10-minute drive from downtown Dalat. Each villa has three to five bedrooms with private bathrooms (tubs and showers), phones, safe-deposit boxes, minibars, coffee- and tea-making equipment and satellite TV. Every villa here has a small backyard, a conservatory, a communal sitting room and a terrace for private dining. All living rooms and some bedrooms have fireplaces. A number of pools scattered about the hotel complex ensures each guest has easy access to one of them. The central villa has a French bistro and a wine bar, and another houses the La Cochinchine Spa, which has outdoor pools and hot tubs with river and mountain views.
✉ Le Lai Street, Dalat ☎ 063-3555888 ✋ US$96–$683, excluding breakfast and taxes 🛈 70 in 13 villas ⬛ ⬜

EMPRESS HOTEL

This particularly attractive hotel—arguably the best in Dalat—has a fine position overlooking Xuan Huong Lake. All rooms are arranged around a sunny courtyard that is a great place for breakfast. Rooms are large, and although the furnishings are dated, the beds are comfortable; the private bathrooms have either tubs or showers, as well as toilets. All rooms have satellite TV, in-house movies, minibars, refrigerators, safe-deposit boxes and phones. Laundry and dry-cleaning services are available. Staff are attentive and courteous, and the restaurant serves Vietnamese and Italian food.

✉ 5 Nguyen Thai Hoc Street, Dalat ☎ 063-3833888 🖐 US$47–$57, including taxes ❶ 27 🆑

GOLF 1

This large, white hotel facing the golf course, half a mile (1km) from downtown Dalat, has recovered its popularity after being briefly overshadowed by Golf 2 and Golf 3 (▷ below). Staff are friendly and helpful, and rooms have satellite TVs, tea- and coffee-making facilities and phones, and private bathrooms with tubs. There's a doctor and nurse on call and a same-day laundry service. The restaurant serves Asian, European and international dishes, plus some Vietnamese specialties.

✉ 11 Dinh Tien Hoang Street, Dalat ☎ 063-3824082 🖐 US$21–$50, including taxes ❶ 36 🆑

GOLF 3

Rooms are comfortable in this central hotel next to Dalat market. Every room has a private bathroom—with a tub in all but the least expensive rooms—as well as a phone, safe-deposit box, minibar, TV, video and CD player and tea- and coffee-making equipment. Hotel amenities include a bar with karaoke, a disco and nightclub, a restaurant serving international food, a beauty salon and a shopping arcade. One drawback is that rooms facing the street are noisy because of their proximity to the market.

✉ 4 Nguyen Thi Minh Khai Street, Dalat ☎ 063-3824082 🖐 US$48–$100, including taxes ❶ 78 🎥 🆑

HANG NGA'S CRAZY HOUSE

If you fancy a fantasy night in a mushroom, a tree or a giraffe, then stay here—an architectural meander through curves, twists and bizarre ornamentation. The guesthouse was designed by Hang Nga, whose father, Truong Chinh, was one of the triumvirate who took power after the death of Ho Chi Minh. Trees are entwined among the concrete structure, and there is an art gallery in the grounds (▷ 136). Rooms have satellite TV, minibars and phones, and the furniture is sturdy, if not particularly comfortable. There's a café and bar and a rooftop barbecue restaurant, and laundry and dry cleaning services are also available.

✉ 3 Huynh Thuc Khang Street, Dalat ☎ 063-3822070 🖐 US$47–$84, including taxes ❶ 9 🆑

HOTEL DU PARC

www.hotelduparc.vn
Hotel Du Parc (formerly the Novotel and the Mercure) faces the post office and is near the Sofitel (▷ below), with which it shares its management and many facilities, including golf, tennis and the restaurants and bars. Its restored rooms are comfortably furnished and have satellite TVs, in-house movies, phones, minibars and safe-deposit boxes. There is a lobby restaurant, and breakfast is available; the landmark Café de la Poste is just over the road.

✉ 7 Tran Phu Street, Dalat ☎ 063-825777 🖐 US$28–$48, excluding taxes ❶ 140 (20 nonsmoking) 🆑

SOFITEL DALAT PALACE

www.sofitel.com
This rambling old building was built in 1922, and in 1995 was restored to its former glory, with new curtains, furniture, statues, gilt mirrors and chandeliers in every room. The view over Xuan Huong Lake to the hills beyond is superb,

and the extensive hotel grounds are beautifully laid out. Rooms have private bathrooms with tubs, minibars, satellite and cable TV and safe-deposit boxes. Baby-sitting services are available, and there are indoor and outdoor playgrounds. Guests can get a discount on green fees at the nearby golf course and play on the hotel tennis courts. The restaurant and brasserie serve local and international food, and there's a bar and a piano bar.

✉ 12 Tran Phu Street, Dalat ☎ 063-3825444 🖐 US$119–$175, excluding breakfast and taxes ❶ 43 (5 nonsmoking) 🆑

DANANG

BAC MY AN FURAMA RESORT

www.furamavietnam.com
This 5-star beach resort is beautifully designed and furnished, and has a fabulously opulent foyer and two swimming pools. All rooms have balconies or terraces and overlook the ocean, the tropical garden or the freshwater lagoon, and all have satellite TV with in-house movies, bathrooms, minibars, safe-deposit boxes and tea- and coffee-making facilities. Two rooms are equipped for guests with disabilities, and there are a large number of office services. There are two restaurants; light snacks are available at the Lagoon Bar. Fitness fans can enjoy watersports, mountain biking, and beach volleyball. There is a free shuttle to Danang, the Marble Mountains and Hoi An.

✉ 68 Ho Xuan Huong Street (5 miles/ 8km from Danang) ☎ 0511-3847888 🖐 US$172–$260, excluding taxes ❶ 198 🏖 🎥 🆑

BAMBOO GREEN CENTRAL

www.bamboogreenhotel.com.vn
In the heart of town, within reach of the Museum of Champa Sculpture (▷ 138–139), this highrise hotel has a restaurant, a nightclub, tour-arranging and laundry services, and a fitness center offering massage, sauna and steam room. Guest rooms are plain but pleasant and have phones, TVs and minibars.

✉ 158 Phan Chu Trinh Street, Danang ☎ 0511-3822996 ⚑ US$37–$43, including taxes ⓘ 46 ⛔ ♿

BAMBOO GREEN RIVERSIDE

There are pleasant river views from this efficiently run hotel near the Han River bridge, which leads to My Khe beach. The two-bedded rooms have phones, minibars, satellite TVs and private bathrooms with tubs. General services include Internet access, air reservations and car rental, laundry and airport transfer. The restaurant serves Vietnamese, European and Asian food, and there's a karaoke bar and a massage room, as well as a 24-hour ATM outside the hotel's main door. Another hotel in the Bamboo group, with similar amenities, is the Bamboo Green Harbourside, close to the cathedral (177 Tran Phu Street; tel 0511-3822722).

✉ 68 Bach Dang Street, Danang ☎ 0511-3832591 ⚑ US$119–$175, including taxes ⓘ 40 ♿

DANANG RIVERSIDE

www.danangriversidehotel.com.vn
Comfortable, smart-looking and spacious bedrooms are available in this modern, 14-floor hotel in Danang. Although it is not in the center of the city, restaurants, bars and other amenities, apart from those in the hotel, are within walking distance on the other side of the bridge.

✉ 30 Tran Hung Dao, Danang ☎ 0511-3946666 s ♿ US$40–$60 ⓘ 107 ♿

MY KHE BEACH HOTEL

This hotel faces the beach and is set back a little on the other side of the quiet beach road. Rooms are in blocks, among the sea pines. The suites have sea views, sitting rooms and double and single beds; 27 less expensive rooms have garden views. All have phones, satellite TVs and private bathrooms. Conroy's Bar, one of three eating outlets here, offers sandwiches, hamburgers and cold beer, as well as seafood. There are tennis and

badminton courts, a steam bath, sauna and massages.

✉ 241 Nguyen Van Thoai Street, My Khe ☎ 0511-3836125 ⚑ US$30–$95, including taxes ⓘ 45 in 5 villas ♿

TOURANE

www.vietnamstay.com/hotel/tourane
Simple red-roofed chalet houses sit one road back from the famous China Beach, with rooms designed in French colonial style. All rooms have satellite TVs, phones and private bathrooms. There are garden views from 20 rooms, sea views and balconies from the more expensive rooms and five suites. The restaurant serves Asian and European food, and there are tennis and badminton courts, tour and laundry services, massages, a sauna and a steam bath.

✉ My Khe Beach, Phuoc My Ward, Son Tra District, 1 mile (2km) from Danang ☎ 0511-3932666 ⚑ US$45–$70, including taxes ⓘ 33 in 5 chalets ♿

HOI AN
ANCIENT HOUSE RESORT

www.ancienthouseresort.com
This very beautiful resort hotel is built in the style of Hoi An's ancient houses, with a clay-tile roof and Chinese lanterns, and is set around a small pretty garden with a series of landscaped ponds. All the rooms are decorated in white, with Marelli fans and bronze lamps. The room facilities include a minibar, phone, cable TV and private shower or bath. Behind the hotel, in the grounds, is a traditional wooden house divided into three: an area for living, another for worship, and a warehouse. Next to it is a building where *pho* noodles are made to supply the town's restaurants. The resort includes a billiards room, sauna and spa and a restaurant and coffee bar. Conveniently, there is also a free shuttle to the town and beach. The resort also offer a free bicycle rental service.

✉ 61 Cua Dai Street, Hoi An ☎ 0510-3923377 ⚑ US$65–$69, excluding taxes ⓘ 52 (nonsmoking on request) ✉ ⛔ ♿

GOLDEN SAND RESORT & SPA

www.swiss-belhotel.com
Occupying nearly 0.25 miles (0.5km) of beach and with a huge pool, this family-friendly hotel complex includes the Sands Kitchen, open all day for Western and Asian food, a pub that opens in the evening with a happy hour for food and, from 10–11pm, drinks. Various buffets are held according to the day of the week. The hotel also offers a cookery class, which takes in a visit to the local market. If you're looking for just pure relaxation, there is the Scentual Spa, which offers various treatments. Staff training, it is expected, will raise overall the standards of service at a resort that is popular with Australians and Germans.

✉ Cua Dai Beach, Hoi An ☎ 0510-3927550 ⚑ US$109–$190, excluding taxes ⓘ 212 ≈ ♿

HA AN HOTEL

www.haanhotel.com
In the heart of the French quarter, the Ha An is a family-run boutique hotel with a white balustraded balcony and pleasant gardens. The rooms are attractively decorated and have ethnic-minority drapes on the walls; rooms around the front yard, opposite an open-air café, are a little larger. All have private bathrooms and phones, and complimentary bottled water and fruit are provided. There is a communal seating area with TV, Internet and e-mail access, a laundry service, a restaurant and bar and a beauty salon.

✉ 6–8 Phan Boi Chau Street, Hoi An ☎ 0510-3863126 ⚑ US$54–$103, including taxes ⓘ 25 ♿

HOI AN BEACH RESORT

www.hoianbeachresort.com.vn
Choose between Vietnamese-style houses and villa rooms in this quiet, attractively designed resort with its own stretch of private beach between the De Vong River and Cua Dai Beach. The spacious rooms are simply designed, with large, private bathrooms; some have small terraces or balconies overlooking

the river. All have satellite and cable TV, phones, safe-deposit boxes, minibars, tea- and coffee-making equipment, and there are extra touches such as free bottled water, umbrellas and slippers. The large restaurant overlooks the river and there are two pools, a beauty salon, volleyball and badminton courts, a sauna and steam bath, and laundry and baby-sitting services. Activities include parasailing and jet- and water-skiing, and there is a speedboat to take guests to Cham Island. A free shuttle travels between the hotel and the frenetic streets of Hoi An.

✉ Cua Dai Beach, Hoi An ☎ 0510-3927011 🖐 US$54–$103, including taxes 🛈 110 🏊 📺 ⚓

HOI AN RIVERSIDE RESORT
www.hoianriverresort.com
This resort, just a five-minute bicycle ride from the beach, faces the Thu Bon River, enjoying wonderful views. The dark, slate-lined swimming pool is surrounded by white umbrellas, white mattressed seats and hammocks, all set in landscaped gardens. Standard rooms have balconies, wooden floors and ethnic-minority drapes, and all have private showers, satellite TV, phones, minibars, Internet access and safe-deposit boxes. The resort is owned by Khaisilk (▷ 26) and has a store selling the company's products. There's a badminton court, billiards room, spa and fitness center, and you can take Vietnamese cooking lessons, sometimes visiting the market with the chef to buy ingredients. Vietnamese and international dishes are served at the Song Do restaurant, which has river views, and there is a bar by the pool.

✉ 175 Cua Dai Road, Hoi An ☎ 0510-3864800 🖐 US$80–$100, including taxes 🛈 60 🏊 📺 ⚓

LIFE HERITAGE RESORT
www.life-resorts.com
This secluded luxury resort has rooms overlooking the gardens or

the river and the Senses restaurant for fine dining as well as Café Vienna for informal meals. There is an attractive bar and a variety of activities are available, including boat tours, bicycle rental, daily tai chi sessions and a superb spa. The infinity pool is another attraction.

✉ 1 Pham Hong Thai Street, Hoi An ☎ 0510-3914555 🖐 US$122–$186, including taxes 🛈 94 ⚓

MINH A
The Minh A is a welcome alternative to the area's top-of-the-range resorts. It is a 200-year-old family house, next to the busy market, where guests are really made to feel part of the family. Each of the four rooms, which is separated from its neighbor by panels, is individually laid out and has a fan. The bathrooms have four separate showers and toilets and are communal. The family room has a view of the market and the bougainvillea-covered house opposite; another room houses a shrine to Quan Cong, the god of war, and has a tiny balcony overlooking the orchid-filled courtyard and furnished with a minuscule table and two chairs. Credit cards are not accepted.

✉ 2 Nguyen Thai Hoc Street, Hoi An ☎ 0510-3861368 🖐 US$17–$30, excluding breakfast, including taxes 🛈 4

VINH HUNG 1
www.vinhhungresort.com
An attractive, 125-year-old building with a splendidly ornate reception room, decorated with dark wood in Chinese style, this popular hotel has a range of rooms. Some are large and traditionally furnished, with private bathrooms and small tubs; others (in the downstairs area) are rather small and lack a window, with showers only. All have phones, minibars, and satellite and cable TV; there's a laundry service and a restaurant serving Asian and European food.

✉ 143 Tran Phu Street, Hoi An ☎ 0510-3861621 🖐 US$80–$90, including taxes 🛈 6 🏊 ⚓

Above *Sofitel Dalat Palace*

VICTORIA HOI AN BEACH RESORT
www.victoriahotels-asia.com
This appealing resort is laid out like a traditional fishermen's village, with clay-tiled houses, streets and ponds on the white-sand beach between the sea and the river delta. All rooms, some with balconies, have sea or river views, and are decorated with Japanese, French or Vietnamese themes. Phones, satellite TVs, minibars, safe-deposit boxes and coffee- and tea-makers are provided in every room. Le Annam restaurant is excellent and the buffet dinners offer above-average food. The hotel has a library, laundry, tour-arranging services and a free shuttle between the hotel and town. There are children's activities and tennis courts, and free bicycles.

✉ Cam An Beach, near Cua Dai Beach ☎ 0510-3927040 🖐 US$110–$280, excluding taxes 🛈 100 🏊 📺 ⚓

HUÊ
CENTURY RIVERSIDE
www.centuryriversidehue.com
White steps lead up to the entrance of this imposing hotel, whose foyer is decorated with chandeliers and sturdy columns. The more expensive rooms have fabulous river views, and all have bathrooms with tubs, complimentary fruit and bottled water, satellite TV, minibars, refrigerators and phones. Vietnamese and Western dishes are served at the three restaurants;

there is a bar, tennis courts, bicycle and motorcycle rental, a tour desk, a beauty salon, massage and a laundry service.

✉ 49 Le Loi Street, Huê ☎ 054-3823390
🖐 From US$93, excluding taxes ⓘ 135
🏊 🛇 🛇

DONG LOI
www.hoteldongloi.com
This inexpensive family-run hotel is surrounded by Internet cafés, shops and restaurants. All rooms have small private bathrooms, phones and cable TV; the most expensive have bathtubs. Some rooms are darker than others, but all are individually decorated, spotlessly clean and comfortable. Breakfast is served at the delightful La Carambole Restaurant next door. The hotel can arrange tours, as well as bicycle, car and motorcycle rental. It provides Internet access and a laundry service.

✉ 119 Pham Ngu Lao Street, Huê
☎ 054-3822296 🖐 US$20–$40, including taxes ⓘ 65 🛇

HOTEL SAIGON MORIN
www.morinhotel.com.vn
The Morin, which faces the Perfume River, is the oldest, grandest and most famous hotel in Huê. It was built in 1901 by the eponymous Mr. Morin, a French businessman. It is set around a large courtyard filled with wrought-iron furniture; this is where diners sit for the hotel's

Below *Coco Beach Resort, Mui Ne*

buffet nights (▷ 172). All rooms are large, comfortable and carpeted. All have private bathrooms, plus extensive minibars and snack bars, tea- and coffee-making equipment, high-speed Internet access, safe-deposit boxes, phones and satellite TV. The hotel also provides complimentary fruit baskets and bottled water. Services include airport pickup, car rental, a 24-hour ATM, baby-sitting, same-day laundry service, an arts and crafts shop, a beauty salon, massage and sauna, billiards and pool. The in-house tour service can arrange a variety of trips for guests, including a boat journey with traditional Huê folk music. Asian, Vietnamese, European and Huê specialties are served in the two restaurants, while the Garden Bar offers snacks and drinks, as well as the nightly barbecue.

✉ 30 Le Loi Street, Huê ☎ 054-3823526
🖐 US$82–$102, excluding taxes ⓘ 184
🏊 🛇 🛇

HUONG GIANG
(PERFUME RIVER HOTEL)
www.huonggianghotel.com.vn
This hotel has a superb setting on the river, and its rooms are comfortable, despite the heavy wooden, lacquered imperial-style furniture. The more expensive rooms overlook the river and are decorated with mother-of-pearl while the less expensive rooms are designed in bamboo. All rooms have private bathrooms, albeit rather spartan ones, plus satellite TV, minibars, phones and safe-deposit boxes. The Royal Restaurant is decked out with heavy red furniture and decorated columns; it specializes in Huê dishes. The Hoa Mai has a menu of Vietnamese, Asian and European food, as well as local specialties and the riverfront terrace bar has great views. Other facilities include sauna and massage, tennis courts, a post office, film-processing, laundry and dry cleaning, a tour desk and a hairdressing and beauty salon.

✉ 51 Le Loi Street, Huê ☎ 054-3822122

🖐 US$80–$250, excluding taxes ⓘ 165
🏊 🛇 🛇

LA RÉSIDENCE HÔTEL AND SPA
www.la-residence-hue.com
A classic hotel, this beautiful colonial villa prides itself on its first-class service, excellent cuisine in its Le Parfum restaurant (▷ 172) and an environmentally conscious spa. La Résidence, once the home of the French governor of Huê, overlooks the Perfume River, providing some stunning views. Nearly all rooms have a large balcony and a river view. There are a number of suites each of which is themed: Suite d'Ornithologue, as the name suggests, gives the occupant the feeling of a bird sanctuary, while Voyage en Chine takes you on a journey through ancient China. Relax in the hotel's comfortable bar, Le Gouverneur, and admire the fresco created by Roland Renauc, a locally based French artist.

✉ 5 Le Loi Street, Huê ☎ 054-3837475
🖐 From US$98, excluding taxes ⓘ 122
(7 suites, all nonsmoking) 🏊 🛇

SPORTS 1 HOTEL
www.huesportshotel.com
The Sports Hotel is probably the best budget hotel in the center of Huê, close to restaurants and bars, with clean and comfortable rooms and free use of the Internet. Onward travel arrangements and local tours can be made at the travel desk in the lobby. Bedrooms have cable TV, bathrooms and telephones.

✉ 15 Pham Nga Lao Street, Huê ☎ 054-3828096 🖐 US$32–$39, including taxes ⓘ 29 🛇

KONTUM
DAKBLA 1 HOTEL
Set in attractive grounds, this hotel has a small restaurant and a jetty on the riverbank. The friendly, helpful staff have a basic understanding of English and French. Rooms, although drably decorated, are large, and have private bathrooms, minibars, phones and satellite TVs. The restaurant on the first floor

serves good, reasonably priced food, and the hotel provides a taxi service, tennis courts, karaoke and dancing. The hotel is the first building on the right as you cross the bridge into Kontum.

✉ 2 Phan Dinh Phung Street, Kontum ☎ 060-7386334 🖐 US$25–$29, including taxes 🛈 42 ⬡

LANG CO
LANG CO BEACH RESORT
www.langcobeachresort.com.vn
The green-roofed villas of the resort are set back from the beach on the Lap An lagoon, on the beautiful Lang Co peninsula. The hotel has a large outdoor pool, a bar and a 300-seater restaurant, which serves French, Vietnamese, Chinese and Huê royal court dishes. Rooms are based on traditional Huê design, and are equipped with satellite TVs, phones (with bathroom extensions) and safe-deposit boxes. Tennis courts, a beauty and hairdressing salon, health and fitness club, sauna and laundry services are available, and there are facilities for guests with disabilities.

✉ National Route 1A, 22 miles (35km) from Danang Airport ☎ 054-3873555 🖐 US$20–$110, including taxes 🛈 76 ⬡ ⬡ ⬡

THANH TAM RESORT AND HOTEL
www.thanhtamresort.com.vn
This comfortable collection of bungalow accommodations north of Lang Co village overlooks the sea. Amenities are limited, but they do have a good seafood restaurant. Sports facilities include windsurfing, volleyball and badminton. The helpful tour desk will reserve onward tickets to most destinations.

✉ Central Lang Co Beach ☎ 054-3874456 🖐 US$25–$50, excluding breakfast and taxes 🛈 25 ⬡

MUI NE
BAMBOO VILLAGE BEACH RESORT
www.bamboovillageresortvn.com
Attractive, simple bamboo huts are scattered around a lovely shady spot at the top of the beach. The most expensive cabins have two beds, small bathrooms and private balconies that look out onto the beach. Rooms are rustic but comfortable, and have satellite TVs and phones. There are also 14 "lodges," which are in fact rooms, but these are not as inviting. Transportation can be arranged here to Ho Chi Minh City or to the airport. On site there is an excellent restaurant, two swimming pools (one with Jacuzzi), a children's play area, table tennis and pool, a library, Internet access and water sports such as windsurfing and paddlesurfing. Comfortable and self-contained, this is a good place for families.

✉ Km 11.8, Ham Tien, Phan Thiet, Mui Ne ☎ 062-3847007 🖐 US$98–$190, including taxes 🛈 65 ⬡ ⬡ In top-rate rooms only

COCO BEACH RESORT
www.cocobeach.net
Thatched wooden cabins and three two-bedroom villas face the beach in a tranquil setting, with a swimming pool, a children's wading pool and a play area. Coco Beach is well run by German owners and was the first resort on Mui Ne; competition has since stepped up, but it remains among the best. Rooms can be dark, but have private terraces. Villa bathrooms have tubs; cabin bathrooms have enclosed shower stalls. All rooms provide mosquito nets, minibars, hot water and phones. There are two restaurants: Champa, a French restaurant, open afternoons and evenings, and the Paradise Beach Club restaurant, whose yellow-and-white striped chairs are right on the beach, and which is open all day. The resort shop sells souvenirs and crafts, and a library has books in English, French and German. Also available are a flight reservation desk and Internet access. The resort is very child-friendly and provides baby-sitting and bottle-cleaning and sterilization, plus games and videos for older children.

✉ 58 Nguyen Ninh Chiau, Phung Haum Tian, Phan Thiet, Mui Ne ☎ 062-3847111 🖐 US$110–$270, including taxes 🛈 34 ⬡ ⬡

FULL MOON BEACH
www.windsurf-vietnam.com
Accommodations at Full Moon Beach are in a variety of brick and bamboo rooms; the most attractive rooms have a sea view and constant breeze. Bamboo suites are a little dark, but have two double bedrooms each, plus bathrooms with mosaic floors. The brick rooms are more comfortable, with low-slung, Japanese-style beds and low ceilings. Only the four-person villas have air-conditioning. There's Internet access and a pool, and the resort is next to Jibe's restaurant and bar and the windsurfing and kiteboarding center.

✉ 84 Nguyen Dinh Chieu, Phan Thiet, Mui Ne ☎ 062-3847008 🖐 US$48–$90, including taxes 🛈 27 (including cabins) ⬡ ⬡

MIA RESORT
www.miamuine.com
This Australian-owned resort has been designed in an attractive style, with simple and cool cabins and rooms surrounded by glorious vegetation. There's a small pool close to the beach and a good restaurant and bar. The costlier cabins have mosquito nets and cloths draped on the walls; upper floors have air-conditioning, the lower floors fans only. Bathrooms have walk-in hot showers (except for the top-range bungalows, which have tubs). Cable TV and phones are supplied. The Sandals is the main restaurant, alongside the beach, and there's also the Beachfront Bar terrace. Home furnishings are sold in the shop, and there's a spa, Internet and watersports. Bicycles and motorcycles are available to rent. You can have a massage in the beach pavilion or in your room.

✉ 24 Nguyen Dinh Chieu, Ham Tien ward, Phan Thiet ☎ 062-3847440 🖐 US$85–$170, including taxes 🛈 30 ⬡ ⬡

NOVOTEL OCEAN DUNES & GOLF RESORT

www.novotel.com

Strictly speaking, this resort is not really on Mui Ne, but it does have a beach setting and its own private stretch of sand. The rooms are comfortable and plushly furnished, with private bathrooms with bathtubs, tea- and coffee-making equipment, safe-deposit boxes, minibars, TVs, slippers and bathrobes, and private balconies. The hotel provides a laundry service, and there are two swimming pools, several restaurants, a bar, tennis courts and a gym. For those on a romatic getaway, it's also possible to dine by candlelight on the beach by arrangement. Guests are given a 20 percent discount on green fees at the adjacent Ocean Dunes Golf Club.

✉ 1 Ton Duc Thang Street, Phan Thiet, Mui Ne ☎ 062-3822393 ✋ From US$53, excluding taxes 🛏 135 (11 nonsmoking) 🏊 ⚙

ROMANA RESORT & SPA

www.romanaresort.com.vn

Set on a private mountain, with the ocean as a backdrop, the resort's spa is one of its main attractions. All the rooms face the sea, as does the Panorama restaurant. Food is also available at the Laguna bar and there is a billiards room as well.

✉ Phu Hai, Mui Nee ☎ 062-3741289 ✋ US$78–$203 including taxes 🛏 64 (and 28 villas and 4 suites) 🏊 ⚙

NAM CAT TIEN NATIONAL PARK
FOREST FLOOR LODGE

www.vietnamforesthotel.com

Luxury tented accommodations and wooden lodges make up the new Forest Floor Lodge in the National Park. A variety of activities is organized at extra cost, including forest treks, birding trips, a night safari and boat trips. Transportation from Ho Chi Minh City can also be arranged (see hotel website).

✉ Tan Phu District ☎ 061-3669890/ 3669580 ✋ US$112 🛏 15 ⚙

NHA TRANG
BAO DAI'S VILLAS

www.vngold.com/nt/baodai

These French colonial villas, on a small promontory, were built in 1923 for Emperor Bao Dai and his wife, Queen Nam Phuong. They now form a guest resort with magnificent views over the harbor and islands. The large villa rooms are essentially big studios with bedrooms, sitting rooms and dining areas in an open-plan space. The furniture is heavy and the bedspreads are gold-colored. All rooms have minibars, phones, satellite TV and private bathrooms with tubs. A restaurant overlooking the bay serves seafood, or you can eat barbecued food at the open-air beachside eatery. Motorcycle and bicycle rental, Internet, tennis courts and fishing tours are all available, and there's a laundry service.

✉ Tran Phu Street, Nha Trang (approach to Cau Da village) ☎ 058-3522222 ✋ US$18–$80, including taxes 🛏 48 ⚙

BLUE HOUSE

Down a quiet alley, this neat, blue building is run by a welcoming family (with little English) and is excellent value for money. Rooms are large and clean, and come with minibar and TV; those with air-conditioning are more expensive. Breakfast is taken in a pleasant terrace area.

✉ 12/8 Hung Vuong Street, Nha Trang ☎ 058-3824505 ✋ US$8–$12, excluding breakfast 🛏 14 ⚙ Some rooms

EVASON ANA MANDARA

www.six-senses.com

In Nha Trang's finest beach resort guests are pampered from head to toe. Bungalows designed in native wood and rattan are set amid extensive tropical foliage on the beach off Nha Trang's main boulevard. The 17 villas have 35 garden-view rooms, 11 sea-view rooms, and more expensive deluxe rooms and suites. All rooms have a private terrace, king-size or twin beds, bathtubs, phones, safe-deposit boxes, satellite TV, minibars, and coffee- and tea-makers. There are two pools, one with a Jacuzzi, a tennis court, and several places to eat. The Pavilion restaurant, with veranda tables overlooking the gardens and Nha Trang Bay, serves Vietnamese and international food; the poolside Beach restaurant and bar specializes in seafood, which can be cooked to guests' liking or presented the chef's way. Private meals can also be provided on the villa terrace. The Six Senses Spa has a sauna, steam baths and treatment rooms where a whole range of therapies is on offer, plus activities such as tai chi and aikido. Among guest services are fax, translation and Internet access, laundry and dry cleaning, an air-conditioned library, a craft shop and travel and tour information. Airport transfer can be arranged at 24 hours' notice, for US$10 per person.

✉ Tran Phu Street, Nha Trang ☎ 058-3522222 ✋ US$167–$213, excluding breakfast and taxes 🛏 74 🏊 ⚙

NHA TRANG LODGE

www.nhatranglodge.com

Most rooms in this 14-floor building dominating the main road in Nha Trang overlook the beach, and some have extraordinary sea views. Rooms are comfortable, if rather small, with phones, satellite TV, minibars and private bathrooms. Service is efficient, and guests have the use of a pool, tennis courts, a disco, casino, billiards room and car rental, plus massage, sauna, steam bath, business amenities and an ATM in the foyer. The on-site restaurants serve Vietnamese, Asian and international dishes.

✉ 42 Tran Phu Street, Nha Trang ☎ 058-3521900 ✋ US$43–$57, including taxes 🛏 121 🏊 📺 ⚙

QUE THAO (PERFUME GRASS INN)

www.perfume-grass.com

Rooms are basic, but stylish, in this quiet little hotel in Nha Trang. It's efficiently run by the family owners and has a range of accommodations whose prices depend on whether you would like air-conditioning, bathtubs and breakfast. All rooms have private toilets and hot showers. There is an Internet service in the reception area. Advance reservation is recommended. Good breakfasts are served at a restaurant across the street.

✉ 4A Biet Thu Street, Nha Trang ☎ 058-3524286 ✋ US$16–$35, excluding breakfast, including taxes ⓘ 21 ⓢ Some rooms

LA SUISSE HOTEL
www.lasuissehotel.com
This friendly, well-run hotel on five floors sits close to the liveliest part of Nha Trang. The best rooms (VIP) are large and have balconies with sea views. All rooms have bathrooms with tubs. Plants are crowded onto the suite balconies. The top-floor restaurant and open-air bar have fantastic sea views. There is free Internet access.

✉ 34 Tran Quang Khai Street, Nha Trang ☎ 058-3524353 ✋ US$23–$26, including taxes ⓘ 24 ⓢ

VINPEARL RESORT AND SPA
www.vinpearlresort-nhatrang.com
There has been investment and development on Hon Tre on a colossal scale and the sight of another sprawling resort on this tropical island may not appeal to everyone. For those who welcome it, there's a bewildering range of facilities, including a spa, the largest pool in Southeast Asia, restaurants, a children's playground and a casino. Opulent rooms are beautifully finished in dark woods, rattan and marble. All have balconies, some with sea views; those described as "hill view" rooms actually face a blank quarry wall. Phones, minibars, safe-deposit boxes, tea- and coffee-making equipment, radios, satellite TVs and kimonos are all provided. There are rooms equipped for guests with disabilities.

✉ Hon Tre Island (Reception and jetty: 7 Tran Phu Street, Nha Trang) ☎ 058-3598188 ✋ From US$175–$195, including taxes ⓘ 230 🖼 📺 ⓢ

WHALE ISLAND RESORT
www.iledelabaleine.com
A 2.5-hour journey north of Nha Trang brings you to this relaxing resort, among the aquamarine waters of the South China Sea. Bamboo cabins are scattered around the area, and have mosquito nets, fans, shower rooms, sinks and toilets. All sorts of water sports are available, including diving, catamarans, windsurfing and canoeing. Between April and July, you may be lucky enough to see whale sharks offshore. Rates are all-inclusive and the longer the duration of your stay, the lower the rates. Prices do not include transportation from Nha Trang and boat transfer to Whale Island, or meals at the seafood restaurant.

✉ Boat from Dam Mon pier ☎ 058-3840501 ✋ US$43–$64, excluding boat shuttle (US$20) and compulsory dinner (US$25) but including taxes ⓘ 23

YOK DON NATIONAL PARK
SIX SENSES NINH VAN BAY
www.sixsenses.com
This stylishly discreet resort makes the most of Ninh Van Bay's setting, tucking itself between the rocks and mountains and overlooking the coral reef and white-sand beach of the East Vietnam Sea. The scattered villas have large, stand-alone wooden bathtubs, wine cellars, plunge pools, and verandas or floating terraces and sundecks. CDs and in-house video movies are available on request, and standard amenities are minibar, safe-deposit box, tea- and coffee-making equipment, phone and satellite TV. The restaurant serves fusion meals and is open to the fresh air (with retractable screens in case of bad weather). The Six Senses Spa blends into the rocks beside a waterfall, providing every conceivable treatment, and tennis courts, water sports, dive facilities and trekking are available. One part of the restaurant overlooks the pool while its upper level enjoys panoramic views; the bar provides the best vantage point to watch the sun going down over the mountains. There is also boat access from the resort to a private beach where a chef and waiter serve a barbecue.

✉ Ninh Van Bay, accessible by speed boat from Nha Trang (20 min) ☎ 058-3522222 ✋ US$650–$2,000 excluding breakfast and taxes ⓘ 52 📺 ⓢ

Below *Evason Ana Mandarina is a luxurious hideaway with tremendous sea views*

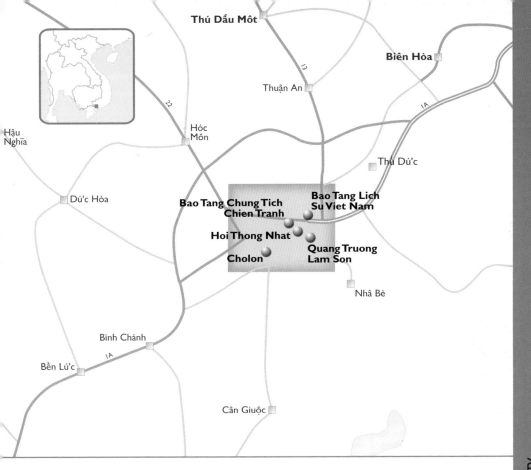

HO CHI MINH CITY

Ho Chi Minh City is New York to Hanoi's Washington, Vietnam's commercial driving force and a hive of activity. The variety and pace of life on the streets, the humidity, the monsoons, the three million or so motorcycles weaving and dodging the human traffic—all demand your full attention and leave you at the end of each day delighted and exhausted in equal measure.

At dawn the markets come alive with the colors of fresh fruit, vegetables and other things you never considered food before; by lunchtime a carbon monoxide haze settles over the city as the maddened and maddening motorcycles repopulate the streets.

Highlights of a visit include the pagodas of Chinatown, the classical French buildings around Lam Son Square, the History Museum and the War Remnants Museum, not forgetting the pleasure of shopping for good deals in the many handicrafts and clothing stores at Ben Thanh Market and Dong Khoi Street.

Unlike the north, Ho Chi Minh city has no cool season, but rather a dry season and a wet one. To avoid the rain and extreme heat the best time to visit is between November and February; or just make sure your hotel has a pool for when things get too hot and humid.

Getting around the city is a nightmare and a joy. Many of the sights are within walking distance of the city center, and for those farther afield you can enjoy the thrills of a motorcycle taxi or a calmer journey by riverboat.

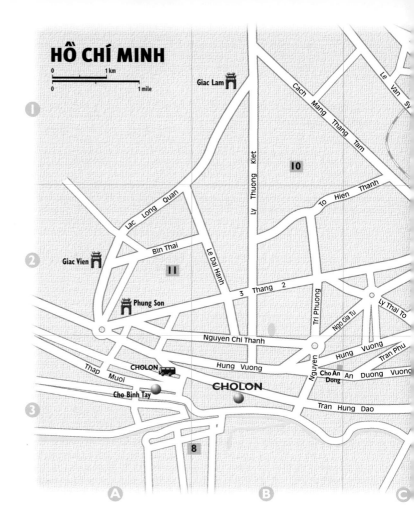

HÔ CHÍ MINH

HO CHI MINH CITY STREET INDEX

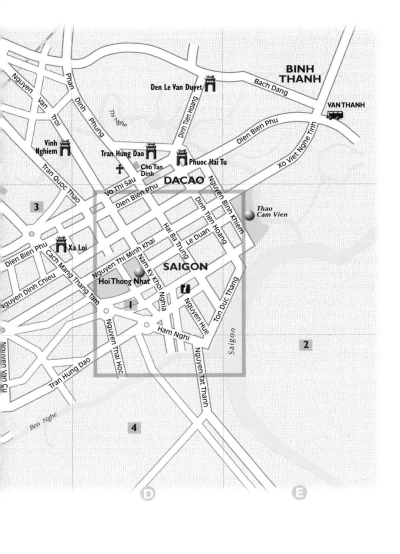

Nguyen Van Troi

Phan Dinh Phung

Nguyen Van

Thi Nghe

Den Le Van Duyet

BINH THANH

Bach Dang

Dinh Tien Hoang

VAN THANH

Dien Bien Phu

Vinh Nghiem

Tran Hung Dao

Cho Tan Dinh

Phuoc Hai Tu

Xo Viet Nghe Tinh

Tran Quoc Thao

Vo Thi Sau

Dien Bien Phu

DACAO

Nguyen Binh Khiem

3

Thao Cam Vien

Dinh Tien Hoang

Hai Ba Trung

Le Duan

Dien Bien Phu

Xa Loi

Cach Mang Thang Tam

Nguyen Thi Minh Khai

SAIGON

Nguyen Dinh Chieu

Hoi Thong Nhat

Nam Ky Khoi Nghia

Nguyen Hue

Ton Duc Thang

Nguyen Thai Hoc

Ham Nghi

Saigon

2

Tran Hung Dao

Nguyen Van Cu

Nguyen Tat Thanh

Ben Nghe

4

D   E

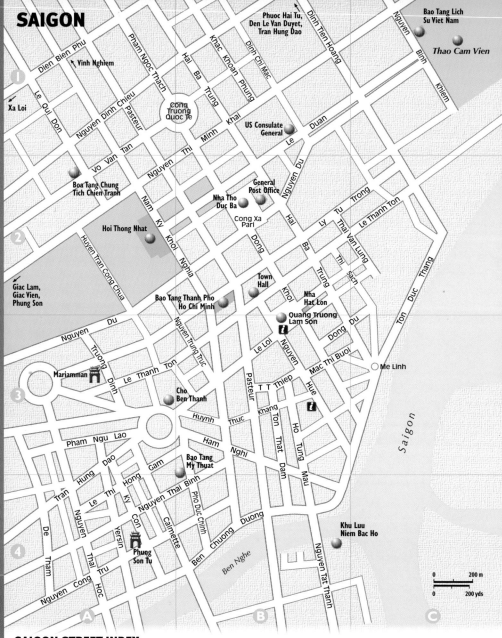

SAIGON

Bao Tang Lich Su Viet Nam

Thao Cam Vien

Phuoc Hai Tu, Den Le Van Duyet, Tran Hung Dao

Vinh Nghiem

Xa Loi

Cong Truong Quoc Te

US Consulate General

Boa Tang Chung Tich Chien Tranh

General Post Office

Nha Tho Duc Ba

Cong Xa Pari

Hoi Thong Nhat

Giac Lam, Giac Vien, Phung Son

Town Hall

Bao Tang Thanh Pho Ho Chi Minh

Nha Hat Lon

Quang Truong Lam Son

Mariamman

Cho Ben Thanh

Me Linh

Saigon

Pham Ngu Lao

Bao Tang My Thuat

Khu Luu Niem Bac Ho

Phung Son Tu

Ben Nghe

0   200 m
0   200 yds

REGIONS | HO CHI MINH CITY • CITY MAP

SAIGON STREET INDEX

BOA TANG CHUNG TICH CHIEN TRANH (WAR REMNANTS MUSEUM)
▷ 190.

BAO TANG MY THUAT
The Fine Art Museum displays a collection of work from the classical period through to socialist realism. Its eclectic mix of art and crafts ranges from ceramics and sculpture to propaganda work and modern art instalations.

The museum building itself, a cream-colored, art nouveau-influenced mansion, is worthy of note; it was constructed early in the 20th century by a wealthy Chinese businessman. Three floors up is a collection of ancient art that contains finds dating from the civilizations of Oc-eo through to the Cham era. More recent collections include attractive Dong Nai ceramics of the early 20th century. The museum's ground-level floor is given over to temporary displays.

Among the most interesting early works is a 12th-century sculpture of Kala, a temple-guarding monster, from My Son (▷ 156)—a fanged beast with a big protuberance for a nose, bulging eyes and forest-thick eyebrows. Sandstone sculptures of Hindu gods include Laksmi, Goddess of Beauty and Good Fortune, a seventh- to eighth-century AD figure found in Soc Trang. Early 20th-century gaunt wooden funeral statues, made by the Tay Nguyen people in the Central Highlands to represent their late relatives, line a corridor.

Go up two floors to find modern lacquered pictures such as the interior of Cu Chi by Quach Phong (1997). There's a small collection of propaganda art posters (undated), which are similar in theme but surprisingly diverse in individual style. A vast, bronze mural by Nguyen Sang (also undated) represents the nation, and there are fascinating drawings of prison riots that were produced in 1973. Some of the most interesting work on show here consists of montages and photography produced by Americans reflecting on the Vietnam War.

In addition to the indoor displays, there are sculptures and contemporary art galleries set up in the museum's backyard.
✚ 186 B4 ✉ 97A Pho Duc Chinh Street, District 1 ☎ 08-38294441 ◷ Tue–Sun 9–5 ✋ 15,000d 🏛 Much of the contemporary art is for sale ❓ Labeling erratic; only general descriptions in English

BAO TANG THANH PHO HO CHI MINH
A stately gray neoclassical building built between 1885 and 1890 for the governor of Cochin-China now houses the Museum of Ho Chi Minh City, the museum of the revolution.

Highlights are the old black-and-white pictures of Saigon, a 19th-century fire engine and a beautiful map from 1921 showing school locations and revealing the former French names of the city's streets. A mummified 19th-century man also on display was found in paddy fields in 2003; his facial expression is reminiscent of the figure in the Edvard Munch painting *The Scream*. Hardware (from helicopters and antiaircraft guns) are displayed in the rear compound.
✚ 186 B2 ✉ 65 Ly Tu Trong Street, District 1 ☎ 08-38299741 ◷ Daily 8–4 ✋ 15,000d ◻ 🏛

CHO BEN THANH
At a chaotic traffic circle, the large, covered, central Ben Thanh Market faces a statue of Tran Nguyen Han, a heroic 15th-century general who fought against the Ming Chinese occupiers. The market is stocked with clothes, household goods, toiletries, souvenirs, lacquerware and embroidery, as well as food, including cold meats and fresh and dried fruits. Prices are not low (local people browse here then buy elsewhere, but the quality is good, the selection excellent, and the sight of all that produce stacked high is unforgettable.

Outside the north gate (Cua Bac), on Le Thanh Ton Street, are tempting displays of fresh fruit and cut flowers. Ben Thanh Night Market opens at dusk and closes after midnight. As the sun sinks and the main market closes, food stands spring up on the surrounding streets, where it's possible to sit in the open and eat well inexpensively.
✚ 186 B3 ✉ Ben Thanh gyratory, at intersection of Le Loi, Ham Nghi and Tran Hung Dao streets, Binh Thanh District ◷ Daily 7–7

Opposite *The Museum of Ho Chi Minh City is housed in a neoclassical building*
Below *Ho Chi Minh City's bus station and the entrance to Ben Thanh Market*

INFORMATION
✚ 186 A2 ✉ 28 Vo Van Tan Street, District 3 ☎ 08-38295587 ⏱ Daily 7.30–12, 1.30–5 💵 15,000d
🏬 Postcards and small Vietnamese souvenirs

TIPS
» Do not underestimate the force of some of the images on display; this is not for the very young or the fainthearted.
» To help you take everything in, you need to devote a few hours to this museum.

BAO TANG CHUNG TICH CHIEN TRANH

Photographs of atrocities and military action, bombs, tanks, planes, deformed bodies—every conceivable reminder of the horrors of modern warfare—are piled from floor to ceiling in the War Remnants Museum. This sobering collection of military hardware, photographs and other items from the Vietnam War presents a graphic account of the conflict from the nation's perspective. In the courtyard are tanks, bombs and helicopters, while inside, photographs and exhibits arranged in rooms around the courtyard record man's inhumanity to man. On the whole, the war is presented exclusively from the North Vietnamese and Viet Cong point of view but, even so, this is one of the most frequently visited sites by Western, and particularly American, travelers in the city. It is certainly hard-hitting as a denunciation of war of any kind.

THE EXHIBITS

The display covers the Son My (My Lai) massacre on March 16, 1968, the effects of napalm and phosphorus, and the after effects of Agent Orange defoliation (a particularly disturbing section, containing bottled malformed human fetuses). Many of the pictures are difficult to view. One of the most repellent, dated 1967, shows an American GI holding up what remains of the body of a Viet Cong soldier, most of whom has been blown away. One of the most interesting rooms is that dedicated to war photographers and their pictures, forming a tribute to those who died pursuing their craft. Unusually, this section depicts the war from both sides. Wall-to-wall images include shots from Robert Capa's last roll of film before the famous photographer was killed by a landmine on May 25, 1954, *Life* magazine's first color coverage of the conflict, and quotes from those who perished during the war. The enduring image of war presented through the camera lens is one of mangled metal, suffocating mud and injured limbs.

The propaganda room contains records of international protests against the war in countries such as Cuba and the Congo. Other displays feature weapons—such as the experimental artillery shell full of darts—and pieces used to punish the enemy, including a guillotine used by the French and tiger cages in which Viet Cong prisoners were kept on Con Son Island (▷ 217).

Below *A US Air Force plane on display at the War Remnants Museum*

BAO TANG LICH SU VIET NAM

The Museum of Vietnamese History occupies a striking and elegant 1928 building with a pagoda-based design. The collection spans a wide range of objects from the prehistoric (300,000 years ago) and the Dong Son periods (3,500BC–AD100), right through to the birth of the Vietnamese Communist Party in 1930. Particularly impressive are the Cham sculptures—the standing bronze Buddha, showing Indian stylistic influence, is probably the finest. There is also a delicately carved Devi (goddess) from the 10th century, and pieces such as the head of Siva, Hindu destroyer and creator, and Ganesh, elephant-headed son of Siva and Parvati, both from the eighth to ninth century AD. Representative pieces from the Chen-la, Funan, Khmer, Oc-eo and Han Chinese periods are also on display, along with items from the various Vietnamese dynasties and some hilltribe objects. Other highlights include the wooden stakes planted in the Bach Dang riverbed to repel the war ships of the Mongol Yuan in the 13th century (▷ 29); a beautiful phoenix head from the Tran Dynasty (13th to 14th century) and a Hgor (big drum) of the Jorai people, made from the skin of two elephants, which once belonged to the Potauoui (King of Fire) family in Ajunpa district, Gia Lai Province. There are fine sandstone sculptures, including an incredibly smooth linga (seventh to eighth century AD) from Long An Province in the Mekong Delta. The linga represents the cult of Siva and signifies gender, energy, fertility and potency.

Other items on display include the preserved body of a 60-year-old woman who died in 1869, which was discovered in the city during work on apartments in 1994, and was subsequently brought here.

INFORMATION
✚ 186 C1 ✉ 2 Nguyen Binh Khiem Street, District 1 ☎ 08-38298146
🕐 Mon–Sat 8–11, 1.30–4, Sun 8.30–4
🖐 15,000d ❓ No photography; labeling in English and French

TIPS
» Water puppet shows are held here daily (▷ 204) for a small fee.
» A research library on the third floor up opens Mon–Sat and has a collection of books on Indochina.

Above *A relief work exhibited at the Museum of Vietnamese History*

INFORMATION

✚ 184 B3 ✉ District 5, west of downtown 🛈 Vietnamtourism, 1037 Nguyen Trai Street ☎ 08-38552855 🛈 Saigontourist, 49 Le Thanh Ton Street, ☎ 08-38298914 ⏰ Mon–Fri 7–11.30, 1.30–5 🚉 Cholon station, serving Long An, My Thuan, Ben Luc, My Tho 🍴 Wide range of Chinese restaurants

INTRODUCTION

Ho Chi Minh City's "Chinatown" is a hectic district given over to bustling markets, fascinating temples and pagodas, and some wonderfully decorated Chinese assembly houses.

Cholon, or Big Market, is an area inhabited predominantly by Vietnamese of Chinese origin (Hoa). The area, southwest of downtown, is worth visiting not only for the bustle and activity, but also because the assembly halls and temples here are the finest in Ho Chi Minh City. As in other towns in Southeast Asia with sizeable Chinese populations, early settlers established meeting rooms that offered social, cultural and spiritual support to members of dialect groups. These assembly halls *(hoi quan)* are most common in Hoi An (▷ 143–144) and Cholon. Vietnamese and Chinese gather in many of the temples, particularly elderly residents, who meet for a chat and tea. Binh Tay Market—a block away in District 6—is Cholon's main and best-known marketplace; you can buy clothes and other goods at the multifloor An Dong Market (intersection of Tran Phu and An Duong Vuong), where the basement has a range of small restaurants. Among other Cholon highlights are Quan Am Pagoda, Tam Son Assembly Hall and the two Thien Hau temples.

WHAT TO SEE

CHO BINH TAY

Along with Ben Thanh Market (▷ 189), the Binh Tay Market, sandwiched between Thap Muoi and Phan Van Khoe streets, is one of Ho Chi Minh City's largest. It is also one of the most exciting markets in the city, with a wonderful array of noises, smells and colors. Though not strictly within the area, Binh Tay has always served as the main market for Cholon; however, in 1991 a five-floor market, An Dong, opened in the district. Binh Tay sprawls out over a large area and is housed in an ocher-colored building decorated with a beautiful dragon mural in blue tiles and topped by a clock tower. On a large central patio are dragon fountains, goldfish-filled ponds and a monument erected in 1930 to mark the contribution of Quach Dam of the Legion of Honor to the building of the Cholon Market.

✉ 184 A3 ✉ Thap Muoi Street ⏰ Daily

Above *Worshipers burning incense in the Thien Hau Temple*

DINH MINH HUONG GIA THANH

The Ming Dynasty Assembly Hall was built by the Cantonese community, which arrived in Saigon via Hoi An in the 18th century. The hall was built in 1789 and dedicated to the Ming Dynasty, but the present building dates largely from an extensive renovation carried out in the 1960s. Among the furniture is a heavy, marble-topped table and chairs that arrived in 1850 from China. In the main hall there are three altars, which, following imperial tradition, are: the central altar, dedicated to the royal family (Ming Dynasty); the right-hand altar, dedicated to two military mandarin officers; and the left altar, dedicated to two civilian mandarin officers. The hall behind is dedicated to the memory of the Vuong family, who built the main hall and whose descendants have lived here ever since; the custodian is third generation. In a small side chapel childless women can seek divine intercession from a local deity, Ba Me Sanh.

✉ 380 Tran Hung Dao Street 🕓 Daily 5.30am–6pm

NGHIA AN ASSEMBLY HALL

A magnificent, carved, gold-painted wooden boat hangs over the entrance to the Nghia An Assembly Hall. To the left, on entering the temple, is a larger-than-life depiction of the horse and groom of Quan Gong, god of war and soldiers. At the main altar are three figures in glass cases. The central, red-faced figure with a green cloak is Quan Cong, a loyal military man who lived in China in the third century. To the left and right are his companions, the fierce-looking General Chau Xuong and the mandarin Quan Binh. On leaving, note the fine gold figures of guardians on the inside of the door panels.

✉ 678 Nguyen Trai Street 🕓 Daily 4am–6pm

CHUA QUAN AM

The Quan Am Pagoda, founded in 1816, is thought to be one of the oldest in the city. Its roof supports four sets of mosaic-encrusted figures, and inside, the main building is fronted with old gold and lacquer panels of guardian spirits. In front of the main altar, which supports a seated statue of A-Pho, the Holy Mother, is a white ceramic statue of Quan Am, the Goddess of Purity and Motherhood (Goddess of Mercy). Quan Am was thrown out by her husband for some unspecified wrongdoing, and, dressed as a monk, took refuge in a monastery. There, a woman accused her of fathering, and then abandoning, her child. Quan Am accepted the blame, taking on the sins of another, and was again turned out. Much later, when on the point of death, she returned to the monastery to confess her true identity. When the Emperor of China heard the tale, he made Quan Am the Guardian Spirit of Mother and Child, and couples without a son now pray to her. Quan Am's husband is sometimes shown as a parakeet, and the goddess usually holds her adopted son in one arm and stands on a lotus leaf (a symbol of purity). The complex also has a series of courtyards and altars dedicated to deities and spirits. Outside, hawkers sell caged birds and vast quantities of incense sticks to pilgrims.

✉ 12 Lao Tu Street (just off Luong Nhu Hoc Street) 🕓 Daily 5.30am–6pm

TIPS

» Most of Cholon's main sights can be visited in half a day on foot.

» Despite Cholon's compact layout, the most relaxing option is to hire a cyclo for a few hours.

» Saigon's Chinatown is a bustling commercial zone. Wander the streets and visit some of the best pagodas and temples in the city.

CHOLON

TAM SON HOI QUAN

Chinese immigrants from Fukien Province built the Tam Son Assembly Hall just off Nguyen Trai Street in the 19th century and dedicated it to Me Sanh, Goddess of Fertility. The bearded general Quan Cong and his red horse are represented in the courtyard; the general is flanked by his military general guardian, Chau Xuong, and his administrative mandarin, Quan Binh. Thien Hau is also represented here, behind the main altar, as is Ong Bon, Guardian Spirit of Happiness and Virtue. Me Sanh herself is shown here surrounded by her daughters.

✉ 118 Trieu Quang Phuc Street 🕓 Daily 4.30am–6pm

CHUA PHO MIEU

Two blocks separate the Thien Hau Temples, both dedicated to Thien Hau, Goddess of the Sea and protector of sailors. Thien Hau was born in China and, as a girl, saved her father from drowning. Her festival is marked here on the 23rd day of the third lunar month. The temple at 710 Nguyen Trai Street, also dedicated to the Buddha, was constructed in the early 19th century, and is one of the largest in the city. An enormous incense urn and an incinerator can be seen through the main doors. Inside, the principal altar supports the gilded form of Thien Hau and a boat. Silk paintings depict religious scenes, and a high-relief frieze shows episodes from the Legends of the Three Kingdoms. In the post-1975 era many would-be refugees prayed here for safe deliverance before casting themselves adrift on the South China Sea. Some who survived sent offerings to the merciful goddess, and the temple has been well maintained since. Over the front door is a picture of a boiling sea peppered with sinking boats. A benign Thien Hau looks down mercifully from a cloud. Migrants from Fukien Province in China built the original temple at 802 Nguyen Trai Street in the 1730s (although the current building is not old). It's less busy than the first, but sometimes worshipers hurry between images of Thien Hau (shown here with a black face) praying for good fortune. Carved dragons curl around the pillars, and to the right of the altars is a frieze of a boat being swamped by a tsunami.

✉ 710 Nguyen Trai Street; 802 Nguyen Trai Street 🕓 Daily 6am–5.30pm

Above *A stand at the Binh Tay Market*
Below *Tam Son Assembly Hall was built by Chinese immigrants*

CHUA BA MARIAMMAN

The Mariamman Hindu Temple houses a statue of Mariamman, Mother of the Universe, who represents power but is also specifically the Goddess of Diseases. She is flanked by her guardians, Maduraiveeran and Pechiamman. About 60 Tamil Hindus live in the city, but Chinese hold this temple sacred, and it is not unusual to see Chinese Vietnamese worshipers clasping incense sticks and prostrating themselves in front of the Hindu deity.

✚ 186 A3 ✉ 45 Truong Dinh Street
🕒 Daily 7–7

CHUA GIAC VIEN

Giac Vien Pagoda is right at the end of a narrow alley off Lac Long Quan Street (beyond No. 247). Similar in layout, content and inspiration to Giac Lam Pagoda (▷ 196), it was built in 1771 and dedicated to Emperor Gia Long (reigned 1802–20). Now restored, Giac Vien is lavishly decorated, with more than 100 carvings of divinities and spirits. Demons and gods jump out around every corner, the aromas and smoke of incense drift through the air, and rich shades gleam in the semi-darkness. Outside, a small pavilion houses urns containing the ashes of the dead.

✚ 184 A2 ✉ Lac Long Quan Street, District 11

CHUA PHUNG SON

Phung Son Pagoda was built at the beginning of the 19th century on the site of an earlier structure and has been rebuilt several times. At one time it was decided to move the pagoda, and all the temple valuables were loaded on to the back of a white elephant. The beast stumbled and the valuables tumbled out into the pond that surrounds the temple. This was taken as a sign from the gods that the pagoda was to stay where it was. The treasures were retrieved, except for a bell, which, it was said, would ring from beneath the water every full and new moon. The sanctuary houses a large, seated gilded Buddha, surrounded by other figures from several Asian and Southeast Asian countries.

✚ 184 A2 ✉ Set back from road at 1408 3 Thang 2 Boulevard 🕒 Daily 5am–7pm

CHUA PHUNG SON TU

This small temple, Phung Son Tu Pagoda, was built just after World War II by immigrants from China's Fukien province. Most notable are the wonderful painted doors with their fearsome bearded armed warriors. Incense spirals hang in the open well of the pagoda, which is dedicated to Ong Bon, the Guardian of Happiness and Virtue; a statue of Ong Bon stands behind the main altar. Among details to look out for are little bat sculptures by the incense-seller's desk to the far right, a white monkey to the left, and a tiger to the right. Farther inside are more tigers in a savannah on the left, and a large, fire-breathing dragon on the right.

✚ 186 A4 ▣ 338 Nguyen Cong Tru Street, District 3 🕒 Daily 5am–7pm

Below *Street vendors outside the Mariamman Hindu Temple*

CHUA VINH NGHIEM

The Vinh Nghiem Pagoda was completed in 1967 and inaugurated four years later. Its Japanese style is a result of the contribution made by the Japan–Vietnam Friendship Association to the construction funds. A statue of Buddha occupies each of the tower's eight stories, and the sanctuary itself is large and airy. On either side of the entrance are two warriors, and inside is a large, Japanese-style Buddha in an attitude of meditation, flanked by two goddesses. Along the walls scrolls depict the Jataka tales.

✛ 185 C1 ✉ 339 Nam Ky Khoi Nghia Street, off Nguyen Van Troi Street, District 3 ◉ Daily 7.30–11.30, 2–6

CHUA XA LOI PAGODA

Food stands surround the 1956 Xa Loi Pagoda, which contains a much-revered multistory tower housing a sacred relic of the Buddha. The main sanctuary contains a large, bronze-coated Buddha in an attitude of meditation. Around the walls paintings depict the previous lives of the Buddha (with an explanation of each life to the right of the entrance). The pagoda is historically rather than artistically important, as it became a focus of dissent against the Diem regime; it was here that several Buddhist monks committed suicide by setting themselves alight. Hundreds of monks and nuns were arrested in a raid on the pagoda in 1963, among them the leader of the Buddhist faith, then aged 80.

✛ 185 C2 ✉ 89 Ba Huyen Thanh Quan Street, District 3 ◉ Daily 7–11, 2–5

DEN LE VAN DUYET

Le Van Duyet (1763–1831) was a Vietnamese general who put down the Tay Son peasant rebellion in the 18th century—an uprising that led to widespread reforms (▷ 31)—and was consequently promoted to marshal by Emperor Gia Long. After his death, Le Van Duyet's reputation was attacked and his tomb pillaged by Emperor Minh Mang, but under Emperor Thieu Tri's reign (1841–47) the tomb was restored, and subsequent renovation work took place in 1937. The main sanctuary contains an assortment of objects, including a stuffed tiger, a miniature mountain, a baleen whale, carved elephants, crystal goblets, spears and other weapons of war. Many of them were the marshal's personal possessions. In front of the temple is the tomb itself, surrounded by a low wall and flanked by two guardian lions and two lotus buds. The pagoda's attractive roof is best seen from the tomb.

✛ 185 D1 ✉ 126 Dinh Tien Hoang Street, Binh Thanh District ◉ Daily 7am–6pm

GENERAL POST OFFICE

The facade of this 1880s building has attractive cornices with French and Khmer motifs, and the names of French men of letters and science. Inside, the high vaulted ceiling and fans create a wonderfully cool atmosphere in which to scribble a postcard. Note the vast old wall map of Cochin China.

✛ 186 B2 ✉ Cong Xa Pari, District 3 ☎ 08-38292291 ◉ Daily 6am–8pm

GIAC LAM PAGODA

The city's oldest pagoda was built in 1744 and is set among fruit trees and vegetable plots. A sacred bodhi tree grows in the courtyard. Blue and white porcelain plates decorate the roof and some of the towers marking burial places of former head monks. Inside, tiers of Buddhas on the main altar are dominated by the gilded Buddha of the Past. A section behind the main temple features rows of funerary tablets, showing pictures of the deceased, and a bust of Ho Chi Minh. At the very back of the pagoda is a hall with murals showing infernal tortures.

✛ 184 B1 ✉ 118 Lac Long Quan Street, 1 mile (2km) northeast of Giac Vien Pagoda ◉ Daily 6am–9pm

KHU LUU NIEM BAC HO

This building at Dragon House Wharf is now the Ho Chi Minh Museum, celebrating the life and exploits of Ho Chi Minh, mostly through pictures and the occasional piece of memorabilia, including clothing. Schoolchildren are brought here to be told of their country's recent history, and visitors of all ages have their photographs taken with the portrait of Bac Ho (Uncle Ho) in the background. Around the back of the museum on an exterior wall are interesting photographs and prints, plus two carriages from early 20th-century Saigon. There's a pleasant, breezy café on the river, and you can watch the boats from the upstairs balcony. A statue of Ho Chi Minh as a young man overlooks the river.

✛ 186 B4 ✉ 1 Nguyen Tat Thanh Street, District 4 ☎ 08-39402060 ◉ Tue–Sun 7.30–11.30, 1.30–4.30 ⚑ 15,000d ▣ ⊞ ❓ Labels in English

Below The Ho Chi Minh Museum celebrates the life of the revolutionary

HOI THONG NHAT

Ngo Dinh Diem's presidential palace, now renamed Reunification Hall, dominates a large park in District 1. The French governor's residence was built here in 1868, and was later renamed the Independence, or Presidential Palace. In February 1962 planes piloted by two of the South's finest airmen took off to attack the Viet Cong, but turned back mid-flight to bomb the palace, in an attempt to assassinate President Diem, in residence since 1954. The President, who held office from 1955 to 1963, escaped with his family to the cellar, but the palace had to be demolished and replaced. (Diem was later assassinated after a military coup.) One of the pilots, Nguyen Thanh Trung, is a Deputy Director General of Vietnam Airlines and still flies.

One of the most memorable photographs taken during the Vietnam War was of a North Vietnamese Army tank crashing through the gates of the palace on April 30, 1975, marking the end of South Vietnam and its government (a similar tank stands in the forecourt). The President and his cabinet were arrested here shortly afterwards.

INSIDE THE PALACE

The hall has been preserved as it was in 1975. In the Vice President's Guest Room there is a lacquered painting of the Temple of Literature in Hanoi (▷ 78–81); the Presenting of Credentials Room contains a fine, 40-piece lacquerwork showing visiting diplomats during the Le Dynasty (15th century). In the basement there are operations rooms, military maps, radios, telephones and other paraphernalia. Upstairs, foreign ambassadors met the President in the Dragon's Head Room (now the Presidential Receiving Room). Next to this is the Vice President's Room, with gold-colored furnishings. The President's living area was at the back, where he had a small cinema, a bar, a dance hall and a casino. Visitors are also shown a poorly made, but nonetheless interesting, film of the revolution.

The palace was rebuilt between 1962 and 1966 and is still filled with fabulously kitsch 1960s furnishings. It was designed according to Chinese geomancy, and even the carpet colors were chosen to calm or stimulate users of the rooms. Don't miss the display of presidential gifts which includes some hollowed elephants' feet.

INFORMATION
✚ 186 A2 ✉ 135 Nam Ky Khoi Nghia, District 3 ☎ 08-73085039 ⏱ Daily 7.30–11, 1–4; hall sometimes closed for state occasions 👋 Adult 15,000d, child (5–15) 2,000d ☕ Two cafés in the grounds and cold drinks on the fourth floor 📖 Pamphlet 5,000d 🎧 Guided tours (in English) every 10 min

Above *The Reunification Hall has been preserved as it was in 1975*

NHA THO DUC BA

The twin-spired, redbrick Notre Dame Cathedral is in the middle of Paris Square, an imposing building overlooking a statue of the Virgin Mary. Built between 1877 and 1880, it is said to stand on the site of an ancient pagoda. Each of the cathedral's towers is 130ft (40m) high, and is topped by an iron spire.
✚ 186 B2 ✉ Cong Xa Pari, District 3 ⊙ Mon–Fri 8–10.30, 3–4; Communion celebrated Sun 5.30am, 6.30am, 7.30am, 9.30am, 4pm, 5.15pm, 6.30pm

PHUOC HAI TU

Behind low pink walls, just before the Thi Nghe Channel, is the Emperor of Jade Pagoda (or Chua Ngoc Hoan), dedicated to the supreme god of the Taoists, though also containing other deities. These include the Archangel Michael of the Buddhists; a Sakyamuni (historic) Buddha; statues of the two generals who tamed the Green Dragon (representing the east) and the White Dragon (representing the west), to the left and right of the first altar respectively; and Quan Am, the Goddess of Mercy, Guardian Spirit of Mother and Child. The statues are, remarkably, made of papier-mâché. The Jade Emperor himself is flanked by guardians known as the Big Diamonds (Tu Dai Kim Cuong), and to his right is Phat Mau Chan De, mother of the Buddhas of north, south, east, west and center, with her two faces and 18 arms. Built by Cantonese worshipers in 1909, the pagoda is a riot of color, with gilded pictographs, woodcarvings and exquisite tilework on the roof. The Hall of Ten Hells, in the sanctuary, has reliefs showing a thousand infernal tortures. In the grounds, women sell birds that are set free to gain merit.
✚ 185 D1 ✉ 73 Mai Thi Luu Street, off Dien Bien Phu Street, District 3 ⊙ Daily 6am–6.30pm

THAO CAM VIEN

The Botanical Gardens run alongside Nguyen Binh Khiem Street, at the end of Le Duan Street,

where the Thi Nghe Channel flows into the Saigon River. They were established in 1864 by French botanist Jean-Baptiste Louis Pierre, and by the 1970s had a collection of nearly 2,000 species, including a particularly fine display of orchids. Following the Vietnam War the gardens went into decline, a situation from which they are still trying to recover. A small zoo in the south quarter of the gardens has live inhabitants and a life-size family of Vietnamese-speaking model dinosaurs.
✚ 186 C1 ✉ 2 Nguyen Binh Khiem Street ☎ 08-38293728 ⊙ Daily 6am–8pm ✋ 15,000d (gardens and zoo)

TRAN HUNG DAO

Not far from the Emperor of Jade Pagoda (▷ left) is the small Tran Hung Temple built in 1932 and dedicated to the worship of the victorious 13th-century General Hung Dao. A series of bas-reliefs depicts the general's successes, and the temple also contains weapons and carved dragons. Tran Hung Dao used a tried and trusted technique to defeat the Chinese in 1288, sinking wooden stakes into the Bach Dang River off the coast of northeast Vietnam. For the second time in less than 500 years the invading Chinese fleet was impaled on the poles and put out of action. Standing in the front courtyard is a larger-than-life bronze statue of this hero of Vietnamese nationalism. A nearby park occupies the former site of the Massiges cemetery, where French military and colonial residents were laid to rest.
✚ 185 D1 ✉ 34 Vo Thi Sau Street, District 1 ⊙ Mon–Fri 6–11, 2–6

US CONSULATE GENERAL AND MEMORIAL

http://hochiminh.usconsulate.gov
Running north of the cathedral is Le Duan Street, the former corridor of power ending at Ngo Dinh Diem's Palace (Reunification Hall, ▷ 197) and lined with the former embassies of France, the US and the UK. One block from the French Consulate

Above The bonsai garden within the Botanical Gardens

was the former US Embassy, a 1960s building that was quickly demolished by the Americans after diplomatic ties were resumed in 1995. The US Consulate General now stands on the site. Outside, a line of hopeful visa applicants forms every day come rain or shine. This office has the distinction of being the busiest overseas US mission for marriage visas, a title for which it vies closely with the US Embassy in Manila. A memorial outside, on the corner of Mac Dinh Chi Street, records the attack by Viet Cong special forces during the Tet Offensive of 1968 and their final victory in 1975. On the other side of the road, a little farther northeast at 25 Le Duan, is the former British Embassy, erected in the late 1950s and now the British Consulate General and British Council.
✚ 186 B1 ✉ 4 Le Duan Street, District 3 ☎ 08-38229433 ⊙ Mon–Thu 8.30–11.30, 1.30–3.30. Closed Fri, Vietnamese and US public holidays

QUANG TRUONG LAM SON

The historic and cultural heart of Saigon is a magnet for shoppers, courting couples, idlers, tourists and thousands of horn-blaring motorcyclists. Lam Son Square is at the center of Saigon in the heart of District 1. Key roads radiate from this point, and it is surrounded by important cultural and historical buildings as well as famous hotels. The Rex Hotel, once a favorite with US officers, stands at the intersection of Le Loi and Nguyen Hue boulevards. This was the scene of the daily press-briefing session during the Vietnam War that came to be known as the Five O'Clock Follies. Following many years of immobility, the crown on the sixth-floor terrace—a popular spot for a drink— has been renovated and is rotating once again.

NORTHWEST OF THE REX

Near the Rex, at the northwestern end of Nguyen Hue Boulevard, is the ornate, yellow and white French colonial City Hall, now home to the Ho Chi Minh City People's Committee. It was built in 1908 and modeled on the Hôtel de Ville in Paris. The building overlooks a statue of Uncle Ho, who offers comfort, or perhaps advice, to a child. This is a popular place for Vietnamese to have their photographs taken, especially newlyweds, who believe Ho confers his blessing on them.

NORTHEAST OF THE REX

At the end of Le Loi Boulevard is the once impressive French-era Opera House, built in 1897 to a design by French architect Ferret Eugene and restored in 1998. It once housed the National Assembly; now it provides a schedule of theater, dance and gymnastics.

Facing the Opera House to the left is the Continental Hotel, built in 1880 and an integral part of the city's history. British novelist Graham Greene (1904–91) stayed here, and the hotel features in his book *The Quiet American*. Journalists, soldiers and others used to gather during the Vietnam War at the so-called Continental Shelf, a veranda, to pick up information. There is also a lovely enclosed garden.

The Continental sits on Dong Khoi Street, formerly known as Tu Do Street and, during the French colonial era, as the rue Catinat. This road stretches from Cong Xa Pari down to the Saigon River and is lined with shops specializing in, or selling silk clothes and accessories, jewelry, lacquerware and household goods. Facing the Continental and adjoining Dong Khoi Street is the opulent Hotel Caravelle, which houses shops selling luxury goods.

INFORMATION

➕ 186 B3 ✉ Bordered by Nguyen Hue and Le Loi boulevards, and by Dong Khoi Street, District 1 🍴 Wide range in the area

TIP

» The Tourist Information Center, on the corner of Lam Son Square at 92–96 Nguyen Hue Street (☎ 08-38226033, www.ticvietnam.com ⏰ Daily 8am–9pm), is a convenient source of information. Call in to collect a free city map and free Internet use. There is also a currency exchange, ATMs, a hotel, tours and train tickets reservation service.

REGIONS | HO CHI MINH CITY • SIGHTS

Above *The French colonial City Hall is now home to the People's Committee*

WALK

COLONIAL SAIGON

Saigon, the name for the capital of Cochinchina, France's colony in Southeast Asia, now covers the area of Ho Chi Minh City designated as District 1. For over two centuries before the arrival of the French, Saigon had been an important commercial center, which in 1698 came under Vietnamese control. It was first attacked by the French in 1859, and their colony came into existence with the Treaty of Saigon in 1862. In the decades that followed Saigon was transformed into an Asian outpost of French culture. This walk focuses on the architectural reminders of French rule.

THE WALK
Distance: 1 mile (2km)
Allow: 1 hour
Start at: Tourist Information Center on the corner of Lam Son Square at 92–96 Nguyen Hue Street
End at: Majestic Hotel, 1 Dong Khoi Street

HOW TO GET THERE
The start point is in the center of Saigon, within walking distance of many of the main hotels, and free city maps can be picked up at the Tourist Information Center.

★ Cross to the other side of Nguyen Hue and pause at the Rex Hotel.

❶ The Rex Hotel (▷ 199, 213) was built by the French in the 1950s and it is worth strolling inside to admire the attractive lobby.

Walk north along Nguyen Hue to take a closer look at the City Hall built by the French and completed in 1908 (▷ 199).

❷ The building's design consciously imitates that of the Hôtel de Ville in Paris, with a wing either side of the central hall and clock tower. The photogenic facade is all visitors can see, as the building is now the city's center of local government and not open to the public.

Cross to the corner where the Vietnam Airlines office is located and then continue by walking back to the Tourist Information Center. From here, turn left on Le Loi, walking to the next corner with the Givral restaurant and, opposite, the Continental Hotel.

❸ The illustrious Continental, completed in 1886 to serve as a hotel for the French, has been restored a little too clinically for some people's tastes (▷ 199, 211–212), losing some of the hotel's character. Famous guests of the past include W. Somerset Maugham (1874–65), André Malraux (1901–76), Graham Greene (1904–91) and Walter Cronkite (b.1916). In Greene's *The Quiet American* this is where Thomas Fowler, the novel's anti-hero, takes his morning tea and first meets the American Pyle. The area outside the hotel, known as place Garnier during French rule, was where the bomb explosion in Greene's novel takes place, and during shooting for the 2002 film *The Quiet American*, the square was used for this scene.

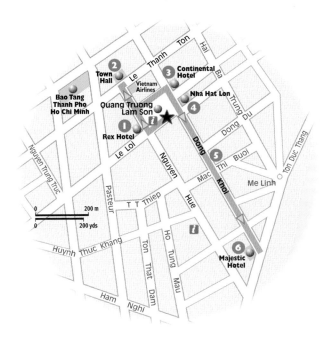

⑥ Between 1951 and 1954 Greene spent a lot of his time in Saigon during the winter months, covering the French war against the Vietnamese for the London *Sunday Times* and France's *Le Figaro*. The writer lived at two locations on Dong Khoi, and when he had to stay in hotels the Majestic (▷ 212) was his favorite. It was built in 1925 and has been sensitively restored with its grand heritage in mind. The lobby area is especially attractive—note the original wooden floor, period elevator and art deco fittings—and there are framed photographs on the walls showing the hotel during different periods of its existence. Greene wrote an early draft of *The Quiet American* while staying here.

WHERE TO EAT AND DRINK

You will pass numerous places on Dong Khoi where food and drink can be enjoyed, but it may be worth waiting until the end of the walk to enjoy a rest and refreshment in one of the outlets, including a comfortable bar at one end of the lobby, in the Majestic Hotel.

Cross the open space in front of the Continental, walking past the entrance to the Opera House.

④ The Opera House (▷ 199) was a French concert hall, built in 1899, and its elegant entrance is worth admiring for its stately staircase, ersatz classical figures and decorative details below the roof.

Walk down the left side Dong Khoi.

⑤ Renamed Dong Khoi ("uprising") by the Vietnamese communists after 1975, this was rue Catinat (named after a French warship which attacked Danang harbour in 1856) when Graham Greene first visited the city in the early 1950s, and he records how part of what captivated him was the French perfumeries along this street. He relished the street's sleazy atmosphere, a far cry from its sophisticated appeal of earlier times. The perfumeries are long gone but you will find on sale pirated copies of *The Quiet American*.

Walk to the bottom of Dong Khoi, facing the river, and cross the road to the Majestic Hotel.

Opposite *The Hotel Continental has had many famous guests*
Below *The reception area of the Rex Hotel*

WHAT TO DO

SHOPPING

APRICOT GALLERY
www.apricotgallery.com.vn
This sister gallery to the one in Hanoi (▷ 84) specializes in famous artists and commands high prices.
✉ 50–52 Mac Thi Buoi Street, District 1 ☎ 08-38227962 🕙 Daily 8.30–8.30

DIAMOND PLAZA DEPARTMENT STORE
Ho Chi Minh City's air-conditioned department store occupies a couple of floors. It sells luxury goods, clothes (including some Western brands), watches, bags and perfumes. There is also a small supermarket, ten-pin bowling complex and a cinema.
✉ Diamond Plaza, 34 Le Duan Street, District 1 ☎ 08-38225500 🕙 Daily 9.30am–10pm

GALLERY DELI
www.vietnamartgallery.com
Attractive Vietnamese art for sale, ranging in price from one dollar to more than a thousand. Shipping can be arranged but it is less expensive to have your purchase securely packed in a tube by the shop.
✉ 44 Dong Khoi Street, District 1 ☎ 08-38224580 🕙 Daily 8am–10pm

GAYA
www.gayavietnam.com
This three-floor shop sells exquisite goods. One floor has a selection of embroidered tablecloths, bamboo bowls, ceramics and large home items such as screens. Another is lined with ethereal and unusual designer items by Parisian Michelle De Albert, Australian Lawson Johnson and Cambodian Romyda Keth. If an item does not fit, the shop will take your measurements and make another in two weeks.
✉ 1 Nguyen Van Trang Street, District 1 ☎ 08-39251495 🕙 Daily 9–9

KHAISILK
www.khaisilkcorp.com
Khaisilk belongs to Mr. Khai's growing retail empire. He has a dozen shops around Vietnam and Saigon branches in the Legend and the Sheraton. Choose from a range of beautifully made quality silks, from dresses to scarves and ties.
✉ 107 Dong Khoi Street, District 1 ☎ 08-38291146 🕙 Daily 8–8

LOTUS GALLERY
www.lotusgallery.com
This expensive gallery showcases works by contemporary Vietnamese

Above Conical rice paper hats for sale

painters. Many are members of the Vietnam Fine Arts Association, and have exhibited around the world.
✉ 67 Pasteur Street, District 1 ☎ 08-38292695 🕙 Daily 8–8

MOSAIQUE
Like its sister store in Hanoi, this cavernous shop is a home accessories parlor, with displays upstairs of exquisitely embroidered wall hangings and table-runners. Many goods come from workshops in the north of the country.
✉ 98 Mac Thi Buoi Street, District 1 ☎ 08-38234634 🕙 Daily 9–9

ORIENTAL HOME
www.madeinvietnamcollection.com
If you are taken with the Imperial style of furniture which is so favored in Huê, this is the place to come. Lamp stands, ceramics and brass ornaments are also displayed in this furnishings and gift emporium. It's an environmentally conscious operation; only natural materials, such as bamboo, rattan and silk, are used in their products.
✉ 2A Le Duan Street, District 1 ☎ 08-39100194 🕙 Daily 9–7.30

PARKSONS DEPARTMENT STORE

The giant Malaysian retail company, Parksons, has opened its first department store in Vietnam and is a useful shopping destination for a general range of products. There is a very good food court and young adults will enjoy a visit to the top floor for the arcades and bowling alley.

✉ 35 bis–45 Le Thanh Ton Street, District 1 ☎ 08-38277635 🕐 Daily 10.30–7

RED DOOR DECO

www.reddoordeco.com

This two-story shop sells stylish, innovative and well-made furniture, fabrics and ornaments. Shoppers can pick up old French Marelli fans of various sizes, dried lotus leaves, some beautiful lamps, cushions or unusual pieces of furniture.

✉ 20A Thi Sach Street, District 1 ☎ 08-38258672 🕐 Mon–Sat 8.30–7.30, Sun 8.30–6

SAIGON CRAFTS

www.saigoncrafts.com

Saigon Crafts has an eye-catching array of lacquered bowls and plates made from wood and bamboo, as well as colorful figures carved from marble. This shop is directly opposite the Bong Sen Hotel and near the Opera House.

✉ 74 Dong Khoi Street, District 1 ☎ 08-38295758 🕐 Daily 8.30–9

SAIGON KITSCH

Communist kitsch items here range from big propaganda poster art to everyday place mats and mugs. You'll also find some good examples of anti-US propaganda material for sale, plus great retro bags and funky jewelry.

✉ 43 Ton That Tiep Street, District 1 ☎ 08-38218019 🕐 Daily 9–8

SONG

www.asiasongdesign.com

This beautiful clothes emporium sells flowing summer dresses from French-born designer Valerie Gregori-McKenzie. There are also other stylish and unique pieces,

accessories and even cookbooks based on her culinary experiences of living in Vietnam.

✉ 76D Le Thanh Ton Street, District, also Ground Floor Eden Mall, 106 Nguyen Hue Street, District 1 ☎ 08-38246986 🕐 Daily 9–8

VIETNAM QUILTS

www.vietnam-quilts.org

The quilts you see displayed in this volunteer-run store are the result of a project designed to develop rural communities by providing training to women. Accessories for sale include aprons, sheets and table sets.

✉ 64 Ngo Duc Ke Street, District 1 ☎ 08-39142119 🕐 Daily 9–7

ENTERTAINMENT AND NIGHTLIFE

163 CYCLO BAR

This friendly venue in the heart of the backpacker district has a bar downstairs and an air-conditioned room upstairs presenting live music—jazz, Latin, flamenco, country and pop—from 8pm nightly. Inexpensive drinks and light meals are served from breakfast onward by friendly and capable staff. Black-and-white photos of the fall of Saigon (in 1975) adorn the walls. Happy hour is between 9am and 6pm.

✉ 163 Pham Ngu Lao Street, District 1 ☎ 08-39201567 🕐 Daily 9am–midnight

APOCALYPSE NOW

Apocalypse Now is one of the most abidingly popular bars with the younger expatriate crowd. The ceiling is decorated with helicopter reliefs, the fans revolving as if they are the helicopter rotors. The large dance floor gets very full and hot and sticky. There is a large screen for sporting events.

✉ 2B–2C Thi Sach Street, District 1 ☎ 08-38256124 🕐 Daily 7pm–midnight

BLUE GECKO

www.bluegeckosaigon.com

Saigon's Australian community has adopted this small bar, so expect cold beer (happy hour is between

5 and 7.30pm) and Australian flags above the pool table. Darts and a TV screen are also available.

✉ 31 Ly Tu Trong Street, District 1 ☎ 08-38243483 🕐 Daily 4.30pm–midnight

CAFÉ LATIN

This very popular, ultramodern bar in downtown Saigon, all sleek steel lines and glass, is a favorite with working expatriates—especially Australians—and is busy every night. Sit at the bar stools or sink into the comfortable sofas that line the walls. There is a restaurant with a balcony upstairs (▷ 207).

✉ 19–21 Dong Du Street, District 1 ☎ 08-38226363 🕐 Daily 9am–midnight

CONSERVATORY OF MUSIC (NHAC VIEN THANH PHO HO CHI MINH)

Traditional Vietnamese music and classical music concerts are performed by the young students who study music here and sometimes by local and visiting musicians.

✉ 112 Nguyen Du Street, District 1 ☎ 08-8243774 🕐 Performances: Mon–Fri from 7pm

LA FENÊTRE SOLEIL

It's a little difficult to find the entrance to this small café, but it is well worth making the effort. In the daytime the place is quiet, with large, comfortable armchairs and is a great place to stop and enjoy a cappuccino or one of the many flavored teas. In the evening there is a different vibe and some fancy cocktails are mixed.

✉ 1st Floor, 135 Le Thanh Ton Street, District 1 ☎ 08-38225209 🕐 Daily 11.30am–midnight

GINGER CLUB

A converted warehouse provides the space for one of Saigon's new nightclubs, attracting a fashionable crowd at weekends. There is a variety of cocktails on the menu, as well as a French house wine, and Asian fusion food.

✉ 88 Ho Tung Mau Street, District 1 ☎ 08-39153691 🕐 Daily 10pm–late

HI-FI NIGHTCLUB

One of the city's larger nightclubs, Hi-Fi's chief attraction is the quality of the international performers who appear here. Tickets sometimes need to be booked in advance.

✉ Lucky Plaza, Level 2, 38 Nguyen Hue Street (alternate entrance at 69 Dong Kho Street), District 1 ☎ 01269-804255 🕐 Thu–Sat 8pm–late 💰 Around 100,000d

HOA VIEN

www.hoavien.vn

Hoa Vien, a vast Czech *bierkeller*, houses Saigon's first microbrewery. Freshly brewed dark and light beer is available by the liter or in smaller measures, and you can tap your own beer: The bar is surrounded by copper kegs. There is also a beer garden (▷ 208).

✉ 28 Mac Dinh Chi Street, District 1 ☎ 08-38290585 🕐 Daily 9am–11pm

LUSH

The bistro-style restaurant is the main draw during the day but at night it is the DJ music, mostly hip hop and contemporary pop hits, that brings in the crowds. By 10pm at weekends the two levels of Lush are crowded; keep an eye on the stiff price of the drinks.

✉ 2 Ly Tu Trong Street, District 1 ☎ 08-38242496 🕐 Daily noon–2am

PURPLE JADE

A stylish lounge bar in a 5-star hotel, Purple Jade offers cozy booths and good live music. Light food is served alongside a drinks menu with some inventive cocktails and rice wines (happy hour is 7–10).

✉ InterContinental Asiana, corner of Hai Ba Trung and Le Duan Streets, District 1 ☎ 08-35209999 🕐 Daily 6pm–midnight

NUMBER FIVE BAR

New premises for an old favorite on the Saigon pub landscape. The bar is now a lot larger but the nightly cocktail specials are still a feature, as is the pool table. This is a popular place for watching major televised sporting events, particularly rugby and soccer, and it regularly organizes golf tournaments.

✉ 43 Mac Dinh Chi Street, District 1 ☎ 08-38256300 🕐 Daily 5pm–midnight

Q BAR

Well positioned under the Opera House, the Q Bar is the haunt of a wide cross-section of Saigon society. The interior is striking: Caravaggio murals adorn some of the walls and there are nooks and crannies for intimate seating.

✉ 7 Lam Son Square, District 1 ☎ 08-38233479 🕐 Daily 6pm–late

ROOFTOP GARDEN

www.rexhotelvietnam.com

Large model elephants, a motley collection of shrubbery and bonsai, and a revolving crown may give this outdoor bar and café a rather shabby air, but that doesn't detract from the hotel's fame as the venue for daily military briefings to the press during the Vietnam War. If you can peer past the leafy decoration there is a great view of Saigon.

✉ Rex Hotel, 141 Nguyen Hue Boulevard District 1 ☎ 08-38292185 🕐 Daily 24 hours

SAIGON SAIGON BAR

www.caravellehotel.com

At this breezy, cool bar there is seating on a patio and on tiny balconies clinging to the edge of the skyscraper, with large chairs from which to enjoy the views. The Saigon Saigon signature cocktail is a mix of vodka, rum, gin, orange juice and pineapple juice, rather swamped by crème de menthe. Snacks and ice cream are available; sandwiches are served at lunchtime, and afternoon tea includes cakes on dainty, tiered dishes. Live music at night is from 8.30pm.

✉ 9th floor, Caravelle Hotel, 19 Lam Son Square, District 1 ☎ 08-38234999 🕐 Daily 11am–late

SAXN'ART CLUB

www.saxnart.com

This is a well-established and popular nightclub where jazz music, whether from local Vietnamese bands or groups from abroad, is the order of the night.

✉ 28 Le Loi Street, District 1 ☎ 08-38228472 🕐 Daily 7pm–midnight

STORM P BAR

www.stormp.vn

Named after the Danish cartoonist Storm Peterson, whose murals run along one wall, this classy bar aspires to create a Scandinavian atmosphere in the heart of Southeast Asia. The endeavor is encouraged by the availability of shots of Gammel Dansk with Enkelt bitters. During happy hour (5–8) Tiger draft is an affordable 17,000d.

✉ 5B Nguyen Sieu Street, District 1 ☎ 08-38274738 🕐 Daily 12–12

VASCOS

www.vascosgroup.com

Still attached to the Camargue restaurant (▷ 207) but now in a new location, this bar has retained its popularity. Friday nights always attract the largest crowd due to the live music; the pizzas from a wood-fired oven are another attraction.

✉ 74/7D Hai Ba Trung Street, District 1 ☎ 08-38242888 🕐 Daily 11am–midnight

WATER PUPPETRY SHOWS

There are two places to enjoy performances of water puppetry in Saigon. In the Museum of Vietnamese History in the Botanical Gardens (▷ 198), there are daily shows in the tiny theater in a covered outdoor area. The advantages of this performance over the Hanoi theater (▷ 87) are that you can get closer to the action, and there is better light and more room for taking photos. At the Golden Dragon Water Puppet Theatre (www.goldendragonwaterpuppet.com) evening performances last 50 minutes.

✉ Museum of Vietnamese History, 2 Nguyen Binh Khiem Street, District 1. Water puppetry 55 B Nguyen Thi Minh Khai Street, District 1 ☎ Museum: 08-38298146. Water puppetry 08-38404027 🕐 Museum: Mon–Sat 8–11, 1.30–4, Sun 8.30–4. Performances: museum Tue–Sun 9, 10, 11am, 2pm, 3, 4. Water puppetry: 5, 6.30 💰 Museum: 15,000d. Water puppetry: daily 30,000d

SPORTS AND ACTIVITIES
DIAMOND SUPERBOWL
This popular complex in the heart of the city is at the top of the Diamond Plaza department store (▷ 202) and has 32 bowling lanes. The top floor has a fast-food outlet, video games and plenty of pool tables for those taking a break from bowling.

✉ Diamond Plaza, 4th Floor, 34 Le Duan Street, District 1 ☎ 08-38257778
🕓 Mon–Sat 10am–1am, Sun 9am–1am
✋ Mon–Fri 9.30am–2pm 20,000d per game, 2pm–6pm 30,000d, 6pm–1am 40,000d

GOLF VIETNAM AND COUNTRY CLUB
www.vietnamgolfcc.com
This 36-hole golfing complex with east and west courses lies north of Ho Chi Minh City. Facilities also include a restaurant, pro shop, tennis and badminton courts and a swimming pool.

✉ Long Thanh My Ward, District 9
☎ 08-62800103 ✋ Green fees: Mon–Fri from US$80, Sat–Sun from US$100

PHU THO RACECOURSE
Races are held Saturday and Sunday afternoons on this course, reopened with financing from a Chinese entrepreneur. Both the winner and the second horse have to be selected to collect winnings.

✉ 2 Le Dai Hanh Street, District 11
☎ 08-39624319 🕓 Sat–Sun noon–5pm
✋ Betting tickets 10,000d; admission 5,000d

Below *Enjoy a round of golf at Song Be Golf Resort*

FEBRUARY
NGHIA ANH HOI QUAN PAGODA FESTIVAL
The Hoa (overseas Chinese) community, together with many local Kinh (Vietnamese), celebrate in honor of Lord Quan Cong with unicorn, lion and dragon dances.

✉ 678 Nguyen Trai Street, District 5
🕓 Fifteenth day of the first lunar month; also 24th day of the sixth lunar month (Jul)

MARCH
ONG DIA TEMPLE FESTIVAL
A celebration of the birth of the Earth genie Phuc Doc Chinh Than.

✉ 125 Le Loi Street, Go Vap District
🕓 Second day of the second lunar month

MAY
THIEN HAU PAGODA FESTIVAL
A festival celebrating Goddess Thien Hau—the goddess of the sea and the protector of sailors (▷ 194).

✉ 710 Nguyen Trai Street, District 5
🕓 Twenty-third–24th day of the third lunar month

SEPTEMBER
NGHINH ONG FESTIVAL
Traditional procession and offerings in honor of the whale cult followed by local fisherfolk.

✉ Hung Thanh hamlet, Can Gio District
🕓 Fifteenth–17th days of eighth lunar month

LE VAN DUYET TOMB FESTIVAL
At one of Ho Chi Minh City's biggest festivals pilgrims flock to the Temple of Marshal Le Van Duyet (▷ 196).

✉ Le Van Duyet Tomb, Binh Thanh District
🕓 Thirtieth day of the seventh lunar month until the first day of the eighth lunar month

SONG BE GOLF RESORT
www.songbegolf.com
This 27-hole course lies in 247 acres (100ha), with lakes and tree-lined fairways, 14 miles (22km) from Ho Chi Minh City on Highway 13. There are also tennis courts, a gym, sauna and children's play area.

✉ 77 Binh Duong Boulevard, Lai Thieu, Thuan An District, Binh Duong Province
☎ 0650-73755802/73756600 ✋ Green fees: Mon–Fri US$47/79/118/142 for 9/18/27/36 holes, Sat–Sun US$71/119/149/173 for 9/18/27/36 holes. Caddy fee US$13–$52, cart rental US$24–$72

SUPERBOWL
This enormous bowling complex has 32 lanes, video arcades and fast-food outlets. It is a great hit with the Vietnamese, especially at weekends, so reserve in advance to be sure of securing a lane.

✉ 43A Truong Son Street, Than Binh District ☎ 08-8850188 🕓 Daily 10am–midnight ✋ 53,000d per person per game, plus shoe rental

HEALTH AND BEAUTY
L'APOTHIQUAIRE
www.lapothiquaire.com
In a century-old French building, this spa has a more comprehensive range of treatments available than any of its competitors. Visitors choose a course that suits their budget as well as their body.

✉ 64A Truong Dinh Street, District 1
☎ 08-39325181 ✋ Facials from 650,000d; body treatments 740,000d–1,000,000d; see website for full price list of all treatments

GLOW
www.glowsaigon.com
Modern and stylish decor helps make Glow one of the more sophisticated spas in the city. There are seven private rooms, four of which are for singles, two for doubles and one a VIP suite. Treatments include massages and facials and there is a hair salon.

✉ Eden Mall, Mezzanine Level, 183 Dong Khoi Street, District 1 ☎ 08-38238368
✋ Massages from US$32

PRICES AND SYMBOLS

The restaurants are listed alphabetically (excluding Le, La, Il and The). The prices given are the average for a two-course lunch (L) and a three-course dinner (D) for one person, without drinks. The wine price is for the least expensive bottle.

For a key to the symbols, ▷ 2.

ASHOKA

This beacon of Indian cuisine has an extensive menu. Its set lunch lists 11 options, with another 19 curry dishes. Highlights in the low-lit, comfortably air-conditioned restaurant are mutton *shami* kebab, prawn vindaloo and *kadhai* fish, which is barbecued chunks of fresh fish cooked in a *kadhai* (a traditional Indian-style wok) with Peshwari ground spices, and sautéed with onion and tomatoes. Try the Coke with ice cream float for dessert.
✉ 17/10 Le Thanh Ton Street, District 1
☎ 08-38231372 🕐 Daily 11.30–2.15,
5–10.30 🖐 Set meals from 150,000d,
Wine 360,000d

AN VIEN

Go down an alley to this intimate three-floor restaurant, which serves the most fragrant rice in

Vietnam. Each room is small and furnished in Vietnamese style. The food is excellent, the service attentive and the interior rich with carpets, tasseled lampshades, silk-embroidered cushions and menus, and bowls of lilies and pink napkins arranged in lotus-leaf style. The *banh xeo*, crispy fried squid, combination "*mam*" special (pickled fish, pork and duck eggs) and steamed eel in a claypot with coconut milk are recommended. A durian- and bean-sweetened porridge and an excellent coconut caramel are on the dessert menu.
✉ 178A Hai Ba Trung Street, District 1
☎ 08-38243877 🕐 Daily 10–10
🖐 L 100,000d, D 120,000d, Wine 300,000d

AUGUSTIN

Prices are reasonable at this small and central restaurant for some of the best and most straightforward French cooking in Saigon. Although tables are quite closely packed together, there is a congenial atmosphere. Try the excellent gratinée onion soup, baked clams, vibrant hot goat's cheese salad and rack of lamb roasted with garlic butter. Their melting Armagnac chocolate cake served with *crème*

Above *Saigon's microbrewery, Hoa Vien Bräuhaus, serves good food*

anglaise makes a magnificent conclusion to your meal.
✉ 10 Nguyen Thiep Street, District 1
☎ 08-38292941 🕐 Mon–Sat 11.30–2,
6–10.30 🖐 L 212,000d, D 300,000d,
Wine 410,000d

AU MANOIR DE KHAI

www.khaisilkcorp.com
The eponymous Mr. Khai, known for his silk empire (▷ 26), has added this French restaurant to his substantial business portfolio. It is set in an elegantly restored villa and garden on which no expense has been spared. Dine among artworks, gilded mirrors and flowers, or alfresco by candlelight, and take your pick from a sublime menu that includes lobster ravioli with truffle soup, Australian lamb dishes, steamed New Zealand mussels with tiger prawns and mayonnaise sauce, and a delicious dessert of hot soufflé with Cointreau or Grand Marnier or chocolate.
✉ 251 Dien Bien Phu Street, District 3
☎ 08-39303394 🕐 Daily 11–1.30,
6–9.30 🖐 L 550,000d, D 1,520,000d,
Wine 800,000d

AU PARC

Facing onto the park in front of the old Presidential Palace, this attractive, European-style café serves light meals on mosaic-covered tables over two floors. Its strawberry crumble and ice cream should not be resisted. Other temptations include lentil salad with roasted tomatoes and cheese, and falafel with tahini sauce. There are 26 sandwich options, from the basic BLT to baked brie with caramelized onions and green apple, and there is a children's menu. A good Sunday brunch is served between 7am and 7.30pm for 215,000d per person.
✉ 23 Han Tuyen Street, District 1
☎ 08-38292772 🕐 Mon–Sat 7am–10.30pm, Sun 8–3.30 ✋ L 204,000d, D 300,000d, Wine 300,000d

BERNIE'S BAR & GRILL

A welcoming, Australian-managed eatery for those who yearn for a hefty burger, sirloin steak or chili con carne. Restaurant seating is upstairs, but the same food is available in the downstairs bar. Breakfast is also served: Try the poached eggs with smoked salmon.
✉ 19 Thai Van Lung Street, District 1
☎ 08-38221720 🕐 Daily 8am–10.30pm
✋ L 200,000d, D 290,000d, Wine 350,000d

BUNTA

Tired after an exhausting walk around Reunification Hall? Bunta is across the road from the entrance and there are over 30 different noodle dishes to choose from. Avoid weekends if possible because local people love this place and getting a table may involve a wait.
✉ 136 Nam Ky Khoi Nghia Street, District 1
☎ 08-38229913 🕐 Daily 6am–midnight
✋ L 120,000d, D 175,000d

CAFÉ LATIN

There's an international feel to the menu of this second-story restaurant, which offers daily specials, sandwiches, bagels and main meals. From its galaxy of intriguing dishes try beer-battered barramundi and tartar sauce, roasted pumpkin, roasted capsicum, feta, endive, olive tapenade, Parmesan toasted wraps, tapenade-crusted lamb cutlets or warm eggplant (aubergine) salad and hot feta dressing. All this delicious food can be rounded off with a selection of desserts such as miniature lime curd tart, mango, coconut praline and vanilla ice creams, or sticky date pudding with toffee sauce and ice cream. Café Latin is a popular venue for watching sporting events on television and can become very busy at these times.
✉ 19–21 Dong Du Street, District 1
☎ 08-38226363 🕐 Daily 9am–midnight
✋ L 160,000d, D 270,000d, Wine 335,000d

CAMARGUE

www.vascosgroup.com
Camargue, one of Saigon's longest-running restaurants, has moved to a new location without changing its identity. There is still an open-air dining room upstairs and Camargue continues to serve consistently excellent food from an international menu with a strong French influence. Professional waitstaff provide diners with appetizers that verge on the unusual—green lentil cappuccino served with crunchy duck and pistachio dumplings, or gently sautéed scallops with a rum butter sauce. The perfectly grilled and sliced duck breast, *pommes sarladaises* and béarnaise sauce perfumed with raspberry vinegar, is recommended. Follow with the excellent white chocolate parfait with fresh raspberries and an almond pastry.
✉ A Hai Bo Trung Street, District 3
☎ 08-35204888 🕐 Daily 9–4, 6–11
✋ L 450,000d, D 600,000d, Wine 500,000d

CAY BO DE

This is Saigon's most popular vegetarian eatery. In the heart of backpacker land, it serves very good food at amazing prices. The Mexican pancake, vegetable curry, rice in coconut and braised mushrooms are classics. There's also a wide choice of soups and stir-fried dishes. It is a struggle to spend more than 30,000d per head.

✉ 175/6 Pham Ngu Lao Street, District 1
☎ 08-38371910 🕐 Daily 7am–11pm
✋ L 45,000d, D 65,000d

CEPAGE

There is fine dining upstairs but the same menu of modern European cuisine is attracting the majority of customers to the more informal and über-cool lounge area at ground level. Imaginative and interesting food, including a raw tuna starter, and popular steaks and seafood such as sea bass cooked wih leeks in Japanese wood paper. There are also vegetarian starters and main courses.
✉ 22 Le Thanh Ton Street, District 1
☎ 08-38238733 🕐 Daily 7.30am–midnight (Sun ground floor only)
✋ L 300,000d, D 600,000d, Wine 410,000d

COM NIEU SAIGON

The theatrics that accompany the serving of the specialty baked rice have earned this informal restaurant something of a reputation. One waiter smashes the earthenware pot before tossing the contents across the room to his nimble-fingered colleague standing by the table. The staff are well trained in this startling skill, and will safely deliver to your table a good selection of soups and salads. Steamed clams with onion and ginger and the kidney are recommended. Deep-fried cow's womb and duck's feet are more challenging additions to a vast menu.
✉ 6C Tu Xuong Street, District 3
☎ 08-39326388 🕐 Daily 9am–10pm
✋ L 90,000d, D 135,000d

CUC GACH QUAN

www.cucgachquan.com.vn
Tucked away down an alleyway (see website's map), this homey restaurant in a restored old French house is well worth seeking out for its delightful rustic-style decor and traditional Vietnamese food of a consistently high standard. The tofu dishes are especially recommended. Cuc Gach Quan is becoming well known and reservations need to be made to be sure of a table,

particularly at weekends. There is a French wine list.

✉ 10 Dang Tat Street, District 1
☎ 08-3848014 🕐 Daily 7am–10.30pm
🖐 L 50,000d (set menu), D 250,000, Wine 500,000d

LA FOURCHETTE

French posters and prints decorate this excellent and authentic little French bistro, where there's a warm welcome and a range of well-prepared dishes in generous portions at fair prices. The glorious selection of meals includes pâté de fois gras imported from France; clams with butter, garlic and parsley; beef tenderloin from Australia; local beef with a myriad sauce options (the local steak is as tender as any import); and fried squid with cognac.

✉ 9 Ngo Duc Ke Street, District 1
☎ 08-38298143 🕐 Daily 11.30–2.30, 6.30–10 🖐 L 210,000d, D 380,000d, Wine 365,000d

HOA TUC

This restaurant offers contemporary Vietnamese cuisine at reasonable prices and in a pleasant setting where the elegant decor adds a touch of style. Eat indoors with air conditioning or outside in the fresh air in a tea garden. To find Hoa Tuc, go through the yellow arch and it is just past the Refinery, on your left.

✉ 74 Hai Ban Trung Street, District 1
☎ 08-38251676 🕐 Daily 11–10
🖐 L 200,000d, D 300,000d, Wine 400,000d

HOA VIEN

www.hoavien.vn

Saigon's first microbrewery has set up shop in an amazing vast Czech-style *bierkeller*. The food here has improved dramatically in recent years and is very helpful for soaking up the alcohol. Sitting among the huge, glistening copper tanks, you can tuck into smoked chicken drumsticks, beer garden sausages, grilled salmon with bacon, Czech-style fried cheese, steamed goat's ribs with beer, Australian steak with pepper or fried squid with tempura.

✉ 28 bis Mac Dinh Chi Street, District 1
☎ 08-38290585 🕐 Daily 9am–11pm
🖐 L 110,000d, D 220,000d, Wine 200,000d

HOI AN

Hoi An is located in a beautiful replica of a traditional Hoi An house—a theme repeated in the interior decoration and in the staff uniforms. This is a sister (and almost neighboring) restaurant of Mandarin (▷ 209) and meets the same exacting standards. The menu has a wide and varied selection of dishes, such as tiny rice custards with crumbled shrimp, delicious sautéed lobster in tamarind sauce, grilled beef with lemon grass and roasted duck with pepper sauce.

✉ 11 Le Thanh Ton Street, District 1
☎ 08-38237694 🕐 Daily 5.30pm–11pm
🖐 Set meals from 637,000d, Wine 800,000d

INDOCHINE

An unabashedly long menu covering just about all Vietnamese specialties is found at this themed restaurant, with staff dressed in costume and menus in the shape of conical hats. Enjoy house specials such as baby clams in white wine or grilled duck breast with orange or pepper sauce. Choose from a selection of salads such as chicken and banana-flower salad and grapefruit salad with shrimp and pork, which can be followed by steamed and fried crustacea and fish; the squid is especially succulent. Staff are attentive and service is efficient.

✉ 32 Pham Ngoc Thach Street, District 3
☎ 08-38239256 🕐 Daily 11.30–2, 5.30–10
🖐 L 160,000d, D 245,000d, Wine 330,000d

LE JARDIN

European visitors flock to this excellent little French restaurant, which is part of the French Cultural Institute, with a small, shaded garden and fairly priced food. Particularly good options include the beef skewers with cumin seeds and the apple crumble and ice cream. On your second visit opt for the red mullet with aniseed sauce or moussaka followed by profiteroles.

✉ 31 Thai Van Lung Street, District 1
☎ 08-38258465 🕐 Mon–Sat 11–2, 5–9.30 🖐 L 105,000d, D 180,000d, Wine 330,000d

JAVA

Rich smoothies such as the Fountain of Youth (a strawberry and cherry concoction), Watermelon Wavelength and Big Bold Banana are mixed for around 45,000d each in the inviting environment of this glass-fronted café. Rattan furniture, sofas and low-hung camouflage-print lamps make this a popular spot for expatriates. Java is a useful stop for breakfast or brunch, serving snacks such as bagels with cream cheese and smoked salmon, and muffins.

✉ 38–42 Dong Du Street, District 1
☎ 08-38230187 🕐 Daily 7.30am–11.30pm
🖐 L 60,000d, D 245,000d, Wine 100,000d

KABIN

Reserve a window table at Kabin for the best views while enjoying authentic Chinese cuisine. Appetizers include spicy beef and salmon and vegetable salad; the menu of main courses divides itself into barbecued and marinated dishes (duck, prawn), an expensive selection of bird's nest soup, abalone seafood and meat-based clay-pot dishes. The hot and sour seafood soup is a delight.

✉ Renaissance Riverside Hotel, 8–15 Ton Duc Thang Street, District 1 ☎ 08-38220033
🕐 Daily 11–2, 6–10.30 🖐 L 350,000d, D 550,000d, Wine 500,000d

LEMONGRASS

www.bongsencorporation.com

The restaurant in Nguyen Thiep Street has been a firm favorite with visitors for many years. Queue for a sparkling new branch high up in the Palace Hotel. The waitresses wear a form of traditional wedding dress and every night from 7–9.30pm there is live traditional music. Both restaurants share the same menu: Try the lemongrass seafood soup, one of the spring roll choices and the baked prawns in garlic. Start or end your meal with a drink at the open-air bar on the floor above the restaurant.

✉ 4 Nguyen Thiep Street, District 1 ☎ 08-38220496; ✉ 14th Floor Palace Hotel Saigon ☎ 08-38291520 ⏰ Daily 11–10 ✋ L 120,000d, D 310,000d, Wine 350,000d

MANDARIN

One of the finest Vietnamese restaurants in Saigon serves up a mix of exquisite flavors from across the country in an elegant setting enhanced by richly colored silk tablecloths. The delicious deep-fried crab spring rolls are served on a bed of artfully carved carrot flowers. To follow, the mullet fish in a clay pot is a good option. The expensive set menus are recommended for special occasions.

✉ 11A Ngo Van Nam Street, District 1 ☎ 08-38229783 ⏰ Daily 5.30pm–10pm ✋ L 410,000d, D 600,000d, Wine 750,000d

MUMTAZ INDIAN RESTAURANT

The decor is nothing to write home about, but this is a good-value Indian restaurant with a large menu that will suit meat-eaters and vegetarians alike. Individual dishes, especially for nonvegetarians, are not large but, for good for two or more people sharing. Diners on their own should consider the set-menu thalis. A takeout service, with delivery to your hotel, is available for no extra charge.

✉ 226 Bui Vien, Pham Ngu Lao Ward, District 1 ☎ 08-38371767 ⏰ Daily 10–10 ✋ L 160,000d, D 250,000d. Set meals 95,000d (vegetarian), 115,000d (nonvegetarian)

NAM PHAN

Mr. Khai of Khaisilk fame (▷ 26) certainly knows how to bring out the best in old buildings. Moved from its former location, Nam Phan is now housed in a four-story restored villa. The style of the place is sumptuous but the decor is elegant. Described by the owners as "high-end," the individual dishes are delicious, though the menu is oddly put together and makes it

rather difficult to construct a full meal. The mix includes young pork rib with fermented galangal, stuffed squid with ground meat and tomato soup, trademark triangle spring rolls and delicious banana cake with coconut cream.

✉ 34–34A Vo Van Tan, District 3 ☎ 08-39333636 ⏰ Daily 11–3, 5–11 ✋ L 320,000d, D 460,000d, Wine 550,000d

NINETEEN

This lavish incarnation of what was formerly the acclaimed Port Orient restaurant is furnished with ostrich-feather seating and imported Cararra marble. It serves what is regarded by many locals as the best buffet in town. There's sushi, Chinese dim sum, cheeses and an array of puddings. Wine, which is included in the price, flows freely.

✉ Caravelle Hotel, 19 Lam Son Square, District 1 ☎ 08-38234999 ⏰ Daily 6am–10pm ✋ L 592,000d, D 1,170,000d

OPERA

Overlooking the busy Lam Son Square, this restaurant also has the option of alfresco dining. The open-style kitchen and wood-burning pizza oven inspire confidence in the quality of the food while the esthetically pleasing decor, in the form of earth-tone bricks, relaxes the mind. Besides pizza and pasta, specialties include pan-fried sea bass, roasted prawns, deep-fried calamari and the aromatic *bosso buco* from Milan. The Sunday brunch (1,260,000d with free-flowing champagne and 840,000d with Prosecco) is popular with the city's expat community and foodies with an appetite for oysters, roast beef and pork.

✉ Park Hyatt, 2 Lam Son Square, District 1 ☎ 08-38241234 ⏰ Daily 6am–10.30am, noon–2.30pm (3.30pm at weekends), 6pm–11pm ✋ L 390,000d, D 600,000d, Wine 800,000d

PHO HOA PASTEUR

Pho Hoa Pasteur is probably the best known of all *pho* restaurants, and is packed with customers and dizzying aromas. The *pho* is good

but costs more than average; it comes in 10 options and is served inside the small restaurant, where tables are tightly arranged. Chinese bread and wedding cake (*banh xu xe*) provide the only alternatives in this specialist restaurant.

☎ 08-38256802 ⏰ Daily 9am–10pm ✋ L 50,000d, D 65,000d

POMODORO

www.pomodoro-vietnam.com

A congenial and unpretentious Italian eatery, this is popular with expatriates as well as visitors. There is a choice of 10 starters (including Parma ham) and just as many salads. Vegetarians can enjoy a plate of *melanzane alla parmigiana* (eggplant/aubergine with a cheese and tomato sauce) or one of the pizzas while, meat eaters have dishes such as *bistecca di manzo* (beefsteak with Italian herbs and homemade noodles). An unashamedly partisan wine list makes no concessions to non-Italian choices.

✉ 77 Hai Ba Trung Street, District 1 ☎ 08-38238998 ⏰ Daily 10am–10.30pm ✋ L 280,000d, D 400,000d, Wine 400,000d

RESTAURANT 13

Locals, expatriates and travelers rate this very informal restaurant a hit. It serves fresh, well-cooked Vietnamese dishes such as chicken

Below *A chef serves a prawn salad*

in lemongrass (no skin, no bone)—a great favorite—and beef *(bo luc lac)* that melts in the mouth. If you have a strong stomach, other dishes from the vast menu, which does not list prices, are dough-wrapped crayfish, steamed fallopian tube with onion and sautéed heart and liver with garlic. Vegetarians, soup-lovers and squid-eaters have their own options too.

✉ 13 Ngo Duc Ke Street, District 1
☎ 08-38239314 ◷ Daily 9am–10pm
✋ L 70,000d, D 140,000d, Wine 400,000d

SANTA LUCIA
This popular downtown Italian restaurant is in a convenient spot on the main boulevard. Dishes include pancakes filled with ricotta and spinach and baked in béchamel sauce, and *carpaccio de vitello*—thin slices of raw veal served with olive oil, garlic and Parmesan cheese. Most of the pasta-based meals are served in large portions, but the tasty ravioli dishes are smaller. Piped opera music completes the effect.

✉ 14 Nguyen Hue Boulevard, District 1
☎ 08-38226562 ◷ Daily 9.30am–11pm
✋ L 130,000d, D 250,000d, Wine 470,000d

SKEWERS
www.skewers-restaurant.com
The decor is rustic but elegant and the Mediterranean-style food is of a consistently high standard, making Skewers one of the most reliable places for a good meal in Ho Chi Minh City. The menu has many of the dishes you would expect to find in a southern European restaurant—Greek salad, falafel, beef carpaccio, couscous, goat's cheese tart, osso bucco, moussaka—plus a very appealing wine list.

✉ 9A Thai Van Lung Street, District 1
☎ 08-38224798 ◷ Mon–Fri 11.30–2,
6–11, Sat–Sun 6–11. ✋ L 280,000d,
D 500,000d, Wine 500,000d

SQUARE 1
Vietnamese-inspired latticework and brick patterns provide a colorful and relaxed setting for this chic restaurant. There are two

kitchens, Western and Vietnamese, but diners can still mix and match and expect their orders to arrive at the same time. Highlights include Nha Trang oysters, *wagyu*, New Zealand and Australian beef, wok-based Vietnamese specialties and a rare lotus stem salad. Set lunches range from tasty vegetarian (192,000d) to a steak-based one (480,000d).

✉ Park Hyatt, 2 Lam Son Square,
District 1 ☎ 08-38241234 ◷ Daily 11–11
✋ L 360,000d, D 950,000d, Wine
1,100,000d

TAM NAM
Appealing modern decor sets off this centrally located restaurant, as does the menu of carefully prepared Vietnamese favorites. For some personal space it is worth trying to reserve the table by the window on the upper floor; those on the ground floor, lining one side, are open to human traffic coming and going.

✉ 44 Nguyen Hue Street, District 1
☎ 08-38248514 ◷ Daily 8am–11pm
✋ L 250,000d, D 350,000d, Wine 400,000d

TEMPLE CLUB
You can catch an intriguing and evocative glimpse of colonial living in this beautifully furnished club and restaurant, open to nonmembers. Laid out in French colonial style, it exudes understated chic, with carved doorways, exposed brickwork, purple silk lanterns in the bar area and stunning wooden screens. The food is superb: Examples are Huê-style spring rolls, deep-fried soft-shell crab, grilled tiger shrimp and simmered crab in coconut juice. Bizarrely, you can also order fish and chips. The chocolate whiskey mousse is sinful. It's advisable to reserve a table in advance at this popular place.

✉ 29–31 Ton That Thiep Street, District 1
☎ 08-38299244 ◷ Daily 11am–midnight
(L 11–2, D 5.30–10.30) ✋ L 140,000d,
D 200,000d, Wine 320,000d

TIB
Tib is a little pocket of Huê in Saigon, furnished in the dark

wood so favored by that city. The extensive menu has a good selection of Huê specialties, including such standout dishes as crumbled shrimp wrapped with fresh rice paper and stir-fried vermicelli with crab. The atmosphere is convivial and the restaurant, which is down an alley off the main road, is popular with Vietnamese families. The incredible wine stock is a bonus.

✉ 187 Hai Ba Trung Street, District 3
☎ 08-38297242 ◷ Daily 11–10
✋ L 130,000d, D 300,000d, Wine 390,000d

WILD HORSE SALOON
Unmissable with its monumental beer-barrel facade, this Tex-Mex restaurant is a popular spot for a Sunday roast dinner. You can dine at solid wood tables on pasta, superb steaks, burgers, Mexican meatballs, crab cakes or Texas-style rack of lamb. The Sunday roast of pork, chicken, beef or lamb is served with boiled vegetables, roasted potatoes, gravy, stuffing, crackling and apple sauce. The separate bar area, entered through a massive, cut-out beer barrel, shows sports on TV. There is also live music.

✉ 8A1/2D1 Thai Van Lung Street, District 1
☎ 08-38277786 ◷ Daily 10.15–2, 4.30–12
✋ L 130,000d, D 200,000d, Wine 340,000d

XU
www.xusaigon.com
Xu serves enjoyable modern Vietnamese cuisine, whether for a spot of lunch at the downstairs bar or, for a more formal meal and a cocktail lounge, upstairs under quiet lighting. What could be called signature dishes include heart of palm confit and tamarind beef; nonmeat eaters will enjoy the vegetarian choices. Seafood is a special attraction and the first Friday of each month is devoted to oysters flown in from Australia, Europe and North America. There is live music on Thursday nights.

✉ Level 1, 71–5 Hai Ba Trun Street, District
1 ☎ 08-38248468 ◷ Daily 7am–11pm
✋ L 190,000d, D 400,000d, Wine 400,000d

STAYING

PRICES AND SYMBOLS

The prices are for a double room for one night including breakfast, unless otherwise stated. All the hotels listed accept credit cards unless otherwise stated. Note that rates can vary widely throughout the year.

For a key to the symbols, ▷ 2.

ARC EN CIEL

This is the best hotel in Cholon (▷ 192–194), and there is a bonus in that it is within walking distance of all the major Chinatown pagodas. Run by Saigontourist, it has four restaurants and a rooftop bar with fine views. Standard rooms have TVs, minibars and firm mattresses, but not much of a view. The bathrooms are small; some rooms have bathtubs. Superior rooms, with bigger bathrooms, cost an extra US$5. Reception has the only safe-deposit box.

✉ 52–56 Tan Da Street, District 5
☎ 08-38554435 💵 From US$40, including taxes ⓘ 86 🅢

BONG SEN

www.hotelbongsen.com
The standard rooms at this well-run hotel in the shopping district are small. They have TVs, minibars, phones and showers. Superior rooms (only slightly more expensive) are larger and have bathtubs in the bathrooms. The most expensive rooms have city views. A laundry, airport transfers, massages and a steam room are available.

✉ 117–123 Dong Khoi Street, District 1
☎ 08-38291516 💵 US$50–$130, excluding taxes ⓘ 127 🅨 🅢

BONG SEN HOTEL ANNEX

www.bongsenhotel2.com
Rooms in this well-managed, central hotel are very small and decorated with attractive photographs. Bathrooms are adequately sized, and the complimentary drinking water is a bonus for a hotel in this class. Rooms with city views cost an extra US$5. All rooms have a TV, minibar and phone, and there's a laundry service, car rental and airport transfer. The restaurant, the Co Noi, is on the eighth floor.

✉ 61–63 Hai Ba Trung Street, District 1
☎ 08-38235818 💵 US$38–$43, excluding taxes ⓘ 57 🅢

CARAVELLE

www.caravellehotel.com
One of the city's top hotels sits in the heart of downtown. It incorporates the old Air France

Above *The Rex Hotel illuminated at night*

Caravelle hotel, onto which extra floors have been added (there are 24 floors in total). All rooms have tea- and coffee-making equipment, a phone, minibar and cable TV. The hotel's restaurant, Nineteen, serves an excellent buffet lunch and dinner (▷ 209), and Saigon Saigon (▷ 204), the rooftop bar, draws the crowds until the early hours. Boutiques, a pool, a health center and treatments give this luxurious hotel added appeal. One room is specially equipped for guests with disabilities.

✉ 19 Lam Son Square, District 1
☎ 08-38234999 💵 US$156–$250, excluding breakfast and taxes ⓘ 335 (140 nonsmoking) 🅰 🅨 🅢

CONTINENTAL

www.continentalvietnam.com
Built in 1880 and renovated in 1989, the Continental is an integral part of the city's history, facing the Opera House in central Saigon. The whole place has an air of faded colonial splendor. Its large but dated rooms are in need of an upgrade, but the hotel's character shines through. Hotel facilities include a business center, fitness room and

pool, car rental, airport transfer and a baby-sitting service. All rooms have a phone, cable TV, minibar and private bathroom.

✉ 132–134 Dong Khoi Street, District 1
☎ 08-38299201 💲 US$80–$130, excluding taxes 🛈 83 🏊 🍴 🔄

DUXTON

www.saigon.duxtonhotels.com

This stylish boutique hotel in the middle of Saigon is one of the nicest places to stay in the city. Beds are beautifully made with cushions and silk bedspreads, and top-of-the-range rooms come with large desks, complimentary fruit and attractive black marble bathrooms hung with flower prints. All rooms have tea- and coffee-making equipment, cable TV, ironing board and iron, a safe-deposit box and minibar, and in the health center—with its waterfall shower—there's a sauna, Jacuzzi, steam room and spa (with different opening hours for men and women). There's also The Grill, an all-day dining restaurant and The Bar, which also does an afternoon tea service (2–6pm). There is a casino as well.

✉ 63 Nguyen Hue Boulevard, District 1
☎ 08-38222999 💲 US$100–$155, excluding taxes 🛈 198 rooms (28 nonsmoking) 🏊 🍴 🔄

EQUATORIAL

www.equatorial.com

A free shuttle takes you to this rather out-of-the-way hotel between Cholon and downtown Saigon. Rooms are large and airy, with high ceilings, terraces and views of the hotel garden, and all have a phone, cable TV, tea- and coffee-making equipment, minibar and voice mail. The Equatorial has the biggest ballroom in the city; exhibits and conferences are regularly held here. The swimming pool has a sunken bar, and there's a gym and Japanese, Chinese and Western restaurants.

✉ 242 Tran Binh Trong Street, District 5
☎ 08-38397777 💲 US$70–$200, excluding breakfast and taxes 🛈 333 (nonsmoking on request) 🏊 🍴 🔄

GRAND

www.grandhotel.vn

This 1930s building in the heart of the shopping district has been extensively renovated; happily, the stained glass and marble staircase have largely survived the process. The attractive pool (try to get a poolside room) is surrounded by a plant-filled patio. Rooms all have cable TV, in-house movies, a minibar, phone and safe-deposit box. The hotel can arrange car rental and a laundry service. There is a 12th-floor restaurant, the Belle Vue, with panoramic views, a coffee shop and patisserie, a beauty salon, a sauna, a steam bath, Jacuzzi and massage. Nonresidents can use the swimming pool for US$3.

✉ 8 Dong Khoi Street, District 1
☎ 08-38230163 💲 US$115–$170, including taxes 🛈 128 (1 floor nonsmoking) 🔄 🏊

HONG HOA

www.honghoavn.com

There are three types of room in this airy, well-run family hotel in the heart of the backpackers' district. The least expensive is small and has no refrigerator or TV; the mid-priced rooms have a bathtub; and the most expensive are the largest, with a balcony and satellite TV, but a shower only. Downstairs is a supermarket and banks of computers with email connection.

✉ 185/28 Pham Ngu Lao Street, District 1
☎ 08-38361915 💲 US$17–$25, excluding breakfast, including taxes 🛈 9 🔄

LEGEND

www.legendsaigon.com

The Legend overlooks the river and has Saigon's most ostentatious foyer, with large bronze horse statues dominating the entrance and two golden phoenixes guarding the lobby bar. Business clients favor this hotel. The Legend's three restaurants serve a mix of Asian food. Other facilities include a massage and fitness center, a staffed children's play area and a jazz bar with live music from Tuesday to Sunday. The Sunday

lunch buffet in the Atrium Café is very good. Rooms have tea- and coffee-making equipment, cable TV with in-house movies, a minibar, phone and voice mail, and there are baby-sitting and laundry services. Two rooms are equipped for guests with disabilities.

✉ 2A–4A Ton Duc Thang Street, District 1
☎ 08-38233333 💲 US$130–$160, excluding breakfast and taxes 🛈 283 (42 nonsmoking) 🍴 🏊 🔄

LINH

This is a well-priced, small and very friendly family-run hotel in the middle of the Pham Ngu Lao budget area. All rooms have two beds and a small private bathroom with a shower. There is free Internet access for guests and an amazing range of amenities, given the price, including cable TV, air conditioning, hot water, phone and refrigerator.

✉ 40/10 Bui Vien Street, District 1
☎ 08-38369641 💲 US$36–$60, excluding breakfast, including taxes 🛈 6 🔄

MAJESTIC

www.majesticsaigon.com

Built in 1925, this riverside hotel has been tastefully restored. The top-of-the-range rooms have wooden floors and queen-size beds, plus fantastic river views from their balconies. All have minibars, phones, safe-deposit boxes and cable TV. From the eighth-floor M Bar (4pm–1am) there are magnificent views of the river and the docks beyond. There is a restaurant on the seventh floor, serving European cuisine, and a café and lounge area at ground level. Breakfast is served on the fifth floor and with the option of open-air tables overlooking the river.

✉ 1 Dong Khoi Street, District 1 ☎ 08-38295517 💲 US$170–$250, excluding taxes 🛈 175 (and a smoke-free wing) 🏊 🍴 🔄

MÖVENPICK

www.moevenenpick-hotels.com

This well-run hotel has a Japanese restaurant and a Chinese one, a café and an open-air bar on the seventh floor. Mövenpick is close to the airport but too far to walk from the city center so taxis are necessary. The hotel is sited on the former headquarters of the CIA during the Vietnam War.

✉ 252 Nguyen Van Troi Street, Phu Nhuan District ☎ 08-384449222 🖐 US$100–$160, including taxes 🛈 267 ⛱ 📶

NEW WORLD

www.newworldsaigon.com

Business travelers make up a large position of the guests at this hotel on the edge of District 1 and close to Ben Thanh Market. Staff are efficient, friendly and speak English. The striking lobby is surrounded by glass, and has dusted gold and beige columns and a domed atrium; this lavish style is matched in the bedrooms, which have private marble bathrooms and writing desks, as well as standard amenities such as safe-deposit boxes, cable TV with in-house movies, phones and minibars. Eating options include a restaurant serving a choice of Chinese and Western food, a patisserie and a bakery, and there's a dry-cleaning service, an ATM, a nightclub, a gym, floodlit tennis courts, a jogging track and a health center. The Executive Floor is excellent value with breakfast, afternoon tea and refreshments available all day.

✉ 76 Le Lai Street, District 1 ☎ 08-38228888 🖐 US$130–$200, excluding breakfast and taxes 🛈 533 (4 floors nonsmoking) ⛱ 🍸 📶

RENAISSANCE RIVERSIDE

www.marriott.com/hotels

This popular, well-run riverfront hotel has Vietnam's highest atrium. Rooms are comfortable and have cable TV, voicemail, a minibar and a safe-deposit box. Those with a river view cost extra. The rooftop pool, which is open to nonresidents for US$10, has fabulous views, and there are sauna, massage and health club rooms. The restaurant serves Western and Eastern food, and you can take afternoon tea (daily 3.30–6pm) at the lobby café, served

on tiered chrome cake stands, or wine and cheese between 5pm and midnight. Hotel services include baby-sitting and laundry. Two rooms are equipped for guests with disabilities.

✉ 8–15 Ton Duc Thang Street, District 1 ☎ 08-38220033 🖐 US$160–$200, including taxes 🛈 336 (208 nonsmoking) ⛱ 🍸 📶

REX

www.rexhotelvietnam.com

The historically important Rex Hotel (▷ 199) in the heart of Ho Chi Minh City has unusual interior design. The large lobby is decorated entirely in wood, furnished with numerous wicker chairs, and dominated by the ceiling, a vast replica of a Dong Son drum. Superior rooms have small bathtubs and face an internal courtyard; deluxe rooms are double the size, but those on the main road are noisy. Interior deluxe rooms are similar, but some have private balconies. All have phones, cable TV and minibars, and the hotel can provide airport transfer and a laundry service. The Mimosa Club has an open-air pool, a rooftop tennis court, a fitness center with massage, sauna and steam rooms, and a beauty salon. Four rooms are equipped for guests with disabilities. In addition to its restaurants and cafés, guests can also visit the Bingo Club, a gaming center with slot machines, gaming tables and video games: Remember to bring your passport, as the Bingo Club is open only to foreign visitors.

✉ 141 Nguyen Hue Boulevard, District 1 ☎ 08-38292185 🖐 US$150–$160, excluding taxes 🛈 227 ⛱ 🍸 📶

SHERATON SAIGON HOTEL & TOWERS

www.sheratongrandtower.com

This smart hotel is sandwiched into a downtown street and has proved popular since it opened in late 2003. The Saigon Café serves very good lunches and dinners, and Level 23 is a must for an evening drink, not least for the wonderful views across Saigon. There's also a restaurant,

nightclub and bars, and there is live entertainment in The Lounge. The hotel also has shops, a pool, a spa, and squash and tennis courts. Baby-sitting and laundry services are available. Modern, stylish rooms are equipped with coffee- and tea-makers, minibars and cable TV, and all have private bathrooms with both tubs and showers. Some rooms are equipped for guests with disabilities.

✉ 88 Dong Khoi Street, District 1 ☎ 08-38272828 🖐 From US$150, excluding breakfast and taxes 🛈 483 (nonsmoking on request) ⛱ 🍸 📶

SPRING

www.springhotelvietnam.com

In a central position near several excellent restaurants, the Spring hotel is comfortable and well run by friendly and helpful staff. Top-of-the-range rooms have king-size beds; standard rooms are only slightly smaller, but the bathrooms are much smaller and space is tight. Other in-room amenities include TVs and in-house movies, minibars, refrigerators, safe-deposit boxes and phones. Hotel guests have free Internet use and local phone calls. There's a restaurant and bar, a laundry service and car rental, and tours can be arranged here.

✉ 44–46 Le Thanh Ton Street, District 1 ☎ 08-38297362 🖐 US$40–$77, excluding taxes 🛈 45 📶

SOFITEL PLAZA SAIGON

www.sofitel.com

This smart, fashionable and comfortable hotel surpasses many other large hotels in the city because of its superb design. The more expensive rooms have balconies, and all have minibars, phones and cable TV. The Provençal restaurant often hosts cooking classes, and there's a free shuttle to downtown Saigon. Laundry and baby-sitting services, massage, a sauna and steam room are available.

✉ 17 Le Duan Street, District 1 ☎ 08-38241555 🖐 US$140–$170, excluding breakfast and taxes 🛈 322 (35 nonsmoking) ⛱ 🍸 📶

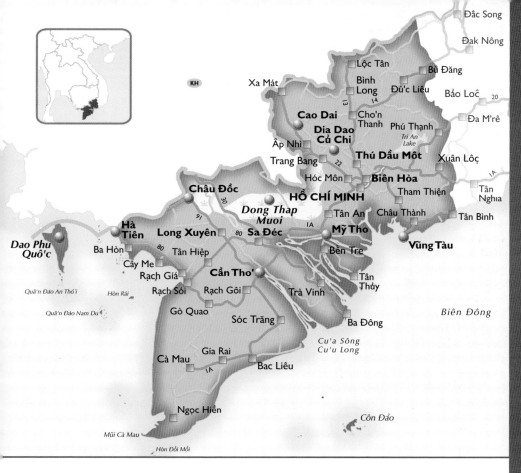

Đắc Song
Đak Nông
Lộc Tân
Bình Long
Bù Đăng
Đức Liễu
Bảo Loc   20
Đa M'rê
Xa Mát
KH
Cao Dai
Dia Dao
Củ Chi
Chợ'n Thanh
Phú Thạnh
Trí An Lake
Ấp Nhì
Thú Dầu Một
Xuân Lộc
Trang Bang
Hóc Môn
Biên Hòa
Tham Thiện
Tân Nghĩa
Châu Đốc
HỒ CHÍ MINH
Dong Thap Muoi
Tân An
Châu Thành
Tân Bình
Hà Tiên
Long Xuyên
Sa Đéc
Mỹ Tho
Ba Hòn
Tân Hiệp
Bến Tre
Vũng Tàu
Dao Phu Quô'c
Cây Me
Cần Thơ'
Tân Thủy
Quâ'n Đảo An Thô'i
Hòn Rái
Rạch Giá
Rạch Sỏi
Rạch Gôi
Trà Vinh
Biên Đông
Quâ'n Đảo Nam Du
Gò Quao
Sóc Trăng
Ba Đông
Cu'a Sông
Cu'u Long
Cà Mau
Gía Rai
Bac Liêu
Ngọc Hiền
Côn Đảo
Mũi Cà Mau
Hòn Đồi Mồi

THE SOUTH

Densely populated, densely green and densely fertile, the south of Vietnam and especially the vast Mekong Delta is the country's chief food source, producing rice, fruit, vegetables, sugarcane, and fish from its fish farms. The area has had its bad times—occupied by the French and by the Cambodians and showered repeatedly with defoliants through the war with Americ—but the place is now blossoming in ways that few people might have imagined. A visit to the area is a visit to the river delta, with river trips, farm visits, riverside towns and villages, floating markets, wildlife spotting and sunbathing on the delta's beaches.

At its best between November and April, the dry season, when it is hot, sultry and verdant, the region outside of these months can also be gray, muddy and occasionally dangerous as the river, laden with rainwater and silt, floods fields and carries off bridges and livestock.

Highlights of a visit to the region include Con Dao National Park, set among an archipelago of tiny islands with coral reefs, rare birdlife and, in season, female green turtles. For nature lovers, there is also the undeveloped and pristine Phu Quoc Island, while the Cu Chi Tunnels, inhabited for months on end by the Viet Cong in their struggle to unify their country, constitute one of the most popular excursions from Ho Chi Minh City.

Transportation around the area is slow and leisurely and inevitably water-borne, but minibuses are cheap and frequent and the best fun of all is to rent a car or bicycle and wander the tiny lanes of the area, discovering quiet villages, watching unhurried villagers tend their fields of rice and vegetable and absorbing the slow and peaceful pace of life.

BA CHUC

On the road skirting the Cambodian border between Chau Doc and Ha Tien is an ossuary housing the bones of 1,000 Vietnamese, killed in 1978 by Cambodia's Khmer Rouge. Skulls are stacked up in a glass-sided memorial, and each section is categorized by gender and by age—from young children to grandparents.

✚ 286 C11 ✉ 24 miles (38km) south of Chau Doc

CAN THO AND FLOATING MARKETS

▷ 218–219.

CAO DAI GREAT TEMPLE

▷ 220–221.

CHAU DOC AND SAM MOUNTAIN

▷ 222–223.

CON DAO

Con Dao is a tiny archipelago of 14 islands. The biggest and only permanently settled island is Con Son, with a population of about 6,000. A trading post was set up here between 1702 and 1705 by the East Indies Trading Company; in 1773 it became home to Emperor Gia Long and mandarin families, fleeing after their defeat by the Tay Son. In 1832 Con Dao was ceded to the French by Emperor Tu Duc. The jails here were built in 1863 by Admiral Bonard to hold political prisoners—up to 12,000 of them—and the government of South Vietnam later put them to the same use. A museum on Con Son (Bao Tang Tong Ho Tinh, daily 8–4) occupies the former prison governor's house and has items relating to the island's past. Three prisons are open, including one with life-size models and recreations of the horrific conditions. The infamous "tiger cages," where prisoners were chained and tortured, still stand.

Con Dao National Park offers such activities as snorkeling, forest walks, swimming and birding, and it's also the most important sea turtle nesting site in Vietnam; several hundred female green turtles *(Chelonia mydas)* come ashore every year to lay their eggs.

In the forests more than 1,000 plant species have been identified, several unique to Con Dao, and there's valuable timber and medicinal plants. This is the only place where you can see the rare pied imperial pigeon *(Ducula bicolor)*, and one of few places that are home to the red-billed tropicbird *(Phaethon aethereus)*. The extremely rare brown booby *(Sula leucogaster)* inhabits the most remote island, Hon Trung (Egg Island), a one-hour boat ride away, and there are thousands of seabirds.

✚ 286 D13 ☎ 064-3830437 👆 Prison: 2,000d. Tour: 45,000d 🚢 Passenger ships from Vung Tau weekly (overnight); tickets from shipping office, 2 Le Loi Street, Vung Tau ☎ 064-3838684 ✈ Vietnam Airlines and Air Mekong flights from Saigon daily

for the one-hour journey, around US$70 one way

CU CHI TUNNELS

▷ 224.

DAO PHU QUOC

▷ 225.

DONG THAP MUOI

▷ 226.

HA TIEN

▷ 227.

HON CHONG

Hon Chong is a popular beach with cafés behind the casuarina trees. Hang Pagoda (Chua Hang), inside a cave, houses a Buddha of 100 hands among the many Buddha images. From the Ham Trem Resort it is a 15-minute walk to the Hang Pagoda; a path through the temple leads to Bai Duong beach.

✚ 286 C12 ✉ 19 miles (30km) east of Ha Tien 🚌 From Ha Tien to Rach Gia, then *xe ôm*, or get off bus at Ba Hon and take *xe ôm* from there 💻

INFORMATION

www.canthotourist.com.vn

✚ 286 D12 🛈 Can Tho Tourist, 20
Hai Ba Trung Street ☎ 0710-3821852
🕓 Daily 7am–8pm 🚌 Nguyen
Trai Street; connections with Saigon
✖ Airport 6 miles (10km) from town.
Flights from Saigon and Hanoi 🍴 Local
seafood specialties; several along
waterfront and Restaurant Alley (Nam Ky
Khoi Nghia Street) 💻 Internet cafés on
Vo Van Tan Street 🖱 Tours by Victoria
Can Tho and Can Tho Tourist. Private tours
from Saigon

INTRODUCTION

From this pleasant and breezy Mekong town you can visit the famous river markets, where fruit and vegetables swing from locals' staves as they ply the waters selling their wares.

Can Tho is a large and rapidly growing commercial city in the heart of the Mekong Delta, with strong vestiges of French influence apparent in broad, tree-lined boulevards and elegant buildings. It is also the most welcoming and agreeable of the delta towns and is easily explored on foot. Hai Ba Trung Street, alongside the river, is the heart of town, where, at dusk, families stroll in the park in their best clothes. This pleasant, leafy promenade is dominated by a giant, silver-colored statue of Ho Chi Minh. Phan Dinh Phung Street is the main commercial route, a couple of blocks west, and to its west again is Hoa Binh Boulevard, the main thoroughfare, which becomes 30 Than 4 Boulevard and runs out toward the bus station.

A small settlement was established at Can Tho at the end of the 18th century, although the town did not prosper until the French took control of the delta a century later and rice production for export began to take off. During the Vietnam War the city was used as an important US base, and thousands of GIs made their temporary home here. Can Tho's university was founded in 1966, and a rice research institute was established here, based at O Mon, 15 miles (24km) away on Highway 91. Like the International Rice Research Institute (IRRI), its more famous counterpart at Los Banos in the Philippines (to which it is attached), one of the Can Tho institute's key functions is developing rice hybrids that will flourish in the varied conditions of the delta. Rice-husking mills still form a large part of the city's industry and contribute to its economy.

WHAT TO SEE
FLOATING MARKETS

The river markets near Can Tho are bustling confusions of boats, goods, vendors, customers and tourists. From their boats the market traders attach samples of their wares to bamboo poles, which they hold out to attract customers. Up to seven vegetables can be seen dangling from the staves—winter melon, pumpkin, green onions, giant parsnips, grapefruit, garlic, mangoes, onions, and Vietnamese plums—and the boats are usually piled

Above *The Cai Rang floating market is a short distance from Can Tho*

high with one or two of the products. Housewives paddle their sampans from boat to boat, haggling over prices and gossiping. At the back of the boats, the domesticity of life on the water can be seen, down to the washing hung out to dry. Phung Hiep has a snake market (on land), and yards where fishing boats and rice barges are made.

✉ Phung Hiep, 20 miles (33km) from Can Tho; Phong Dien, 9 miles (15km) downriver; Cai Rang, 4 miles (7km) south of Can Tho 🕐 Daily; busiest 6–9am ✋ Trips to the floating markets can be booked through Can Tho Tourist or through one of the very many private operators offering various deals and packages. Compare prices and confirm in detail exactly what is being offered 🚢 Sampans available to rent in Hai Ba Trung Street

CHUA ONG PAGODA
Chua Ong Pagoda, facing the riverfront park, dates from 1894 and was built by Chinese from Guangzhou. Unusually for a Chinese temple it is not free-standing but part of a row of buildings. The right side of the pagoda is dedicated to the Goddess of Fortune, and the left side belongs to the fierce and warlike General Ma Tien, whose unsmiling statue stands here. The layout is a combination of the classic pagoda style, with a small, open courtyard where the incense smoke can escape, and the meeting-house style introduced by the Chinese in Southeast Asia, with its own language school.
✉ 34 Hai Ba Trung Street

MUNIRANGSYARAM PAGODA
Two monks conduct prayers twice a day (5am and 6pm) in this pagoda built in 1946 to serve the city's Khmer residents. This is a Khmer Hinayana Buddhist sanctuary; it houses a seated figure of Siddhartha Gautama (the historical Buddha), meditating under a bodhi tree.
✉ 36 Hoa Binh Boulevard

Left *A vendor at the Cai Rang floating market*
Below *The statue of Ho Chi Minh on Hai Ba Trung Street*

REGIONS THE SOUTH • SIGHTS

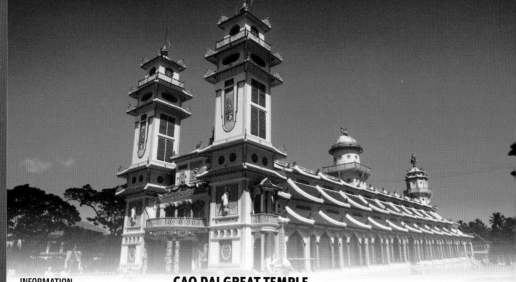

INFORMATION

286 D11 ✉ 2 miles (3km) east of Tay Ninh, 60 miles (96km) northwest of Saigon ⏰ Prayer ceremonies daily 6am, noon, 6pm, midnight; visitor access to balcony 🚌 Tay Ninh; connections from Mien Tay via Cu Chi 🚗 Private tour from Saigon (which includes Cu Chi)

TIPS

» Do not enter the central portion of the nave—keep to the side aisles—and do not wander in and out during services.
» Remove your shoes before going on to the balcony to watch the ceremonies.
» Do not wear sleeveless tops or shorts.

Above *The Great Temple is dominated by its twin towers*
Opposite *Worshipers sitting between ornately carved pillars inside the temple*

CAO DAI GREAT TEMPLE

THE GREAT TEMPLE

Idiosyncratic Cao Dai Great Temple is the main place of worship of the Cao Dai religion (▷ 16), built in 1880 and set within a large complex of schools and administrative buildings. The twin-towered cathedral is European in inspiration but with distinct Asian features. On the facade are figures of Cao Dai saints in high relief, and at the entrance is a painting depicting French writer Victor Hugo (1802–85) flanked by the Vietnamese poet Nguyen Binh Khiem (1492–1587) and the Chinese nationalist Sun Yat-sen (1866–1925). Sun Yat-sen holds an inkstone, symbolizing the link between Confucianism and Christianity. There are nine columns and nine steps to the cathedral, representing the nine steps to heaven.

INSIDE THE GREAT TEMPLE

After removing shoes and hats, women enter through a door to the left, men to the right, and they then proceed down their respective aisles toward the altar, usually accompanied by a Cao Dai priest dressed in white with a black turban. During services the priests don red, blue and yellow robes, signifying Confucianism, Taoism and Buddhism respectively. Senior officiates wear colored robes sporting an embroidered divine eye.

Rows of pink pillars entwined with green, horned dragons line the nave, leading up to the main altar, which supports a large globe on which is painted a single staring eye—the divine, all-seeing eye. The ceiling is blue and dotted with clouds and sparkling stars, representing the heavens, and the domes are covered in a riot of dragons and vegetation in pink, orange and green. Open, lattice-work windows pierce the walls, each with a divine eye as its centerpiece. Above the altar is the Cao Dai pantheon: At the top, in the center, is Sakyamuni Buddha; next to him, on the left, is Lao Tzu, master of Taoism; and left of Lao Tzu is Quan Am, goddess of mercy, sitting on a lotus blossom. On the other side of the Buddha statue is Confucius. The red-faced Chinese god of war and soldiers, Quan Cong, is shown to the right. Below Sakyamuni Buddha is the poet and leader of the Chinese saints, Li Ti Pei; below him is Jesus Christ and on the next level down Jiang Zhia, master of Geniism.

At the back of the cathedral is a sculpture of Pham Com Tac, one of the religion's founders, who died in 1957. He stands on flowers, surrounded by huge, brown snakes, and is flanked by his two assistants—one the leader of spirits, the other the leader of materialism.

CHAU DOC AND SAM MOUNTAIN

The busy, commercial frontier town of Chau Doc straddles the giant crossroads of the Mekong. An important pilgrimage center at Sam Mountain is riddled with religious relics. Chau Doc (formerly Chau Phu) is an attractive, bustling riverside town on the Hau or Bassac River and an important trading center for nearby agricultural communities. Until the mid-18th century this was part of Cambodia, but was given to the Nguyen Lord Nguyen Phuc Khoat after he helped quash an insurrection in the area. A large Khmer population still lives in the area, as well as the largest Cham settlement in the delta. Chau Doc District (a separate province for a while) is the seat of the Hoa Hao religion, founded in Hoa Hao village in 1939, with up to 1.5 million adherents.

The Vietnamese flock to Sam Mountain (Nui Sam), a barren hill honeycombed with tombs, sanctuaries and temples. Walk or drive up the hill, 3 miles (5km) southwest of town from Nguyen Van Thoai Street, for outstanding views of some of Vietnam's most fertile land.

MAIN SIGHTS

The Tay An Pagoda, facing the road at the foot of the hill, dates originally from 1847 but has been extended twice. It has an eclectic mixture of styles—Chinese, Islamic, perhaps even Italian—and inside more than 200 statues include elephants and green monsters.

Nearby, along the road to the right, is the rather featureless Chua Xu Temple, originally dating from the late 19th century but rebuilt in 1972. Revered by the Vietnamese, it honors the Holy Lady Xu, whose statue is in the new pagoda. The 23rd to 25th days of the fourth lunar month are the Holy Lady's festival, when crowds come to see the statue washed and reclothed.

On the other side of the road is the tomb of Thoai Ngoc Hau (1761–1829), a local hero of the resistance against the French, but more noted as a canal-building and swamp-draining engineer.

Hang Pagoda is a 200-year-old temple halfway up Sam Mountain (take the road to the right; entrance at street level). On the first level are vivid cartoons of the tortures of hell, while the second is at the mouth of a cave, home, during the last century, to a woman named Thich Gieu Thien. Her likeness and tomb can be seen in the first pagoda. She came here after leaving her lazy and abusive husband in Cholon and lived as an ascetic, supposedly waited on by two snakes.

Sampans take visitors from the ferry terminal near Victoria Chau Doc Hotel to Phu Hiep, a Cham village on the opposite bank of the river, which has some historic mosques.

INFORMATION
✚ 286 C11 ✉ An Giang Province, on border with Cambodia 🚌 Le Loi Street; connections with Saigon, Long Xuyen, Can Tho 🚢 Ferries from Phnom Penh, Ha Tien 🚗 Private tours from Saigon

TIPS
» Sam Mountain is one of the holiest sites in southern Vietnam and is very crowded on auspicious days.
» The daily ferries along the 56-mile (90km) Vinh Te Canal to Ha Tien are a fascinating way to see village life; take plenty of water and food.

Opposite *Huts in the floating village at Chau Doc*
Below *The Tay An Pagoda dates from the 19th century*

REGIONS · THE SOUTH · SIGHTS

INFORMATION
www.cuchitunnel.org.vn

✠ 286 D11 ✉ 25 miles (40km) northwest of Saigon ☎ 08-37946442
◷ Daily 7–5 💰 Ben Dinh (Cu Chi 1): 80,000d. Ben Duoc (Cu Chi 2): 65,000d
🚌 Cu Chi town; connections from Mien Tay and Ham Nghi stations, Saigon. Honda *ôm* or infrequent Ben Suc bus to tunnels 🍴 Snacks and ice cream
🎁 Souvenirs, flags and bottles of snake wine 🚐 Private tours from Saigon; daily with Kim Tours (www.kimtours.net)

TIPS
» The Cu Chi Tunnels (Dia Dao Cu Chi) are too narrow for most Westerners, but a short section has been especially widened to allow visitors to share the experience. Tall or large people might still find it a claustrophobic squeeze.

» Cu Chi 1 (Ben Dinh) is more popular with the tourist trade; Cu Chi 2 (Ben Duoc) attracts fewer visitors and has more original tunnels.

CU CHI TUNNELS

The 124-mile (200km) complex of tunnels at Cu Chi (Dia Dao Cu Chi) was excavated by Viet Minh and Viet Cong fighters over 25 years of conflict. Work began on the network of tunnels under Cu Chi town back in 1948, when the Viet Minh needed to find a way of escaping superior French weaponry and to communicate with each other in secret. Between 1960 and 1970 the network was expanded by the Viet Cong and used for storage as well as for refuge. The tunnels contained sleeping quarters, hospitals and schools, and were originally only 32in (80cm) high; some have been made bigger for larger Western visitors. The width of the tunnel entry at ground level was 9in by 12in (22cm by 30cm).

When the Americans first discovered this network they tried a variety of means to remove it. CS gas was pumped down tunnel openings, and explosives were set; river water was pumped in, and German shepherd dogs were sent to detect air holes (subsequently smothered in garlic to deter them). Craters testify to the carpet-bombing that was also employed. Some 40,000 Viet Cong were killed in the tunnels over the course of 10 years. Later, realizing the tunnels might also yield valuable intelligence, American commanders sent in volunteer "tunnel rats" to capture prisoners.

AN EXPERIENCE
In Cu Chi 1, visitors are shown film footage of the tunnels during the Vietnam War before being taken underground to see some of the rooms and the booby traps that were encountered by GIs. The Viet Cong survived on cassava alone for up to three months at a time; here, and at Cu Chi 2, you will be encouraged to taste some, dipped in salt, sesame, sugar and peanuts.

In Cu Chi 2, visitors are invited to a firing range to try their hand with AK47s or a revolver for 20,000d a round. In the grounds of Cu Chi 2 is a pagoda, built in 1993 and devoted to the memory of the dead. Relatives of those who are still missing attend the pagoda, which is inscribed inside with the names of about 50,000 Vietnamese dead. Murals on the walls include imagery of the self-immolation of Buddhist monks in Saigon in 1963. The sculpture behind the temple is of a massive teardrop cradled in the hands of a mother.

Between the two sites is the Cu Chi military cemetery, where 10,000 soldiers are buried. There is a vast, gray, brutalist mural depicting the Vietnam War. Inside the cemetery gates is a large statue of a father weeping over the fallen body of his son.

Below *A basic kitchen in the Cu Chi Tunnels*

DAO PHU QUOC

Phu Quoc Island, fringed by beaches and an aquamarine sea, produces some of the best fish sauce in Vietnam. This remote, tropical island, off the southwest coast, is Vietnam's largest island and remains largely undeveloped. White, sandy beaches line much of its coastline; forested hills and pepper farms are found inland. There are only a few resorts, and although new additions are planned the pace of development is slow due to the lack of power and water supplies to much of the island. Phu Quoc's northernmost tip lies just outside Cambodian territorial waters but within sight of its coast, and has in the past been disputed, claimed and reclaimed by Thai, Khmer and Viet powers. Refugees from the Khmer Rouge regime came to live at the northern town of Ganh Dau and Cambodian is still spoken here.

MAIN ATTRACTIONS

Dai Bau is a strip of white sand overlooking Turtle Island (Hon Doi Moi), 20 miles (32km) from Ganh Dau. The water is clear but there are no facilities. The dazzling, white sands of Sao Beach, on the southeast coast, are worth visiting by motorcycle, but poor signposting can make it hard to find. There's a restaurant at the back of the beach. Inland are wooded areas protected against clearance and development, and streams and waterfalls that lose their drama in the dry season but still provide relaxing spots to swim and walk.

Around the island, millions of fish can be seen laid out to dry—all destined to be made into fish sauce *(nuoc mam)*. Before being bottled they are fermented, and you can watch the process at the fish sauce factory in Duong Dong, where 95 massive wooden barrels act as vats, each containing fish and salt weighing 15 tons (14 tonnes) and ringing in the till at more than US$5,000 a barrel. If the sauce is made in concrete vats, the flavor is lost and so the sauce is less expensive.

About 6 miles (10km) south of Duong Dong is the Phu Quoc Pearl Gallery (daily 8–5.30; tel: 077-3980585; www.treasuresfromthedeep.com). Just offshore, 10,000 South Sea pearls are collected each year. A video demonstrates the farming operation, and in the gallery the pearl-culturing process is illustrated and oyster meat can be tasted. Pearl necklaces are available for sale.

About 100 yards (90m) south of the pearl farm on the coastal road are two whale dedication temples (Lang Ca Ong, ▷ 230). In front of one is a crudely sculpted whale statue. Boat trips are arranged from the resorts around the An Thoi islands, off the southern coast, where you can swim and snorkel.

INFORMATION

✛ 286 B12 Daily ferry from Ha Tien; daily high-speed boat service from Rach Gia ✕ Connections with Saigon and Rach Gia ▢ Beach and hotel restaurants; café at Phu Quoc Pearl Gallery
☞ Phu Quoc Explorer, To 5, Kp 8, Duong Dong ☎ 077-3994695; www.phuquocexplorer.com

TIPS

» The roads are poor and only the one between Duong Dong and Ham Ninh is metaled.
» Motorcycles and cars with drivers can be rented from most resorts.

Above *Palm trees, white sand and blue waters at Long Beach on Phu Quoc*

INFORMATION

www.dongthaptourist.com

🗺 286 D11 🛈 Dong Thap Tourist Company, 178 Nguyen Hue Street, Cao Lanh ☎ 067-3852136 🕓 Mon–Fri 7–5 👋 Tours from Saigon are costed according to the numbers involved 🚌 Buses from Saigon to Ly Thuong Kiet Street, Cao Lanh 🚤 Boat trips to main sites arranged by Dong Thap Tourist Company or private tours from Saigon

TIP

» During the wet season (September through November) water levels rise dramatically and all transportation around the Plain of Reeds is by boat.

DONG THAP MUOI

The vast Plain of Reeds is a swamp that extends for miles north of Cao Lanh, capital of Dong Thap Province, toward Cambodia. A rich diversity of birdlife thrives in the Mekong wetlands, where subterranean Viet Cong hiding places still survive.

In the rural districts Vietnamese houses are built on the highest land available, and during the wet season of a good year the floor remains inches above the rising waters. When the sky is gray the isolated plain can seem like the end of the earth, but is, in fact, an important habitat, teeming with wildlife.

BIRD SANCTUARIES

Tam Nong Bird Sanctuary (in Tram Chim National Park—Khu Bao Ton Chim Tam Nong) is a 20,000-acre (8,000ha) reserve, 28 miles (45km) northwest of Cao Lanh, and is home to 182 species of bird at various times of year. Its most famous resident is the red-headed crane *(Grus antigone sharpii)*, rarest of the 15 known crane species, and the world's tallest flying bird. Between August and November these spectacular creatures migrate across the Cambodian border, but in any month, particularly at dawn and dusk, they are a magnificent sight. Floating rice grows in the area, its leaves on the surface and its roots in the mud as much as 15ft (5m) down. So much energy is needed to grow the stalk, however, that little is left for the rice.

Storks and ibises can be seen at the White Stork Sanctuary (Vuon Co Thap Muoi), 27 miles (44km) northeast of Cao Lanh, near Thap Muoi. Again, dawn and dusk are the best times, when the sky is darkened by tens of thousands of birds flying off to feed or coming home to roost.

XEO QUYT BASE

Signs at My Long point to Xeo Quyt, a hidden Communist base (daily 8–5) 4 miles (6km) off the main road, 12 miles (20km) northwest of Cao Lanh. There was so little vegetation cover here that fast-growing eucalyptus trees were planted, but even these took three years to provide sufficient cover. The waterlogged ground prevented tunneling, so waterproof chambers sealed with plastic and resin were sunk into the mud. This base was stocked with rice, water and candles, and the Communists coordinated their resistance from here for almost 15 years of the Vietnam War. Despite frequent land and air raids the US forces never found or damaged the base. A 25-minute tour along narrow canals passes the underground shelters, offices and residences of party members. The sampans are paddled by women in Viet Cong dress; they make their way among the forest ferns and water hyacinth.

Below *A woman in Viet Cong dress paddles a sampan at Xeo Quyt*

HA TIEN

This small Mekong Delta town, huddled along the riverfront, has several temples and tombs and gives access to beaches and Phu Quoc Island.

Ha Tien lies west of a lagoon called East Lake (Dong Ho), which is bridged by a floating pontoon built by US Army engineers. Its riverside promenade, with a stilted café, is one of the most attractive in the delta. Ha Tien's history is strongly influenced by its proximity to Cambodia, to which the area belonged until the 18th century. There were Khmer incursions into the area in the late 1970s, and bitter resentments remain on both sides of the border.

Follow Phuong Thanh Street to the end to visit the Cotton Rose Hibiscus Pagoda (Chua Phu Dung) on Tomb Mountain (Nui Lang). In 1730, newly widowed Nguyen Nghi fled invaders from Laos and landed in Ha Tien with his son and 10-year-old daughter, Phu Cu, who dressed as a boy in order to attend school. She later became the second wife of Mac Cuu, the provincial governor, but after years of happy marriage begged her husband to let her become a nun, and in response Mac Cuu built the Cotton Rose Hibiscus Pagoda, where his wife spent the rest of her life in prayer and contemplation.

In 1708, Mac Cuu established a Vietnamese protectorate under waning Khmer rule. Den Mac Cuu is a temple built between 1898 and 1902 at the foot of Tomb Mountain, and is dedicated to him and his clan. To the left of the altar house a map locates the tombs of clan members. Mac Cuu's own tomb lies a short distance up the hill along a path leading from the right of the temple.

Behind Tomb Mountain is Lang Mo Ba Co Nam (Tomb of Great Aunt Number Five). The honorary title was given to Mac Cuu's three-year-old daughter, who was buried alive. The tomb has become an important shrine to many Vietnamese, who seek the girl's divine intercession in times of family crisis. Two beautiful blue phoenixes standing on turtles flank the tomb of Great Aunt Number Five.

INFORMATION

✚ 286 B12 🚌 Southeast edge of town; connections with Saigon, Rach Gia, Can Tho 🚢 Ferry to Chau Doc 📷 🏁 Private tour from Saigon

TIP

» The Cambodian border about 1 mile (2km) beyond Thach Dong Pagoda is not an authorized crossing point for foreigners.

Above *A pontoon bridges East Lake*

REGIONS THE SOUTH • SIGHTS

INFORMATION

✚ 286 D12 ✉ 44 miles (71km)
southwest of Saigon 🚌 Ben Xe My Tho,
Ap Bac Street; connections with Saigon,
Can Tho, Chau Doc, Vinh Long, Cao Lanh
🚢 Ferry to Chau Doc from Ben Tre ferry
terminal; ferry to islands from Le Thi Hong
Gam Street 🍴 Good restaurants on
Trung Trac Street; noodle stands at night
on Le Loi Street and Le Dai Han Street
intersection ☛ Island tours arranged
by Tien Giang Tourist Company, 08, 30/4
Street, My Tho ☎ 073-3873184; private
tours from Saigon

TIPS

» Prices for island tours vary according to
the number of people; expect to pay about
US$45 to charter a boat for a few hours.
» Try the honey tea on one of the islands.
The honey is made from the longan flower,
and a splash of kumquat juice is added to
balance the flavor.

MY THO AND THE ISLANDS

My Tho sits on the banks of the Tien River, a distributary of the mighty
Mekong, about 25 miles (40km) from the South China Sea. Dominating
its river promenade is a statue of Nguyen Huu Huan, a resistance fighter
who was captured by the French in 1875 and put to death. The town has
a turbulent history, having been Khmer until the 17th century, when the
advancing Vietnamese took control of the surrounding area. In the 18th
century Thai forces annexed the territory, before being driven out in 1784.
Finally, the French gained control in 1862.

Nowadays, a quiet, rural way of life continues among the fruit trees in
this riverside market town, where you can watch rice-paper, rice "popcorn,"
coconut candy and honey in production.

AROUND MY THO

Vinh Trang Pagoda, at 60 Nguyen Trung Truc Street (daily 8–4) is entered
through an ornate, porcelain-encrusted gate. The pagoda was constructed
during 1849 in a mix of Chinese, Vietnamese and colonial styles, and its fairy-
tale facade sits incongruously next to the encroaching forest. Not far from
My Tho, the hamlet of Ap Bac was the site of the first major victory of the
Communists against the Army of the Republic of Vietnam, which showed
that without direct US involvement there was no prospect of the ARVN
defeating the Communist forces.

THE ISLANDS

There are four islands in the Tien River between My Tho and Ben Tre—Dragon,
Tortoise, Phoenix and Unicorn—which can be visited as part of a tour or by
renting a boat. Dragon (Tan Long) Island lies immediately opposite My Tho
and is a relaxing place to wander. It is especially noted for its longan crop, but
there are many other fruits to sample here, as well as honey and rice whiskey.
Phoenix Island (Con Phung) is about 2 miles (3km) from My Tho. It's also
known as the Island of the Coconut Monk, who established a retreat here
shortly after World War II and developed a religious movement with elements
of Buddhism and Christianity. He is said to have meditated for three years on
a stone slab, eating nothing but coconuts. Persecuted by government and
Communists, the monastery has fallen into disuse.

On Tortoise Island (Con Qui) there is an abundance of dragon fruit, longan,
banana and papaya. Here visitors are treated to singing accompanied by a
guitar and Vietnamese monochord.

Below *Navigating Tortoise Island's
waterways*

SA DEC

A road lined with brick kilns leads to this small and friendly town, whose main avenues—Nguyen Hue, Tran Hung Dao and Hung Vuong—and attractive colonial villas reveal a lasting French influence. French author Marguerite Duras (1914–96) was born here, and parts of the 1992 film adaptation of her novel *The Lover* were filmed by the riverside on Nguyen Hue Street. Duras' childhood home is across the river and can be reached by sampan from the covered market.

Phuoc Hung Pagoda, at 75/5 Hung Vuong Street, is a splendid Chinese-style pagoda constructed in 1838 and decorated with fabulous animals assembled from pieces of porcelain rice bowls. Old turtles plod round the courtyard amid the greenery.

Tu Ton Rose Garden (Vuon Hong Tu Ton), at 11/5 Vuon Hong Street (daily 6am–8pm), is west of Sa Dec and can be reached either on foot or by Honda *ôm* to Tan Qui Don village. This 14,800-acre (6,000ha) nursery borders the river and harbors more than 40 varieties of rose and 540 other types of plant, from medicinal herbs to beautiful and exotic orchids.
🔳 286 D12 ✉ 12 miles (20km) west of Vinh Long 🚌 Southeast of town; connections with Vinh Long, Long Xuyen 🍴 🚗 Private tour from Saigon

SOC TRANG

Straddling a narrow branch of the Mekong, Soc Trang is a sprawling and scruffy town with many Khmer residents. On the fourth day of the 10th lunar month (usually December) it takes on a carnival atmosphere for the Khmer *Ooc-om-bok* festival, culminating with a river boat race.

At the top end of town on Nguyen Thi Minh Khai Street is the Kleang Pagoda, a temple in traditional Cambodian style, perched on a two-level terrace. Vivid colors adorn the windows and doors; inside is a golden Sakyamuni statue with an electric halo.

About 2 miles (3km) out of Soc Trang is the Matoc Pagoda (Maha Tup in Khmer). To get to it, follow Le Hong Phong Street and fork right after the fire station. The main pagoda is on the right and is decorated with bright murals; it has been restored with donations from the Vietnamese and Khmer diaspora. Thousands of fruit bats roost in the trees behind the pagoda and at dusk they are an impressive sight as they fly off to find food, blackening the sky.

Also behind the pagoda are the monks' living quarters and the tombs of two five-toed pigs. Living examples can be seen in the pens, where they are lovingly cared for by the monks.
🔳 286 D12 🚌 101C Nguyen Chi Thanh Street; connections with Ca Mau, Can Tho, Rach Gia, Saigon 🚢 Ferry from Tra Vinh 🚗 Private tour from Saigon

TRA VINH

This attractive capital of the province of the same name has huge trees—some much more than 100ft (30m) tall—lining almost every street. It is home to a large Khmer population and has 140 Khmer temples.

Hang Pagoda is about 3 miles (5km) south of town, and Giong Long Pagoda is 27 miles (43km) southeast. Although neither is particularly noteworthy architecturally, both provide the awe-inspiring sight of hundreds of storks resting in their grounds and wheeling around their pointed roofs at dawn and dusk.
🔳 286 D12 🚌 Nguyen Dan Street; connections with Vinh Long 🍴 🚗 Private tour from Saigon

VINH LONG

Escape from the bustle of Vinh Long to An Binh Island and experience a tranquil way of life in the Mekong Delta. The small floating market at Cai Be will be of interest to those unable to make it to Can Tho.

The capital of Vinh Long Province is a busy and somewhat ramshackle town on the banks of the Co Chien River. It was one of the focal points of the spread of Christianity in the Mekong Delta, and in addition to its interesting temples and pagodas there is a cathedral and Catholic seminary in town. There is also a Cao Dai church near the second bridge leading into town from Saigon and My Tho.

River trips from Vinh Long, taking in the surrounding islands and orchards, are very enjoyable but can be expensive owing to Cuu Long Tourist's monopoly. Local boatmen risk the fine to take visitors for a much lower price. There is a small floating market and an attractive church at Cai Be, about 6 miles (10km) from Vinh Long.

An Binh Island is a 10-minute ferry ride from Phan Boi Chau Street and provides a splendid example of a typical delta landscape. The island can be explored either by boat, paddling down narrow canals, or by following the dirt tracks and teetering across monkey bridges— single bamboo poles with, if you are lucky, a flimsy handrail.

Sights on the island include the ancient Tien Chau Pagoda and a *nuoc mam* (fish sauce) factory, and the welcoming residents will also show you popcorn made from rice, rice-paper production and a lovely bonsai garden.

Nguyen Van Tam, also known as Mr. Tiger, is the island's oldest resident, and owns a flourishing orchard with bonsai trees, which can be visited on a tour (Green Island Tour, Binh Tuan 1 Hamlet, Hoa Ninh Village, tel 070-859859). If you stay overnight in a homestay on An Binh Island, you can get up at dawn to witness the beautiful sunrise and be ready to go paddling around the narrow channels of the island in a sampan.
🔳 286 D12 ℹ Cuu Long Tourist, 1 Thang 5 Street ☎ 070-3823616; www.cuulongtourist.com 🚌 1A Dinh Tien Hoang Street, 3 miles (5km) from downtown; connections with Saigon, Can Tho, My Tho, Long Xuyen, Rach Gia, Sa Dec 🚗 Range of excursions arranged by Cuu Long Tourist, 1 Thang 5 Street, or private tour from Saigon

INFORMATION

www.vungtautourist.com.vn
✚ 287 E12 ℹ 207 Vo Thi Sau Street
☎ 064-3856445 🕐 Mon–Fri 7–11.30,
1.30–5 🚌 192 Nam Ky Khoi Nghia Street;
connections with Saigon, Bien Hoa, Binh
Khanh 🚢 Halong Street; hydrofoil from
Ham Nghi Street Wharf, Saigon

TIPS

» There are many Honda *ôms* and taxis in town but few cyclos.

» Distances within town are quite short and can be covered comfortably on foot.

VUNG TAU

This hub of the country's oil industry and significant fishing port is also a popular coastal resort, packed with visitors every weekend.

Vung Tau sits on a rocky promontory between two hills, Nui Lon (Big Mountain) to the north and Nui Nho (Small Mountain) to the south. Vietnamese day-trippers flock here for its cooling breezes and beachfront, and the town enjoys a high level of prosperity based on oil, trade and its role as capital of Ba Ria-Vung Tau Province. As Cap Saint-Jacques, it began developing as a seaside resort at the beginning of the 20th century, but with the exception of Bai Sau (Back Beach), the beaches are narrow and have little or no sand. Bai Sau lies on the east side of town, 1 mile (2km) southeast of the center, and has a 3-mile (5km) stretch of sand, exposed to the wind and the South China Sea. The surf is usually good—sometimes ferocious.

TOWN SIGHTS

At 12 Tran Phu Street (the coast road) is Bach Dinh (daily 7–5), built in the early part of the last century as a summer residence (Villa Blanche) for French Governor-General Paul Doumer on the site of an old fort. It's now a museum for the Hon Cau, or Vung Tau, ceramics, dating from the Qing Dynasty, that were salvaged in 1990–91 from a Chinese trading junk that sank near Con Dao Island in around 1690. The find was highly significant not only for its size—48,000 pieces in all—but also because it represents some of the first pieces of standing, as opposed to flat, ceramics to come from China. This collection consists of vases, goblets and small statues; some are encrusted with coral and some retain their original elegant blue and white glaze. The building is rather fine, with a mosaic frieze running under the eaves. It has a glorious outlook and beautiful gardens with colorful *cay su* trees, a type of Vietnamese rhododendron.

The Whale Dedication Temple (Lang Ca Ong), at 77A Hoang Hoa Tham Street, is sumptuously adorned in red and gold and dedicated to the whale, the patron god of Vung Tau fisherfolk (worship of the whale was inherited from the Cham). The temple was built in 1911 and contains a number of whale skeletons in cabinets behind the main altar. The whale skeleton to the right of the altar dates from 1931, while the central skeleton is believed to date from 1848. Whale and dolphin bones are brought to the temple and worshiped before being cremated: The marine mammals are credited with saving drowning sailors and fisherfolk. A number of photographs show the annual whale dedication ceremony.

Above *A statue of Tran Hung Dao*
Opposite *Drying fish on the beach*

PHU QUOC ISLAND

This drive takes you around the southern part of Phu Quoc Island and on the way you will see white-sand beaches, pagodas, a pearl farm, a prison and picturesque fishing villages. Cars and motorcycles are readily available for hire (▷ 55) but if you drive yourself by motorcycle, consider carrying a face mask, as the unpaved roads can throw up uncomfortable amounts of dust in dry weather.

THE TOUR
Distance: 34 miles (55 km)
Allow: 3 hours
Start/end at: Duong Dong

HOW TO GET THERE
For transport details to Phu Quoc,
▷ 225.

★ In Duong Dong stop at the junction that is a couple of hundred yards past the post office on your right. Sung Hung Pagoda is on your left.

❶ Sung Hung Pagoda is the most interesting of the many pagodas dotted around the island. It was built over a hundred years ago—the actual year is not known—and is

landscaped with trees, including a giant banyan. Facing the small lotus-filled pond in the courtyard is a statue of the goddess Quan An Bo Tat. A Buddha statue stands serenely on the altar inside the temple.

Continue on the road heading south from Duong Dong, hugging the coast for most of the way to An Thoi. At first you will pass a cluster of resort hotels on what is known as Long Beach. About 6 miles (10km) from the center of Duong Dong make a stop at the Phu Quoc Pearl Farm, which is on your right.

❷ The pearl farm (▷ 225) has a small café, and a deserted stretch

of beach is directly opposite. One hundred yards (90m) south stand two whale dedication statues.

From the pearl farm the dirt road continues south, staying very close to Long Beach. Stay on this road until you reach a T-junction. Turn right at the junction and join the paved, inland road that connects Duong Dong with An Thoi. A short way along this road stop at the Coconut Tree Prison on your left.

❸ The prison was built by the French but maximum use of it was not made until the Vietnam War, when the Americans used it as a secure, and notorious, detention center for Viet Cong prisoners,

Above *Inviting hot springs at Suoi Chanh*
Opposite *A fishing boat pulled up on an idyllic and deserted beach on the island*

holding up to 40,000 inmates. A part of it is still used as a prison and the main point of interest is the monument that stands opposite it by the side of the road.

It is a short run into the coastal village of An Thoi; park at one of the hotels. An Thoi is where ferries from the mainland dock.

4 The An Thoi archipelago is a popular place for diving and snorkeling, and boat trips to the islands depart from the harbor. There are a number of hotels here so you could stay overnight if a boat trip means a late return. Fish sauce factories are also located here and most of them can be visited.

Leave An Thoi by the road you arrived on but, instead of returning on the coastal dirt road that you traveled down to get here, stay on the paved road that heads inland back to Duong Dong. Stay on this road for most of the way back to Duong Dong but before entering the town take the turning on your right for Ham Ninh and look for large concrete gates on the left side of the road that lead to Suoi Tranh waterfall.

5 There is a small entrance fee and a 10-minute walk along a path through the jungle to reach the waterfall and the adjoining rock pools. Swimming in the pools is allowed and it is a very relaxing spot even though the waterfall itself is quite small and not very dramatic.

Stay on the road heading east to the fishing village of Ham Ninh on the coast, 12 miles (19km) from Duong Dong.

6 The water at Ham Ninh is remarkably shallow, hence the very long jetty that stretches out into the sea. Villagers mostly make their living from fishing and diving for sea pearls. The village is also noted for its fresh crabs, which are the chief attraction of any meal here.

Head back on the same road to Duong Dong, though there is the option of heading south down the east coast from Ham Ninh to stop at breathtakingly beautiful beaches. The dirt road, though, is bumpy and only suitable for motorcycles.

WHEN TO GO
The months of November through May are the best time for diving and snorkeling; trips are not usually available outside of this period.

WHERE TO EAT
There are places to eat at An Thoi and Ham Ninh.

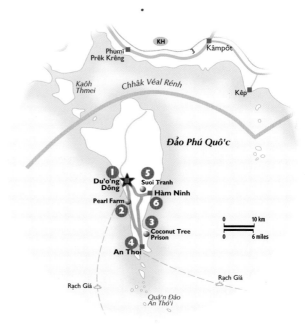

CAN THO

CAN THO WATER PARK

Young children should enjoy a visit to this water park for its slides. It is usually busy only at weekends.
✉ Lot D1, Cai Khe Ward ☎ 071-3763343 🕐 Daily 9am–6pm 💰 35,000d–55,000d

COOKERY CLASSES

www.victoriahotels-asia.com
Kitchen staff take you to the local market in the early morning to buy produce for these cookery courses. On returning to the hotel, the Vietnamese chef explains all the ingredients and helps you prepare a dish for lunch.
✉ Victoria Can Tho, Cai Khe Ward ☎ 071-3810111 💰 US$42 (minimum 2 people). Reservations must be made by 9pm the previous night

LADY HAU BOAT TRIP

www.victoriahotels-asia.com
The *Lady Hau* is a converted wooden ship that embarks on a sunrise breakfast cruise to Cai Rang floating market. The 3.5-hour trip involves taking a sampan up narrow creeks and visiting a noodle factory and an orchard. A romantic sunset cruise with cocktails and snacks also leaves at 5.30pm.
✉ Victoria Can Tho, Cai Khe Ward ☎ 071-3810111 💰 Sunrise cruise: US$50 per person (minimum 4 people). Sunset cruise: US$30 per person (with cocktail)

TRANSMÉKONG

www.transmekong.com
The company's converted wooden rice barge, *Bassac*, can sleep 12 passengers in six air-conditioned cabins with private bathrooms. Each cabin has two beds, cotton sheets, a bedside table, slippers and an elegant white ceramic bowl for the sink. Prices include dinner and breakfast, entry tickets to visited sights, a French- or English-speaking guide on board and access to a small boat.

Above *River trips are arranged by Victoria Chau Doc Spa*

✉ 97/10 Ngo Quyen, P. An Cu, Can Tho ☎ 071-3829540 💰 2-day/1-night cruise between Cai Be and Can Tho: 1 to 2 passengers US$290 per person; 3 or more passengers US$238 per person. Single cabin supplement US$90

VICTORIA CAN THO SPA

www.victoriahotels-asia.com
The relaxing massage cabins at the colonial-style resort of the Victoria Can Tho are situated near to the Mekong River. You can hear the chug of the boats as you lie on thin mattresses covered in crisp, white cotton and strewn with delicate, pink orchids, while you enjoy the healing and calming treatments. These range from the 45-minute gentle Vietnamese massage or hand and foot reflexology to the Victoria massage package of reflexology, body massage, oil massage and

head massage. There's also a sauna that needs an hour's notice.

✉ Victoria Can Tho, Cai Khe Ward ☎ 071-3810111 ◷ Daily 10–10. Reserve in advance ✋ From US$23

CHAU DOC
RAINBOW DIVERS
www.divevietnam.com
This British-owned diving company can be contacted through any of the local hotels. The dive season runs from mid-November to early June, and divers can see excellent corals around the cluster of islands off the south coast, plus varied sea life to the north. PADI courses are available.

✉ Rainbow Bar, next to Kim Hoa Resort ☎ 090-8781756 ✋ Introductory 2-day course with 2 dives US$284.

VICTORIA CHAU DOC SPA
www.victoriahotels-asia.com
Massage beds are mounted on platforms and surrounded by four-poster hangings at this Victoria hotel. Choose from a foot and hand massage, head and shoulder massage or the full Victoria massage. Every hotel guest gets a free 10-minute massage. River trips aboard *Le Jarai* are arranged by the hotel.

✉ Victoria Chau Doc, 32 Le Loi Street ☎ 076-3865010 ◷ Daily 9–9 ✋ From US$23 (head and shoulder massage)

MY THO
VAM HO BIRD SANCTUARY
On an islet by the Ba Lai River, the sanctuary is noted for the large numbers of storks and black-crowned night herons. Small boats take visitors through the mangrove forest. It is best to arrange a tour from a company in Ho Chi Minh City that includes an overnight stay in a nearby town, because the ideal time to see the birds is after dusk.

✉ Ben Tre Province ☎ 075-3858669 ✋ 15,000d

TRA VINH
BA DONG BEACH
During the week you will largely have this beautiful, white-sand

FESTIVALS AND EVENTS

APRIL
BOAT FESTIVAL
The Khmer New Year is celebrated with ritual and frantic boat racing on the Maspero River, a tributary of the Mekong River.

✉ Soc Trang Province ◷ Fifth–seventh days of third lunar month

SEPTEMBER
LE NGHINH ONG
An annual festival that commemorates the whale starts on the beach and finishes at the Lang Ca Ong (Whale) Temple.

✉ Vung Tau ◷ 15th–17th days of eighth lunar month

beach to yourself, although there are plans to develop its potential as a resort destination. Buses run to Duyen Hai from Tra Vinh and from there it is a short ride on a motorcycle taxi to the beach.

✉ Duyen Hai, 55km (34 miles) east of Tra Vinh

VUNG TAU
BINH CHAU THERMAL SPRINGS
Immerse yourself in a communal or a private pool—but be careful where you bathe; in places the sulfurous water bubbles out of the springs at 179°F (82°C). The Cu Mi Hotel, nearby, provides lodging, a restaurant and massage.

✉ 70km (43 miles) from Vung Tau ✋ Admission to springs 20,000d

GREYHOUND RACING
Greyhound racing has been

operating in Vietnam for several years. There are 12 races held every Saturday evening. The 437-yard (400m) track and stand for 5,000 spectators are maintained to the highest standards, and the dogs are in excellent condition.

✉ Lam Son Stadium, 15 Le Loi Street ☎ 064-3807309 ◷ Sat 7.15pm–10.30pm ✋ 25,000d

SURF BAR
This beach-style bar at the Vang Tau Beach Club, opposite Sammy hotel (▷ 242), is very popular on weekends when live music plays. A party atmosphere prevails but it is always a relaxing watering hole for cocktails and light meals.

✉ 08 Thuy Van Street ☎ 064-3526101 ◷ Daily 9am–late

Above *Boat races take place during the Boat Festival at the Khmer New Year*

PRICES AND SYMBOLS

The restaurants are listed alphabetically (excluding Le, La, Il and The). The prices given are the average for a two-course lunch (L) and a three-course dinner (D) for one person, without drinks. The wine price is for the least expensive bottle.

For a key to the symbols, ▷ 2.

CAN THO

BELLEVUE RESTAURANT

Set on the Golf Can Tho Hotel's 11th story, the tiny Bellevue is attractive and has a more appetizing menu than its on-site sister, The Golf (▷ below). There are excellent views from a small, external balcony along a large stretch of the river. The French menu includes pumpkin soup with cream among the starters, main courses such as stuffed duck's leg with pineapple, and a choice of desserts such as orange cream.

✉ Golf Can Tho Hotel, 2 Hai Ba Trung Street, Can Tho ☎ 071-3812210 ⊕ Daily 7am–10pm ⍩ L 160,000d, D 250,000d, Wine 340,000d

THE GOLF RESTAURANT

This large and rather anonymous, but friendly, hotel restaurant with high ceilings serves a mainly conventional Vietnamese menu of fried squid salad, steamed pigeon with lotus beans and steamed duck with sautéed orange, as well as a range of spaghetti and other pasta dishes. The house sandwiches are rather expensive.

✉ Golf Can Tho Hotel, 2 Hai Ba Trung Street, Can Tho ☎ 071-3812210 ⊕ Daily 6am–11pm ⍩ L 140,000d, D 200,000d, Wine 290,000d

NAM BO

This delightful French house provides the best (and most popular with visitors) setting for eating in Can Tho town. The balcony seating area overlooks the market clutter and the riverside promenade, while the dishès are a mixture of Vietnamese and French cooking. Among the best items are pumpkin-flower soup, a tasty fried calamari in tamarind sauce, sautéed frogs' legs with mushrooms, and shrimp with mango sauce. The Can Tho delicately fried spring rolls are a must, and are served with a beautifully carved carrot and tomato decoration. Snake meat, for those who wish to try it, Western dishes for children and vegetarian options are all available.

✉ 50 Hai Ba Trung Street, Can Tho ☎ 071-3823908 ⊕ Daily 6am–11pm ⍩ L 120,000d, D 190,000d, Wine 220,000d

Above *Le Bassac restaurant terrace in Ha Tien*

RESTAURANT HOANG CUNG

Though large and a little impersonal, the Hoang Cung provides good-value for the money. The menu combines straightforward dishes, such as baked onion soup and breaded pork chops with mashed potatoes, with the more unusual — shark's fin and crab-meat soup, fish bladder and deep-fried eel. The dessert menu is limited to fruit.

✉ Saigon Can Tho, 55 Phan Dinh Phung Street, Can Tho ☎ 071-3825831 ⊕ Daily 6am–11pm ⍩ L 140,000d, D 190,000d, Wine 400,000d

SPICES RESTAURANT

www.victoriahotels-asia.com

A sampan stuffed with flowers and jars of goodies is the focal point of this restaurant. Their Vetnamese dishes range from a spinach soup served with *banh xeo* (savory pancakes), pork ribs and steamed sea bass to a less substantial crab bisque soup garnished with Parmesan cheese and aioli. There is also a good menu of international dishes, with starters such as a lobster salad, main items like chicken with port sauce, potato croquettes and vegetables, and

cooling desserts like a milkshake with apricot and pineapple sorbet.
✉ Victoria Can Tho, Cai Khe Ward, Can Tho ☎ 071-3810111 🕐 Daily 6am–10pm (6–10, 12–2, 7–10) 🍽 Vietnamese menu L US$20, US$27; International menu L US$17, D US$23; Wine 500,000đ

CHAU DOC
LA BASSAC
www.victoriahotels-asia.com
The extravagant French and Vietnamese menus at this riverside restaurant outstrip the setting, which has the air of a conservatory and is pervaded by cheesy instrumental love tunes. Ignoring this, tuck into a delicious meal of duck liver parfait with Cumberland sauce and melba toast, followed by rack of lamb coated in Mekong herbs, sweet-potato purée and pork wine reduction, or spaghetti with flambéed shrimp in vodka paprika sauce. Leave room for the sublime frozen strawberry yogurt in meringue on an orange Grand Marnier sauce. Alternatively, try the shrimp paste on sugarcane, or the eel and banana-blossom fondue. The menu includes low-fat options, indicated by a heart symbol.
✉ Victoria Chau Doc, 32 Le Loi Street, Chau Doc ☎ 076-3865010 🕐 Daily 6am–10pm 🍽 L 200,000đ, D 320,000đ; Wine 480,000đ

HA TIEN
HAI VAN
Open-fronted, bright and airy, this popular café on the main riverfront road serves a reasonable selection of Chinese, Vietnamese and international cuisine. All the traditional Vietnamese dishes are available here, with additions such as fried eel with chili and lemongrass and sweet and sour lobster ribs with rice. Those who prefer Western fare can order omelets with bread and butter.
✉ 4 Tran Hau Street, Ha Tien ☎ 077-3850344 🕐 Daily 6am–11pm 🍽 L 100,000đ, D 180,000đ

TRUNG NGUYEN CAFÉ
You can sit at this small, stilted wooden café overlooking the river

and the pontoon bridge, surrounded by pink bougainvillea, and watch the world go by, refreshed by a light river breeze. If you're not afraid of experimenting with new tastes, you could try the weasel coffee. Beer is also sold.
✉ Nguyen Van Hai Street, Ha Tien 🕐 Daily 7am–9pm 🍽 L 75,000đ, D 90,000đ

HON CHONG PENINSULA
TAN PHAT RESTAURANT
This restaurant on the waterfront of Hon Chong Peninsula's main town serves excellent seafood dishes, including succulent squid cooked in ginger. It's a real treat to sit out under the moonlight next to the dock, where fishing boats are moored, and to eat while listening to water lapping against wet wood, chattering families on board and the tinny sounds of fishing gear and boats knocking each other in the evening tide.
✉ Binh An 🕐 Daily 7am–9pm 🍽 L 75,000đ, D 120,000đ

MY THO
BANH XEO 46
A small, local restaurant on the main riverfront street, around the corner from the Chuong Duong hotel. The Banh Xeo 46 specializes in *banh xeo*, divine savory pancakes filled with bean sprouts, mushrooms and prawns. It also serves crab claws fried with rice flour. Look for the local specialty, *hu tieu my tho*—a spicy soup of vermicelli, sliced pork, dried shrimps and fresh herbs.
✉ 11 Trung Trac Street, My Tho ☎ 073-3874696 🕐 Daily 6am–9pm 🍽 L 65,000đ, D 100,000đ

PHU QUOC
ALANIS COFFEE DELI
Easy to find, as it's on the main road into Duong Dong, this immaculately clean deli is deservedly popular with travelers who appreciate a good coffee, an iced peppermint tea or a smoothie, while tucking into delicious cakes and sandwiches in air-conditioned comfort. Ideal for a light meal; the

proprietors, who double up as the staff, are friendly and informative.
✉ 98 Tran Hung Dao Street, Phu Quoc ☎ 077-3994931 🕐 Daily 8am–7pm 🍽 L 65,000đ

TROPICANA RESORT RESTAURANT
Tropicana is one of the island's best restaurants with a sunny terrace and a well-stocked, semi-enclosed bar, allowing relaxed alfresco dining overlooking the sea. From the list of Vietnamese and European favorites, enjoy succulent stir-fried squid, braised shrimps in coconut milk, Italian spaghetti dishes or a range of other alternatives from the set menus. The restaurant, which is next to the pool, also offers covered dining.
✉ Duong Dong, Phu Quoc ☎ 077-3847127 🕐 Daily 6.30am–10pm 🍽 L 100,000đ, D 160,000đ, Wine 300,000đ

VUNG TAU
CAY BANG
Vung Tau's most celebrated seafood restaurant is well worth the detour of 2 miles (3km) northwest from Bai Truoc and the middle of town. People will travel for many miles just to eat here, and it is usually packed on Sundays and very busy during the rest of the week. Crab, squid and fish specialties are served in a rough and ready setting overlooking the sea.
✉ 69 Tran Phu Street, Bai Dau Beach ☎ 064-3838522 🕐 Daily 10am–9pm 🍽 L 130,000đ, D 175,000đ

TOMMY'S
www.tommysvietnam.com
Tommy's restaurant and bar, run by Australian Glen and his wife Trang, has long been a favorite spot with visitors—and now there is a second restaurant. Come here for burgers and steaks and a friendly, hospitable atmosphere. The bar is the place to go for major sporting events on television.
✉ 03 Bacu Street, Vung Tau ☎ 064-3515181 ✉ 94 Ha Long Street ☎ 064-3853554 🕐 Daily 8am–11pm 🍽 L 100,000đ, D 200,000đ, Wine 200,000đ

PRICES AND SYMBOLS

The prices are for a double room for one night including breakfast, unless otherwise stated. All the hotels listed accept credit cards unless otherwise stated. Note that rates can vary widely throughout the year.

For a key to the symbols, ▷ 2.

CAN THO

GOLF CAN THO HOTEL

www.vinagolf.vn

Although the Golf Can Tho Hotel is the tallest in town, lacks for nothing in facilities and is excellent value, it possesses little charm. Rooms are large, plainly decorated and well equipped with minibars, safe-deposit boxes, phones, cable TVs and balconies overlooking the river. The restaurants provide fine dining, and the views from the Windy Restaurant on the ninth floor are superb. Other facilities include a massage center with sauna and steam bath, a karaoke bar, nightclub, beauty parlor and car rental and laundry services.

✉ 2 Hai Ba Trung Street, Can Tho ☎ 071-3812210 🖐 US$115–$130, including taxes ⓘ 101 🍴 📶 ♿

HOA BINH HOTEL

This is a comfortable, quiet, budget hotel, just 10 minutes' walk from the riverside promenade, next to a bank with an ATM machine and around the corner from an excellent bakery. Rooms are simply furnished and could do with updating, but at this price represent good value as they all have air conditioning, fans, spacious bathrooms with piping-hot water and limited satellite TV.

✉ 5 Hoa Binh Avenue, Can Tho ☎ 071-3820536 🖐 US$32–$50, including taxes ⓘ 56 ♿

SAIGON CAN THO

www.saigoncantho.com.vn

In this comfortable, central business hotel run by Saigontourist, standard rooms have balconies, and the larger rooms have desks as well; all have cable TV with in-house movies, a minibar and phone, and guests receive complimentary fruit and a welcome drink on arrival, and free mineral water every day. The restaurant is open 24 hours. A small sauna, massage and steam-bath area is laid out in small cabins; massages are discounted by 10 percent for hotel residents.

✉ 55 Phan Dinh Phung Street, Can Tho ☎ 071-3825831 🖐 US$38–$62, excluding taxes ⓘ 46 ♿

VICTORIA CAN THO

www.victoriahotels-asia.com

One of the most beautiful hotels in Vietnam has a riverside garden location, a breezy, open reception area, and an emphasis on comfort. The focal point is the floodlit pool, flanked by the lobby bar

Above *Saigon-Phu Quoc Resort*

and restaurant. Elegant rooms are equipped with coffee- and tea-makers, a minibar, safe-deposit box, phone and cable TV. Guests staying in suites receive rice, rice wine, pineapple and dragonfruit jam and incense sticks. Other facilities include a tennis court and massages, plus baby-sitting and laundry services. The *Lady Hau*, a remodeled rice barge, runs sunrise and sunset cruises (▷ 234). A shuttle usually takes guests from the Ninh Kieu jetty on Hai Ba Trung Street in town to the little peninsula on the banks of the Hau River. The hotel can arrange transport to and from Saigon and the airport.

✉ Cai Khe Ward, Can Tho ☎ 071-3810111 ✋ From US$147, excluding taxes ❶ 92 🏊 📺 🌀

CHAU DOC
CHAU PHO
Although not situated in the town center, this is a comfortable hotel with good room facilities: fridge, satellite TV, telephone, room safe, iron and ironing board.

✉ Trung Nu Vuong Street, Chau Doc ☎ 076-3564139 ✋ US$32–$50, including taxes ❶ 38 🌀

TRUNG NGUYEN
www.trungnguyenhotel.com.vn
A short walk from the bus station, the bedrooms in this friendly, budget hotel are small but clean and well maintained; some have balconies overlooking the busy market (which starts very early in the morning). This is good value for the money.

✉ 86 Bach Dang Street, Chau Doc ☎ 076-3561561 ✋ US$20, including taxes ❶ 15 🌀

VICTORIA CHAU DOC
This old, cream building with its riverfront pool is the perfect place in which to relax and look out over the busy, three-way Mekong intersection on which the hotel sits. The best room is the junior suite, whose balcony faces the tributary heading to Phnom Penh. Solid-wood lampstands, desks, gold-

colored curtains and champagne in the minibars are added extras; cable TV and in-house movies are standard. Superior rooms are just as attractive as the suites but smaller; some rooms have showers but no bathtubs. Oscar, the white-faced gibbon rescued from a Saigon animal market, plays with guests in the grounds, and the hotel offers baby-sitting, laundry, sauna and massage services. The Victoria Group runs a speedboat from Saigon to Can Tho, from Can Tho to Chau Doc and on to Phnom Penh.

✉ 32 Le Loi Street, Chau Doc ☎ 076-3865010 ✋ From US$125, excluding taxes ❶ 92 🏊 📺 🌀

CON DAO
SAIGON CONDAO HOTEL
www.saigoncondao.com
The Saigon Condao Hotel is a Saigontourist property in converted French buildings on the Con Dao waterfront. The seven villas with a total of 36 rooms overlook the sea in tropical, landscaped gardens. Facilities include sauna, massage, tennis courts and karaoke. All rooms have satellite TV, in-house movies, a minibar and phone, and the hotel provides same-day laundry, car rental, and a tour and travel desk. The restaurant serves international, Asian and seafood specialties.

✉ 18 Ton Duc Thang Street, Con Dao ☎ 064-3830155/3830345 ✋ US$50–$85, including taxes ❶ 36 📺 🌀

HA TIEN
HA TIEN
This is the most comfortable hotel in Ha Tien which has an attractive restaurant. The bedrooms come with a mini bar, separate shower and bath as well as telephone, and there is also a sauna and steam room; massages can be booked.

✉ 36 Tran Hau Street, Ha Tien ☎ 077-3851563 ✋ US$25–$50, including taxes ❶ 32 🌀

TO CHAU
The views are the main attraction of this small hotel on the riverfront. Rooms are very large but very

spartan, though they all have air-conditioning, TV, minibar and private bathroom with hot water. The best rooms are those with a view of the To Chau River, as these have balconies. The friendly owner and his family speak a little English.

✉ 56 Dong Ho Street, Ha Tien ☎ 077-3852148 ✋ US$12–$25, including taxes ❶ 11 🌀

HON CHONG PENINSULA
GREEN HILL GUESTHOUSE
Just above Duong Beach, perched on a hill, this all-white guesthouse is the friendliest, most pleasant place to stay on the peninsula. Run by the welcoming, English-speaking owner, Tuyen, the building is enhanced by lush bougainvillea. All rooms have a private bathroom with tub and hot water. Some of the top-of-the-range rooms have balconies, and all enjoy panoramic views of the bay. Three deluxe rooms can accommodate up to four people. Vietnamese meals are cooked by Tuyen's wife in the restaurant (open 6am–midnight), and he serves great milky coffee.

✉ 905 Hon Chong, Binh An ☎ 077-3854369 ✋ US$25–$40, excluding breakfast; no taxes ❶ 9 rooms 🌀

MY LAN
The large, clean rooms in this secure, gated hotel on the beach road are excellent value for money. Housed in smart, new cabins, they have ultra-clean, white-tiled floors, TVs and ceiling fans, as well as air-conditioning, shower units and suitcase holders. The open-fronted, 24-hour restaurant serves a good breakfast; its menu is in Vietnamese only, but some staff speak basic English. Dinner options include fried squid, fried rice with shrimp and crab soup.

✉ Opposite Duong Beach, Hon Chong ☎ 077-3759044 ✋ US$20–$30, including taxes ❶ 24 🌀

LONG HAI
ANOASIS BEACH RESORT
www.anoasisresort.com.vn
Scenically, this is one of the most

appealing of all Vietnam's resorts, set in 32 acres (13ha) of tropical trees and unspoiled vegetation, with views of the mountains and the ocean. It belonged to the last emperor of Vietnam. Cabins are scattered through a parkland setting with wide views over the sea. Rooms are attractively finished, and everything is on a generous scale, with baths big enough for two, and comfortable and attractive furnishings. Phones, cable TV, minibars and balconies or decks are standard. There's a good restaurant (although it's not especially good value for the money), a gigantic pool, a private beach, tennis courts, massage and a jetty, and the resort provides airport transfers and a laundry service. To reach Anoasis, you can take a *xe ôm* from Ba Ria or the Vung Tau hydrofoil and then taxi or motorcycle.

✉ 2 miles (3km) east of Long Hai ☎ 064-3868227 ✋ From US$85, excluding taxes ⓘ 15 cottage cabins, 12 family cabins, 17 pavilion rooms, 2 ocean villas ⌇ ◈

MY THO
CHUONG DUONG

By far the best hotel in town, the Chuong Duong is a large hotel occupying a prime riverside location in front of the erstwhile hydrofoil ferry. All rooms overlook the river and are decorated in beige and diluted orange, and all have a private bathroom, satellite TV and minibar. The in-house restaurant has a long menu including Mekong specialties such as stir-fried sea cucumber with Chinese mushrooms, plus a range of Euro-Asian, Chinese and Vietnamese dishes; some of its tables overlook the river.

✉ 10 30 Thang 4 Street, My Tho ☎ 073-3870875 ✋ US$33–$42, including taxes ⓘ 27 ◈

PHU QUOC
KIM HOA RESORT

This small resort has wooden bungalows on a clean strip of sand, each with one double and one single bed. The bathrooms have showers without units. There are also more basic rooms that are not on the beach, but which have small bathrooms. Standard in-room amenities are refrigerators, satellite TV and phones. The resort has a restaurant specializing in seafood dishes, and can arrange fishing, snorkeling and sightseeing trips, as well as car and motorcycle rental. Free pickup is available from the airport.

✉ Khu Pho I, Duong Dong ☎ 077-3848969 ✋ US$30–$47, including taxes ⓘ 56 ◈ Some rooms

MANGO BAY

www.mangobayphuquoc.com
This welcoming, Australian-owned resort has a number of different bungalows and rooms, a beachfront restaurant serving fresh seafood and Vietnamese and Western dishes, and a beach bar. There are eight rammed-earth bungalows with fans, tiled floors and bamboo furniture, and three traditional Phu Quoc fishermen's bungalows. The five rooms have a wonderful, large communal veranda. Some rooms have outdoor bathrooms in bamboo-enclosed patios. The resort can arrange night squid-fishing, a free small boat, swimming and snorkeling equipment, fishing trips, car and motorcycle rental, and pays 50 percent of the taxi fare from the airport, or the full fare for a moto taxi.

✉ On Lang Beach, Phu Quoc ☎ 0903-7382207 ✋ From US$65, excluding breakfast, including taxes ⓘ 31

SAIGON-PHU QUOC RESORT

www.sgphuquocresort.com.vn
Overlooking the sea on a hillside garden, cabins and villas surround an attractive swimming pool in this pleasant resort. All rooms have satellite TV, phone, minibar, private bathroom with tub or shower and safe-deposit box. The costlier President Suite has two TVs, a computer, a kitchenette and a Jacuzzi; the VIP is less expensive, brighter and better, with a sea view and bathtub. An enviable list of facilities includes a reasonably priced restaurant serving international food, Internet access, play equipment, a beauty salon, motorcycle rental, fishing, tennis, massage, snorkeling, horseback riding and bicycling. Baby-sitting and laundry services are available. A shop in the lobby sells clothes and crafts. Airport transfers are included in the price. One cabin is equipped for guests with disabilities.

✉ 1 Trang Hung Dao Street, Duong Dong, Phu Quoc ☎ 077-3846999 ✋ US$129–$389, excluding taxes ⓘ 90 ⌇ ◈

SASCO BLUE LAGOON RESORT

www.sasco-bluelagoon-resort.com
The medium-priced Blue Lagoon offers comfortable bedrooms in a modern resort (it opened in 2006) situated close to a pleasant stretch of beach, which is kept clean by hotel staff. The best accommodations are in the sea-facing villas, although the rooms in the main building are fine for a short stay. There is a well-maintained garden area, a decent-size swimming pool and helpful staff. Reservations must be paid in advance for the whole period of the booking.

✉ 64 Tran Hung Dao Street, Duong Dong, Phu Quoc ☎ 077-3994499 ✋ From US$65, including taxes ⓘ 75 ⌇ ◈

TROPICANA RESORT

Here you'll find high-quality wooden cabins and rooms in a tropical garden next to the beach. There is a pool and a good restaurant. Cabins have terraces with seating, large glass doors, rustic wooden fittings, mosquito nets and good hot showers. No boat tours are offered, but one-day motorcycle rental is available at 100,000d; for 400,000d you can rent a four-wheel drive with driver. Two-way airport transfer is available free; travel from the port is 200,000d.

✉ Duong Dong, Phu Quoc ☎ 077-3847127 ✋ US$40–$50, including taxes ⓘ 35 ⌇ ◈

VINH LONG
CUU LONG

Set back from the Tien river with a huge, green, glass-fronted facade, the Cuu Long is well maintained and its comfortable, carpeted rooms all have private bathrooms, with tubs and showers, and a balcony. There is a large restaurant, WiFi connections and a travel service (Cuu Long Tourist), and massage and tennis courts are available. The hotel is in a convenient spot, opposite the wharf where boats leave for An Binh Island.

✉ 1 1 Thang 5 Street, Vinh Long ☎ 070-3823616 ✋ US$48–$52, including taxes ① 34 💲

MEKONG HOMESTAYS

www.cuulongtourist.com
Facing Vinh Long town in the Co Chien River, a tributary of the Mekong, is a large island that is further sliced into smaller islands by ribbons of narrow canals. Cuu

Below *Enjoying the sea at Phu Quoc Island*

Long Tourist runs homestays on one of these islands, An Binh—a wonderful way to immerse yourself in local life. The accommodations are basic, with camp beds, shared bathrooms and mosquito nets, and include a home-cooked dinner made from the fruits of the delta (elephant-ear fish with abundant greens, including mint, spring rolls, and beef cooked in coconut). Evening drinks are taken on the patio or terrace or on the riverfront, chatting with the owner. Travel is by sampan or on foot down the winding paths that link the communities. The packages, either two days/one night or three days/two nights, include bicycle rides through the countryside and visits to villages to see local cottage industries and daily agricultural life. The boat trip, transfers, dinner and local guide are all included in the price.

✉ Cuu Long Tourist, 1 Thang 5 Street, Vinh Long ☎ 070-3823616 ✋ US$54–$65, including one breakfast ① 11 homestays

VUNG TAU
GRAND HOTEL

www.grandhotel.com.vn
An excellent restoration project has brought this hotel, in a great position overlooking the sea, back to its former glory, without affecting its general look. Rooms are comfortable and clean, and all have satellite TV, safe-deposit box, phone, minibar, tea- and coffee-making facilities, Internet access and private bathroom. The more expensive rooms have welcome extras such as complimentary fruit, flowers and mineral water, and free use of the swimming pool and fitness center. The 350-seat restaurant serves Asian and European dishes, or you can relax over a drink in the lounge bar or on the terrace. Other hotel services include tennis courts, a steam bath, massages, laundry, dry-cleaning services and car rental.

✉ 2 Nguyen Du Street, Vung Tau ☎ 064-3856888 ✋ US$90–$95, excluding taxes ① 59 🏊 🍸 💲

PALACE

www.palacehotel.com.vn

This renovated and expanded hotel, just a few minutes' walk from Bai Truoc (Front Beach) and close to popular bars and restaurants, offers comfortable rooms and efficient service. Rooms have a minibar, phone and cable TV, and there is an attractive swimming pool under the shade of a tamarind tree. A gym, massage facilities and a tennis court are available, and the restaurant serves European and Asian dishes and seafood.

11 Nguyen Trai Street, Vung Tau 064-3856411 From US$90, including taxes 94

PETRO HOUSE

www.petrohouse-vungtau.com

Central, comfortable and decorated in colonial style, this boutique hotel has full amenities, including a swimming pool, a business center, a casino and Ma Maison, a good French restaurant. Rooms have cable TV and phones. Though not on the beach, this is one of the most popular choices in town.

63 Tran Hung Dao Street, Vung Tau 064-3852014 US$52–$60, including taxes 75

REX HOTEL

www.rexhotelvungtau.com.vn

Nicely positioned opposite the beach and with an outdoor pool, as well as a tennis court and a small gym, this is a good place to stay in Vung Tau. Rooms have either sea views or face the city. The service is reliable and staff are helpful.

91 Le Quy Don, Vung Tau 064-3852135 US$52–$60, including taxes 75

ROYAL HOTEL

The Royal occupies a prime seafront site facing Bai Truoc (Front Beach), and some of its rooms have spectacular views. The decoration is slightly old-fashioned, but all rooms have a private bathroom with tub, minibar, safe-deposit box, phone, satellite TV and in-house movies. The pool is shared with the adjoining Rex Hotel, and there is a seafood restaurant, a Japanese restaurant, car rental and airline reservation desk. The hotel can arrange tours of Vung Tau.

36 Quang Trung Street, Vung Tau 064-3859852 US$48–$60, including taxes 53

Above *Petro House hotel where amenities include the Monte Carlo casino*

SAMMY

www.sammyhotelvt.com

Easily the best hotel along the Back Beach (Bai Sau), Sammy is a large and very comfortable place, somewhat glitzy and known for its efficient service, good views, business facilities and its highly recommended Chinese restaurant. Rooms have a minibar, safe-deposit box and cable TV, and there's a beauty salon, nightclub, massages and sauna, and a laundry service. Customers also have use of the Ocean Park swimming pool, opposite, at reduced prices.

157 Thuy Van Street, Bai Sau (Back Beach), Vung Tau 064-3854755 US$40–$50; US$57 sea view (less on weekdays), excluding breakfast, including taxes 119 (nonsmoking on request)

SON THUY RESORT

The beach is within walking distance of the hotel and the resort has its own pool and tennis court. Accommodation is in the form of groups of bungalows, set back from the road, and families are especially welcome here.

165C Thuy Van Street, Vung Tau 064-3523460 US$38–$75, including taxes 40

PRACTICALITIES

Practicalities gives you all the important practical information you will need during your visit from money matters to emergency phone numbers.

PRACTICALITIES VIETNAM

TIME ZONES

Vietnam is 7 hours ahead of Greenwich Mean Time, 12 hours ahead of New York and 15 hours ahead of Los Angeles.

CITY	TIME DIFFERENCE	TIME AT 12 NOON VIETNAM
Amsterdam	-6	6am
Auckland	+3	3pm
Bangkok	0	12 noon
Berlin	-6	6am
Brussels	-6	6am
Chicago	-13	11pm*
Dublin	-7	5am
Johannesburg	-5	7am
London	-7	5am
Madrid	-6	6am
Montréal	-12	12 midnight*
New York	-12	12 midnight*
Paris	-6	6am
Perth, Australia	+1	1pm
Rome	-6	6am
San Francisco	-15	9pm*
Sydney	+3	3pm
Tokyo	+2	2pm

* = the previous day

WEATHER
CLIMATE

» Vietnam stretches more than 1,118 miles (1,800km) from north to south, and the weather in the two principal cities, Hanoi in the north and Saigon in the south, is very different. Average temperatures tend to rise the farther south you go. The exceptions to this rule are the interior highland areas, where the altitude makes it much colder.

» **In the north**, winter is November through April, with temperatures averaging 61°F (16°C), and little rainfall. The summer runs May until October. It can be very hot, with an average temperature of 86°F (30°C), along with heavy rainfall and the occasional typhoon.

» **Central Vietnam** has a transitional climate, midway in the country. Huê has a reputation for particularly poor weather; it is often overcast, and an umbrella is needed whatever the month—even during the short "dry" season between February and April.

» **In the south**, temperatures are fairly constant all year—77°F (25°C) to 86°F (30°C)—and the seasons are determined by the rains. The dry season runs from November through April (when there is virtually no rain whatsoever) and the wet season from May through October. The hottest months are March and April, before the rains have broken. Typhoons are common in coastal areas between July and November.

» **In the hill resorts** of Dalat, Buon Me Thuot and Sapa, nights are cool throughout the year, and in the "winter" months, between October and March, it can be distinctly chilly, with temperatures falling to 39°F (4°C). Even in the hottest months of March and April, the temperature rarely exceeds 79°F (26°C).

WHEN TO GO

» Climatically, the best time to visit Vietnam is from December through March, when it should be dry and not too hot. In the south, days are warm and evenings are cool. The north and highlands are chilly, but should be dry, with clear blue skies.

» The visitor industry's busiest season is November through May, when hotel prices rise and reserving flights can be a problem.

» Travel in the south and the Mekong Delta can be difficult at the height of the monsoon season (particularly September, October and November).

» The central regions and north sometimes suffer typhoons and tropical storms from May through November. Huê is at its wettest from September to January.

DOCUMENTS
CUSTOMS AND DUTY-FREE

» Visitors can bring unlimited foreign currency but it must be declared on their customs forms.

» The duty-free allowance is 100 cigarettes, 400 cigars or 1.76oz (50g) of tobacco, 50fl oz (1.5 liters) of spirits, perfume and jewelry for personal use, and personal gifts for friends and relations.

» All luggage entering (and leaving) Vietnam is X-rayed.

» You may not import weapons, illicit drugs, pornographic material, anti-government literature, photographs or movies, or culturally unsuitable children's toys.

» Export of wood products or antiques (anything that appears to be more than 20 years old) is forbidden. If the product you have bought is antique, or looks antique, it may require an export permit from customs (General Department of Customs, 162 Nguyen Van Cu Street, tel 04-48727033; www.customs.gov.vn).

VISAS

» Valid passports with visas issued by a Vietnamese embassy are required by all visitors, irrespective of citizenship. Citizens of Thailand, Philippines, Malaysia, Singapore and Indonesia receive a free 30-day visa upon arrival. Japanese passport holders will get a free 15-day visa upon arrival. Time needed to process a visa varies from country to country and according to the type of visa required.

» Visa regulations are ever changing, so check well before you are due to travel. Usually it is possible to extend visas within Vietnam but not during Party Congresses. Check your visa carefully: Any incorrect details

HANOI
TEMPERATURE

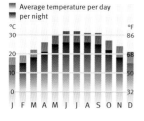

RAINFALL

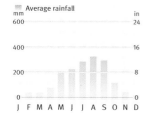

HO CHI MINH CITY
TEMPERATURE

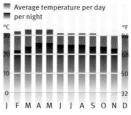

RAINFALL

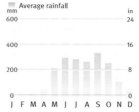

HUÊ
TEMPERATURE

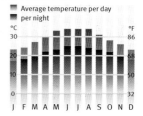

RAINFALL

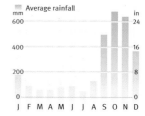

WEATHER WEBSITES		
ORGANIZATION	**NOTES**	**WEBSITE**
AccuWeather.com	A simple but effective weather site with five-day forecasts for 800 cities worldwide.	www.accuweather.com
The Weather Channel	Key in Ho Chi Minh City or Hanoi for a five-day forecast.	www.weather.com
	Note the heat index—although the temperature may be 92°F (33°C),	
	it might actually feel much hotter.	

will be noticed by the sharp-eyed immigration officers.

» Tourist visas (US$45) generally take five to seven days. Travel agencies will probably add their own mark-up, but you may find it worth paying to avoid one or two journeys to an embassy.

» Visas are also available on arrival in Vietnam but they need to be applied for before you leave your home country. Several online agencies (www.myvietnamvisa. com, for example) will arrange this, for a fee of around US$20 (you can pay using PayPal and avoid giving a credit card number), and you will be emailed a letter of authorization, which needs to be shown at the airport before boarding your plane. When you arrive in Vietnam head for a Visa On Arrival Desk, not the normal immigration line, and your entry visa will be stamped in your passport. You can then join the normal immigration line. It shoul dbe said that your Vietnamese embassy is unlikely to approve of this procedure; many travelers feel more secure having a visa stamped in their passport before they travel.

» If you plan to stay for a while, or make a trip to Laos or Cambodia and then return to Vietnam, a multiple-entry visa will make life much simpler.

» Visas are normally valid only for arrival by air, at Noi Bai (Hanoi), Tan Son Nhat (Saigon) and Danang International Airport.

» The standard tourist visa is valid for one month for one entry (mot lan) only. For a fee, you can extend it for one month at tour operators. Your hotel may also do it for you for a small extra charge. Some agencies say it takes one to three days; others say it takes a week.

» A visa valid for one month can usually be extended only for one month. A further one-month extension may be possible.

» Those wishing to enter or leave Vietnam by land must specify the border crossing when applying. It is possible to alter the point of departure at immigration offices in Hanoi and Saigon.

» Business visas are valid for three months (US$60) or six months (US$110) and usually enable multiple entry (nhieu lan). It costs US$85 for a three-month multiple-entry visa extension and US$140 for a six-month extension.

WORKING IN VIETNAM

» Officially, anyone working in Vietnam should have a business visa and a work permit. In practice, however, authorities take a fairly relaxed view of foreigners working in Vietnam for short periods. Those with specific skills, notably computer skills and English-language teaching, will not find it hard to get work—but you need relevant qualifications.

» If you plan to work in Vietnam, contact your embassy, which will

be able to provide the most up-to-date information.

» www.ukti.gov.uk/export is a British government agency dealing with developing business in different countries. It provides free up-to-date information.

» www.business-in-asia.com has some excellent information about working in Vietnam or investing in businesses there.

» Voluntary work is best organized in advance through agencies such as Voluntary Service Overseas, www.vso.org.uk. People with specific skills, and those available for four months or more, are of greatest use.

» The first port of call for further information should be the NGO Resource Centre, La Thanh Hotel, 218 Doi Can, Hanoi, tel 04-38328570, fax 04-38328611; www.ngocentre.org.vn.

TRAVEL INSURANCE

» Insurance is crucial and should cover you in case of theft, loss of possessions or money (often including cash), the cost of medical and dental treatment, cancellation of flights, delays in travel arrangements, accidents, missed departures, lost baggage, lost passport, personal liability and legal expenses.

» Check the small print; some policies exclude "dangerous activities" such as scuba diving, horseback riding or even trekking.

EMBASSIES IN VIETNAM

COUNTRY	ADDRESS	TELEPHONE AND WEBSITE
Australia	8 Dao Tan Street, Hanoi	tel 04-37740100 www.vietnamembassy.gov.au
	Landmark Building, 5B Ton Duc Thang Street, Ho Chi Minh City	tel 08-32518100
Canada	31 Hung Vuong Street, Hanoi	tel 04-37345000
	The Metropolitan, 235 Dong Khoi Street, Ho Chi Minh City	tel 08-38279899
France	57 Tran Hung Dao Street, Hanoi	tel 04-39445700
	27 Nguyen Thi Minh Khai Street, Ho Chi Minh City	tel 08-35206800; www.ambafrance-vn.org
New Zealand	63 Ly Thai To Street, Hanoi	tel 04-38241481 www.nzembassy.com/viet-nam
United Kingdom	Central Building, 31 Hai Ba Trung Street, Hanoi www.ukinvietnam.fco.gov.uk	tel 04-39360500;
United States	7 Lang Ha Street, Hanoi	tel 38505000; http://vietnam.usembassy.gov

VIETNAM EMBASSIES AND CONSULATES ABROAD

COUNTRY	ADDRESS	WEBSITE
Australia	6 Timbarra Crescent, O'Malley, Canberra, ACT 2606, tel 0061 2-6286846	www.vietnamembassy.org.au
	Vietnam General Consulate, Suite 205, Level 2 Edgecliff Centre, New South Head Road, Double Bay, Sydney, NSW 2008, tel 0061 2-9327 2539/0061 2 9327 1912	www.vietnamconsulate.org.au
Canada	470 Wilbrod Street, Ottawa, Ontario K1N 6M8, tel 001 613-2360772	www.vietnamembassy-canada.ca
France	62–66 rue Boileau, 75016 Paris, tel 0033 1-4414640	http://embassyvietnam.org/ embassy-of-vietnam-in-paris
Hong Kong	15/F Great Smart Tower, 230 Wan Chai Road, Wan Chai, tel 00852 25914517	www.vietnamconsulate-hongkong.org
South Africa	87 Brooks Street, Brooklyn, PO Box 13692, Hatfield 0028, Pretoria, tel 0027 12 3628119	www.vietnamembassy-southafrica.org
United Kingdom	12–14 Victoria Road, London W8 5RD, tel 0044 20 7937 1912	www.vietnamembassy.org.uk
United States	1233 20th Street, NW Suite 400, Washington, DC 20036, tel 001 202/861-07377	www.vietnamembassy-usa.org/
	Consulate General of Vietnam, 1700 California Street, Suite 430, San Francisco, CA 94109, tel 001 415/922-1577	

» Not all policies cover ambulance, helicopter rescue or emergency flights home.

» Find out whether your policy pays medical expenses direct to the hospital or doctor, or whether you have to pay and then claim the money back later. If the latter applies, keep all records.

» If you have something stolen, make sure you get a copy of the police report, as you will need this to substantiate your claim.

WHAT TO TAKE

» Items such as light shirts and shorts can be bought cheaply in Vietnam, but good-quality underwear and socks cannot. Inexpensive shoes are also available, as are bags for extra purchases.

» Take long-sleeved shirts for cool evenings, severely air-conditioned restaurants and to prevent sunburn.

» Long trousers and socks deter mosquitoes in the evening.

» Warm clothing is necessary for upland areas in winter.

» Women may prefer dresses rather than jeans when traveling, for easier access to squat toilets.

» Bring good walking boots, especially if traveling to the Central Highlands and northern Vietnam.

» Bring any prescription drugs needed and bring your own supply of sanitary products.

» Earplugs are useful to combat the high noise levels in the cities.

» Other useful items include passport photographs, a small first-aid kit, a flashlight, insect repellent, photocopies of your passport and visa, a strong padlock to lock bags in hotel rooms, and a money belt.

» Bring sunscreen because a good brand is likely to cost just as much, if not more, in Vietnam, and local brands are likely to be inferior.

» Batteries are widely available, but memory cards are sold only in larger cities. Bring a universal adapter.

WHAT NOT TO TAKE

» Bottled water is widely available. You will only need water filters if trekking in remote areas.

Below *Don't forget to take your camera*

MONEY

CASH

» The unit of currency is the dong.
» Bills in circulation are in denominations of 500, 1,000, 2,000, 5,000, 10,000, 20,000, 50,000, 100,000, 200,000 and 500,000 dong. Coins of 200, 500, 1,000, 2,000 and 5,000d are also in circulation.
» The 500,000 bills are now made of polymer to make them more durable and less easily counterfeited. They also have diamond markings to enable people with visual impairments to distinguish between them.
» Check the exchange rate closer to the time of your visit as rates can vary. The exchange rate at the time of writing was (approximately) US$1 = 20,000d; £1 = 33,000d.
» You cannot bring dong into the country, so take US dollars and/or travelers' checks and convert them when you are in Vietnam. You should also take at least one credit/debit card to use at an ATM.
» Any amount of foreign currency can be taken into or out of Vietnam, although amounts of more than US$3,000 must be declared on the customs form.
» Do not take dong out of the country—it is illegal and the cash cannot be converted overseas.
» It is quite difficult to convert dong back into US dollars even inside Vietnam.
» By law, shops should accept only dong, but in practice this is not enforced and dollars are accepted almost everywhere.
» ATMs are plentiful in Saigon and Hanoi and can also be found in other major visitor centers.
» Many of the larger hotels have ATMs installed.
» It is best to travel with US dollars as a backup. Clean (that is, unmarked) US$100 bills receive

Above *Bundles of Vietnamese dong at a bank*
Opposite *A Vietcombank ATM*

the best rates. Bills that are dirty or slightly marked will be politely but firmly returned.
» Small US$ bills receive slightly lower rates.
» US$ can be changed in banks, in larger hotels and in gold or jewelry shops.
» Do not change money in the street or if approached by strangers.
» The best rates are offered by the banks (Vietcombank, in particular, offers good rates).
» Banks in the main towns also change other major currencies,

10 EVERYDAY ITEMS AND HOW MUCH THEY COST	
Pizza	50,000d
Western breakfast	From 40,000d
Imported beer	25,000d
Local beer	8,000d
Bowl of pho	20,000d
Local coffee/cappuccino	13,000d/40,000d
Motorcycle taxi	10,000d
Car taxi	From 30,000d
Internet access	From 4,000d per hour
Preloaded SIM card	From 50,000

including sterling, HK$, Thai baht, Swiss francs, euros, A$, S$, CAN$ and yen.

» Try to pay for everything in dong, not in US$. Prices are usually lower in dong, and in remote areas people may be unaware of the latest exchange rate. Also, to most Vietnamese 15,000d is a lot of money, while US$1 means nothing.

» VAT (IVA) of 10 percent and sales tax of 5 percent are added to some hotel and restaurant bills. These are non-refundable.

» www.oanda.com/converter/classic enables you to select a currency and convert it.

CREDIT CARDS

» These are increasingly widely accepted. Major credit cards taken are Visa, MasterCard, Amex and JCB.

» Large hotels, expensive restaurants and medical clinics invariably take credit cards, but there may be a surcharge of between 2.5 and 4.5 percent, depending upon the card that you use (Visa and MasterCard: 3 percent; Amex: 4.5 percent).

TRAVELERS' CHECKS

» Travelers' checks are best denominated in US$ and can be cashed only in banks in the major towns. A commission of 2 to 4 percent is payable if cashing into dollars, but not if you are converting them direct to dong. When cashing travelers' checks, take proof of purchase and your passport to the bank.

TIPPING

» Tipping varies widely. Vietnamese do not normally tip if eating in small family restaurants but may tip extravagantly in expensive bars. Foreigners normally leave the small change, and this is perfectly acceptable and appreciated. Big hotels and some restaurants add a 5 to 10 percent service charge and the government tax of 10 percent to the bill.

WIRING MONEY

» Western Union has hundreds of outlets in Vietnam, with transfers available in dong or dollars. The principal agents are Asia Commercial Bank, Vietinbank and Vietnam Bank for Agriculture, and they are open during normal Monday to Friday banking hours. The offices for Saigon, Hanoi and Huê are as follows:

Agribank
26–8 Cua Dong, Hoan Kiew District, Hanoi
Tel 04-39233220
Open Mon–Fri 7.30–4.30

Vietinbank
165–9 Ham Nghi Street, Nguyen Thai Binh, District 1, Ho Chi Minh City
Tel 08-38210089
Open Mon–Fri 8–4.30

Vietinbank
2 Le Quy Donst, Hue
Tel 054-3825102
Open Mon–Fri 8–4.30

PRACTICALITIES ESSENTIAL INFORMATION

HEALTH

» Health care in Vietnam varies, with some very good private and government clinics and hospitals. There are Western hospitals in Hanoi and Saigon (▷ 252).
» You should see your doctor or travel clinic at least six weeks before your departure for general advice on travel risks, malaria and vaccinations.
» Make sure you have travel insurance, get a dental check, and know your blood group. If you suffer a long-term medical condition, such as diabetes or epilepsy, make sure someone knows or that you have a Medic Alert bracelet giving this information.
» Wear a shirt and hat and put on plenty of sunscreen.

MALARIA

» Vietnam is a high-risk country.
» Symptoms can resemble an attack of influenza; you may feel lethargic and have a headache. In the worst cases, fits are followed by coma and death.
» All clinics in Vietnam can test for malaria quickly and reliably. If you come down with a fever, get tested as quickly as possible.

Below Hitching a ride

» Malaria exists in rural areas, but there is no risk in the Red River Delta, the coastal plains north of Nha Trang, Hanoi, Saigon, Danang, Nha Trang, Quy Nhon or Haiphong. But always check the latest advice before you travel and be careful as late changes to your itinerary may take you outside "safe" areas.
» Treatment is with drugs and may be oral or intravenous, depending on the seriousness of the infection.
» Remember ABCD: awareness (of whether the disease is present in your area), bite avoidance, chemoprophylaxis (use of chemicals to prevent disease), diagnosis.
» Prevention is best summarized as B and C: bite avoidance and chemoprophylaxis. Wear clothes that cover arms and legs and use insect repellents. Use a mosquito net dipped in permethrin as both a physical and chemical barrier at night.
» Guard against malaria with the correct anti-malarials. Specialist advice is required as to which type to take; Malarone, Lariam (mefloquine) and doxycycline are available.

DENGUE FEVER

» Dengue fever is transmitted by mosquitoes that bite during the day, and can be contracted throughout Vietnam.
» It can cause a severe, flu-like illness, with fever, enlarged lymph glands, lethargy and muscle

pains. Two or three days' illness are followed by a short period of recovery, then a second attack.
» Local children are prone to the much nastier hemorrhagic form of the disease, but this is rarely contracted by Westerners.
» The traveler's version of the disease is usually self-limiting and requires only rest and recuperation.
» Mosquito repellent should be applied and limbs covered 24 hours a day.
» Check your accommodations for flowerpots and shallow pools of water, as these are where the dengue-carrying mosquitoes breed.

MOSQUITO REPELLENTS

» DEET (Di-ethyltoluamide) is the gold standard. Apply the repellent every four to six hours but more often if you are sweating heavily.
» If a non-DEET product is used, check who tested it. Validated products (tested at the London School of Hygiene and Tropical Medicine and the Centers for Disease Control and Prevention in Atlanta; www.cdc.gov) include Mosiguard, non-DEET Jungle Formula and non-DEET Autan.
» Citronella must be applied very frequently (hourly) to be effective.
» If you are a popular target for insect bites or develop lumps quite soon after being bitten, carry an Aspivenin kit. This pump suction device is available from many pharmacists and draws out some

VACCINATION CHART	
VACCINATION	RECOMMENDED
Polio	Yes, if none in last 10 years.
Tetanus	Yes, if none in last 10 years (five doses are enough for life).
Typhoid	Yes, if none in last three years.
Yellow fever	The disease does not exist in Vietnam. However, the authorities may wish to see a certificate if you have recently arrived from an endemic area in Africa or South America.
Rabies	Yes, if traveling to jungle and/or remote areas.
Hepatitis A	Yes, the disease can be caught easily from food/water.
Japanese encephalitis	May be advised for some areas, depending on the duration of the trip and proximity to rice-growing and pig-farming areas.
BCG	It is not known how much protection this vaccination gives the traveler against lung tuberculosis, but it is currently advised in the absence of any better alternative.

of the allergic materials to provide quick relief.

HEPATITIS
» Hepatitis—inflammation of the liver—can be contracted virally anywhere in Vietnam.
» The most obvious symptom is a yellowing of the skin or of the whites of the eyes; before this there may be itching and tiredness.
» Early on, depending on the type of hepatitis, a vaccine or immunoglobulin may reduce the duration of the illness.
» There are vaccines for hepatitis B (which is spread through blood and unprotected sex) and A. Unfortunately, there is no vaccine for hepatitis C, or the increasing list of other hepatitis viruses.

TUBERCULOSIS
» This disease is still a significant problem in Ho Chi Minh City and many other areas.
» Symptoms include coughing, tiredness, fever and lethargy.

» Have a BCG vaccination before you go and see a doctor early if you have a persistent cough, cough blood, have a fever or suffer unexplained weight loss.

SARS
» Each year there is the possibilty that avian flu or SARS might occur. Check the latest news reports.
» If there is a problem in an area you are due to visit, seek expert advice.

DIARRHEA
» One survey found that up to 70 percent of travelers may suffer diarrhea during their trip. It should last only a short while, but if it lasts longer, or if there is blood or pain, get specialist medical attention.
» Try to prevent diarrhea by drinking only bottled water and avoiding ice cubes. Be wary of salads (you don't know what they have been washed in), reheated foods, food that has been left out in the sun and unpasteurized dairy products.

Above *Fresh fruit is refreshing while spending time on a beach*

LUNG FLUKE
» Avoid eating undercooked or raw crabs, as these contain a fluke (a flattened worm) that travels to the lungs.

SEXUAL HEALTH
» Unprotected sex can spread HIV, hepatitis B and C, gonorrhea, chlamydia, painful recurrent herpes, syphilis and warts.
» The risk of disease is significantly decreased with the use of condoms.
» ▷ 255 for more information.

PHARMACIES
» There are pharmacies in every town and they are increasingly better stocked.
» In larger cities, such as Hanoi, staff will often speak English.
» Be aware of counterfeit medicines and those past their sell-by date.

FURTHER INFORMATION
Centers for Disease Control and Prevention (USA)
www.cdc.gov
This US government site gives excellent advice on travel health and has useful disease maps and details of disease outbreaks.

HEALTHY FLYING
» Visitors to Vietnam may be concerned about the effect of long-haul flights on their health. The most widely publicized concern is deep vein thrombosis, or DVT. Misleadingly called "economy class syndrome," DVT is the forming of a blood clot in the body's deep veins, particularly in the legs. The clot can move around the bloodstream and could be fatal.
» Those most at risk include the elderly, pregnant women and those using the contraceptive pill, smokers and people who are overweight. If you are at increased risk of DVT see your doctor before departing. Flying increases the likelihood of DVT because passengers are often seated in a cramped position for long periods of time and may become dehydrated.

To minimize risk:
Drink water (not alcohol)
Don't stay immobile for hours at a time
Stretch and exercise your legs periodically
Do wear elastic flight socks, which support veins and reduce the chances of a clot forming

EXERCISES
1. Ankle Rotations	2. Calf Stretches	3. Knee Lifts
Lift feet off the floor. Draw a circle with the toes, moving one foot clockwise and the other counterclockwise	Start with heel on the floor and point foot upward as high as you can. Then lift heels high, keeping balls of feet on the floor	Lift leg with knee bent while contracting your thigh muscle. Then straighten leg, pressing foot flat to the floor

Other health hazards for flyers are airborne diseases and bugs spread by the plane's air-conditioning system. These are largely unavoidable but if you have a serious medical condition seek advice from a doctor before flying.

HOSPITALS

Consultation rates vary but usually start at around US$40 for a consultation with a foreign doctor, and half that for a Vietnamese doctor.

HOSPITAL	ADDRESS	CONTACT
Hanoi		
Eye Hospital	85 Ba Trieu Street	04-39438004
Hanoi Family Medical Practice	109–112 Van Phuc	04-38430748
	24-hour medical service, including intensive care	04-38430748
	and dental care.	www.vietnammedicalpractice.com
Hospital Bach Mai	Giai Phong Street	04-38693731
	English-speaking doctors. A dental service is also available.	www.bachmaihospital.org
Huu Nghi (Friendship Hospital)	Tran Khanh Du Street	04-39722231
International Hospital	Phuong Mai, Dong Da	04-35771100
		www.hfh.com.vn
International SOS	1 Dong Thai Mai	04-39340666
	Open 24 hours for emergencies, routine and	www.internationalsos.com
	medical evacuation. Dental service.	
Ho Chi Minh City		
Cho Ray Hospital	201B Nguyen Chi Thanh Street, District 5	08-38554138
	The largest hospital, with 24-hour emergency care.	
Columbia Asia	1 No Trang Long Street, Quan Binh Thanh	08-38030678
(Gia Dinh International Clinic)	An American-run emergency clinic with medievac	(08-38238888 24-hour emergency)
	and general practice services.	www.columbiaasia.com
Columbia Asia	8 Alexandre de Rhodes Street	08-38238455
(Saigon International Clinic)	International doctors offering a full range of services.	(08-38238888 24-hour emergency)
		www.columbiaasia.com
Franco-Vietnamese Hospital	6 Nguyen Luong Bang, District 7, Saigon South	08-54113333, 08-54113500
	This new and fully equipped hospital offers international	www.fvhospital.com
	medical care and is equipped to deal with emergency cases.	
Emergency Ambulance service		08-54113500
Ho Chi Minh City Family	Diamond Plaza, 34 Le Duan Street	08-38227848
Medical Practice	Well-equipped practice; emergency and evacuation	(09-13234911 24-hour emergency)
	service with Western doctors. Full range of services	www.vietnammedicalpractice.com
	including tropical disease specialists and dental services.	
International Medical Center	1 Han Thuyen Street (facing the cathedral), District 1	08-38272366
	English-speaking French doctors.	
International SOS	167A Nam Ky Khoi, District 3	08-38298424 (24-hour emergency)
	Comprehensive medical and dental service.	www.internationalsos.com
Koseikai Dental Office	Saigon Tower, 29 Le Duan Street	08-38235918
	Japanese facilities with Japanese and Japanese-trained	
	Vietnamese staff.	

World Health Organization
www.who.int
The WHO site has links to the WHO Blue Book on travel advice, listing diseases in different regions of the world and vaccination schedules, and specifying countries with yellow fever vaccination certificate requirements and malarial risk.

Department of Health Travel Advice (UK)
www.dh.gov.uk

Look for Health Advice for Travelers. Also available as a free booklet, the T6, from UK post offices. Lists vaccine requirements for each country.

Health Protection Agency (UK)
www.hpa.org.uk
Up-to-date malaria advice for travel around the world. Specific advice about the right drugs for each location and information for those who are pregnant, suffering from epilepsy or traveling with children.

Medic Alert (UK)
www.medicalert.org.uk
The website of the foundation that produces bracelets and necklaces for those with existing medical problems. Write your key medical details on paper inside the bracelet.

Tropical Medical Bureau (Eire)
www.tmb.ie
This Irish-based site has a good collection of general travel health information and disease risks.

PRACTICALITIES | ESSENTIAL INFORMATION

BASICS

ELECTRICITY

» Voltage is generally 220V (frequency 50Hz), but in some places 110V is still in use. Always ask before plugging anything in.

» Plugs are usually for two small round pins; some are for two flat pins. A number of top hotels now use three-square-pin sockets. Bring a universal adaptor.

LAUNDRY

» All hotels and guesthouses offer a laundry service. The more expensive the hotel, the more expensive the laundry, with a 10 percent VAT (IVA) and 5 percent service charge added in the more expensive places.

MEASUREMENTS

Most clothes marketed to Westerners are made for export and come in US, UK and European sizes; otherwise sizes are small, medium, large and extra large. In US terms, women's small is size 6, medium is size 8, large is size 10 and extra large is 12–14 (in UK terms, that's 8, 10, 12 and 14–16 respectively).

PUBLIC TOILETS

» Toilets in hotels, guesthouses and restaurants are Western-style, and the majority are clean, though there are exceptions.

» In some small Vietnamese restaurants there are squat toilets, and you will need to bring your own toilet paper.

» In hotels and restaurants there is plenty of toilet paper, soap and individual hand towels. Women's bathrooms are often decorated with frangipani buds floating in bowls.

SMOKING REGULATIONS

» Smoking is permitted throughout Vietnam.

» Some hotels offer nonsmoking rooms and floors. A few restaurants have nonsmoking sections.

CHILDREN

» Diapers are available in supermarkets in large towns. In more remote regions, such as the north, the Central Highlands and smaller towns, take them with you.

» Vietnam is a tropical country, so children should wear hats, long-sleeved clothing and high-factor sunscreen.

» Children's menus do exist in some restaurants, and knives and forks can always be provided. If your child does not take to Vietnamese food, most destinations have international restaurants and, if all else fails, there is always rice. Fruit and vegetables from markets will ensure that no one starves.

» Some hotels are child-friendly. Good options include Evason Ana Mandara, Nha Trang (▷ 180), the Furama Resort, Danang, and the Victoria Hotel Group.

» Many of the cities have playgrounds, although these are likely to be basic.

» Neither children nor adults should drink the tap water in Vietnam. Bottled water is cheap and available everywhere. Some hotels supply it free of charge.

» Children should always be accompanied in the sea.

» Children receive reductions in the price of rail, bus and air travel (▷ 50–54).

CONVERSION CHART

From	To	Multiply by
Inches	Centimeters	2.54
Centimeters	Inches	0.3937
Feet	Meters	0.3048
Meters	Feet	3.2810
Yards	Meters	0.9144
Meters	Yards	1.0940
Miles	Kilometers	1.6090
Kilometers	Miles	0.6214
Acres	Hectares	0.4047
Hectares	Acres	2.4710
Gallons	Liters	4.5460
Liters	Gallons	0.2200
Ounces	Grams	28.35
Grams	Ounces	0.0353
Pounds	Grams	453.6
Grams	Pounds	0.0022
Pounds	Kilograms	0.4536
Kilograms	Pounds	2.205
Tons	Tonnes	1.0160
Tonnes	Tons	0.9842

PLACES OF WORSHIP

» Vietnam is mainly a Buddhist country (▷ 16–17).

» Mass is held in the Roman Catholic churches in the main towns in Vietnam, including St. Joseph's Cathedral (Hanoi), Dalat Cathedral, and Notre Dame Cathedral (Saigon).

Below *Cao Dai Great Temple, Tay Ninh*

LOCAL WAYS

CULTURAL ISSUES

Vietnam is relaxed and easygoing with regard to conventions, and it is rare to cause offence unwittingly. The main complaint Vietnamese have of foreigners is that some wear dirty and torn clothing. Backpackers come in for particularly severe criticism, and the term *tay ba lo* (Western backpacker) is a contemptuous one.

SOCIAL ETIQUETTE

» Shoes should be removed before entering temples and before going into people's houses.
» Modesty should be preserved, and excessive displays of bare flesh are not good form, particularly in temples and private houses.
» Shorts are fine for the beach and travelers' cafés but not for smart restaurants.
» Kissing and cuddling in public are likely to draw wide attention, not much of it favorable, but walking hand-in-hand is now accepted as a common, if slightly eccentric, Western habit.
» Hand-shaking among men is a standard greeting (often with both hands for added cordiality). Although Vietnamese women will consent to the process, it is often clear that they would prefer not to.
» The head is held by some to be sacred, and people would rather you didn't pat them on it, which amazingly some visitors do.
» Vietnamese who meet you for the first time will always ask how old you are, whether you are married and whether you have children.
» Vietnamese names are written with the surname first, followed by the first name. Thus, Nguyen Minh is informally addressed not as Nguyen but as Minh.
» When addressing strangers of the same age, use *anh* (for a man) or *chi* (for a woman). When you know the first name use *anh* Minh, for example.
» When addressing your senior or someone of uncertain age, use *ông* for a man or *bà* for a woman.

» It is perfectly acceptable to address someone as Mr Minh or Ms Hanh, for example.

POLITICAL AND RELIGIOUS ACTIVITY

» Do not take photographs of military installations.
» Involvement in politics, possession of political material, business activities that have not been licensed by appropriate authorities or nonsanctioned religious activities (including proselytizing) can result in detention.
» Sponsors of small, informal religious gatherings such as Bible-study groups in hotel rooms, as well as distributors of religious materials, have been detained, fined and expelled, according to the US State Department.
» Foreigners are free to attend Christian services. In Saigon, one or two services in the Notre Dame Cathedral are in French and in English; in Protestant churches, which are found across the country, all services are in Vietnamese.
» Vietnam is predominantly a Buddhist country.
» Ancestor-worship is widely practiced and animism (the belief in, and worship of, the spirits of inanimate objects such as venerable trees, the land, mountains and so on) is widespread.

SLEEPING RULES

» Government restrictions limit the range of homestays and bed-and-breakfast accommodations. In a few

places, such as the Mekong Delta and the northwest, some private homes are licensed to accept foreigners, but this tends to be at the discretion of the police.
» If you wish to stay at a friend's house, this is normally permitted, but your hosts will need to take your passport and arrival form to their local police station.

SEXUAL ETIQUETTE

» Police and People's Committee regulations in some towns require a foreigner traveling with a Vietnamese spouse to bring a marriage certificate in order to share a hotel room.
» The age of consent in Vietnam is 18.
» There are rules and regulations relating to Vietnamese guests of the opposite sex being in your hotel room, though if the guest is your partner hotels are generally relaxed. However, in Hoi An and in international hotels in big cities, which are under police scrutiny, you may have to rent a second room.
» There are no legal restraints for two people of the same sex cohabiting in the same room.
» There are several bars in central Saigon that are popular with gay clients: www.utopia-asia.com is an Asian resource for gays and lesbians. The site includes a list of scams and warnings in Vietnam as well as gay-friendly bars in Hanoi and Saigon.

Below *Khmer monks chatting to a visitor at the Khmer Khleng Pagoda in Soc Trang*

FINDING HELP
CRIME

» Bag- and jewelry-snatching is a common problem. Do not take any valuables onto the streets of Saigon. Possessions are safer in all but the most disreputable hotels than on the streets.

» Do not wear expensive jewelry or watches, or carry wallets, cellphones or handbags.

» Thieves work in teams in central Saigon, often with women carrying babies and begging as a decoy.

» Beware of people who obstruct your path (pushing a bicycle across the sidewalk (pavement) is a common ruse) while your pockets are being emptied from behind.

» Take particular care in Nha Trang and Hanoi.

» Stick to tried and trusted cyclo drivers after dark or, better still, go by taxi. Never take a cyclo in a strange part of town after dark.

» If you are robbed, report the incident to the police for insurance purposes, but don't expect any further action.

» If you are arrested ask for consular assistance and English-speaking staff immediately.

EMERGENCY PHONE NUMBERS	
Police	113
Fire	114
Ambulance	115

TRAVEL ADVISORIES

www.travel.state.gov/travel

The US State Department's continually updated travel advisories on its Travel Warnings and Consular Information Sheets page.

www.fco.gov.uk/travel

The UK Foreign and Commonwealth Office's travel warning section, which is regularly reviewed and updated.

SAFETY ISSUES
LANDMINES

» Unexploded ordnance is still a threat in some areas. Do not stray too far from the beaten track or unearth pieces of suspicious metal.

» The Technology Center for Bomb and Mine Disposal (BOMICO), a department of the Engineering Command of the Ministry of Defense, estimates that 7 to 8 percent of land is affected. It is thought that there are between 350,000 and 800,000 tons of war-era ordnance in the ground. All Vietnam's provinces are affected, but especially the DMZ and the south.

» According to the International Campaign to Ban Landmines, 66 people were killed in 2002 and 100 injured in mine/unexploded ordnance incidents. BOMICO estimates that 1,110 people die and 1,882 are injured every year. It is thought that between 1975 and the end of 2000, 38,849 had been killed and 65,852 injured.

Above Police officers in Hanoi

HIV AND AIDS

» UNAIDS (the Joint United Nations Programme on HIV/AIDS) reports that while HIV incidence among the adult population is low (4 percent), rates could be as high as 65 percent among intravenous drug abusers, and sexual transmission is expected to become the dominant mode of HIV transmission in Vietnam in coming years.

» Between 40 and 50 new infections are reported every day in Vietnam according to the website www.unaids.org.vn.

» Like the other countries of Southeast Asia, Vietnam is thought to have the potential for "rapid increase" in the HIV/AIDS epidemic.

» The first reported case of AIDS was in 1990.

» Although 80,000 cases of HIV have so far been reported, it is believed that about 280,000 people, 2,500 of whom are children, were living with HIV or AIDS by the end of 2009.

» In Dong Nai Province, where body art is fashionable, tattooing is believed to be a major cause of transmission of HIV.

» AIDS is found in all 61 of Vietnam's provinces. Urban and border regions have the highest incidence, topped by Quang Ninh Province, Haiphong and Saigon. Provinces such as Quang Binh and Quang Tri, in the center of the country, are least affected.

DRUGS

» Illegal drugs are common and inexpensive, and the use of hard drugs by Vietnamese is a rapidly growing problem, with a 400 percent increase in drug seizures over the previous year in 2001. In 2009, five people were sentenced to death for trafficking marijuana.

» It is not uncommon to see drug abusers injecting themselves in back alleys, but periodically bars and nightclubs are closed for a few weeks in response to the problem.

» Attitudes to drug traffickers are harsh; the death penalty is usually reserved for Vietnamese and other Asian carriers.

OPENING TIMES AND TICKETS

DISCOUNT TRAVEL

» Discounted fares for young people or senior citizens are rarely offered by the airlines operating within Vietnam.

» Bus and car companies are less forthcoming with their discounts.

» Vietnam Airlines charges children under two 10 percent of the adult ticket price; those aged 2–12 pay 75 percent of the adult ticket price.

» The railways allow children under five to travel free and charge 50 percent of the adult fare for those aged 5–10.

» The traveling café Open Tour bus tickets and tours (▷ 50) are free for children under two, but those aged 2–10 pay half the adult price.

» Buses, especially when crowded, may not be suitable for small children.

TOURIST OFFICES

» The national tourist office is called Vietnam National Administration of Tourism: Vietnamtourism (www.vietnamtourism.com). Its role is to promote Vietnam as a tourist destination rather than to provide practical tourist information.

» Many of the 61 provinces in Vietnam have a branch office of the state-run tourist company.

» Visitors to its offices can find some information and maps but are more likely to be offered organized tours.

» Good tourist information is also available from the many tour operators around the country; most are happy to offer advice as well as tours.

Right *Tourists cruise out over the waters off Ha Long Bay in one of the many junks there*

NATIONAL HOLIDAYS	
January 1	(But not known as New Year's Day in Vietnam)
Late January–March	*Tet* (first to seventh day of the new lunar year)
February 3	Founding Anniversary of the Communist Party of Vietnam
April 30	Liberation Day of South Vietnam and Saigon
May 1	International Labor Day
May 19	Anniversary of the Birth of Ho Chi Minh; most state
	institutions shut, but the private sector carries on
September 2	National Day
September 3	President Ho Chi Minh's Anniversary

OPENING TIMES	
Banks	Mon–Fri 8 or 8.30 –4; some close 11–1.
Shops	Daily 8–8; some stay open a further hour or two, especially in visitor areas.
Supermarkets	Daily 8–8.
Offices	Mon–Fri 7.30–11.30, 1.30–4.30.
Museums and galleries	Times vary according to each place, but most are open all day, every day. Some are closed on Mondays.
Restaurants, cafés and bars	Daily from 7 or 8am; some open earlier. By law bars must close by midnight.
Churches	Open only during services; otherwise there may be a caretaker who will let you in.

STATE AND PRIVATE TOUR OPERATORS		
OFFICE	ADDRESS	TELEPHONE/WEBSITE
Ba Ria-Vung Tau Tourist Corporation	207 Vo Thi Sau Street	064-3856445
Buon Me Thuot Daklak Tourist Office	53 Ly Thuong Kiet Street	050-3852246; www.daklaktourist.com.vn
Can Tho Tourist	20 Hai Ba Trung Street	071-3824221; www.canthotourist.vn
Cao Bang Tourist	Phong Lan Hotel, 83 Be Van Dan Street	026-3385226
Cao Lanh Dong Thap Tourist Company	2 Doc Binh Kieu Street	067-3855638; www.dongthaptourist.com
Dalat Tourist	10 Quang Trung Street	063-3810324
Danang Tourist Office	17 Tran Ke Xuong Street	0511-3868626; www.danangtourist.vn
Danang Tourist Information Centre	10 Hai Phong Street	0511-3887750; www.ticvietnam.com
Ha Giang Tourist Company	Tran Hung Dao Street	019-3875288; www.hagiangtrade.gov.vn
Haiphong Tourism	18 Minh Khai Street	031-3822616; www.haiphongtourism.gov.vn
Hanoi Tourist	18 Ly Thuong Kiet Street and 30A Ly Thuong Kiet Street	04-38243011; www.hanoitourist-travel.com
Hanoi Tourist Information Centre	7 Dinh Tien Hoang Street	04-39263366; www.ticvietnam.com
Ho Chi Minh City Tourist Information Centre	7 Dinh Tien Hoang Street	04-39263366; http://ticvietnam.com
Hoi An Tourist Office	Truong Minh Hung Street	974-676593; www.hoian-tourism.com
Sapa Tours	6 Muong Hoa Street	020-3873625; http://sapaluxurytravel.com
Vinh Long Tourism	1 1/5 Street	070- 3823529; www.cuulongtourist.com

COMMUNICATIONS
INTERNET

» Vietnam has a long way to go to catch up with nearby countries in terms of Internet communication. The first wave of cybercafés was closed down by the authorities, but emailing is now easy and access to the Internet from within Vietnam is not a problem. Broadband is now available in many places in Hanoi and Saigon and in some main cities.

» Many of the large hotels offer broadband access.

» Many travelers' cafés in Hanoi and Saigon, and in other main towns, such as Sapa, Huê, Hoi An and Nha Trang, provide e-mail access, as do hotels and guesthouses.

» Cybercafés are rare because many hotels, except for high-end ones, now offer free Internet access, and WiFi is increasingly common.

» Rates for receiving, sending and printing emails have fallen as competition has spread, and are currently around US$3 per hour in the two main cities (more in smaller places). Business centers in top hotels charge a lot more.

MAIL

» Generally, postal services are good. International aerograms take about two weeks in each direction. Every town has a post office, as does every district in every city, and provincial capitals have two general post offices: one for the province and one for the town.

» Post offices tend to keep long opening hours: daily 7am–9pm (smaller offices close for lunch).

» Postal deliveries are seven days a week and stop only on official national holidays.

» General post offices in the major cities can send parcels overseas and usually offer packing services for a small additional fee.

» To send letters and parcels from Vietnam costs: 100g airmail letter to Europe 77,000d, to the US 95,000d; 1kg surface parcel to Europe 334,000d, to the US 424,000d; postcard to Europe 11,500d, to the US 13,500d.

» Outgoing packages are opened and the contents checked by the censor before being allowed out.

» Incoming parcels are rarely delivered to the door; a note is sent to summon you to the post office, where you must show your passport and pay a fee, before the parcel is produced and opened by customs officers.

» All major international courier companies have offices near the big general post offices.

» Post offices offer domestic telegram services—useful for getting messages to people who are not on the telephone. There is also an express mail service, EMS, which delivers letters or small packages the following day.

» Post offices in Saigon, Hanoi, Huê, Hoi An, Nha Trang, Dalat and Danang provide poste restante facilities. Ask your correspondent to print your surname—for example, Chris ARNOLD, c/o Poste Restante, GPO, Hanoi.

TELEPHONE AND FAX

» All post offices can provide international telephone and fax services. The cost of calls has been greatly reduced, but some post offices and hotels will still charge a minimum of three minutes; hotels also add their own surcharge. Note that you start paying for an overseas call from the moment you ring, even if the call is not answered.

» A one-minute international call from a post office costs from US$1.50 depending on the country called and the time of the call.

» Before you leave home, try to establish, from your mobile phone provider, the cost of making international calls from Vietnam.

» Local calls are inexpensive or even free of charge in some hotels.

» Most shops or cafés will let you call a local number for 2,000d: Look for the blue sign *"dien thoai cong cong"* (public telephone).

» To make a domestic call, dial 0 + area code + number.

» Equal tones followed by long pauses indicate that the telephone

Above *Broadband is available in many large hotels*

is ringing. Equal tones separated by equal pauses, or short pauses separated by short tones mean that the line is engaged.

» All towns and areas have telephone codes.

» Telephone numbers that begin with 091 or 090 are cellphone numbers.

» Sending a one-page fax abroad costs around US$3.

CELLPHONES

» Most, but not all cellphones with global roaming work in Vietnam, and coverage is improving. Check with your provider before you travel.

» Calls on global roaming phones from within Vietnam are charged as international, so it may be cheaper to buy a pay-as-you-go SIM card from Vinaphone or Mobiphone (around 50,000d). Their offices are found near every big post office.

» Top-up cards (minimum value of 100,000d) are available—just look for the sign.

USEFUL NUMBERS	
Vietnam international code	0084
Directory inquiries	116
Operator-assisted domestic long-distance calls	103
International directory inquiries	143
General information service	1080
International operator	110

MEDIA

NEWSPAPERS

» The English-language daily *Vietnam News* (http://vietnamnews. vnagency.com.vn) is widely available and covers Vietnamese and foreign news selectively. It has especially good sports pages. The Sunday edition is worth reading for its cultural stories, and is particularly good on the traditions of ethnic minorities. Inside the back page of the *Vietnam News* is an excellent "What's on" section, recommended for visitors interested in cultural events in Hanoi and Saigon.

» The *Saigon Times Daily* (http:// english.thesaigontimes.vn) is more business-oriented.

» There are several weeklies, of which the *Vietnam Investment Review* (www.vir.com.vn) is the best.

» The monthly *Vietnam Economic Times* (www.vneconomy.com.vn/ eng) is very thorough and remains forthright in its views.

» The *Viet Nam News Agency* (www.vnagency.com.vn) is Vietnam's official news agency.

» The *Saigon Times* (http:// english.thesiagontimes.vn) has an interesting news summary with full listings of what's on.

» The *Saigon Today* network (www. saigontoday.net) is a great round-up of local news, with photo galleries of events around town, stretching back for more than a year—an excellent way to get a real feel for Saigon.

» One- or two-day-old editions of the *Financial Times, International Tribune, USA Today, Le Figaro* and some weeklies, such as *The Economist, Time* and *Asiaweek*, are available in Saigon and Hanoi.

TELEVISION

» There is news in English on the TV once in the evening, mainly covering Party members' visits to factories, presentations of medals to Heroic Mothers and meetings of People's Committee personnel.

» All foreign films are dubbed over with a single monotone voice, except on cable TV, which is available in many hotels and features a full range of cable options—normally CNN, Star Sport, BBC World, HBO, Cinemax and Star Movies.

BOOKS

Books on the region

» *Travellers' Literary Companion to Southeast Asia* (Alastair Dingwall, 1994). Experts on Southeast Asian language and literature select extracts from novels and books by Western and regional writers. The extracts are brief, but give a good overview of what is available.

» *Vietnam: Rising Dragon* (Bill Hayton, 2010). Written in an engaging style, it questions the issues behind Vietnam's ongoing economic and social development.

» *All the Wrong Places: Adrift in the Politics of the Pacific Rim* (James Fenton, 2000). British journalist James Fenton entertainingly recounts his experiences in Vietnam, Cambodia, the Philippines and Korea.

» *The Archaeology of Mainland Southeast Asia: From 10,000BC to the Fall of Angkor* (Charles Higham, 1989). Best summary of changing views of the archeology of the mainland.

» *In Search of Southeast Asia: A Modern History* (D. J. Steinberg et al., 1987). The best standard history of the region, examining and assessing general processes of change and their impacts, from the arrival of the Europeans in the region.

History

» *The Sacred Willow: Four Generations in the Life of a Vietnamese Family* (Mai Elliott, 1999). Recounts the history of Vietnam through the life of the Duong family from the 19th century to the tragedy of the boat people. Vietnam as seen through Vietnamese eyes.

» *The Deprat Affair: Ambition, Revenge and Deceit in French Indo-China* (Roger Osborne, 1999).

The extraordinary story of Jacques Deprat, a brilliant young geologist, who may have been guilty of professional deceit. A useful insight into colonial society and mores in the first two decades of the 20th century.

» *The Vietnam Wars* (Justin Wintle, 1991). An examination of all Vietnam's many conflicts.

Novels

» *Saigon Tea* (Graham Reilly, 2004). Danny Canyon from Glasgow ends up in Ho Chi Minh City and suffers culture shock while grappling with the local mafia.

» *The Quiet American* (Graham Greene, 1954). A remarkably prescient novel about America's experience in Vietnam, set in and around Saigon as the war between the French and the Viet Minh intensifies.

» *Saigon* (Anthony Grey, 1983). An entertaining novel covering events of the 20th century.

» *The Sorrow of War* (Bao Ninh, 1993). A wartime novel by a North Vietnamese soldier; an account of emotions during and after the war.

Travel and geography

» *The Voyage from London to Indochina* (Crosbie Garstin, 1928). Hilarious, irreverent account of a journey through Vietnam.

» *A Dragon Apparent: Travels in Cambodia, Laos and Vietnam* (Norman Lewis, 1951). One of the finest of all travel books. It details Lewis' account of his visit to Vietnam just a few years prior to the French defeat at Dien Bien Phu in 1954, and captures the twilight years of the Indochinese empire. He fraternizes with the French colonialist rulers and hitchhikes around in their transportation. His narrative reports encounters with these characters, with wildlife and with the *moi* (savages or slaves), as the French called the ethnic minorities living in the highlands.

» *The Great Railway Bazaar: By Train Through Asia* (Paul Theroux, 1975). Theroux's graphic account of one

American's attempt to travel by rail between Saigon and Huê.

War in Vietnam

» *Hell in a Very Small Place: The Siege of Dien Bien Phu* (Bernard B. Fall, 1967).

» *The Last Valley: Dien Bien Phu and the French Defeat in Vietnam* (Martin Windrow, 2004). A detailed account of this key 1954 battle.

» *Australia's Vietnam War* (Jeff Doyle, with Jeffrey Grey and Peter Pierce, 2002). Discusses Australia's role in, and motives for, joining the Vietnam War.

» *Fire in the Lake* (Francis Fitzgerald, 1972). A Pulitzer prize-winning, readable account of the US involvement in the war.

» *Dispatches* (Michael Herr, 1977). An acclaimed account of the Vietnam War written by a correspondent who experienced the conflict firsthand.

» *American Tragedy: Kennedy, Johnson and the Origins of the Vietnam War* (David Kaiser, 1999). Based on recently opened archives; a penetrating insight into America's involvement in Vietnam.

» *Vietnam: A History* (Stanley Karnow, 1983, revised 1991, second edition, 1997). A comprehensive and readable history.

» *The White House Years* (Henry Alfred Kissinger, 1979). The first volume of the memoirs of America's best-known 20th-century diplomat covers the first President Nixon term and ends with the Paris Peace Accord of 1973. *Years of Upheaval* (1982), covers the turbulent months from Kissinger's visit to Hanoi in February 1973 to Nixon's resignation in August 1974; and *Years of Renewal* (1998), the concluding volume, covers the end of the Vietnam War and collapse of the South.

» *Vietnam: A Reporter's War* (Hugh Lunn, 1985). Australian reporter Hugh Lunn's year in Vietnam with Reuters between 1967 and 1968, including an account of the Tet Offensive.

» *In Retrospect: The Tragedy and Lessons of Vietnam* (Robert S. McNamara and Brian Van de Mark, 1997). McNamara was US Secretary for Defense from 1961 to 1968. This is his cathartic account of the war.

» *The Tunnels of Cu Chi* (Tom Mangold and John Penycate, 1985). A compelling account of the building of the tunnels and of the Viet Cong who fought in them.

» *Chickenhawk* (Robert Mason, 1983). An excellent autobiography of a helicopter pilot.

» *The Human Stain* (Philip Roth, 2000). Not ostensibly about the Vietnam War at all, but it has an excellent account of American war veterans coming to terms with their traumas and with the country that shunned them.

» *A Bright Shining Lie* (Neil Sheehan, 1989). A meticulously researched 850-page account of the Vietnam War, based around the life of Lieutenant Colonel John Paul Vann.

» *Two Cities: Hanoi and Saigon* (Neil Sheehan, 1992). A short but fascinating book that tries to link the past with the present in a part autobiography, part travelog, part contemporary commentary.

» *River of Time* (Jon Swain, 1996). An account by a war correspondent who speculates that American generals saw the war in Vietnam as a rehearsal for future conflict in Europe against the Red Army.

» *A Wavering Grace: A Vietnamese Family in War and Peace* (Gavin Young, 1997). Young's account of the war in Vietnam, where he was a reporter, told through the lives of a Vietnamese family.

» *Vietnam Now: A Reporter Returns* (David Lamb, 2003). War reporter Lamb returns to journalism in Hanoi in 1997 and documents the social revolution since the end of the war. All the more readable for presenting one of the few up-to-date accounts of contemporary Vietnam.

MAPS

» www.lib.utexas.edu/maps Up-to-date maps showing relief, political boundaries and major towns. Search for Vietnam and cities of interest.

» www.maps.google.com. Enter Vietnam in the search box, which takes maps from their current atlas of the world.

» Vietnam maps can be bought in the UK from Stanfords, 12–14 Long Acre, London WC2E 9LP, tel 020 7836 1321; www.stanfords.co.uk. There is another branch in in Bristol.

USEFUL WEBSITES

www.asiasociety.org
Homepage of the Asia Society.

www.cpv.org.vn
The Communist Party of Vietnam's website.

www.hrw.org
Human Rights Watch reports on police and military brutality against ethnic minorities.

www.amnesty.org/en/region/viet-nam
News and information about Vietnam from Amnesty International.

www.mofa.gov.vn
Ministry of Foreign Affairs website, with Vietnam's interpretation of world events.

www.pata.org
The Pacific Asia Travel Association.

www.thingsasian.com
A huge online collection of historical, cultural and travelog articles.

www.vdic.org.vn
Vietnam Development Information Center.

SHOPPING

Since the gradual liberalization of the Vietnamese economy began in 1986, shopping here has become increasingly varied and enjoyable. You will find a wide range of designer clothing, high-quality handicrafts, ceramics, lacquerware and silk goods, including tailor-made silk dresses and shirts, at relatively low prices. Some visitors even need to buy extra luggage to take home all their purchases! The main shopping destinations are Hanoi, Ho Chi Minh City and Hoi An. A word of warning: It is against Vietnamese law and international wildlife convention laws (CITES) to buy and trade in marine turtle products.

BASICS

The majority of shops and markets in Vietnam are open from early in the morning to late at night every day of the week. They do not close for lunch. Most shops now accept internationally recognized credit cards. Shops and markets accept US dollars and Vietnamese dong; at markets your change will be returned in dong. There is no sales or government tax on shop purchases. Bargaining is expected in markets and in shops except where price tags are used.

Export of wood or antiques is strictly controlled, and anything antique or antique-looking may be seized upon at customs unless you have a license. If your purchase is antique or antique-looking, you will need to get an export license from the Customs Department (▷ 245), although this can be a time-consuming process. If you buy through a reputable shop, they can handle the paperwork for you. If you are buying a reproduction, then you need to make sure it states this on your receipt.

ANTIQUES

In Ho Chi Minh City, most antiques shops are on Dong Khoi, Mac Thi Buoi and Ngo Duc Ke streets. For the knowledgeable, there are bargains to be found, especially Chinese and Vietnamese ceramics. Also available are old watches, colonial bric-a-brac, lacquerware and carvings. To look for items off the beaten track, spend an hour or so browsing the shops in Le Cong Kieu Street, which is not marked on any maps but runs between Nam Ky Khoi Nghia and Pho Duc

Chinh streets, just south of Ben Thanh Market. Here you may find interesting items of furniture, statuary and ceramics. Bargaining is expected and can deliver some pretty good deals.

Along Hang Khay and Trang Tien streets and the south edge of Hoan Kiem Lake are Hanoi's main antiques outlets. Shops sell silver ornaments, porcelain, jewelry and carvings. Much is not antique and not all is silver; bargain hard.

Remember that you need a license to take antiques out of the country (▷ 245).

ART AND ART GALLERIES

Contemporary art in Vietnam, as elsewhere in Southeast Asia, has benefited from an upsurge in interest from young Asian collectors with plenty of money. Exhibits in Hong Kong, New York, Paris and London have helped bring contemporary Vietnamese art to a wider public. Galleries have opened in all the major cities of Vietnam, and although much of the work displayed is purely commercial, artists now have the chance to show pictures that would, not long ago, have been considered subversive. Vietnam has three art colleges: one in Saigon, one in Huê, and the School of Fine Arts in Hanoi, which was founded by the French in 1925.

Although most Vietnamese painting is still conservative in subject, idiom and medium, some painters of the younger generation, including Dao Hai Phong, Tran Trong Vu and Truong Tan, are experimenting with more abstract ideas; in the more liberal artistic climate of the 21st century, their work is more expressive and less clichéd than that of 15 or 20 years ago. Even established artists such as Ly Quy Chung, Tran Luu Hau and Mai Long are taking advantage of their newly found artistic freedom to produce exciting experimental

work; Trinh Cung and Tran Trong Vu are noted for their abstract paintings, and Nguyen Thanh Binh's famous but faceless schoolgirls in *ao dais* (long, flowing tunics worn over trousers) hang in drawing rooms across Asia and Europe. The popularity of this theme has been seized upon by many lesser artists. Among the most respected artists of the older generation are Professor Nguyen Thu, Colonel Quang Tho and Diep Minh Chau, whose work draws heavily on traditional Vietnamese themes, particularly rural landscapes, but also episodes from recent history: the battle of Dien Bien Phu, life under American occupation and pencil sketches of Ho Chi Minh. Traditional art forms such as watercolor paintings on silk and lacquerwork are still popular.

Ho Chi Minh City has acquired something of a reputation for its galleries, and a number of contemporary artists have a considerable international following. There are also countless shops that do nothing but reproduce works of art and are willing to turn their hand to anything. They will produce an oil portrait from a crumpled passport photograph, paint a stately home from a postcard, or a grand master from a photograph in a magazine. There is also a lot of lively original work inexpensively available in shops around Pham Ngu Lao and in the Dong Khoi area.

Hanoi has a few art galleries and shops. These are scattered around the Hoan Kiem Lake area. Leading Vietnamese contemporary artists are represented, and paintings are sold in US dollars. Prices are high for Vietnam but not for the Western contemporary art trade.

Many galleries in Hoi An sell original works of art. Vietnamese artists have been inspired by its old buildings, which are instantly recognizable even when distorted into shapes and hues on canvas or silk. The more serious galleries are clustered near one another on Nguyen Thi Minh Khai Street, west of the Japanese Bridge.

CERAMICS

Vietnam has a ceramics tradition going back hundreds of years. There has been a renaissance of this art since the 1990s, and shops selling new and antique (or antique-looking) ceramics abound on the main shopping streets of Dong Khoi and Le Thanh Ton in Ho Chi Minh City. Much is in traditional Chinese-style blue and white, and there is also a very attractive celadon green, often with a crackled glaze. Other styles and finishes are coming to the fore as local craftspeople brush the dust off old ideas and come up with new ones.

DEPARTMENT STORES

Ho Chi Minh City now has several good, air-conditioned department stores selling everything from electrical goods and cellphones to clothes, jewelry, make-up and food. Prices for some of these items are equivalent to prices in the West or just a little lower. The range or quality of clothes, however, is more limited than would be expected in a Western department store, with a few exceptions where Western-brand clothes are sold. Western-style supermarkets are usually found inside the department stores, selling everything from cornflakes and milk to liquor and toiletries. All supermarkets require you to leave your bags in lockers at the entrance to the stores.

FASHION

Beautiful and affordable women's clothes are now sold in designer and clothes stores in Hanoi and Saigon in particular. Vietnam has produced a number of exciting fashion designers in the past few years (▷ 26), and there is a growing number of stylish stores in the fashionable cathedral shopping area in Hanoi. These sell jackets, dresses, handbags, scarves and shoes—a phenomenon that has appeared over a remarkably few years. The greatest concentration of shops is in the Hoan Kiem Lake area, especially on Nha Tho, Nha

Chung, Hang Trong and Hang Gai streets. Imported luxury goods are sold in the Sofitel Metropole Hotel's Louis Vuitton outlet.

Tailors charge low prices and can produce skirts, shirts and jackets from patterns and photographs, but quality does vary considerably. It's worth shopping around. Demand for speedy work can create enormous strain on staff and a poorer quality end product, so if you are in town for a few days it pays to do your clothes shopping on the first day. This will also give you time to accommodate second or third fittings, which may be necessary.

Hoi An is now the main place to get clothes made. Its tailors are renowned—there are reckoned to be more than 140—and they will produce finished silk or cotton clothing in 24 hours. The quality of the stitching varies from shop to shop so see some samples first. As the range of fabrics can be limited, some people choose to bring their own. Note that Thai silk costs more than Vietnamese silk, and Hoi An silk is quite coarse.

The *ao dai* is an unforgiving garment, exquisite on a slender frame but often unsuited to larger builds. Most fabrics are synthetic, but in the bigger markets there is a lot of excellent coarse Vietnamese silk and imported cotton and wool.

Dong Khoi is the street paved with silk in Ho Chi Minh City, with many excellent clothing stores. The Russian Market (Tax Department Store) has some good men's and women's clothes, and the Saigontourist Department Store on the corner of Le Thanh Ton and Dong Khoi streets also has a wide selection. Vietnamese silk and traditional dresses are sold in the shops on Dong Khoi Street and in Ben Thanh Market. On Le Thanh Ton the shops opposite the town hall (People's Committee) are particularly good. Western-style fashions are sold in the stores lining Hai Ba Trung Street from District 1 right through District 3. However, if you are female and a UK size 12,

American size 10 or European size 40 or above, or an average-sized male Westerner or larger, you'll find it difficult to buy anything that fits in these stores. There are luxury outlets such as Prada in the Hotel Caravelle and Armani, Gucci and Versace in the Sheraton.

Inexpensive T-shirts bearing the image of Ho Chi Minh or the yellow star of the Vietnamese flag are sold for a couple of dollars from stall-holders in tourist hubs.

HANDICRAFTS

Handicrafts include embroidered and woven fabrics, lacquerware (▷ below), mother-of-pearl inlaid screens and ceramics (▷ 261). There are a number of handicraft shops along Dong Khoi Street and Nguyen Hue Boulevard in Ho Chi Minh City, and in Hanoi most of the shops selling handicrafts, including those made by ethnic minorities, are in the Old Quarter.

Ethnic minority products, fabrics, wickerware and jewelry are best bought in the uplands (where they are least expensive), but many of these items are available in Hanoi and Ho Chi Minh City. Cham fabrics, for example, are available in Saigon, while those of the Thái and Hmông minorities can be seen in Hanoi.

Hang Gai Street in Hanoi is well equipped for the foreign souvenir-hunter and stocks excellent ethnic goods, fabrics and lacquerware. Hats of all descriptions abound.

As the tourist industry has developed, so the number of handicrafts and hand-woven fabrics on sale in Hanoi has increased. You'll find a wide range of interesting pieces on sale around the popular cathedral shopping cluster of Nha Tho, Ly Quoc Su and Nha Chung streets, Hang Khay Street, on the southern shores of Hoan Kiem Lake, and Hai Gai Street.

Good-quality water puppets are sold in Hanoi's water puppetry theater and inside the Temple of Literature (▷ 78–81). Masks are sold around Hoan Kiem Lake and in the Old Quarter.

In Ho Chi Minh City you can buy elaborately decorated model wooden ships in District 1, on the intersection of Hai Ba Trung and Ca Ba Quat.

HOME FURNISHINGS AND FURNITURE

This is a relatively new industry in Vietnam, but locally produced furniture and home furnishings are already having a significant impact on the global market. Craftsmanship is good, and many of the items are beautifully finished. Much of the wood is imported, as Vietnam's own resources have been severely depleted. Leading stores can be found in Hanoi, Ho Chi Minh City and Hoi An.

JEWELRY

This is another industry that has flourished in Vietnam in recent years. At the inexpensive end of the market, there is a cluster of gold and jewelry shops around Ben Thanh Market in Ho Chi Minh City and also in the International Trade Center on Nam Ky Khoi Nghia Street. In these stands, because skilled labor is so inexpensive, you'll rarely have to pay more than the weight of the item in silver or gold.

At the higher end of the market, there is a Bulgari outlet in the Caravelle Hotel, in District 1.

JUNK

Junk collectors will have a field day in Saigon and Hanoi. Many knickknacks were left behind by the French, Americans and Russians: old cameras, watches, cigarette lighters (most Zippos are fake), 1960s Coca-Cola signs and 1930s Pernod ashtrays. However, much is now reproduction, and to separate the authentic from the fake will require some specialist knowledge.

LACQUERWARE

The art of making *son mai* (lacquerware) is said to have been introduced into Vietnam after Emperor Le Thanh Ton (ruled 1443–59) sent an emissary to the

Chinese court to investigate the process. Lacquer is a resin from the son tree *(Rhus succedanea or R. vernicifera)*, which is then applied in numerous coats (usually 11) to wood (traditionally teak), leather, metal or porcelain. Prior to lacquering, the article must be sanded and coated with a fixative. The final coat is highly polished with coal powder. The piece may then be decorated with an incised design, painted, or inset with mother-of-pearl. If mother-of-pearl is used, appropriately shaped pieces of lacquer are chiseled out and the mother-of-pearl inset. This method is similar to that used in China, but different from those of Thailand and Burma. Designs in the north show Japanese influences, apparently because Japanese artists were employed as teachers at the École des Beaux Arts in Hanoi in the 1930s.

Lacquerware is plentiful and inexpensive, but remember that lacquer pictures are heavy to carry about and so should be bought near the end of a trip. Small lacquer trinkets, such as boxes and trays, are more portable and make ideal presents. These are ubiquitous in Hanoi, Ho Chi Minh City (on Nguyen Hue Boulevard and Dong Khoi Street in District 1) and Hoi An.

MARKETS

Every town and city in Vietnam has its markets. These bustling and fascinating affairs are the lifeblood of communities. Sellers come from far and wide, offering a vast array of the fruits of the earth and sea.

Secondhand goods and household items are also sold, and it is possible to eat well and at very little cost in most markets.

At Ho Chi Minh City's Ben Thanh Market (▷ 189) hundreds of stalls set up at sunset. The markets of the northwest are the most spectacular, drawing ethnic minority traders from the surrounding hills in their bright, intricately designed traditional clothing.

The Hang Be Market on Gai Ngu Street in the Old Quarter of Hanoi sells foodstuff live and dead, and functions in a swirl of cooking smells. The big Dong Xuan Market on Dong Xuan Street is a covered market selling mostly clothes and household goods.

Below *Colored lacquer jars*

Classical Vietnamese theater (known as *hat boi*—*hat* means to sing and *boi* means to gesture or pose) shows close links with the classical theater of China. Emperor Tu Duc (ruled 1848–83) had a troop of 150 female artists and employed stars from China in a series of extravagant productions. Since partition in 1954, this has been replaced by what might be termed "revolutionary realist" theater. Vietnam's repertoire of performance arts in the Western, classical tradition is limited to occasional productions at the opera houses in Hanoi and Ho Chi Minh City. There is one dedicated jazz club and a conservatory of music in Ho Chi Minh City. Some restaurants and a handful of expat bars have live music. In Hanoi, there is also one dedicated jazz club, and restaurants with live music such as Cay Cau (▷ 89). You can listen to folk music performed on traditional instruments by players in traditional dress at venues in Hoi An and Huê. Nightlife in Vietnam divides into two categories—Western and Vietnamese—though the edges are becoming increasingly blurred with time. Visitors tend to have a good meal, then head to a bar, often one with Western music, for a drink or two. Western-style bars, with cold beer, contemporary music and pool, are easy to find in the main towns but are virtually non-existent elsewhere. The locals go for a meal and then either to a darkened café or into a karaoke bar for an hour or two. They tend to prefer nonalcoholic drinks and huge numbers of cafés exist to cater to this market.

WATER PUPPETRY

The most original theatrical art form in Vietnam is *mua roi nuoc* (water puppet theater). Vietnam is famous for its water puppetry and it has exported this art internationally to much acclaim. You can see performances at the Water Puppetry House in Hanoi; a small show is also staged at the Museum of Vietnamese History in Ho Chi Minh City. The most famous and active troop is based in Hanoi, and in total there are about a dozen groups.

Water puppetry seems to have originated in northern Vietnam during the early years of the last millennium, when it was associated with the harvest festival. An inscription in Nam Ha Province mentions a show staged in honor of King Ly Nhan Ton in 1121. By the time the French began to colonize Vietnam at the end of the 19th century, the art form had spread to all the major towns of the country.

As the name suggests, this form of theater uses the surface of the water as the stage. Puppeteers, concealed behind a bamboo screen symbolizing an ancient village communal house, manipulate the characters while standing in 3ft (1m) of water. The puppets—some more

than 1.5ft (0.5m) tall—are carved from water-resistant sung wood, which is also very lightweight, and then painted in bright shades. Most need one puppeteer to manipulate them, but some require three or four.

Plays are based on historical and religious themes: the origins of the Viet nation, legends (for instance, the Lake of the Restored Sword, ▷ 74), village life and acts of heroism. Figures spout water when

required (and sometimes shower audience members), and they perform with great gusto, mischief and complex choreography. On occasion in Hanoi, the shows are accompanied by fireworks—especially during battle scenes—and live music supplied by folk-opera singers and traditional instruments. Performances usually begin with the clown, Teu, taking the stage. He acts as a linking character between the various scenes.

Below *Water puppeteers at the end of a show in Hanoi*

Since the 1980s Vietnamese writers have turned their attention from revolutionary heroes to commentary on political and social issues of the day, and consequently many plays have been censored or edited by the authorities.

VIETNAMESE BARS

A common type of Vietnamese bar is the *bia hoi*. *Bia hoi* is draft beer (fairly weak) but fresh and thirst-quenching. At around 4,000d for a half-pint glass, it is also good value. *Bia hoi* bars are usually occupied by men and consist of a handful of tables and plastic chairs. They often sell simple food dishes—*bo luc lac* (diced steak with fries), for example. *Bia ôm* are literally translated as "cuddle" bars—another integral part of Vietnamese social fabric. In a Vietnamese *bia ôm*, the women drink beer with the men; however, they are more popular with Asian customers than Westerners.

WESTERN BARS

Most smarter hotels catering to visitors have bars. There are numerous Western-style bars in Ho Chi Minh City, Hanoi and Hoi An. A smattering are found in other places where there are tourist attractions. Dalat has a handful of bars and clubs but these are mainly connected to the bigger hotels.

There are a few bars in Huê and some in Mui Ne, although the vast majority in Mui Ne are attached to the hotel resorts along the beach. Nha Trang's nightlife is focused around a few streets where the inexpensive hotels are to be found, and caters to visitors who have come for the sun, sea, sand and diving. There are more upscale bars which are attached to the more expensive hotels.

CAFÉS

Cafés serving nonalcoholic drinks are a popular choice among Vietnamese. Young romantic couples sit in virtual darkness listening to Vietnamese love songs—often played at a deafening volume—while sipping coffee. The furniture tends to be rather small for the Western frame, but these cafés are an agreeable way of relaxing after dinner in a more typically Vietnamese setting.

CLUBBING

Clubs, as Westerners understand them, do not exist in Vietnam. The more well-heeled hotels have discos that are popular with businessmen, while in Hanoi and Ho Chi Minh City there are two Apocalypse Now venues that play Western music and have large dance floors. Some bars have areas that convert to dance floors later in the evening and during the early hours; in Saigon, these are often found in the Pham Ngu Lao area.

TICKETING AND INFORMATION

To buy tickets in Vietnam it is best to go direct to the box office (▷ individual listings for opening hours). To find out about specific events, check the daily publication *Vietnam News*, which has a "What's On" section. Also check www. ticketvn.com for online booking.

Above *Streetside cafés in Hoi An*

SPORTS AND ACTIVITIES

There is no shortage of sports and activities to try in Vietnam, whether you fancy trekking through the national parks, windsurfing or dicing in Nha Trang or enjoying a round of golf. Other popular pursuits include birding and cookery classes.

BICYCLING

Vietnam has great tracts of flat land, making bicycling a popular activity. The main hindrance is traffic on the roads; to avoid this, plan any bicycling tours off-road or on minor roads, not Highway 1. Many bicyclists prefer to bring their own all-terrain or racing bicycles, but it's also possible to rent from tour organizers. Tour operators in Ho Chi Minh City and Hanoi arrange a multitude of tours.

BIRDING

Vietnam may not seem like the first choice for a birding trip, but for those in the know it has become one of the top birding destinations of the region, thanks to its 10 endemic species, the highest number of any country in mainland Southeast Asia. Around 850 species have been recorded in Vietnam, and in a three-week intensive birding trip it should be possible to tick off around 250 to 300.

The best time of year for birding is November through May.

In Nam Cat Tien National Park, in the central region, there are an estimated 230 bird species. Endangered birds include Germain's peacock-pheasant, green peafowl and the orange-necked partridge, as well as bar-bellied and blue-rumped pitta, red, black and banded broadbill, and orange-bottomed trogon. Woolly-necked stork, Siamese fireback, scaly-bottomed partridge and woodpeckers can also be seen. Close to Dalat, in the Central Highlands, is Mount Lang Bian, where it's possible to see silver pheasant, Indochinese cuckooshrike, Eurasian jay, yellow-billed nuthatch, Mugimaki flycatcher, cutia and red crossbill. The endemic collared laughingthrush and the Vietnamese greenfinch can also be seen here. Closer to the town of Dalat, the rare and endemic grey-crowned crocias have been spotted. In Bach

Ma National Park, near the coast in the central region, more than 330 bird species have been recorded, including the Annam partridge, crested argus, coral-billed ground-cuckoo, Blyth's kingfisher, ratchet-tailed treepie and sultan tit. At Tam Dao, north of Hanoi, the grey laughing thrush, chestnut bulbul, black-chinned yuhina and fork-tailed sunbird make regular appearances. Cuc Phuong National Park, south of Hanoi, has more than 300 recorded species and attracts the gray peacock-pheasant; bar-bellied, blue-rumped and eared pitta; white-winged magpie; limestone wren- babbler; Fujian niltava; and pied falconet. In the Mekong Delta area, especially around the Plain of Reeds, there are several bird sanctuaries where it's possible to see wetland species (▷ 226).

COOKERY CLASSES

Cookery classes have not caught on in Vietnam in quite the way they have in Thailand, but the number of places offering classes and food tours is increasing, including hotels and restaurants in Hanoi, Saigon and Hoi An. Some operators run tours that include either half a day or a whole day of cooking.

GOLF
In the 1930s, Emperor Bao Dai laid a golf course in Dalat, and after a period of dormancy the game has enjoyed a resurgence. It remains chiefly an expatriate game, and the first courses to be opened in the 1990s were able to command colossal fees. There are currently 14 courses (some internationally designed and also foreign-owned), with a number of others planned or under construction, and green fees are now lower. Most are in southern Vietnam; the top two courses are in Dalat in the Central Highlands and in Phan Thiet on the coast.

GREYHOUND RACING
Dog racing is popular in Vietnam as it is the only legalized gambling available in the country. The Australian-financed greyhound stadium at Vung Tau is a popular venue for races every Saturday night (▷ 235).

HORSEBACK RIDING
Horseback riding is organized by a few tour operators in Dalat in the central region and in Sapa in the north. Excursions, which can vary in duration from one day to several days, are accompanied by guides and, in the case of longer trips, by support vehicles.

KAYAKING
Kayaking in Vietnam is virtually synonymous with Halong Bay and Lan Ha Bay. Although there are a few kayaks in places like Mui Ne and Ba Be Lakes, these are locally made and designed for gentle recreational use. Anyone wishing to kayak in earnest should head straight for Halong Bay, where operators arrange special-interest tours (▷ 114–117).

SOCCER
The Vietnamese are passionate about soccer and many children long to be players as adults. The Vietnamese league includes players and coaches from abroad.

SWIMMING
Many Vietnamese hotels have outdoor swimming pools, and those in Sapa, high in the mountains of northwestern Vietnam, have indoor ones. Pools vary in size: Beach resorts tend to have larger pools, while those in Ho Chi Minh City's hotels are generally tight for space. Rooftop pools provide stunning views. Outside Ho Chi Minh City is a waterpark that is hugely popular with Vietnamese families.

TENNIS
Luxury hotels offer tennis facilities. Courts can be found in Ho Chi Minh City, Can Tho and Phu Quoc in the south; Danang, China Beach, Dalat, Hoi An, Huê, Lang Co, Phan Thiet, Nha Trang and Long Hai in the central region; and Sapa in the north.

WALKING
There are plenty of opportunities for walking and trekking. The main focus is Sapa, in the north, but some trekking is organized around Dalat. Around Sapa, the stunning scenery and way of life provide ample opportunity for trekking through the hills and staying with local people. There are walks of varying durations, demanding different fitness levels and degrees of stamina. At several national parks you can trek and stay overnight. The main national parks are Ba Be and Cuc Phuong in the north; Cat Ba, on Cat Ba Island in Halong Bay; Bach Ma, close to the coast and near Huê; Yok Don, in the Central Highlands; and Nam Cat Tien, southwest of Dalat. Walking out of a town or city into the countryside can be a delightful experience, as you wander past paddy fields, buffalo and ducks. Trekking can be done alone or through tour

operators; homestays with families from ethnic minorities must be arranged through a tour operator. There are no accurate maps available for walkers in Vietnam.

WATERSPORTS
Diving takes place mainly between January and November; the height of activity is during the dry season, January through May. The biggest dive resort is Nha Trang; smaller resorts are Whale Island, Danang, Con Dao and Phu Quoc.

Windsurfing, kitesurfing and other watersports are popular in Mui Ne, which offers just about perfect conditions throughout the year. The wind is normally brisk over many days, and the combination of powerful wind and waves enables good kitesurfers to get airborne for several seconds at a time. Equipment and training are offered by a couple of outlets (▷ 168). Windsurfing is popular in Nha Trang, but the conditions are not quite in the same class as at Mui Ne.

Opposite *The areas of flat land are good for bicycling*
Below *Vietnam has several dive resorts*

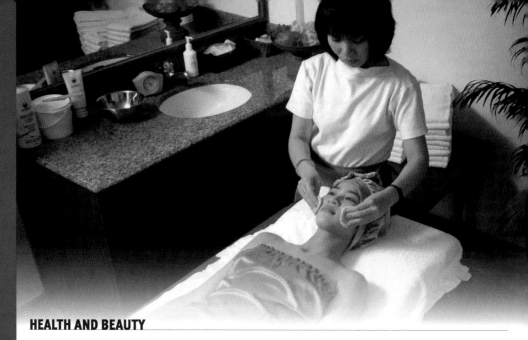

HEALTH AND BEAUTY

Save some time for relaxing while you are in Vietnam—you'll find a wide range of beauty salons and pampering services.

Spa treatments can be expensive, but prices are lower than those charged in major Western cities.

SPAS AND HOT SPRINGS
There are only a few authentic spas in Vietnam, but several places call themselves spas and many hotels offer spa facilities. The country's top spas are the Six Senses Spa at the Ana Mandara in Nha Trang (▷ 180) and at the Evason Hideaway at Ana Mandara on an island off Nha Trang (▷ 169). The Six Senses Spa has also opened at the Ana Mandara Villas Dalat and Spa (▷ 174) in Dalat. The Shiseido Spa at the

VinPearl Resort and Spa is on Hon Tre Island, also off Nha Trang. Many hotels offer massage, treatments and therapies. Ho Chi Minh City has a growing number of spas.

At Thap Ba Hot Springs (▷ 169), near Nha Trang, and at Binh Chau, near Vung Tau, there are thermal baths with mud and mineral water. As a bonus, prices are very low. (Take care at Binh Chau—at some places the water is hot enough to cook an egg!)

MASSAGE PARLORS
In Ho Chi Minh City and Hanoi, central areas are full of hair salons and foot-massage parlors. Some are sleazy, but you can tell this from the outside. Generally they are good value for money. Visitor magazines available at most hotels are bursting with advertisements, which can give you an idea of the best deals.

Above *Many hotels offer spa facilities*
Opposite *Tet festival masks*

FOR CHILDREN

The Vietnamese adore children, and give them a lot of attention, hugs and pats. In the north, pinching the cheeks of babies is a sign of love and affection. At the same time, Vietnam is not particularly well geared up to activities for children, and only the more expensive hotels offer specifically child-friendly facilities. Many activities, however, will appeal to both adults and children.

CHILDREN'S ACTIVITIES
Children in particular are likely to enjoy a water puppetry performance with its cast of attractive and lively characters, fireworks and loud

music. The water park outside Ho Chi Minh City will also delight youngsters, as will boat trips along the Mekong River or some of the country's other waterways. Some

attractions offer concessions for children; where this is the case, details are listed in the admission information under individual entries in this guide.

Vietnam has countless festivals celebrating ancient heroes, gods and legends with joyful or solemn ceremonies throughout the lunar calendar. Some of the country's major festivals are listed below. The following website converts from the Gregorian calendar to the lunar calendar: www.vietnamtourism.com/e_pages/tourist/festival.asp.

TET

Tet is the traditional Vietnamese New Year and comes some time between late January and March. Its name is the shortened version of *tet nguyen dan* (first morning of the new period). This is the time to forgive and forget, and to pay off debts. It is also everyone's birthday—the Vietnamese tend not to celebrate their birthdays, but everyone adds one year to their age at *Tet*. Enormous quantities of food are consumed, new clothes are bought, houses are painted and repaired, and kumquat trees are brought into homes; until a government-imposed ban in 1995, firecrackers were lit to welcome in the new year. As a Vietnamese saying has it: "Hungry all year, but *Tet* three days full."

It is believed that before *Tet* the spirit of the hearth, Ong Tao, leaves on a journey to visit the palace of the Jade Emperor, where he must report on family affairs. To ensure that Ong Tao sets off in good cheer, a ceremony is held before *Tet (Le Tao Quan)*, and during his absence a shrine is constructed *(Cay Neu)* to keep evil spirits at bay until his return. On the afternoon before *Tet (Tat Nien)* a sacrifice is offered at the family altar to dead relatives, who are invited back to join in the festivities.

Great attention is paid to preparations for *Tet* because the first week of the new year is believed to dictate your fortunes for the year to come.

The first visitor to the house on New Year's morning should be an influential, lucky and happy person, so families take care to arrange a suitable caller.

Visitors to Vietnam should be aware that the entire country is on the move at *Tet* and international

flights are reserved months in advance as overseas *Viet Kieu* return to Vietnam for the celebration. All domestic transportation and hotels throughout the country are reserved for days before and after *Tet*.

🕓 Movable, start of the new lunar year: Aug 31 (2012), Aug 21 (2013), Aug 10 (2014)

THANH MINH

During the New Year of the Dead, or Feast of the Pure Light, the Vietnamese walk outdoors to evoke the spirit of the dead, and family shrines and tombs are traditionally cleaned and decorated. The festival takes place in April.

🕓 Fifth or sixth day of the third lunar month

TRUNG NGUYEN

Wandering Souls Day, in August, is one of the most important festivals in Vietnam. During this time, prayers can absolve the sins of the dead, who leave hell and return, hungry and naked, to their relatives. The Wandering Souls are those with no homes to go to. There are celebrations in Buddhist temples and homes, food is placed out on tables, and ghost money is burned.

🕓 Movable, 15th day of the seventh lunar month: Feb 10 (2013), Jan 31 (2014)

TET TRUNG THU

The Mid-Autumn Festival, particularly celebrated by children, is based on various legends. One tells of a Chinese king who went to the moon and, on his return, wished to share what he had seen with the people on earth.

In the evening of the festival, families prepare special food, including sticky rice, fruit and chicken, to be placed on the ancestral altars. Moon cakes (egg, green bean, and lotus seed) are baked (with some variations on these ingredients, such as chocolate, offered by some of the smarter hotels), lanterns are made and painted, and children parade through towns with music and lanterns. The festival is particularly celebrated in Hanoi, where toy shops in the Old Quarter go to town decorating stores with lanterns and masks.

🕓 Movable, 15th day of the eighth lunar month: Sep 30 (2012), Sep19 (2013), Sep 8 (2014)

EATING

Vietnam's food is a major part of its appeal. This unique cuisine has developed over many centuries, absorbing a variety of national influences, such as Chinese and French, and adding them to local ingredients like *nuoc mam* (fish sauce), green leaves and chilies, with a dash of innovative flair. The result is some of the most exciting, original and tasty food available anywhere between Paris and Beijing.

In Vietnam you will find a wide selection of eating places, ranging from smart local, French and international restaurants to humble food stands, which offer exceptional meals. The accent is on local, seasonal, fresh produce, and rich pickings from the sea along Vietnam's 1,250-mile (2,000km) coastline, which are available far inland. Hearty stews are the tradition in the more remote north; along the coast, the tendency is toward salad dishes. Restaurants generally offer regional cuisines, though some specialize.

MEALS AND MEALTIMES

Breakfast is usually eaten between 6am and 7am and traditionally consists of a bowl of *pho* (▷ What to Eat, opposite). Hotels tend to serve breakfast up until about 10am; here you may be offered a cooked breakfast (eggs, bacon, tomatoes) or a simpler meal of bread or croissant with preserves. Lunch is eaten soon after 11am and is the most substantial meal of the day; restaurants catering to visitors carry on serving until 2pm. Dinner is a smaller meal for the Vietnamese, but restaurants serve evening meals between 5pm and 11pm, except in remote areas, where dinner may be served only until about 9.30.

All Vietnamese food is dipped, whether in fish sauce, soya sauce, chili sauce, peanut sauce or the particularly pungent prawn sauce *mam tom*. Each new course is served with a new set of dips. Your waiter can advise you on picking the right dip for your dish. Many restaurants provide fish sauce, chili sauce and rice as part of the price of the meal. More expensive establishments charge extra for rice.

Dessert choices in Vietnamese restaurants are usually limited to fruit, ice cream, *banh flan* (crème caramel) or *che* (beans and dried fruit in a sweet or savory syrup).

WHERE TO EAT

It is possible to eat out at very little cost in Vietnam, especially outside Hanoi and Saigon. Peripherals such as furniture, service and ambience are regarded as distractions from the main task of plowing through plates, crocks, casseroles and tureens of piping-hot meats, vegetables and soups. Smarter restaurants, particularly those serving foreign cuisine, can prove quite expensive, especially if wine is served. Some restaurants add 5 percent service charge and the government tax of 10 percent to the bill. But with judicious shopping around it is not hard to find excellent value for money, particularly in small, family-owned restaurants.

For day trips, an early morning visit to the markets will produce a picnic fit for a king. Hard-boiled quails' eggs, thinly sliced garlic sausage and salami, pickled vegetables, beefsteak tomatoes, cucumber, pâté, cheese, warm baguettes and fresh fruit will feed four for around a dollar a head.

There are vegetarian restaurants in Vietnam, most serving tofu dressed to look like meat rather than specific vegetarian dishes. In other restaurants be wary when ordering apparently vegetarian dishes, as vegetables are often cooked with pork, beef or prawns.

CHILDREN

Given the large proportion of the population aged 16 and under, it isn't surprising that, in the main, Vietnamese restaurants have no problem catering to children. Indeed, any restaurant frequented by Vietnamese families is likely to have children running around everywhere. Lively and exuberant behavior is generally tolerated and taken as a matter of course. In most places the waitstaff will make a big fuss of Western children, especially those with fair hair. In the smarter establishments, such as those in hotels, unruly children may not be as popular.

If your children do not develop a taste for Vietnamese food, try eating at restaurants with a mixed or exclusively international menu, where children can enjoy the standard fare of pizzas, pastas, burgers and sausages.

ETIQUETTE

Dinner table etiquette is pretty informal: Meals are generally a family occasion, and an opportunity

for conversation. It's impolite to start before everyone has been served rice, and to take too much of one dish for yourself. Dishes are set in the middle of the table for all to dip into with their chopsticks: Take one or two pieces at a time. Spoon soup into your bowl and eat it with your spoon or put your bowl to your lips. It's acceptable to hold your rice bowl up to your mouth and shovel the rice in with your chopsticks.

Nose-blowing is seen as unhygienic: If you must, turn away from the table. It's considered bad manners to use one of the readily available toothpicks without covering your mouth.

The practice of tipping varies widely. The locals do not normally tip if eating in small family restaurants but may tip extravagantly in expensive bars. Foreigners normally leave small change, which is quite acceptable and is appreciated by the waitstaff.

WHAT TO EAT

» *Pho* is a noodle soup made from stock flavored with star anise, ginger and other spices and herbs; individual recipes often remain a closely guarded secret. *Pho* is served with chicken or beef and is eaten in the morning and often in the evening, but rarely at lunchtime. *Pho* restaurants offer plates of fresh green leaves—mint, cinnamon, basil, spiky *ngo gai*—and some extras such as bean sprouts, chopped red chilies, barbecue sauce and sliced lemons, so that patrons can make their own versions.

» *Com tam* (broken rice) is served in street stands, which do a brisk trade at breakfast and lunch. In many cities they are abandoning their tiny plastic stools in favor of tables and chairs. The steamed, broken rice is eaten with fried chicken, fish, pork and vegetables; soup is normally included in the price of the dish.

» The most common type of spring roll is deep-fried (*cha gio* in the south, *nem ranh* in the north), but

there are also delicious fresh or roll-it-yourself versions, such as *bi cuon* or *bo bia*. Essentially, these are salads with prawns or grilled meats wrapped in rice paper. Customers can roll their own, but it's not easy, and you can end up with sagging versions that collapse into your lap.

» There is a bewildering variety of seafood on offer. One particularly tasty dish is crab in tamarind sauce, combining a fusion of flavors such as sour tamarind, garlic and scallion (spring onion); to eat it you must be willing to crack and suck the meat from the farthest recesses of the crab's claws and legs.

» The tiny nests of the brown-rumped swift *(Collocalia esculenta)*, also known as the edible-nest swiftlet or sea swallow, are collected for bird's-nest soup throughout Southeast Asia.

The semi-oval nests are made of silk-like strands of saliva secreted by the birds, which when cooked in broth soften and become a little like noodles. The nests are believed to have aphrodisiac qualities, and the Vietnamese Emperor Minh Mang (reigned 1820–1840) is said to have owed his extraordinary vitality to his inordinate consumption of bird's-nest soup. Red nests are the most highly valued. Collecting the nests is a profitable but extremely precarious business that involves climbing rickety ladders to cave roofs, sometimes in almost total darkness save for a candle strapped to the head.

FRUITS OF VIETNAM

» The custard apple, or sugar apple *(Annona squamos)*, has a scaly green skin that you squeeze to reveal the flesh inside. This is then scooped out with a spoon.

» Durian *(Durio zibethinus)* is a large, prickly fruit with yellow flesh, infamous for its pungent smell; in fact, it is banned from many hotel rooms. Nevertheless, if you can overcome the smell the durian has an alluring taste, and durian-flavored chewing gum, ice cream and jams are available.

» Jackfruit *(Artocarpus heterophyllus)* is similar in appearance to durian, but its yellow flesh is smoother. The fruit tastes slightly like custard.

» Mango *(Mangifera indica)* comes in hundreds of different varieties with subtle variations in flavor, and is delicious with sticky rice and a sweet sauce.

» Mangosteen *(Garcinia mangostana)* is a small fruit in a hard, purple shell. Cut or squeeze the shell to reach its sweet, white flesh.

» Papaya *(Carica papaya)*, introduced into Southeast Asia in the 16th century, is large, round or oval, and yellow- or green-skinned, with bright, orange flesh and a collection of round, black seeds in the middle.

» Pomelo *(Citrus grandis)* is a large, round fruit with dense, green skin, thick pith, and flesh not unlike that of the grapefruit, but less acidic.

» Rambutan *(Nephelium lappaceum)* is bright red and hairy—*rambut* is the Malay word for "hair"—and has slightly rubbery but sweet flesh.

» Salak *(Salacca edulis)* is a small, pear-shaped fruit with a rough, brown, scaly skin and yellow-white, crisp flesh. It is related to the sago and rattan trees.

» Tamarind *(Tamarindus indicus)* comes as brown seed pods with dry, brittle skins, or a brown, tart-sweet fruit whose flesh has a high tartaric acid content and is used to flavor curries, jams, jellies and chutneys, as well as for cleaning brass and copper.

DOG MEAT

Westerners may be taken aback by some of the dishes on offer in northern restaurants. One establishment advertises its specialty with the question: "Who can resist a steaming bowl of broth with a pair of dog's paws?" Dog meat *(thit chó* or *thit cay)* is an esteemed delicacy in the north of Vietnam, but is usually served only in specialist outlets at certain times of the month. These tend to be shacks on the edge of a town, and you are unlikely to order dog meat inadvertently in a standard restaurant.

BEER

Locally produced fresh beer is called *bia hoi*. It is cold and refreshing, and weak and inexpensive enough to drink in quite large volumes. As a rule, beer is consumed in small sidewalk (pavement) cafés, where patrons sit on plastic stools. Most of these *bia hoi* cafés also serve simple and inexpensive food, and almost all their customers are men. As the beer is fresh it has to be consumed within a short period of brewing. As a result, most towns, even quite small ones, have their own breweries, and each community imparts to its beer its own local flavor.

Unfortunately, bars and restaurants do not sell *bia hoi* as its low price—just 5,000d per pint (half liter)—offers them little benefit. Hence bar customers have a choice of Tiger, Heineken, Carlsberg, San Miguel, 333, Saigon Beer or Huda. All are brewed in Vietnam, but many visitors prefer to stick to the local beers (333, Saigon and Huda), which are the most inexpensive brands and considered by many to have more distinctive flavors than the mass-produced international brands. This is not always possible, however, as many bars and restaurants stock only the more expensive beers.

WINE

Rice and fruit wines are produced and consumed in large quantities in upland areas, particularly in the north of Vietnam, though rice wines are fairly widely available throughout the country. There are two types of rice wine: *ruou nep* and *ruou de*. *Ruou nep* is a viscous wine made from sticky rice. It comes in different colors—purple and white—as a result of the different types of rice used to make it. Among Vietnam's ethnic minorities, who are recognized as masters of rice wine, *ruou nep* is drunk from a ceramic jar through a straw. This communal drinking is an integral part of the way of life of the Montagnards, and no doubt contributes substantially to the strengthening of clan ties. A word of warning: It is possible to become very drunk on *ruou nep* without realizing it. *Ruou de* is a rice spirit and is also very strong.

There is a very wide range of fruit wines but unless you make a real effort it can be quite hard to find them. Wines are made from just about all upland fruits, including plum, strawberry, apple and, of course, grapes—but grape wine in Vietnam is generally disappointing. Most restaurants offer New and Old World wines and some offer the local Dalat wine, which is not very highly rated by wine experts, but has the advantage of being inexpensive. The other fruit wines on offer are fiery and warm, strong and, by the bottle, cost very little.

Snake wines are another variant enjoyed in Vietnam. Chinese tradition holds that snake wines increase virility, and as a result they are normally found in areas with large Chinese populations. In fact snake wine is, strictly speaking, a spirit, rather than a wine. Other wines are made using the bodies and parts of sea horses, geckos, silkworms and honey bees.

SOFT DRINKS

Soft drinks and bottled still and sparkling mineral water are widely available. It is probably not wise to drink tap water (▷ 251).

Tea and coffee are sold everywhere, but if you are used to American or European beverages the local versions can be an acquired taste. The Vietnamese tend to drink coffee black, but restaurants catering to the tourist trade are always happy to provide milk. There are also some unusual coffee flavors that take some courage to sample—for example, coffee that has passed through the innards of a weasel!

MENU READER

Ordering Vietnamese food can be a daunting prospect, but knowledge of a few key words will help you work out what's available on the menu, order what you want and avoid any embarrassing blunders. This menu reader will help you translate some common words, dishes and ingredients.

Above *A range of Vietnamese dishes at a buffet*

MEAT (THIT)
bò kho stewed beef
bò nhúng dam beef dipped in vinegar
bò nuong lá lot/mo chài grilled beef wrapped in vegetable leaf/pork fat
bò tung xeo sliced grilled beef
bún mang vit duck with bamboo-shoot noodles
bún thit nuong grilled pork and noodles
cánh gà chiên nuoc mam fried chicken wings in fish sauce
càri gà chicken curry
cha giò thit/tom pork/shrimp spring rolls
chân gà rút xuong boneless chicken-feet salad
dua dau heo pickled pork
ech frog
ech chiên bo frog fried in butter
ech lan bôt deep-fried frog
gà chicken
gà nuong grilled chicken
gà quay roasted chicken
goi gà/gà xé phay chicken salad
heo sua quay roasted young pork
lap xuong Chinese sausage
nem chua pickled pork wrapped in vegetable leaf
nem nuong grilled pork rolls
oc snails
oc hap gung snails steamed with ginger
oc len xào dua snails with coconut milk
oc nhoi pork-stuffed snails
thit bò beef
thit dê goat
thit gà chicken
thit heo pork

thit vit duck
vit duck
vit lap dry duck
vit quay roasted duck

FISH/SEAFOOD (CÁ/HAI SAN)
cá com chiên dòn deep-fried anchovy
cá hap steamed fish
cá lóc nuong dat sét grilled trout wrapped in clay
cá lóc nuong lá chuoi grilled trout wrapped in banana leaf
cá lóc nuong trui trout grilled in straw
cá tai tuong chiên xù deep-fried fish
cá trê chiên cham mam gung fried catfish with ginger sauce
com hen mussel rice
cua crab
cua hap bia crab steamed in beer
cua hap gung crab steamed with ginger
cua rang me tamarind crab
goi hen xào dhe mussel salad with star fruit
goi tôm ngó sen lotus stem and shrimp salad
hào song raw oyster
khô muc trôn buoi dried squid mixed with grapefruit
lau cá fish hot pot
lúon eel

muc squid
muc tuoi lan bot chiên deep-fried squid
muc xào stir-fried squid
nghêu nuong grilled clam
nuoc nam fish sauce
sò shellfish
sò nuong/hap grilled/steamed shellfish
tôm shrimp
tôm càng nuong grilled lobster
tôm hap bia shrimp steamed in beer
tôm hùm lobster
tôm nuong grilled prawn
tôm sú hap nuoc dua tiger prawns steamed in coconut

SOUP (CANH/XÚP)
canh chua cá sour fish soup
canh rau vegetable soup
cháo gà chicken rice soup
cháo hen mussel rice soup
cháo trang hot vit muoi rice soup with salted duck eggs
cháo vit duck rice soup
hoành thành wonton soup
pho soup with flat, white, rice noodles
xú bong bóng cá fish soup
xúp cua crab soup
xúp mang cua crab and asparagus soup

NOODLES (MÌ)
bánh canh fat round rice noodles
bún bò hué Huê beef noodles
hu tíu pork noodles
mì quang Quang Nam noodles
mì vit tiem Chinese duck noodles
mì xào giòn crispy fried noodles

RICE/VEGETABLES (COM/RAU CAI)
bap/ngô corn
bông bí xào fried pumpkin flower
bông cai cauliflower
bông cai xào fried cauliflower
cà chua tomato
cà rot carrot
cai bó xôi xào toi spinach fried with garlic
com chiên Duong Chau Cantonese fried rice
com niêu rice in clay pot
dau beans
dau hu tofu
dua chua pickled vegetable
dua leo cucumber
giá bean sprouts
hành tây onion
khoai tây potato
mang bamboo shoot

nâm mushroom
oi Da Lat green pepper
rau muong spinach
rau muong xào toi morning glory fried with garlic
rau sà lách lettuce

OTHER BASICS
bánh mì bread
cha giò spring rolls
mien vermicelli
nuoc tuong soya sauce
trung egg

DRINKS
cà phê dá iced coffee
cà phê den black coffee
cà phê sua dá milky iced coffee
cam vat orange juice
mot chai bia bottle of beer
mot chai nuoc suoi bottle of mineral water
mot lon bia can of beer
nuoc chanh lemon juice
nuoc dua coconut
ruou de rice wine
sinh to thom pineapple shake
trà/chè (N) tea
noc huan sparkling water

FRUIT/OTHER DISHES (TRÁI CÂY/CÁC MÓN KHÁC)
bánh khoái Hué sizzling cake
bánh xèo sizzling cake
trái/qua bó avocado
trái/qua buoi grapefruit
trái/qua cam orange
trái/qua chanh lemon
trái/qua choi banana
trái/qua chôm rambutan
trái/qua dào peach
trái/qua du dû papaya
trái/qua dua hau watermelon
trái/qua mân/roi plum
trái/qua nhan longan
trái/qua quyt mandarin
trái/qua thóm/dua pineapple
trái/qua vai lychee

COOKING METHODS
chiên/rán fried
hap steamed
luoc boiled
nuong grilled
quay roasted

Accommodation options in Vietnam range from luxury suites in 5-star hotels and spa resorts to small, family hotels (mini-hotels) and homestays with local people. The types of places to stay are limited in range, partly due to the country's as yet underdeveloped tourism industry; but it is possible for accommodations to offer a real insight into Vietnamese life, and to be an invaluable part of the whole Vietnam experience.

RESERVATIONS

Nearly all hotels have a website or an email address that can be used to make reservations and to check offers, though in most cases the best rates are found through one of the many speicalist reservation websites. It's worth reserving in advance, especially if you plan to tour the country. Reservations are essential during peak times, especially December through March, during busy festivals such as *Tet* (Vietnamese New Year), Christmas, December 31 and Easter.

HOTELS

A star classification is awarded to hotels by the Vietnam National Administration of Tourism (VNAT), and while this may not tally with the requirements expected in other countries, modern hotels in Vietnam are comfortable and well run and, by international standards, offer good value for money. Most staff speak English in the top establishments, but not in less expensive or more remote hotels—although most places employ someone with a smattering of a foreign language.

» High-quality hotels and luxurious beach resorts are steadily increasing in number: You can expect standards to match, and often exceed, comparably priced accommodations in other parts of the world. New establishments, especially small ones not linked to international hotel brand names, are especially worth seeking out.

» If you pay more than US$30 for a room, facilities should include private bathroom (though not necessarily with a bathtub), air-conditioning, minibar, TV, phone and usually a safe.

» If you pay less than US$30, you can expect the same facilities. Occasionally there may be no minibar, but the room should have a private bathroom, possibly with only a plastic showerhead and with or without a bath/shower cubicle.

Above *A line of beach huts at Ca Na*

» Sheets, towels and mosquito nets (where necessary) are always provided. Many hotels also have ceiling fans as well as air-conditioning. In some inexpensive hotels pillows are made from foam rubber.

» Vietnam is a tropical country. In the listings sections of this guide, swimming pools are outdoors unless otherwise stated.

Hotels at the lower end of the price range usually offer quite good value for money. In particular, private mini-hotels are worth seeking out. These are family-run, and the owners often take a close interest in their guests and are willing to advise on local sightseeing. Staying in mini-hotels is a good way to get to know Vietnamese people.

» Mid-range and tourist hotels may provide good breakfasts, which are often included in the price.

» However, many luxury and top-range hotels charge extra for breakfast, and also add value-added tax (VAT) and a service charge.

» The majority of hotels (apart from private mini-hotels) have restaurants, where standards vary widely. Most hotels have a laundry service; the more expensive the hotel, the greater the charge, and VAT and a service charge will also be added.

BEACH RESORTS

There are luxurious five-star beach resorts in Nha Trang, Mui Ne, Hoi An and Danang, some with spa facilities of very high standards, where you can enjoy excellent service and food in beautiful surroundings. Many resorts have private beaches or at least a beachfront area, and the vast majority have swimming pools.

BOATS

It's possible to spend a night on a boat in Halong Bay or on the Mekong Delta. Standards on the boats range from fairly luxurious to basic. Most guests reserve their stays through tour operators, but you can make arrangements in Halong City or Cat Ba Island for Halong Bay (▷ 114–117), and through hotels and tour operators in Can Tho for a Mekong River trip (▷ 218–219).

GUESTHOUSES

Guesthouses differ slightly from hotels and mini-hotels in that guests are made to feel like members of the family. It's quite common for guests to be invited to eat with the owners. For long-staying visitors, the guesthouse is usually a very economical option.

HOMESTAYS

» In places such as Sapa and Mai Chau, in the northern uplands, you can stay in an ethnic minority stilt house. In general, this type of accommodation is quite strictly controlled by the Vietnamese authorities, and minority houses are out of bounds in most of the Central Highlands. Don't expect luxuries; the host families have precious few themselves. You are likely to sleep on a rush mat with a hard pillow; bathrooms are basic and consist of a cold shower and a hole-in-the-ground lavatory.

» Make your reservation through a tour operator or through the local tourist office—do not simply turn up in a village, as you will not be welcome.

» In the Mekong Delta, you can stay on farms and in orchards. This is an interesting way to see an attractive part of rural Vietnam, and here guests sleep on camp beds and share a Western-style bathroom with hot and cold water.

NATIONAL PARKS

National parks offer a wide range of accommodations, from air-conditioned bungalows to shared dormitory rooms or campgrounds where, sometimes, it is possible to rent a tent.

SERVICED APARTMENTS

Large towns have serviced apartments, which are ideal for people staying in one place for a considerable period of time, as they are generally cheaper than hotels for long stays.

» Some hotels in Ho Chi Minh City rent out their own serviced apartments, many for fairly short periods (a few days), although the shorter the rental period, the higher the price per night.

» Apartment sizes vary from a cramped single bedroom to a more spacious four bedrooms, and prices generally vary according to the facilities available.

CHECKING IN AND OUT

» It is perfectly acceptable to ask to see a room before taking it. This is especially recommended in the event of any confusion over the provision of "twin" (two-bed) rooms or "double occupancy" rooms, where two guests may share one bed for no extra charge.

» You will be asked to show your passport at the reception desk when you check in and a photocopy will be taken.

» Check-out time varies from hotel to hotel.

» Hotels are generally willing to store your luggage for you until the end of your check-out day.

PRICING

» Many hotels do not charge anything for the cost of local telephone calls, and some will also offer daily, complimentary bottled water.

» Larger and more expensive hotels add 10 percent VAT and a 5 percent service charge to the price. Smaller hotels generally quote all-inclusive prices.

» Credit cards are widely accepted.

» Although room rates are still sometimes quoted in US dollars, all places accept Vietnamese dong. Tipping is not expected in hotels.

ONLINE RESERVATIONS

www.asiatravel.com/vietnam
www.expedia.com
www.ebookers.com
www.asiarooms.com

Outside Saigon, Hanoi, Huê, Hoi An, Nha Trang, Dalat and other visitor centers, language can be a problem for those who have no knowledge of Vietnamese, although you are likely to find a smattering of English wherever there are visitor services.

Vietnamese is not easy to pick up and pronunciation can sometimes present difficulties, but it is worth making an effort, and the Vietnamese are delighted when foreigners try to speak in their language.

» Vietnamese uses six tones and has 12 vowels and 27 consonants—pronunciation is varied by the use of diacritical marks.

» As in other tonal languages, one word can mean many things depending upon the tone used: "ma," for example, can mean horse, cheek, ghost, grave or rice seedling.

» Vietnamese is written in a Roman alphabet, so place and street names are recognizable.

» Vietnamese–English and English–Vietnamese dictionaries are inexpensive and widely available in most towns.

» English is the most useful foreign language; visitors can find themselves asked to clarify some point of pronunciation or grammar.

» French is still spoken by the more elderly and educated.

SOUNDS

TONAL SOUNDS

There are six tonal sounds in Vietnamese, which apply to a selection of vowels: a, e o and u. These tones depend on voice pitch and change in pitch.

The mid tone is unmarked but other tones are represented by various additional characters.

For instance, "á" indicates that the voice rises sharply from middle range; "ò'" indicates that the voice lowers from middle range, and "o?" tells the speaker to use a rising tone. The "ã" represents the voice starting low, rising sharply but broken by a stop, and the "o'" starts low and drops even lower.

VOWEL SOUNDS

a	as in rather
ă	as in cut
â	as in hum
e	as in egg
ê	as in say
i	as in bin
y	as in be
o	as in saw
ô	as in so
ơ	as in blur
u	as in rule
ư	as in put

CONSONANT SOUNDS

ch	as in child
-ch	as in eke (end position)
d	as in zip
d-	as in dad
g	as in gad
gi	as in zip
kh	as in king
ng	as in singer
nh	as in onion
ph	like an "f"
r	like a "z" in the north of the country like a "r" in the south
th	as in ten
tr	as in train
x	like an "s"

VOCABULARY

BASICS

yes	da co
no	da khong
please	lam on/xin
thank you	cam on
excuse me	xin loi
good night	chuc anh/chi ngu ngon
Where is the toilet?	Nha ve sinh o dau?

INTRODUCTIONS

hello or goodbye
xin chao

How are you?
Ong/ba khoe khong?

I'm fine, thanks
Cam on, toi khoe

What's your name?
Ong/ba ten la gi?

My name is...
Toi ten la...

How old are you?
Ong/ba bao nhieu tuoi?

Are you married?
Ahn/chi lap gia dinh chua?

Do you have children?
Ong/ba co con khong?

I'm glad to see you
Rat han hanh duoc gap ong/ba

This is my wife/husband
Day la nhatoi

daughter
con gai

son
con trai

What is your job?
Ong/ba lam nghe gi?

PROFESSIONS

I'm a...	Toi la...
...doctor	bac si
...nurse	y ta
...teacher	giao vien
...student	hoc sinh
...engineer	ky su
...journalist	nha bao
...lawyer	luat su
...secretary	thu ky
...clerk	vien chuc/ van phong
...worker	cong nhan
...farmer	nong dan
...scientist	khoa hoc gia
...tourist	khach du lich

NATIONALITIES

Which country are you from?
Ong/ba la nguoi nuoc nao?

I am...	Toi la nguoi...
...American	My
...Australian	Uc
...Austrian	Ao
...British	Anh
...Chinese	Trung Quoc
...Danish	Dan Mach

...Dutch ...Ha Lan
...French ...Phap
...German ...Duc
...Indian ...An Do
...Irish ...Ai Nhi Lan
...Italian ...Y
...Japanese ...Nhat
...Norwegian ...Na Uy
...Swedish ...Thuy Dien
...Swiss ...Thuy Si

EMERGENCIES

emergency .... khan cap/cap cuu
fire .... dam chay/lua
flood .... lut/lu lut
help .... giup/giup do
accident .... tai nan
ambulance .... xe cuu thuong
backache .... dau lung
broken .... hu
cut .... cat
dentist .... nha si
disease .... benh tat
dizzy .... chong mat
doctor .... bac si
eye .... mat
fever .... sot
headache .... nhuc dau/dau dau
hospital .... benh vien
ill .... benh/om/dau
injured .... bi thuong
medicine .... thuoc
nurse .... y ta
pharmacy .... hieu thuoc tay
sick .... benh/om/dau

CONSULAR

consulate .... lanh su quan
embassy .... su quan/toa dai su
interpreter .... nguoi phien dich/
thong dich vien
passport . ho chieu/giay thong hanh

CRIME

arrest .... bat giam
credit card .... the tin dung
luggage .... hanh ly
police officer .... canh sat
police station .... tram canh sat
robbed .... bi cuop
traveler's checks ..... ngan phieu du
lich
wallet .... vi/bop

TAKING A TRIP

I want a ticket to...
Toi muon mot ve di...

How much is a ticket?
Bao nhieu tien mot ve?
return-ticket
ve khu hoi
one-way ticket
ve mot chieu
I want to go to...
Toi muon di den...
Is there a bus to Hanoi?
Co chuyen xe buyt di Ha Noi
khong?
Does this bus go to Sapa?
Xe nay co di den Sapa khong?
When is the next train?
Chuyen xe lua ke tiep vao luc nao?
How long does the trip take?
Hanh trinh mat bao lau?
I want the next train to Hue
Toi muon mot chuyen tau som nhat
di Hue
I want to go by express train
Toi muon mot chuyen tau toc hanh
What time does the train arrive?
Xe lua den luc may gio?
What time will the train depart?
Xe lua se khoi hanh luc may gio?
The train is late
Chuyen xe lua bi te
The train has been cancelled
Chuyen xe lua bi huy

USEFUL WORDS

airport .... phi truong
boat .... thuyen
bus station .... ben xe
car .... xe hoi/oto
church .... nha tho
ferry .... pha
ferry station .... ben pha
flight .... chuyen bay
market .... cho
museum .... vien bao tang
pagoda .... chua
post office .... buu dien
ship .... tau
train .... xe lua/tau hoa

DIRECTIONS

Where is the...? .... o dau...?
railway station .... ga xe lua
school .... truong hoc
university .... truong dai hoc
Could you show me the way
to...?
Ong/ba co the chi toi duong toi...?
Is it far? .... Co xa khong?
Is it near? .... Co gan khong?

go straight .... di thang
turn left .... queo/re trai
turn right .... queo/re phai
crossroads .... nga tu
intersection .... nga ba
traffic circle .... bung binh

COLORS

black .... den
blue .... xanh da troi
brown .... nau
green .... xanh la cay
gray .... xam
orange .... cam
pink .... hong
purple .... tim
red .... do
white .... trang
yellow .... vang
color .... mau
dark .... dam
light .... nhat/lat

NUMBERS

1 .... mot
2 .... hai
3 .... ba
4 .... bon
5 .... nam
6 .... sau
7 .... bay
8 .... tam
9 .... chin
10 .... muoi/mot chuc
11 .... muoi mot
12 .... muoi hai
15 .... muoi lam...etc
20 .... hai muoi
21 .... hai muoi mot
30 .... ba muoi...etc
100 .... mot tram
101 .... mot tram le mot
.... (or mot tram mot)
200 .... hai tram...etc
1,000 .... mot nghin/mot
.... ngan
10,000 .... muoi nghin/
.... muoi ngan
100,000 .... mot tram nghin
1,000,000 .... mot trieu

DAYS AND TIME

morning .... buoi sang
noon .... trua
afternoon .... buoi chieu
evening .... buoi toi
night .... ban dem

day time	ban ngay
today	hom nay
yesterday	hom qua
tomorrow	ngay mai
day	ngay
week	tuan
weekend	cuoi tuan
month	thang
year	nam

one o'clock	mot gio
two o'clock	hai gio
three o'clock	ba gio
four o'clock	bon gio...etc

Sunday	chu nhat
Monday	thu hai
Tuesday	thu ba
Wednesday	thu tu
Thursday	thu nam
Friday	thu sau
Saturday	thu bay
spring	mua xuan
summer	mua ha/he
autumn	mua thu
winter	mua dong

MONTHS

January	thang gieng
February	thang hai
March	thang ba
April	thang tu
May	thang nam
June	thang sau
July	thang bay
August	thang tam
September	thang chin
October	thang muoi
November	thang muoi mot
December	thang muoi hai

RESTAURANTS

Can I have the menu please?
Xin cho toi xem thuc don?

I'm a vegetarian
Toi an chay

No chili, please
Xin dung cho ot

I'd like some rice
Toi muon mot it com

Do you have traditional food?
Co mon an truyen thong khong?

Do you have any special dishes? Mon nao la dac san cua quan?

It's delicious
Rat ngon

I'm thirsty
Toi khat nuoc

Cold water, please
Cho toi xin mot coc nuoc lanh

No ice
khong da

Is the water safe to drink?
Nuoc uong co sach khong?

SHOPPING

I'd like to buy some clothes
Toi muon mua mot it quan ao

How much is it?
Gia bao nhieu?

It's too expensive
Mac qua

Can you lower the price?
Co bot khong?

Oh, it's still very expensive
O, van con mac lam

Is 10,000 dong OK?
10,000 dong, duoc khong?

Can I have a look?
Toi co the xem duoc khong?

Do you have one in a bigger size?
Ong/ba co co lon hon khong?

Sorry, I don't like it
Rat tiec, toi khong thich

Do you have another one?
Ong/ba co cai khac khong?

I will take this one
Toi se mua cai nay

They don't/It doesn't fit me
No khong vua voi toi

It's too small
No nho qua

USEFUL SHOPPING WORDS

bag	gio xach
book	sach
cigarette	thuoc la
clothes	quan ao
duty free	mien thue
fabric	vai
film (camera)	phim
gas/petrol	xang
handicraft	do thu cong
hat	non
jacket	ao khoac
matches	que diem
paintings	tranh
pottery	do gom
raincoat	ao mua
razor	dao cao
sandals	dep
shampoo	xa-phong goi dau

shoes	giay
skirt	vay dam
socks	vo
souvenir	do luu niem
supermarket	sieu thi
T-shirt	ao pun ngan tay

VIETNAMESE ADDRESSES

Large buildings with a single street number are usually subdivided 21A, 21B, 21C etc; some buildings may be further subdivided 21C1, 21C2, 21C3 and so on. So, if you are standing at 21 Hai Ba Trung Street and want number 31, it may be as far as two blocks away.

An oblique (/) in a number, as in 23/16 Dinh Tien Hoang Street, means that the address is to be found in a small side street *(hem)*, in this case running off Dinh Tien Hoang Street by the side of No. 23; the house in question will probably be signed 23/16 rather than just 16. Usually, but by no means always, a *hem* will be quieter than the main street, and it may be worth looking at a guesthouse with an oblique number for that reason (especially in the Pham Ngu Lao area of Saigon).

An address sometimes contains the letter F followed by a number, as in F6; this is short for *phuong* (ward, a small administrative area). Q in an address stands for *quan* (district); this points you in the right general direction and is important in locating your destination, as a long street in Hanoi or Saigon may run through several *quan*. In suburban and rural areas districts are known as *huyen*—Huyen Nha Be, outside Saigon, for instance. Note that there are no zip codes (post codes) in Vietnam.

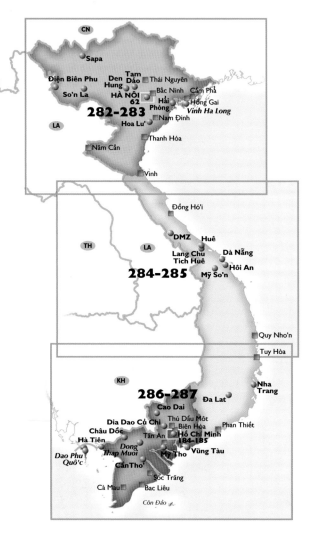

CN

Sapa

Điện Biên Phu
Den
Hung
Tam
Đảo
Thái Nguyên
So'n La
HÀ NỘI
62
Bắc Ninh
Cẩm Phả
Hải
Phòng
Hồng Gai
Vinh Ha Long
LA
Nam Định
Hoa Lu'
Nâm Cần
Thanh Hóa

282-283

Vinh

Đồng Hó'i

DMZ
Huê

TH
LA
Lang Chu
Tich Huê
Dà Nẵng
Hôi An

284-285
Mỹ So'n

Quy Nho'n

Tuy Hòa

KH
Nha
Trang

286-287
Đa Lat

Cao Dai

Dia Dao Cú Chi
Thú Dầu Môt
Biên Hòa
Phan Thiết
Châu Dốc
Tân An
Hồ Chí Minh
Hà Tiên
184-185
Dong
Thap Muoi
Mỹ Tho
Vũng Tàu
Dao Phu
Quố'c
CầnTho'
Sốc Trăng
Cà Mau
Bac Liêu
Côn Đảo

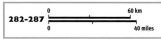

282-287

0		60 km
0		40 miles

	Motorway (Expressway)		Featured place of interest
	National road	■	City / Town
	Regional road		Built-up area
	Minor road		Railway
	Track	✈	Airport
	International boundary	621 ▲	Height in metres
--	Administrative provincial boundary	⌂	Ferry route

MAPS

Map references for the sights refer to the atlas pages within this section or to the individual town plans within the regions. For example, Huê has the reference ✚ 285 E6, indicating the page on which the map is found (285) and the grid square in which Huê sits (E6).

Xinxu

Litang

Silong

Wuming

Nanning

CN

Longmin

You Jiang

Wuxu

 hà Quảng

Hà Quảng

Trà Lĩnh

Trùng Khánh

Mã Phục

hông hồng

Quảng Noa

Nguyên Bình

Cao Bằng

Phục Hoa

Xijin Sk

Lingshan

BẰNG

Ắc Bó

Ngã Sơn

Năm Nàng

Dawangtan Sk

Phác

Na Ri

Thạch An

Qin Jiang

AN

Lam Son

Thất Khê

Văn Mịch

Fengdinghe Sk

322

Qinzhou

c

Cảnh Cung Ngân Sơn

4A

279

Bình Gia

Van Lang

Đồng Đăng

Banli

Sifang Ling

Naban Sk

u'o'ng

Võ Nhai

IB

Bắc Sơn

Văn Quán

Lang So'n

Ningming

NGUYÊN

LẠNG SO'N

Chi Lăng

Đồng Mỏ

Lộc Bình

Na Du'o'ne

1462

Shiwan Dashan

Fangcheng

Qinzhou Wan

Beihai Gang

Beihai

hái Nguyên

Trai Câu

379

Yên Thế

Hữu Lũng

Hồ Cầm So'n

Cẩm Sơn

Pỏ Đòn

Đình Lập

Bình Liêu

Quảng Thành

Hải Ninh

hò Yên

Nhã Nam

Kép

Lục Ngạn

31

Khe Giảm

Nà Péo

QUẢNG

Quảng Hà

Hiệp Hòa

Bắc Giang

BẮC GIANG

So'n Đong

Bãi Liêu

Tiên Yên

Đ Vĩnh Thự'c

a Phúc

Lục Nam

Tuần Mậu

Ba Chẽ

Đầm Hà

ồng

BẮC NINH

Chí Linh

Vàng Danh

279

Lọng So'n

NINH

18

Đái Xuyên

Cẩm Phả

Đ Thanh Lân

Bắc Ninh

Phả Lại

Đồng Triều

Uông Bí

Mồng Du'o'ng

Cẩm Phả

Đ Cô Tô

ền Viên

Thuận Thành

Hải

Kim Môn

Vũ Dai

HẢI PHÒNG

Đ Quan Lạn

an Diễn

Mỹ Vẫn

Du'o'ng

An Hải

Hồng Gai

Vịnh Ha Long

Châu Giang

Tứ Lộc

HẢI HU'NG

Yen Hu'ng

HẢI PHÒNG

Ninh Thanh

Kiến An

Tiên Lãng

Đao Cát Bà

y Tiên

Phù Tiên

Ninh Giang

Vĩnh Bảo

Đồ So'n

Beibu Wan

HU'NG YÊN

Hu'ng Yên

Đồng Hu'ng

NAM

Hà Nam

THÁI BÌNH

Vũ Thu

Thái Thủy

Vịnh Bắc Bộ

Vụ Bản

Tiền Hải

Lú'

Nam Định

Ninh

Nghĩa Hu'ng

Xuân Thủy

BÌNH

Yên Định

Bìm So'n

Kim So'n

Nha Thơ Chanh Toa

Phat Diem

Nga So'n

Rạng Đông

ậu Lộc

Lạch Tru'ong

hanh Hóa

Sầm So'n

ang Lợi

Gia

Hòn Mê

Haikou

Haikou

Nghi So'n

ái

u'

Quèn

Dongfang

CN

Hainan Dao

n Hội

Đà Nẵng,
Quy Nho'n

Đà Nẵng,
Quy Nho'n

Manila

Kim Đôi

Hà Tĩnh

Cầm Xuyên

Voi

Sanya

Hồ Kẻ
Gỏ

Kỳ Anh

M Ròn

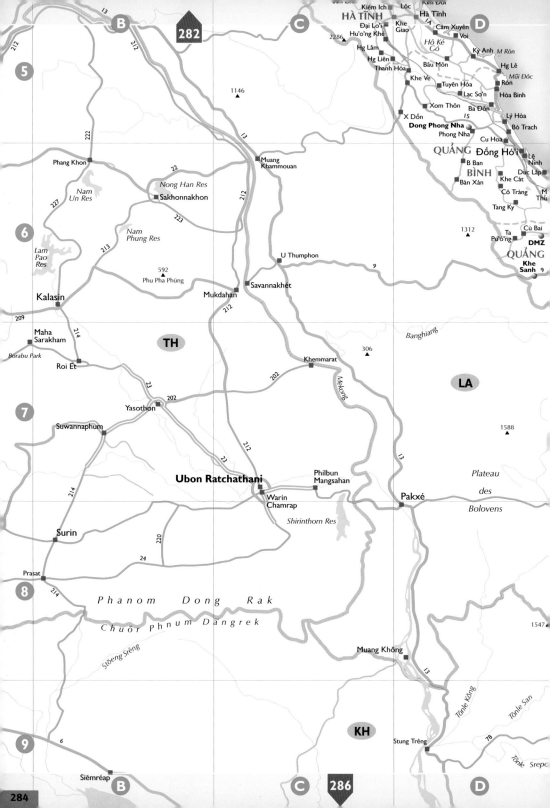

212

13

B

212

282

C

Kim Đồi
Kiềm Ich   Lộc
HÀ TĨNH   Hà Tĩnh
Đại Lo'i   Khe   Cầm Xuyên
Hu'o'ng Khè   Giao   Voi
2286   Hô Kẻ   D
Hg Lâm   Gô   Kỳ Anh   M Ròn

5

1146

222

13

Phang Khon

22

227   Nam
Un Res   Nong Han Res
Sakhonnakhon
223

Lam
Pao
Res

Nam
Phung Res

6

213

592
Phu Pha Phùng

Kalasin

209

214

Maha
Sarakham

Bôrabu Park

Roi Et

Muang
Khammouan

212

U Thumphon

Savannakhet

Mukdahan

212

TH

23

202

Yasothon

7

Suwannaphum

214

Ubon Ratchathani

212

Warin
Chamrap

Surin

220

Shirinthorn Res

24

Prasat

214

8

Phanom   Dong   Rak

Chuòr phnum Dǎngrek

Stoeng Srêng

9

6

Siêmréap

B

286

C

D

Hg Liên   Bàu Môn
Thanh Hóa   Khe Vè   Tuyên Hóa   Hg Lê
Lac So'n   Mũi Độc
Ròn
Xom Thôn   Hòa Bình
Ba Đôn
15   Lý Hòa
X Dôn
Dong Phong Nha   Bô Trach
Phong Nha   Cu Hoa
QUẢNG Đồng Hó'i
B Ban   Lệ
BÌNH   Ninh
Bàn Xán   Đúc Lập
Khe Cát
Cô Tràng   M
Thủ
Tang Ky

1312   Cù Bai
Ta   DMZ
Pu'o'ng   QUẢNG
Khe
Sanh   9

U Thumphon

9

Banghiang

306

LA

Khemmarat

202

Mekong

1588

13

Philbun
Mangsahan

Pakxé

Plateau

des

Bolovens

1547

Muang Không

13

Tônle Kông

Tônle San

KH

Stung Trêng

78

Tônle Srepc

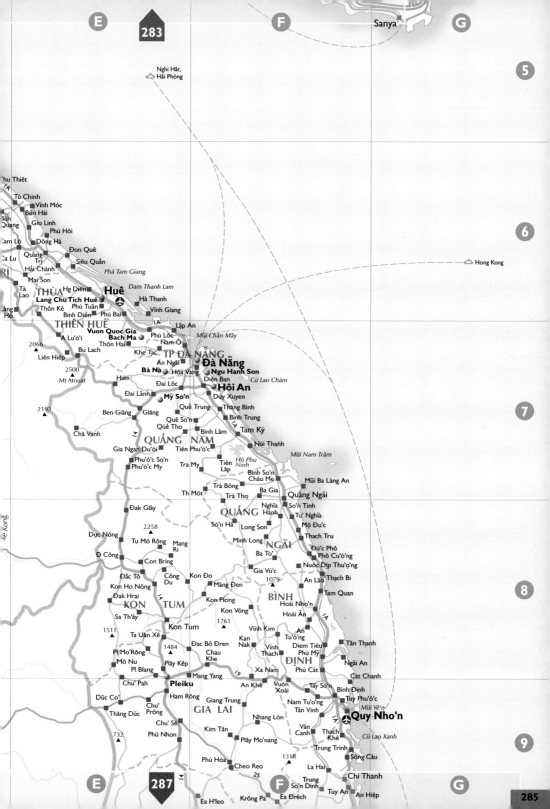

Sanya

5

Nghi Hâr,
Hải Phòng

6

Hong Kong

Thu Thiêt
Tù Chinh
Vĩnh Mốc
Bến Hải
Bên Gio Linh
Quảng Phú Hối
Cam Lô Đông Hà
Ca Lu Quảng Đon Quê
Trị Siêu Quần
Hải Chánh
Mai Sơn
Tà Huy Diên Phá Tam Giang
Lao THUA Đam Thanh Lam
ng Tô Lang Chu Tich Huê Huê Hà Thanh
Hô THIÊN HUÊ Thôn Kê Phú Tuân Vĩnh Giang
Bình Diên Phú Bài
A Lu'ới Vuon Quoc Gia Phú Lốc Lập An
2066 Bach Ma Thôn Hai Nam Ô Mũi Chân Mây
Liên Hiệp Bu Lach Khe Tạc TP ĐÀ NĂNG
2500 Ấn Ngãi Đà Nẵng
Mt Atouat Hiên Bà Nà Hòa Vang Ngu Hanh Son
Đai Lãnh Đại Lốc Diện Ban Cù Lao Chàm
2193 Mỹ So'n Hôi An
Ben Giang Giãng Quê Trung Duy Xuyen
Chã Vanh Quê Sơn Thăng Bình
Quê Thọ Bình Trung
QUẢNG NAM Bình Lâm Tam Ký
Gia Ngan Du'ói Tiên Phu'ớc Núi Thanh
Phu'ớc So'n Tra My Tiên Hô Phu Mũi Nam Trâm
Phu'ớc My Lập Ninh
Trà Bông Bình So'n
Th Một Châu Me Mũi Ba Làng An
Đak Glây Trà Thọ Ba Gia Quảng Ngãi
QUẢNG Nghĩa So'n Tinh
2258 Hành Tư' Nghĩa
Dục Nông Tu Mô Rông So'n Hà Long Son Mô Đu'c
Đ Công Mang Minh Long Thạch Tru
Ri Ba To' Đu'c Phô
Con Bring Phô Cu'ò'ng
Đắc Tô Công Kon Đo Gia Vu'c Nu'óc Dip Thu'o'ng
Kon Ho Nông Du Măng Đen 1079 An Lão Thạch Bi
Đak Hrai Kon Plong Tam Quan
Sa Th'ầy KON TUM Kon Vông BÌNH Hoài Nho'n
1511 1761 Vĩnh Kim Hoài Ân
Ta Uân Xê Kon Tum An Tân Thanh
Pl Mo'Rông 1484 Đac Bô Đren Kan Tu'ờng Diem Tiêu Ngãi An
Mô Nu Chau Nak Vĩnh Phù Mỹ Cát Chanh
Pl Blang Plây Kêp Khe Thạch ĐỊNH
Chư' Pah Mang Yang Xa Nam Phù Cát
Dũc Co' Pleiku An Khê Vuôn Tây So'n Bình Định
Ham Rông Xoài Nam Tu'o'ng Tuy Phu'ớc
Thăng Dũc Chư' Giang Trung Tân Vinh Mũi Yê'n
Prông GIA LAI Nhang Lón Quy Nho'n
Chư' Sẻ Văn Thạch
732 Phũ Nhon Kim Tân Plây Mo'nang Canh Khê Cù Lao Xanh
Trung Trinh
1318 La Hai Sông Câu
Phú Hòa Cheo Reo Trung Chí Thanh
25 So'n Dinh
Ea H'leo Krông Pa Ea Đrêch Tuy An An Hiệp

7

8

9

Phú Hòa   Cheo Reo   1318   La Hai   Sông Câu

E   **F**   Chí Thanh   **G**   **9**

Trung
Ea H'leo   Krông Pa   Ea Đrếch   So'n Dinh
     Tuy An   An Hiệp

Ea Sup   Ea Ta   Ea Hô   Tây So'n   Hòa Hội   **Tuy Hòa**

Bản Đôn   Ea Ta   Tam Giang   **PHÙ YÊN**
Vuon Quoc Gia   Bản Giang   Krong Buk   Ma Nha   *Mũi Nay*
Yok Don   Lan   Cu Ngar   B Poan   B E Klô'p   Đại Lãnh

Buôn Mê   Hòa   Ea Lô'p   26   Vĩnh Yên
Thuôt   Đak Nam   Tiê'n   M'Đrac   B Guynh   Vạn Ninh   *Mũi Ganh*
   Krông   B Krong   1731   *B Đ Hòn*
   Pach   Pach   Ninh Sim   *Gôm*

Đắc   B Ti   **LĂC**   Dục Mỹ   Ninh Hòa
DAC   Mil   Srênh   Krông   Ninh I'ch
Phumĩ   Krông   Giang   Bong   Ninh Phu'ó'c
Dăk Dăm   A Na   So'n   2405   **KHÁNH HÒA**   *Mũi Hòn Thi*
Đức Manh   Thôn   B RêHê   Th Một
Tuy   Đắc Song   Hai   Diên   **Nha Trang**
Đú'c   1580   Thác Trang   Phu'ó'c
   Bù Chét   Đa Tông   Đa Cháy   Diên   Văn Tu Đong   *Hòn Tre*
Bù Đốp   Công Chánh   Kiến Dú'c   14   Cam Tân   Khánh
Tân   Bom Bo   Đak Nông   Lạc Du'o'ng   So'n Hiệp   Cam Đú'c
Thanh Hòa   Phu'ó'c   **Đa Lat**   Phát
Ninh   Long   Bù Đăng   1465   Phú So'n   Chi   Sông Pha   Mã Hoa   Cam Ranh
B R'dang   Minh Hung   Bà Là   Quảng   **NINH**   *Vịnh Cam Ranh*
BÌNH PHUOC   Đú'c Liễu   Đa Đờn   Hiệp   Lạc Lâm   Ninh So'n   *Mũi Đá Vách*
   Vuon Quoc Gia   Đúc Trọng   Nghĩa   Tân Mỹ   Vĩnh Hy
Đồng Phú   **Cat Tien**   **LÂM ĐỒNG**   Đo'n   Hiệp   **THUẬN**   Lợi Hai
   Thi On Than Cao   Di Linh   Du'o'ng   **Po Klong**   Ninh Hai
Tân   B Tac Xong   Tà Nhiên   **Garai**
ảo   Câu Cây   Lợi Tân   Bảo Lộc   Phu'ó'c Hà   **Phan Rang-Tháp Chàm**
Bảo   Phu'ó'ng Lâm   Đa M'rê   Văn Lân   *Vịnh Phan Rang*
Phung   **DONG NAI**   1545   Dinh Hải
Phú Hung   Ma Đa Gui   B'Nom So'Ro'Long   Hải Ninh   *Mũi Dinh*
ắt   Tân   *Tri An*   Phú Thạnh   Vinh Hảo   Cà Ná
Môt   Uyên   *Lake*   An Lâm   Sông Lũy
   Thống   Phú Túc   Tân Phú   Võ Xu   **BÌNH**   Bắc Bình   Tuy Phon
Thủ Dú'c   Nhất Giây   Dâu   Bình Hòa   Tành   Hàm   Lu'o'ng So'n   Bình Thanh
Nhà Bè   Trảng   Gia Kiệm   Gia Ray   Linh   Thuận Bắc   Long Hòa
Biên Hòa   Bom   *Hồ Tri An*   Hàm   *Vịnh Phan Rí*
   Tân   Phong   **Xuân Lộc**   Đú'c Linh   Thuận Nam
Tham Thiện   Long   Xuân Tan   Sông Dinh   **THUẬN**
Phú Mỹ   Thành   Xuân   Tân Minh   Song Phan   **Mũi Né**
   Châu Thành   Hiệp   Đô   Rù'ng La   **Phan Thiết**
Cam Mỹ   Xuân My   Tân   Tân Lập
Bình Giá   Nghĩa   Tân Thuân   *Vịnh Phan Thiết*
   Sô Tây Đú'c   La Gi   Kê Gà
BÀ RỊA-VŨNG-   Tân Thắng   *Mũi Kê Gà*
   TÀU   Tân Bình
   Long Đất   Thuận Biên
ỗ Công Đông   Phu'ó'c Hai
   Châu Thành   Long Hải
Rạch   **Vũng Tàu**
Cùng

Biên Đông

Cung Hậu

Singapore   **E**   **F**   **G**

10   **11**   **12**   **13**

Name	Page	Grid
A Lưới	285	E7
An Châu	286	C12
An Hải	283	D3
An Hiệp	287	F9
Anh Sơn	282	C4
An Khê	285	F9
An Lâm	287	E11
An Lao	285	F8
An Ngãi	285	E7
An Phong	286	C11
An Thái Trung	286	D12
An Trach	286	C13
An Tướng	285	F8
Ấp Nhì	286	D11
Bac Bình	287	F11
Bac Can	283	D2
Bac Giang	283	D2
Bac Hà	282	B1
Ba Che	283	E2
Bac Liêu	286	C13
Bac Mê	282	C1
Bac Ngườn	282	B1
Bac Ninh	283	D2
Bac Son	283	D2
Bac Yên	282	B2
Ba Dôn	284	D5
Ba Dông	286	D12
Ba Gia	285	F7
Ba Hòn	286	C12
Bai Liêu	283	E2
Bà Là	287	E10
Bà Nà	285	E7
Ban Ban	282	C4
Ban Ban	284	D6
Ban Dôn	287	E9
Ba'n E Klô'p	287	F9
Ban Giang Lan	287	E9
Ba'n Guynh	287	F10
Ban Hôn	282	B2
Ba'n Krong Pach	287	F10
Ban Na Mang	282	C3
Ban Phau	282	C4
Ba'n Poan	287	F9
Ban Po Bai	282	A2
Ba'n R'dang	287	D10
Ba'n RêHê	287	F10
Ba'n Tac Xong	287	E11
Ba'n Ti Srênh	287	F10
Ban To	282	A2
Ban Tôm	282	B4
Ban Vay	282	B2
Ban Ve	282	B4
Ban Xan	282	C4
Bàn Xán	284	D6
Ban Xang	282	B4
Bang Khà	282	B3
Bao Ha	282	B2
Bao Lac	282	C1
Bao Loc	287	E11
Bào Phung	287	D11
Bao Yên	282	B2
Bá Thước	282	C3
Ba Tơ	285	F8
Ba Tri	286	D12
Bát Xát	282	B1
Bâu Môn	284	D5
Bên Cát	286	D11
Bên Cau	286	D11
Ben Giang	285	E7
Bên Hái	285	E6
Bên Lức	286	D11
Ben Quang	285	D6
Bên Súc	286	D11
Bên Tre	286	D12
Biên Hòa	287	D11
Biên Quan	282	C3
Bìm Sơn	283	D3
Bình Chánh	286	D11
Bình Dai	287	D12
Bình Diên	285	E6
Bình Dinh	285	F9
Bình Gia	283	D2
Bình Giá	287	E11
Bình Hòa	287	E11
Bình Lâm	285	F7
Bình Liêu	283	E2
Bình Long	286	D10
Bình Luc	283	D3
Bình Sơn Châu Me	285	F7
Bình Thanh	287	F11
Bình Thiên	287	F11
Bình Trung	282	C2
Bình Trung	285	F7
Bom Bo	287	E10
Bó Sinh	282	B2
Bó Trách	284	D5
Bù Chét	287	E10
Bù Dang	287	E10
Bù Dôp	287	D10
Bu Lach	285	E7
Buôn Mê Thuôt	287	E10
Cam Ló	285	E6
Cam My	287	E11
Cam Pha	283	E3
Câm Pha	283	E3
Cam Ranh	287	F10
Cam Son	283	D2
Cam Tân	287	F10
Câm Thuy	282	C3
Câm Xuyên	284	D5
Cà Ná	287	F11
Cân Dước	286	D11
Càng Long	286	D12
Cân Giuôc	287	D11
Can Lôc	282	D5
Cân Thơ	286	D12
Cao Bang	283	D1
Cao Ky	283	D2
Cao Lanh	286	C11
Cát Chanh	285	F9
Ca Tum	286	D10
Câu Cây	287	E11
Cau Kè	286	D12
Cau Ngang	286	D12
Cây Dừa	286	B12
Cây Me	286	C12
Cây Tau Ha	286	D12
Châu Doc	286	C11
Châu Giang	283	D3
Chau Khe	285	F8
Châu Thanh	287	E11
Châu Thành	286	D11
Châu Thành	286	D12
Cha Vanh	285	E7
Cheo Reo	285	F9
Chiêm Hóa	282	C2
Chiêng Khương	282	B3
Chiêng Nhân	282	C3
Chi Lang	283	D2
Chi Lang	286	C11
Chí Linh	283	D2
Chí Thanh	287	F9
Cho Dôn	282	C2
Chợ Lách	286	D12
Chợ Mới	286	C11
Chợn Thanh	287	D11
Chợ Rã	282	D1
Chua Thay	282	C2
Chương My	282	C3
Chư Pah	285	E9
Chư Prông	285	E9
Chư Sê	285	E9
Cia Viên	283	D3
Con Bring	285	E8
Con Cuông	282	C4
Công Chánh	287	E10
Công Du	285	E8
Côn Sơn	282	C4
Cô Tô	286	C12
Cô Tràng	284	D6
Cù Bai	284	D6
Cu Chi	286	D11
Cu Hoa	284	D5
Cu Ngar	287	E9
Dac Bô Dren	285	F8
Da Cháy	287	F10
Dac Mil	287	E10
Dac Song	287	E10
Dac Tô	285	E8
Da Dòn	287	F10
Da Hu Oai	287	E11
Dai Lanh	285	E7
Dai Lanh	287	G9
Dai Lôc	285	E7
Dai Lơi	282	C5
Dài Xuyên	283	E2
Dak Glây	285	E8
Dak Hrai	285	E8
Dak Nam	287	E10
Dak Nông	287	E10
Da Lat	287	F10
Dâm Dơi	286	C13
Dâm Hà	283	E2
Da Mrê	287	E11
Dà Nang	285	F7
Danh Nham	282	C4
Da Phúc	283	D2
Dât Dó	287	E11
Da Tông	287	F10
Dâu Giây	287	E11
Dâu Tiêng	286	D11
Den Hung	282	C2
Diem Tiêu	285	F8
Diên Ban	285	F7
Diên Biên Phu	282	A2
Diên Châu	282	C4
Diên Khánh	287	F10
Diên Phước	287	F10
Di Linh	287	E11
Dinh Hái	287	F11
Dinh Hóa	282	C2
Dinh Lâp	283	E2
Doan Hùng	282	C2
Dô Lương	282	C4
Dơn Dương	287	F10
Dông Chuc	282	C2
Dông Anh	283	D2
Dông Bua	282	C2
Dông Dang	283	D2
Dông Hà	285	E6
Dông Hiêu	282	C4
Dông Hới	284	D6
Dông Hưng	283	D3
Dông Lâm	282	C4

Name	Page	Grid	Name	Page	Grid	Name	Page	Grid	Name	Page	Grid
Mu'ò'ng Loi	282	A3	Ninh Phu'ó'c	287	F10	Phú Tuan	285	E6	Sông Luy	287	F11
Mu'ò'ng Mô	282	A2	Ninh Sim	287	F10	Phú Túc	287	E11	Sông Mã	282	B3
Mu'ò'ng Mu'o'n	282	A2	Ninh So'n	287	F10	Phú Xuân	282	C3	Sông Pha	287	F10
Mu'ò'ng Nhè	282	A2	Ninh Thanh	283	D1	Phù Yên	282	C2	Song Phan	287	E11
Mu'o'ng Sai	282	B2	Nùi Sâp	286	C12	Piêng Pùng	282	C4	Song Thao	282	C2
Mu'ò'ng Tè	282	A1	Núi Thanh	285	F7	Plây Blang	285	E8	So'n La	282	B2
Mu'ò'ng Trai	282	B2	Nuóc Dip Thu'o'ng	285	F8	Plây Mo'Rông	285	E8	Son Linh	282	C5
My Thanh	286	D12				Plây Kêp	285	E8	So'n Nam	282	C2
My Tho	286	D12	Ô Môn	286	C12	Plây Mo'nang	285	F9	So'n Tây	282	C2
My Thuy	284	D6				Pleiku	285	E8	So'n Tinh	285	F8
My Van	283	D3	Pac Bó	283	D1	Pò Dôn	283	D2	Sôp Côp	282	B3
My Xuyên	286	D12	Pac Ma	282	A1				Sôp Cun	282	C3
			Pâc Miâu	282	C1	Quan Ba	282	C1	Só Tây Dú'c	287	E11
Na Du'o'ne	283	E2	Pa Tân	282	A1	Quáng Hà	283	E2	Suôi Nu'ó'c Trong	286	D11
Nà Han	282	C1	Pha Lai	283	D3	Quàng Hiêp	287	F10	Suôi Rùt	282	C3
Na Hang	282	C1	Phan Rang-Tháp Chàm	287	F11	Quang Lâm	282	A2			
Nahia Lô	282	B2	Phan Thiêt	287	E11	Quang Loi	282	D4	Ta Bú	282	B2
Nâm Can	282	B4	Phát Chi	287	F10	Quàng Ngai	285	F7	Ta Cum	282	C3
Nam Dàn	282	C4	Phô Cu'ò'ng	285	F8	Quang Noa	283	D1	Tac Vân	286	C13
Nà Mèo	282	C3	Phô Lu	282	B1	Quáng Thàng	283	E2	Ta Khoa	282	B2
Nâm Ma	282	B2	Phong Châu	282	C2	Quang Tri	285	E6	Tà Lao	285	E6
Nâm Nàng	283	D1	Phong Nha	284	D5	Quàng Xu'o'ng	282	D4	Tam Dao	282	C2
Nam Ô	285	E7	Phong Thô	282	B1	Quan Hóa	282	C3	Tam Giang	287	F9
Nam Tu'o'ng	285	F9	Phô Yên	283	D2	Qué Phong	282	C4	Tam Ky	285	F7
Na Ngoi	282	B4	Phú Bai	285	E6	Qué So'n	285	E7	Tam Nong	286	C11
Na Péo	283	E2	Phuc Am Pin	286	D10	Qúé Tho	285	E7	Tam Quan	285	F8
Nà Phac	283	D1	Phù Cát	285	F8	Qué Trung	285	E7	Tam Thanh	282	C2
Nà Quang	283	D1	Phú Châu	286	C11	Quy Chau	282	C4	Tân An	286	D11
Na Ri	283	D2	Phuc Hoa	283	D1	Quy Hò'p	282	C4	Tân Biên	286	D11
Nà Tàu	282	A2	Phúc Yên	282	C2	Quynh Lu'u	282	C4	Tân Bình	287	E11
Na Tòng	282	A2	Phú Giao	287	D11	Quỳnh Nhai	282	B2	Tang Ky	284	D6
Ngai An	285	F8	Phú Hòa	285	F9	Quy Nho'n	285	F9	Tà Nhiên	287	F11
Ngãi Chõ	282	B1	Phú Hôi	285	E6				Tân Hiêp	286	C12
Ngan Dù'a	286	C12	Phú Hung	287	D11	Rach Cùng	287	D12	Tánh Linh	287	E11
Nga So'n	283	D3	Phú' Lau	282	A3	Rach Giá	286	C12	Tân Ky	282	C4
Ngã So'n	283	D1	Phú Lôc	285	E7	Rach Gôi	286	C12	Tân Lac	282	C3
Nghia Dô	282	B1	Phú Lo'i	286	D12	Rach Sói	286	C12	Tân Lâp	287	E11
Nghia Hành	285	F8	Phú Long	286	C12	Rang Dông	283	D3	Tân Minh	287	E11
Nghia Hiêp	287	F10	Phú Lu'o'ng	282	D2	Ròn	284	D5	Tân My	287	F10
Nghia Hu'ng	283	D3	Phumi Dak Dam	287	E10	Rù'ng La	287	E11	Tân Nghia	287	E11
Nghi Hâr	282	D4	Phú My	287	E11				Tan Phong	287	E11
Nghi Lôc	282	C4	Phù My	285	F8	Sa Déc	286	D12	Tân Phú	287	E11
Ngoc Hiên	286	C13	Phung Hiêp	286	D12	Sám Nám	282	A2	Tân Thang	287	E11
Ngoc Lac	282	C3	Phu Nhon	285	E9	Sâm So'n	283	D4	Tân Thanh	285	F8
Nguyên Binh	283	D1	Phu'ó'c Hà	287	F11	Sao Dò	282	C3	Tân Thanh	286	D11
Nhà Bàng	286	C11	Phu'ó'c Hai	287	E12	Sa Th'ây	285	E8	Tân Thuân	287	E11
Nha Nai	282	C4	Phu'ó'c Hoa	287	D11	Siêu Quân	285	E6	Tân Thu'o'ng	287	E10
Nhã Nam	283	D2	Phu'ó'c Long	286	C12	Sìn Hô	282	A1	Tân Thuy	287	D12
Nhang Lón	285	F9	Phu'ó'c Long	287	E10	Sóc So'n	286	C12	Tan Vinh	285	F9
Nha Trang	287	F10	Phu'ó'c My	285	E7	Sóc Trang	286	D12	Ta Phunh	282	D1
Nho Quan	282	D3	Phu'ó'c So'n	285	E7	So'n Dong	283	D2	Ta Pu'ó'ng	284	D6
Nhu' Xuân	282	C4	Phu'o'ng Lâm	287	E11	So'n Du'o'ng	282	C2	Ta Thiêt Co Rom	286	D10
Ninh Bình	283	D3	Phú So'n	287	F10	Só'n Hà	285	F8	Ta Uân Xê	285	E8
Ninh Giang	283	D3	Phú Tân	286	C11	So'n Hiêp	287	F10	Tây Ninh	286	D11
Ninh Hai	287	F11	Phú Thanh	287	E11	Sông Câu	285	F9	Tay So'n	285	F9
Ninh Hòa	287	F10	Phu Thông	283	D2	Sông Dinh	287	E11	Tây So'n	285	F9
Ninh I'ch	287	F10	Phù Tiên	283	D3	Sông Dôc	286	C13	Thach An	283	D1

Thach Bi	285	F8	Tiên Yên	283	E2	Van Tu Dong	287	F10
Thach Khê	285	F9	Tiêu Cân	286	D12	Viêt Trì	282	C2
Thach Thành	282	C3	Tinh Gia	282	D4	Viêt Vinh	282	C1
Thach Thành	282	C3	Tinh Túc	283	D1	Vinh	282	C5
Thach Tru	285	F8	Trà Bông	285	F7	Vinh Bao	283	D3
Thac Môt	285	F7	Trà Cú	286	D12	Vinh Châu	286	D12
Thac Môt	287	F10	Trai Cau	283	D2	Vinh Giang	285	E6
Thác Trang	287	F10	Trà Linh	283	D1	Vinh Háo	287	F11
Thái Bình	283	D3	Tra My	285	F7	Vinh Hu'ng	286	D11
Thái Hòa	282	C4	Trang Bang	286	D11	Vinh Hy	287	F10
Thái Nguyên	282	D2	Trang Bom	287	E11	Vinh Kim	285	F8
Thái Thuy	283	D3	Trân Thò'i	286	C13	Vinh Lac	282	C2
Tham Thiên	287	E11	Trân Yên	282	C2	Vinh Lôc	282	C3
Thâm Thiên	282	C2	Trà Ôn	286	D12	Vinh Long	286	D12
Than Dai	282	D3	Trà Tho	285	F7	Vinh Móc	285	E6
Thang Bình	285	F7	Trà Vinh	286	D12	Vinh Thach	285	F8
Thang Duc	285	E9	Tri Tôn	286	C12	Vinh Thuân	286	C12
Thanh Ch	282	C4	Trung Dô	282	C4	Vinh Tuy	282	C2
Thanh Hoa	282	C2	Trùng Khánh	283	D1	Vinh Yên	282	C2
Thanh Hóa	282	D4	Trung Liên	282	B1	Vinh Yên	287	G10
Thanh Hóa	284	D5	Trung Nhan	282	D2	Vi Thanh	286	C12
Thanh Hòa	287	D10	Trung So'n Dinh	287	F9	Voi	284	D5
Thanh Hu'o'ng	282	C4	Trung Trinh	285	F9	Võ Nhai	283	D2
Thanh Phú	286	D12	Tuân Giáo	282	B2	Vo Xu	287	E11
Thanh So'n	282	C2	Tuân Mâu	283	D2	Vu Bán	283	D3
Thanh Xuân	282	C5	Tù Chinh	285	E6	Vu Dai	283	E3
Than Uyên	282	B2	Tú Lê	282	B2	Vung Liêm	286	D12
Thât Khê	283	D2	Tú' Lôc	283	D3	Vung Tàu	287	E12
Thi On Than Cao	287	E11	Tu Mô Rông	285	E8	Vuòn Xoài	285	F9
Thô'i Bình	286	C12	Tu' Nghia	285	F8	Vu Thu	283	D3
Thô'i Dong	286	C12	Tu'o'ng Du'o'ng	282	B4			
Thó'i Lai	286	C12	Tu'o'ng Phu'ó'c	287	F11	Xa Mát	286	D11
Thô'ng Nhat	287	E11	Tu Vu	282	C3	Xa Nam	285	F8
Thông Nông	283	D1	Tuy An	287	F9	Xin Mân	282	B1
Thôn Hai	285	E7	Tuy Dú'c	287	E10	Xom Dôn	284	D5
Thôn Hai	287	E10	Tuyên Hóa	284	D5	Xôm Lôm	282	C3
Thôn Kê	285	E6	Tuyên Quang	282	C2	Xom Thôn	284	D5
Tho So'n	282	C4	Tuy Hòa	287	F9	Xuân Hiêp	287	E11
Thôt N'ôt	286	C12	Tuy Phon	287	F11	Xuân Lôc	287	E11
Tho Xuân	282	C3	Tuy Phu'ó'c	285	F9	Xuán My	287	E11
Thuân An	287	D11				Xuân Tan	287	E11
Thuân Biên	287	E11	U Minh	286	C12	Xuân Thuy	283	D3
Thuan Châu	282	B2	Uông Bí	283	D3			
Thuân Hòa	286	C13				Yân Dô	282	C2
Thuân Thành	283	D3	Vàm Co	286	D11	Yên Bái	282	C2
Thú' Ba	286	C12	Van Ban	282	B2	Yên Binh	282	C2
Thu Cúc	282	C2	Vân Canh	285	F9	Yên Châu	282	B3
Thú Dâu Môt	287	D11	Van Diên	283	D3	Yên Dinh	283	D3
Thu Dú'c	287	D11	Vân Dinh	282	D3	Yên Hu'ng	283	D3
Thu'o'ng Bang La	282	C2	Vàng Danh	283	D2	Yên Hung	282	B2
Thu'ò'ng Xuân	282	C4	Van Lân	287	F11	Yên Ly	282	C4
Thu Thiêt	285	D6	Van Lang	283	D2	Yên Minh	282	C1
Thu Thù'a	286	D11	Van Lap	282	C2	Yên Son	282	C2
Tiên Hai	283	D3	Van Mai	282	C3	Yên Thành	282	C4
Tiên Lâng	283	D3	Van Mich	283	D2	Yên Thê	283	D2
Tiên Lâp	285	F7	Van Ninh	287	F10	Yên Viên	283	D3
Tiên Phu'ó'c	285	F7	Van Quán	283	D2			

INDEX VIETNAM

INDEX VIETNAM

PICTURES

The Automobile Association would like to thank the following photographers, companies and picture libraries for their assistance in the preparation of this book.

Abbreviations for the picture credits are as follows: (t) top; (b) bottom; (l) left; (r) right; (c) centre; (AA) AA World Travel Library.

2 AA/J Holmes;
3t AA/J Holmes;
3cr AA/J Holmes;
3cl AA/D Henley;
3b AA/J Holmes;
4 AA/J Holmes;
5 AA/J Holmes;
6 AA/J Holmes;
8 AA/D Henley;
10 AA/D Henley;
11l Evason Hideaway at Ana Mandara;
11r AA/D Henley;
12t AA/J Holmes;
12b AA/D Henley;
13 Jordi Cami/Alamy;
14 AA/J Holmes;
15t AA/J Holmes;
15b Vietnam Photography/Alamy;
16 AA/D Henley;
17l AA/J Holmes;
17r AA/D Henley;
18 Christian Kober/Robert Harding;
19t David Greedy/Lonely Planet Images;
19b Matthew Maran/naturepl.com;
20 AA/J Holmes;
21l Greg Elms/Lonely Planet Images;
21r www.bobbychinn.com;
22 AA/J Holmes;
23t AA/D Henley;
23b Paul Panayiotou/Alamy;
24 Warner Bros/The Kobal Collection;
25l Paramount/The Kobal Collection/ Vaughan, Stephen;
25r AFP/Getty Images;
26l www.ipa-nima.com;
26r AA/J Holmes;
27 Mark Daffey/Lonely Planet Images;
28 Mason Florence/Lonely Planet Images;
29t Laurie Strachan/Alamy;
29b AA/J Holmes;
30 AFP/Getty Images;
31l Reuter Raymond/Corbis Sygma;
31r AA/D Henley;
32 CPA Media;
33l CPA Media;

33r Mary Evans Picture Library;
34 AA/D Henley;
35t AFP/Getty Images;
35b Catherine Karnow/Corbis;
36 Time & Life Pictures/Getty Images;
37l AA/D Henley;
37r Bettmann /Corbis;
38 AFP/Getty Images;
39l Danita Delimont/Alamy;
39r AFP/Getty Images;
40l Jon Arnold Images Ltd/Alamy;
40r Huw Jones/Alamy;
41 AA/J Holmes;
42 AA/D Henley;
43 AA/J Holmes;
44 AA/J Holmes;
45 AA/J Holmes;
47 AA/J Holmes;
48 AA/J Holmes;
49 AA/D Henley;
50 AA/D Henley;
51 AA/D Henley;
52 AA/J Holmes;
54 AA/J Holmes;
55 AA/J Holmes;
56 AA/J Holmes;
57 Toby Adamson/Axiom;
58 Peter Titmuss/Alamy;
59 Daniel Jones/Alamy;
60 AA/J Holmes;
64 AA/J Holmes;
65 AA/J Holmes;
66l AA/J Holmes;
66r AA/J Holmes;
67 AA/D Henley;
68 Andrew Woodley/Alamy;
69 J Holmes;
70 AA/D Henley;
71 AA/D Henley;
72 Peter Treanor/Alamy;
73 AA/D Henley;
74 Beth Wald/Photolibrary.com;
75l Greg Elms/Lonely Planet Images;
75r AA/D Henley;
76 AA/D Henley;
77 AA/J Holmes;
78 AA/D Henley ;
79 AA/D Henley;
80 AA/D Henley;

81t AA/D Henley;
81b AA/D Henley;
82 AA/D Henley;
84 AA/D Henley;
86 AA/D Henley;
88 Restaurant Bobby Chinn;
91 www.greenmango.vn;
92 www.bobbychinn.com;
93 www.hilton.com;
95 www.hotelnikkohanoi.com.vn;
97 AA/D Henley;
98 Mason Florence/Lonely Planet Images;
100 AA/D Henley;
101 AA/D Henley;
102 AA/J Holmes;
103 AA/D Henley;
104 Frederic Soreau/Photolibrary. com;
106 AA/J Holmes;
107 AA/J Holmes;
108 AA/J Holmes;
109 AA/D Henley;
110 AA/D Henley;
111 AA/J Gocher;
112 AA/J Holmes;
113 AA/D Henley;
114 AA/D Henley;
115 AA/J Holmes;
117t Ben Pipe/Alamy;
117b AA/J Gocher;
118 AA/D Henley;
119t AA/D Henley;
119b maggiegowan.co.uk/Alamy;
120 AA/D Henley;
121 AA/D Henley;
122 ©Victoria Hotels and Resorts;
123 Alex Griffiths/Alamy;
124 AA/D Henley;
126 AA/D Henley;
129 Stockbyte;
130 AA/J Holmes;
132 AA/D Henley;
133 AA/D Henley;
134 AA/D Henley;
135 AA/D Henley;
136 Marc Verin/Photolibrary.com;
137 AA/J Holmes;
138 AA/D Henley;
139l AA/D Henley;

139r AA/D Henley;
140 AA/J Holmes;
141l AA/D Henley;
141r AA/J Holmes;
142 AA/J Holmes;
144 AA/J Holmes;
145 Rachel Lewis/Lonely Planet
Images;
147 AA/J Holmes;
149 AA/J Holmes;
150 AA/D Henley;
151 AA/D Henley;
153 AA/D Henley;
154t AA/J Holmes;
154b AA/D Henley;
155 Siegfried Grassegger/
Imagebroker/FLPA;
156 AA/J Holmes;
157 AA/D Henley;
159 AA/J Holmes;
160 AA/D Henley;
161 Colin Brynn/Robert Harding;
162 AA/J Holmes;
163 AA/D Henley;
164 AA/J Holmes;
165 C Boobbyer;
166 www.phattireventures.com;
169 AA/D Henley;
170 Toby Adamson/Axiom;
173 © Ana Mandara;
174 © Furama Hotels and Resorts
International;
177 © Sofitel Hotels & Resorts;
178 © Coco Beach Resort;
181 © Six Senses Resorts
& Spas;
182 Jon Arnold Images/
Photolibrary.com;
187 Tim Hall/Robert Harding;
188 AA/D Henley;
189 Jose Fuste Raga/Photolibrary.
com;
190 AA/D Henley;
191 AA/D Henley;
192 AA/J Holmes;
194t AA/D Henley;
194b AA/D Henley;
195 Alain Evrard/Robert Harding;
196 AA/D Henley;
197 AA/D Henley;
198 Craig Lovell/Eagle Visions
Photography/Alamy;
199 AA/D Henley;
200 JTB Photo/Photolibrary.com;

201 Alain Evrard/Robert Harding;
202 Anthony Giblin/Lonely Planet
Images;
205 Corbis;
206 Stu Smucker/Lonely Planet
Images;
209 Eightfish/Alamy;
211 AA/J Holmes;
214 AA/D Henley;
216 David Henley/Pictures from
Asia;
217 AA/D Henley;
218 Alvaro Leiva
/Photolibrary.com;
219l AA/D Henley;
219r AA/J Holmes;
220 AA/D Henley;
221 AA/D Henley;
222 AA/D Henley;
223 AA/D Henley;
224 AA/D Henley;
225 AA/D Henley;
226 AA/D Henley;
227 AA/D Henley;
228 E Simanor/Robert Harding;
230 John Banagan/Lonely Planet
Images;
231 John Banagan/Lonely Planet
Images;
232 Tim Hall/Robert Harding;
233 Nicholas Pitt/Alamy;
234 © Victoria Hotels & Resorts;
235 Keren Su/China Span/Alamy;
236 © Victoria Hotels and Resorts;
238 AA/D Henley;
241 AA/D Henley;
242 © Petro House;
243 Toby Adamson/Axiom;
244 AA/J Holmes;
247 Toby Adamson/Axiom;
248 AA/J Holmes;
249 AA/D Henley;
250 AA/J Holmes;
251 Andrew Woodley/Alamy;
253 AA/J Holmes;
254 AA/J Holmes;
255 AA/J Holmes;
256 AA/J Holmes;
257 Photodisc;
260 AA/J Holmes;
263 Casal Photography/Alamy;
264 AA/D Henley;
265 David Sutherland/Alamy;
266 © Sofitel Hotels and Resorts;

267 F Jack Jackson/Alamy;
268 © Furama Hotels and Resorts
International;
269 AA/D Henley;
270 AA/J Holmes;
273 © Furama Hotels and Resorts
International, Furama Resort
Danang, Vietnam;
274 AA/D Henley;
275 AA/J Holmes;
281 Robert Francis/Robert Harding.

ACKNOWLEDGMENTS VIETNAM

CREDITS

Series editor
Sheila Hawkins

Project editor
Bookwork Creative Ltd

Design
Low Sky Design Ltd

Cover design
Chie Ushio

Picture research
Alice Earle

Image retouching and repro
Jacqueline Street

Mapping
Maps produced by the Mapping Services
Department of AA Publishing

Text updated by Sean Sheehan

Indexer
Marie Lorimer

Production
Lorraine Taylor

See It Vietnam
ISBN 978-1-4000-0365-5
Third Edition

Published in the United States by Fodor's Travel and simultaneously in Canada by Random House of Canada Limited, Toronto.
Published in the United Kingdom by AA Publishing.
Fodor's is a registered trademark of Random House, Inc., and Fodor's See It is a trademark of Random House, Inc.
Fodor's Travel is a division of Random House, Inc.

Color separation by AA Digital Department
Printed and bound by Leo Paper Products, China
10 9 8 7 6 5 4 3 2 1

Special Sales: This book is available for special discounts for bulk purchases for sales promotions or premiums. Special editions, including personalized covers, excerpts of existing books, and corporate imprints, can be created in large quantities for special needs.
For more information, write to Special Markets/Premium Sales, 1745 Broadway, MD 6-2, New York, NY 10019
or e-mail specialmarkets@randomhouse.com
Important Note: Time inevitably brings changes, so always confirm prices, travel facts, and other perishable information when it matters. Although Fodor's cannot accept responsibility for errors, you can use this guide in the confidence that we have taken every care to ensure its accuracy.

A04723
Maps in this title produced from mapping © MAIRDUMONT / Falk Verlag 2012 and map data
© Footprint Handbooks Limited 2004
Transport map © Communicarta Ltd, UK
Weather chart statistics supplied by Weatherbase © Copyright 2004 Canty and Associates, LLC.